New Zealand Politics and Social Patterns

New Zealand Politics and Social Patterns

selected works by

Robert Chapman

edited and introduced by
Elizabeth McLeay

Victoria University Press

VICTORIA UNIVERSITY PRESS
Victoria University of Wellington
PO Box 600 Wellington
http://www.vup.vuw.ac.nz

Copyright © Robert Chapman 1999
Introduction and editorial matter © Elizabeth McLeay 1999

ISBN 0 86473 361 5

First published 1999

This book is copyright. Apart from
any fair dealing for the purpose of private study,
research, criticism or review, as permitted under the
Copyright Act, no part may be reproduced by any
process without the permission of the publishers.

Every effort has been made to contact the holders of copyright
material reproduced in this book. The publisher would be
grateful to hear from any other copyright holders.

Printed by Publishing Press, Auckland

CONTENTS

Editor's Introduction	1
A Note on the Texts	14
List of Tables and Figures	17

PART ONE: Society and Politics

1	Fiction and the Social Pattern: Some Implications of Recent New Zealand Writing	21
2	Great Expectations: New Zealand Since the War	59
3	No Land is an Island: Twentieth Century Politics	84
4	Patronage in a Changing World	100

PART TWO: Town, City and Country

5	Psephology	115
6	The Sad, Slow End of the Twenties	120
7	The Response to Labour and the Question of Parallelism of Opinion, 1928-1960	132
8	The 'No Change' Election: 1963	163
9	The 1969 Election	168
10	The 1975 Result: How did it Happen and Why?	175
11	The Case of the Pulled Punch: The 1978 Election	200
12	New Zealand Defers Decision: The 1981 Election	208
13	Voting in the Maori Political Sub-System, 1935-1984	226
14	Deaths and Entrances	258

PART THREE: Governing Democratically

15	The Mechanics of Representation	271
16	On Democracy as Having and Exercising a Clear Choice of Government	278
17	The Politics of Division?	288
18	Restructuring Broadcasting	305
19	Political Culture: The Purposes of Party and the Current Challenge	320
20	A Political Culture Under Pressure: The Struggle to Preserve a Progressive Tax Base for Welfare and the Positive State	337

Bibliography of the Published Works of Robert Chapman 367

Editor's Introduction

Robert McDonald Chapman is an historian, poet, editor, reviewer, political scientist, critic of the visual arts, teacher, social and political commentator. He has contributed widely to the intellectual and political life of New Zealand. Hence, although Chapman's work on New Zealand politics and political history is predominantly represented here, it is appropriate that this volume also displays his wider interests in the arts and society. The works included range broadly across the disciplines whilst reflecting three central concerns: the social and political patterns of New Zealand culture; the political continuities and changes from the 1920s onwards; and the nature and problems of New Zealand democracy.

Robert Chapman was born in 1922. He began his academic career as an historian, gaining an MA in History (first class honours) from the University of New Zealand. He lectured in the Department of History at Auckland, becoming an associate professor giving courses on twentieth century New Zealand and the United States. In 1964 he was appointed to the foundation chair in Political Studies at Auckland, a position he held until his retirement in 1988. A key feature of Chapman's leadership of the Department was his development of courses on New Zealand politics and his encouragement of research students to write theses on New Zealand political behaviour and government.

As Professor of Politics, Chapman naturally concentrated more on political analysis than during his earlier years. It would be misleading to imply that there have been divisions between the various facets of Chapman's professional life, however, for the reverse has been the case—he has always retained his wide intellectual interests, and cross-fertilisation of ideas and approaches has been characteristic of his thinking. In part this is because, like us all, Chapman is very much a product of his times. Chapman's early years as a student of political history at the University of Auckland were during a time when learning about New Zealand culture meant approaching it from a range of disciplinary perspectives. Understanding society—and contributing to it—came from creative impulses that were not confined to a particular discipline; and ideas were just as likely to be found in the world outside as in the immediate environment and the literature of one's primary intellectual concentration. In comparison, the contemporary world of ideas and scholarship, especially in academia, is a much more specialised place.

In part, too, during the 1940s and 1950s, and even perhaps well into the 1960s, all kinds of scholarly endeavours on New Zealand were still in their early stages. In one of his early articles Chapman began by disclaiming personal expertise on post-war political and social developments, writing, 'An expert is a man who gets his head above the crowd by standing on a pile of other people's books and, in this case, the books are just not there' (Chapter 2, 'Great Expectations: New Zealand Since the War'). The body of works in any one area was fairly scanty and to do original research on literature, politics and history necessitated scouring the secondary sources from every possible perspective, as well as generating findings from primary data that were often difficult to locate and analyse. Chapman, like all good scholars, did both. Neither has Chapman's reading been confined to history, politics and literature, for he believes that economic literacy is essential for the understanding of government and political behaviour. And the same exists in reverse: 'For the nineteenth century title of economics, political economy, expresses a continuing truth. Politics is to economics as a tightrope walker is to his wire' (Chapter 3, 'No Land is an Island: Twentieth Century Politics'). Thus Chapman's intellectual interests have spanned the traditional disciplinary divides and are characterised by an imaginative and wide-ranging use of sources and ideas. The result has been a unique wisdom and insight not easily attained by those writing from the narrower base of single disciplines or the even more confined perspective of a sub-discipline.

The direction and goals of Chapman's writings and talks have been guided to an unusual extent by his desire to communicate his knowledge and ideas widely, beyond the usual production of academic books and articles. Anyone who is active in research and writing is engaged in dissemination to some extent. For Chapman, however, the task of an academic is not only to teach students, stimulate and supervise postgraduate research and publish academic works but also to educate citizens and enrich the intellectual life of one's society. A political scientist has a particular responsibility to do this because the role of political commentator can be, and should be, an important one. Throughout his life Chapman has given public talks, written articles for newspapers and journals, contributed more talks and commentaries on radio than can now be counted, and appeared on television to speak on political events, especially general elections. He took the role of public educator sufficiently seriously to write also for secondary schools. An excerpt from one of those books, *The Political Scene 1919-1931* (1969), is included here as Chapter 6. This reprint, plus the articles from journals such as the *Listener* and the *National Business Review,* show Chapman's ability to write of complex issues clearly and without condescension to readers coming from a variety of ages and educational backgrounds.

For Chapman, effective communication of information and ideas can be achieved only through the effective use of language. The writings here display his love of the English language. Whether writing for academic, literary or general readers, Chapman crafted his words until they suited the audience and, indeed, satisfied his personal quest for the perfectly balanced phrase, the precise word, the quiet joke and the apt metaphor. Especially in the earlier writings his language appears very different from that of the plain (and frequently careless) styles of contemporary writing. But anyone who enjoys the art and craft of prose will appreciate the care and precision of the writings here.

Chapman has written or co-written four books, edited or co-edited three (including *The Oxford Anthology of New Zealand Verse*, co-edited with J. F. Bennett and published in 1956), co-authored two major reports for government, and contributed a number of very substantial chapters and articles to collections in books and to journals. Many of his political commentaries were never published, however, and many more were published in ephemeral sources. One of the purposes of this book is to make some of these talks and papers accessible. Although radio and television texts could not be included, two previously unpublished talks have been printed here. Others have been taken from books that are no longer in print or from journals or newspapers. Two pieces (the first chapters) are from *Landfall*, one piece is from the *University of Auckland Gazette*, one chapter comprises excerpts from the *National Business Review*, there is an article from the *New Zealand Listener*, and four chapters have been drawn from *Comment*.[1] Two chapters represent Chapman's contributions to official commissions of inquiry. *New Zealand Politics and Social Patterns* contains a fair sample of the breadth of the contributions made by Chapman to political and social analysis.

Chapman began as a political historian and became a political scientist (although he himself has preferred to call his department and discipline the less contestable and perhaps more encompassing 'Political Studies'.) The study of politics thereby gained by his shift in focus, but it might have meant that his scholarly works received less attention than had he remained primarily a writer of history (and, perhaps, literary analysis). For political history tells a story and (like all good stories) tends to be judged on its literary style as well as on its historical analysis. Put simply, the historian's craft is more accessible to more people than that of the political scientist, whose work is likely also to be clouded with the suspicion that it is about 'theory'. The writings included in this collection should help to dispel such suspicions.

Chapman's writings span the half-century of the great and rapid changes which have shaped contemporary New Zealand. To make any sense of the present we need to comprehend the recent past. To this end, the collection offers the reader enlightenment.

Themes

Because there are more themes in this book than can be adequately discussed in this short Introduction, I shall highlight just three: the comparative and international context in which Chapman has researched and explained New Zealand politics and society; the analysis of social and political patterns which provide the intellectual threads of his analyses; and his arguments concerning the nature and problems of New Zealand democracy. These themes appear and reappear throughout the writings and talks published here.

After an illuminating three and a half years studying Australian politics as a research fellow at the Australian National University, Chapman missed the lecturing to students whose experiences and background he had shared. He consciously chose to return home and not to join permanently the academic drift overseas. To remain home (apart from periods of research leave spent abroad) has not meant that he has treated New Zealand political history, political science and literature in an insular way. On the contrary, pertinent insights and well-founded generalisations are derived from examining other states and cultures. Political science is of course an inherently comparative subject; and in this sense Chapman is true to his discipline. Although he never wrote formal comparative political analyses, all of Chapman's work has been enriched by comparative data and ideas. For example, he has long been fascinated with the politics of the United States of America which culminated in spending most of a presidential election year there on a Carnegie Fellowship. This had a major impact on his analysis of New Zealand politics. When studying Maori politics, he looked to the situation of African-American citizens, leading to questions about the relationships between government, ethnicity, political parties, and political behaviour. At a time when most political commentators barely acknowledged ethnic minorities, Chapman was analysing their position. But whether it was the politics of minorities, the role played by constitutional development, the nature of electoral systems and their impact on parties and accountability, the role of the courts, the position of the arts, or the political role of broadcasting in modern societies, Chapman's work on New Zealand has been influenced and disciplined by his knowledge of other societies and polities as well as his own.

New Zealand's position in the world—its trade relations, its military vulnerability in the nuclear age, its relationships with particular geographical areas such as South Africa and the South Pacific—have been central to Chapman's commentaries and analyses of governmental and electoral behaviour. Writing about New Zealand's place in the world in his 1961 article, 'No Land is an Island: Twentieth Century Politics' (Chapter 3), he says, '[W]e live in an age when national differences constitute no more than regional variations on international modes of living. We are different; but not very.' A prescient remark, given turn of the twentieth century internationalisation of world finance and commercial corporations and the convergence of national cultures. New Zealand's foreign relations are of great interest to Chapman, for how can we comprehend domestic politics without also understanding the dynamics of war, commerce, finance, and strategic alliances? At times he wrote directly of these subjects in papers that unfortunately had to be excluded from this collection. For example, throughout his life Chapman has opposed the use of nuclear weapons, and one of his interesting unpublished talks is on the impact on New Zealand of nuclear war.[2] Another article discusses the European Economic Community, General Charles de Gaulle's attitudes towards Britain, and the British government's European and international policies under the then Prime Minister, Harold Wilson.[3]

One of the intriguing aspects of Chapman's work is his analysis of 'social patterns': the behaviour of groups, the order of events, and the social and political structures of contemporary society. He links minutiae and the grand together, micro- and macro-phenomena (in economic jargon). Throughout his lifetime, Chapman has been fascinated with detail and the ways in which the small bits and pieces of life contribute to the overall jigsaw pattern, whether these are the social actions and attitudes depicted by novelists and poets or the social and political attitudes which influence voting behaviour. The detail forms the whole, a picture of a society. Many of the chapters here show Chapman's constant quest to uncover the fit between personal and group experiences on the one hand, and patterns of political behaviour on the other. Many of the assumptions about voting behaviour which have been taken for granted by party strategists, newspaper commentators, twentieth century historians, and political scientists, have been grounded on Chapman's polling booth analysis, grass-roots political behaviour indeed. The data were enriched by Chapman's lifelong love affair with geography and maps, begun when he was using meteorological maps while doing his military service during World War Two. In a recent conversation about this, Robert Chapman remembered 'working amongst isobars and stations denoted by symbols and figures for the points from which the maps derived their weather patterns'.

There are well-known methodological problems of extrapolating from the individual, from a small group or from a geographical area to larger units of analysis such as society or the polity as a whole. Chapman himself, however, in his polling booth research, was aware of the limitations of generalising from the behaviour of small groups to that of society in general. Similarly, he was cautious about generalising downwards: from the behaviour of the group to the individual. He was enthusiastic about the potential of survey research to tap individual attitudes and adapted it to his purposes as soon as the technology was available. At the same time, 'as with most studies dependent on the judgment of humans and numbers, one is soon at the limits of what can be proven' (Chapter 5, 'Psephology').

Above all else, perhaps, Chapman's analysis is systematic. As he said in 1996, it has been grounded on, '[A] study of every electorate from 1908 to 1935 reported in my thesis written in 1946/47 and many grey months in the cellars of Parliament reading newspapers from Invercargill to Whangarei'. He went on to list the historians and sociologists whose work he used, and commented,

> The most subtle social observers, of course, were the short-story writers and novelists of the time. So I drew from them all: writers, historians, economists, and professional social observers alike. Thus my work was seated on some very stout shoulders—and on some young ones [referring to research students] as well.[4]

Not only has Chapman's work been ordered and exhaustive: it has also been accurate in every detail so that his generalisations are always built on rock-solid foundations.

Naturally Chapman has had his critics. Nevertheless, his analyses of elections, governments and electoral behaviour have been highly influential. I note especially his focus on the sectional and social divisions of society, the attention he paid to the non-vote and its significance for party and governmental fortunes, and his steady stream of comments— based on his research findings—on the ineffectualness of enrolment procedures, the frequently unfair drawing of electorate boundaries, and the sadly inadequate administration of the Maori seats. These criticisms have been persuasive and persistent and have had a direct impact on New Zealand political institutions as well as on the study of government and political behaviour.

Chapman's views on the nature of New Zealand democracy flow as undercurrents throughout the first two parts of this book, surfacing in the third. For Chapman, politics in its very essence is conflictual. Political parties express social and economic interests, interests which almost by definition are distinctive interpretations of the world. Chapman acknowledged, however, that societies' interests do not create a simple unidimensional politics based solely on differences between labour and capital, workers and producers, the poor and the rich. Indeed, as Chapman said at a talk in 1996 (where he explained why he had never used the idea of 'swing' to explain movements between parties), 'Politics before MMP and certainly after it have always been multi-dimensional'.[5] Given this, it is the role of political institutions such as parties and the electoral system to reduce and simplify the lines of conflict before the binding decisions of government are attempted. The first-past-the-post electoral system, and the representation in Parliament of two broad-church parties broadly expressing the interests of the centre-left on one side and the centre-right on the other side which that electoral system tends to produce, are the means of achieving this simplification. Broad parties more satisfactorily articulate two sets of policy interests, presenting real alternatives to electors and enabling them to reach a clear verdict for or against a party in government.

Although socially an egalitarian and moderately radical in his social preferences, Chapman has thus been generally conservative about New Zealand political institutions, approving of the basic, Westminster shape (until the introduction of the Mixed Member Proportional electoral system). His appreciation of how institutions found themselves on practice and so accrue legitimacy has led him to support aspects of our polity which have been criticised by others (for instance the two-party system and the uncodified constitution). Chapman appreciates New Zealand's pragmatic, incremental solutions to social and political problems and the quiet successes of some of our institutions. An example is the Maori Seats, created as a temporary part-solution to the problem of uneven numbers and unfair representation in 1867 and still in existence today. But alongside general approval of the basic architecture of the political system goes considerable disquiet about its operation. Uneasiness appears when he considers the disparities of opportunity and resources between Maori and pakeha, the complacency of the socially conservative, the stupidity and venality of some of our politicians, and the imposition of radical political and social reforms which fail to consider the continuities of our social and political culture and the achievements of the past. Naturally, Chapman the political reformer frequently appears in the text— political scientists since classical times have been concerned with normative as well as empirical analysis.

Content

Part One: Society and Politics, contains a selection of Chapman's more wide-ranging writings by bringing together some works on society and the state. The first work (and the earliest of the writings in this collection) is 'Fiction and the Social Pattern: Some Implications of Recent New Zealand Writing'. This article needs no comment from me; it is widely regarded as a seminal work on New Zealand literature and society. Chapter 2, 'Great Expectations: New Zealand Since the War' reprints an article that originated in an address to the New Zealand University Students' Association Congress of January 1962 at Curious Cove in the Marlborough Sounds. The author explores the relationships between government policy (especially economic policy), party behaviour and voting behaviour, going back to the nineteenth century to explain ideologies of the post-war period.

'No Land is an Island: Twentieth Century Politics', was an Auckland University 1960 Winter Lecture. The lectures were published in *Distance Looks Our Way: The Effects of Remoteness on New Zealand*, edited by Keith Sinclair. The topic of the lecture series had been chosen by Harry Scott, then Head of the Psychology Department, who died tragically in a climbing accident shortly after. The book's title was from Charles Brasch's poem, 'The Islands' (ii):

Everywhere in light and calm the murmuring
Shadow of departure: distance looks our way:
And none knows where he will lie down at night.

Here Chapman explores the impact of New Zealand's isolation on its arts and its politics. The impact of the institutions and politics of other states upon New Zealand is also analysed; and the likenesses between New Zealand and other states discussed. The first part of the book concludes appropriately with a chapter which brings together Chapman's historical knowledge and his understanding of the nature of the contemporary state to consider the question of funding of the arts—an issue of continuing relevance today. This paper was presented to an Arts Conference held in Wellington and organised by a leading patron of the arts, Frederick Turnovsky. It was attended by writers and artists, among others, and looked at the policies of the then Arts Council. Chapman's own view is that, in the absence of private sponsorship for the arts, there should be state subsidies.[6]

Part Two traces New Zealand political history between the 1920s and the 1980s. Chapman's MA thesis at the University of Auckland was entitled 'The Significance of the 1928 General Election' (1948) and he has never lost his early fascination with elections: the battles between parties and leaders; the policies argued about; and the patterns created by stable allegiances and shifting loyalties of the voters. His study of electoral behaviour, using both polling booth data and survey research, led him to develop the theory of the sectional basis of New Zealand politics. Thus the title of this section, 'Town, City and Country', is an apt one. The towns, and some of what Chapman called the 'mixed city' areas, were the major battlegrounds of electoral politics, for they contained cross-sections of the voting community and thus were balanced between Labour and National. The single-member constituency, simple plurality electoral system of the pre-1996 period meant that elections were decided in these electorates, the marginal seats. Other significant themes developed by Chapman in his analyses of elections were the significance of non-voting in understanding electoral behaviour and the results of elections and the role played by third (minor) parties in absorbing the votes of the discontented and blunting the effects of the movement of opinion between government and opposition, Labour and National. Furthermore, unlike many other political analysts, Chapman never ignored Maori politics. For him they are a fascinating and significant dimension of our social and historical patterns.

Part Two begins with a brief paper on 'Psephology', the study of the 'nature and habits of the mass electorate'. Here Chapman discusses how American and British political science established the study of voting behaviour. The chapter which follows, 'The Sad, Slow End of the Twenties', applies the psephological craft to three-party politics, an analysis of great interest now when the voting system differs but the results in Parliament are similar. The sectional differences which have for so long fascinated Chapman are employed to interpret the voting results during the 1920s. Chapter 7, 'The Response to Labour and the Question of Parallelism of Opinion, 1928-1960', traces the fortunes of the Labour Party and its passages in and out of government. More importantly, it analyses how electors made their verdicts on the governments of their times and, more particularly, how the Left in politics was treated. Again, sectionalism, non-voting, and third-party voting, are all seen to play their parts. The major thesis, and probably the most controversial one, is that electors move almost as one when they pronounce their verdicts on governments. The chapter includes an important discussion of Maori voters and politics.

The next five chapters study particular elections from the 'non-decision' of 1963 until the bitter, 1981 election, perhaps a turning point in modern politics. (It would have been even better to have included all of Chapman's discussions of particular elections but unfortunately several of the radio talks have been lost.) One of the strengths of the election analyses collected here is their contribution to our historical understanding. As New Zealand faces the issues of the twenty-first century, the world of the mid-twentieth century—of 'credit squeezes', import licences and cuts, national development conferences, a dominant belief that Maori should be assimilated and integrated into the majority culture, and the early years of second-wave feminism—seems a world apart.[7] These election analyses inform us and refresh our memories.

Chapter 13 reprints Chapman's contribution to the *Report of the Royal Commission on the Electoral System: Towards a Better Democracy* (1986) where he analyses the subtleties of the voting patterns in the Maori seats. Part Two ends suitably with a talk Chapman gave to the 1977 Political Studies conference on the topic of by-elections, entitled 'Deaths and Entrances'. Chapman has always been interested in by-elections, and often wrote newspaper articles on specific ones. One of the most interesting findings of this chapter is the habit New Zealand political leaders seem to have adopted of entering Parliament at a by-election.

The six chapters in Part Three: Governing Democratically develop some important normative issues that were only touched on in the earlier chapters. The first chapter with its electoral theme glances backwards. It is a criticism of the administration of the electoral system and also contains a justification of the continued existence of the Maori seats. Next, Chapter 16, 'On Democracy as Having and Exercising a Clear Choice of Government', presents probably the clearest and most persuasive published defence of the single-member constituency, simple plurality electoral system that was voted out in the 1993 referendum. Chapter 17, 'The Politics of Division?', is a fascinating return to the 1981 general election discussed earlier in Part Two. Now, however, the scope is broadened to include the problem of what happens when consensus on the means by which issues are resolved—a vital element of democratic health—diminishes. The chapter illuminates the whole period of the Muldoon years and the character and political motivations of Robert Muldoon himself. Chapman turns his attention again to the marginal seats, showing how Muldoon's refusal to stop the Springbok tour of New Zealand can at least in part be explained by the Prime Minister's pursuit of votes, a strategy that was successful in returning his government to power, albeit by a narrow margin. The origins and rationale of the 'Think Big' policies are also explained. This chapter, with its reference to the rule of law, economic debates, the abandonment of subsidies, and the pursuit of individualism as the basis for social and economic policy, bridges the way to the radical changes of the fourth Labour Government. It is also a summation of the Muldoon years and their legacy to New Zealand political life.

Chapman has always been interested in the mass media, especially its relationship with politics and government. The voter is 'an expert on ... how he feels the last three years have treated him'. Thus governments are judged on their records. Oppositions, however, are largely reliant on the news media:

> The reporting, placing and heading of news stories and, above all, the amount of background analysis of New Zealand trends do much to determine whether

an Opposition can make it plain what its alternatives are, why they were chosen, and how they add up. In this way, the news media are a vital component of the democratic process itself but a component which is, by convention, largely outside the control of the system.[8]

In Chapter 18, 'Restructuring Broadcasting', Chapman sets out a model for effective and competitive television. When the Labour Party went into government in 1972 it set up a commission of inquiry into broadcasting. Chapman became one of the members and was the major author of the extracts included here. The proposals show his concern for quality television and his awareness that structure and control indeed impact on impartiality and quality. In a recent conversation he recalled,

> The changes rapidly became law. A new channel was constructed and both public channels went to colour while radio received its independence and resources. Then the 1975 election introduced Robert Muldoon as Prime Minister and the TV teams were cut down, finance went to bankers' rates, the old loose corporation form returned and the whole system was pointed in an intensified commercial direction. This reversal well illustrates how vital to the nature of the nation's communication systems are the principals as well as the principles of successive governments.

Chapman subsequently chaired the Royal Commission on Broadcasting set up by the Labour Government elected in July 1984.

Chapter 19, 'Political Culture: The Purposes of Party and the Current Challenge', brings together Chapman's views on the significance of the role of political parties in democracies in general and in New Zealand in particular. He argues that Labour and National ideally provide electors with 'alternate parties of government' and that third parties deflect this alternation. Parties provide voters with programmes from which to choose; independent voting, as illustrated by the legislative treatment of such issues as abortion, is ineffectual and incoherent. Party government provides a coherent theory of democratic accountability: governing parties are accountable to the people, to their caucuses, and to their extra-parliamentary party organisations—the latter being the most contested aspect of accountability. But in recent years cabinet had become dominant over caucus and this distorted the accountability process. Through expanding the number of MPs within (or supporting) the political executive, a 'fortress cabinet' had developed. Not only was this a product of the power of numbers, it had also been abetted by the many changes in our society, including the mass media. The fortress cabinets ignored the will of voters, party members and backbench MPs. Thus the normative assumptions about the relationship between party and programme accountability had been undermined. The 1984-1990 Labour government, in particular, by retreating from its historic view of the good state as the positive state, had loosened the link between party and programme.

The last chapter is the most recently written. 'A Political Culture Under Pressure: The Struggle to Preserve a Progressive Tax Base for Welfare and the Positive State' unravels the story of what happened to Roger Douglas's proposal to shift to a flat tax system. The author applies his years of observation and his analytical abilities to studying the published correspondence between Douglas, the Minister of Finance, and David Lange, the Prime Minister, to trace what happened and to explain why. The result is a masterly portrait of two men engaged in a battle of wills. But it is far more than this, for it is also a suitable elegy for the fourth Labour government in particular and accountable party government in a welfare state in general.

Acknowledgements

The compilation and editing of this book has, alas, taken far too long. Without the help I have received throughout, however, it would have taken even longer. First and foremost, Noeline Chapman, Robert Chapman's wife, typist, proof-reader, critic and archivist, has my heartfelt thanks for her help in retrieving texts and dates from her files and her memory. Her advice has been invaluable. Paul Harris, chairperson of the then Department of Politics, Victoria University of Wellington, provided the initial encouragement for this project. Stephen Levine, also a former chairperson, supported and encouraged this work. Peter Aimer, formerly Senior Lecturer at the Department of Political Studies, University of Auckland, helped provide material and critical comments. Andrew Walker conscientiously scanned the material electronically. Theresa Rogers, formerly an administrative assistant at the School of Political Science and International Relations, typed some of the text. Adrienne Nolan, Administrator of the School of Political Science and International Relations, willingly provided the essential expertise at the keyboard and thus made the whole enterprise possible. Fergus Barrowman of Victoria University Press had sufficient faith in this collection to undertake its publication, and his colleague, Rachel Lawson, skilfully escorted the book through its final stages. Finally I should like to thank Robert Chapman for his patience, good humour and forbearance during the editorial process.

Elizabeth McLeay
School of Political Science and International Relations
Victoria University of Wellington
March 1999

Notes

1. *Landfall* is a literary journal begun in 1947 by Charles Brasch. It still exists today. *Comment* was a review of social, political and literary issues published in two series: 1959 until 1970; and 1977 until 1982.
2. 'Preliminary Notes on Political and Communications Aspects of a Northern Nuclear Exchange Scenario and its Effects on New Zealand'. During the 1950s Chapman was president of the Movement Against Nuclear Weapons which advocated a multilateral end to nuclear tests in the atmosphere. He and an Auckland physicist were the authors of a petition to a parliamentary select committee in 1957 which gained a 'most favourable recommendation', but no action.
3. 'Entente Incordiale', *Comment*, Vol. 4, No. 3 (April 1963), pp. 38-45.
4. 'Comment' on Brian Easton's 'The Political Economy of Robert Chapman', a paper presented at the New Zealand Political Studies Association Annual Conference, University of Auckland, July 1996.
5. 'Comment' (1996).
6. Chapman recalls being told at the time by the politicians who attended the Conference that the speakers were not to ask for money.
7. Readers might like to refer also to Chapman's 'From Labour to National', *The Oxford History of New Zealand* (Wellington, 1981), pp. 333-68. This straddles the pieces collected here, discussing governmental and party history from the first Labour government until the defeat of the third Labour government by National under its new leader, Robert Muldoon.
8. 'How is Our Political System Working?', *The Listener* (26 September 1969), p. 11. This article was an Election Preview.

A Note on the Texts

The works included in this book come from a variety of published and unpublished sources. They have been reprinted here as they were in the original; there is no standardisation of spelling or of the abbreviations in the body of the text. Endnotes in the originals have become footnotes, and bracketed references in the body of the original texts have been expanded into footnotes. In general, though, the references have been left as they were. The style of the editor's footnotes is uniform throughout. Editor's footnotes have been placed inside square brackets and end with 'Ed.') Notes have been kept to a minimum and are usually restricted to explanations of people and events where the essential information is not obvious from the context. The notes are also usually confined to New Zealand political events, individuals and publications. Some of the footnotes might appear unnecessary to those who have lived through the events described. Those who were born during the 1970s or later, however, might have a different perspective.

Where necessary, headings have been added to the tables and figures and they have been renumbered (or numbered) to fit with orthodox contemporary style. Material not included (usually a table or a figure) is clearly indicated in the text as '[Omitted]'. Some of the graphs have been left out of this work when they have been either too complex to replicate or when they repeat data that are in the text or are elsewhere in the book.

The very occasional typographical mistake has been corrected with no 'sic' fanfare. (There are almost no misprints or other sorts of errors in Robert Chapman's work.)

Much of the information about MPs and ministers has been taken from the excellent compilation by G. A. Wood (ed.), *Ministers and Members in the New Zealand Parliament*, 2nd edn. (Dunedin, University of Otago Press, 1996).

The sources of the articles included in this selection, their original titles and acknowledgements, are as follows. They are set out here in the order in which they appear in the Table of Contents.

'Fiction and the Social Pattern: Some Implications of Recent New Zealand Writing', *Landfall*, Vol. 7, No. 1 (March 1953), pp. 26-58. Reprinted in Wystan Curnow (ed.), *Essays on New Zealand Literature* (Auckland, Heinemann Educational Books, 1973), pp. 71-98.

'Great Expectations: New Zealand Since the War', originally published as 'New Zealand Since the War: 8. Politics and Society', *Landfall*, Vol. 16, No. 3 (September 1962), pp. 252-77.

'No Land is an Island: Twentieth Century Politics', in Keith Sinclair (ed.), *Distance Looks Our Way: The Effects of Remoteness on New Zealand* (Hamilton, Paul's Book Arcade for the University of Auckland, 1961), pp. 42-62. Reprinted with the permission of Auckland University Press.

'Patronage in a Changing World', unpublished speech, *Arts Conference*, Wellington, April 1970.

'Psephology', *University of Auckland Gazette*, Vol. 5, No. 2 (July 1963), pp. 3-5.

'The Sad, Slow End of the Twenties', Chapter 5, *The Political Scene, 1919-1931* (Auckland, Heinemann Educational Books Ltd., 1969), pp. 54-65.

'The Response to Labour and the Question of Parallelism of Opinion, 1928-1960', in Robert Chapman and Keith Sinclair (eds.), *Studies of a Small Democracy: Essays in Honour of Willis Airey* (Auckland, Blackwood and Janet Paul Ltd. for the University of Auckland, 1963), pp. 221-52. Reprinted with the permission of Auckland University Press.

'The "No Change" Election: 1963', originally published as 'The "No Change" Election', *Comment*, Vol. 5, No. 2 (January 1964), pp. 8-10.

'The 1969 Election', *Comment*, Vol. 10, No. 4 (April 1970), pp. 14-18.

'The 1975 Result: How did it Happen and Why?' compiled from a series of 11 articles on the 1975 general election, *National Business Review* (August-October 1976). The articles reprinted here as subsections of the chapter, and their dates, are as follows: 'Introduction', originally entitled: 'There could be dramatic voter shifts again in 1978' (4 August); 'The stable voter: predictability and surprises' (11 August); 'Delving into the non-vote phenomenon' (15 September); 'The principal reasons we voted the way we did on November 29, 1975' (22 September); and 'How voters responded to Muldoon and Rowling in November 1975' (13 October). The titles of the articles omitted from *New Zealand Politics and Social Patterns* are indicated in footnotes to the text. Reprinted with permission from the *National Business Review*.

'The Case of the Pulled Punch: The 1978 Election', *Comment*, New Series, No. 6 (February 1979), pp. 17-20.

'New Zealand Defers Decision: The 1981 Election', originally published as 'New Zealand Defers Decision: Robert Chapman Reviews the 1981 General Election and Ponders its Consequences', *Comment*, New Series, No. 16 (August 1982), pp. 11-18.

'Voting in the Maori Political Sub-System, 1935-1984', in the Annex to Appendix B, *Report of the Royal Commission on the Electoral System: Towards a Better Democracy* (Wellington, 1986, B-83-108).

'Deaths and Entrances', unpublished paper, *New Zealand Political Studies Association Conference*, University of Auckland, 1977.

'The Mechanics of Representation', *New Zealand Listener* (24 October, 1969), pp. 9 and 27. Reprinted with the permission of the *New Zealand Listener*.

'On Democracy as Having and Exercising a Clear Choice of Government', in J. Stephen Hoadley (ed.), *Improving New Zealand's Democracy* (Auckland, New Zealand Foundation for Peace Studies, 1979), pp. 85-95.

'The Politics of Division?' in Graham Bush (ed.), *New Zealand—A Nation Divided?* (Auckland, The University of Auckland, 1983), pp. 95-110.

'Restructuring Broadcasting', extracts from 'The New Structure', *The Broadcasting Future of New Zealand* (Wellington, Government Printer, 1973), pp. 15-34. This volume contained the recommendations of the Committee on Broadcasting chaired by Kenneth Adam. Robert Chapman was a member of the Committee and was the primary author of the extracts reprinted here. The other members were John Robson and Dorothea Turner. Reprinted with the permission of GP Publications.

'Political Culture: The Purposes of Party and the Current Challenge', in Hyam Gold (ed.), *New Zealand Politics in Perspective*, 2nd edn. (Auckland, Longman Paul, 1989), pp. 14-32.

'A Political Culture Under Pressure: The Struggle to Preserve a Progressive Tax Base for Welfare and the Positive State', *Political Science*, Vol. 44, No. 1 (July 1992), pp. 1-27. Reprinted with the permission of *Political Science*.

Other information about the origins of the works collected here is contained in my Introduction.

Elizabeth McLeay

List of Tables and Figures

Tables		Page
2.1:	The Portion Voting Communist Amongst All Qualified to Vote	61
2.2:	The Possible Sources of Social Credit Support in 1954	65
2.3:	Party Membership of Parliament, 1946-1960, Under Proportional Representation and in Fact	66
2.4:	Goods Available and Election Results, 1954-1960	69
6.1:	Parties, Voting and Sectionalism, 1919 and 1928	121
7.1:	Sectional Differences in Reception of the Left	135
7.2:	Rates of Gain/Loss for the Left, 1928-1960	139
7.3:	Loss of Votes by the Left, 1938 to 1951	140
7.4:	The Left and its Shares of the Whole Vote, 1928-1960 and 1938-1960	141
7.5:	The Sectional Profiles of National and Social Credit	147
7.6:	Country and Independent Country Candidates	149
7.7:	Democratic Soldier Labour—Shares and Averages (1943)	149
7.8:	Two Measures of the Popularity of the Left	152
7.9:	Origins of Non-Voters in the 1951 Strike Election	155
10.1:	Movement of New Changers, 1974	182
10.2:	Final Party Gain/Loss Among New Changers, 1975	183
10.3:	The Choice for Prime Minister in 1975	194
10.4:	The Pull of the Leaders Compared with their Parties	196
11.1:	Net Movements of the Percentages of Valid Votes Cast, 1975-1978 and 1951-1954	206
12.1:	Change in Majorities in Town Seats, 1978 to 1981	212
12.2:	Net Movements in the Maori Seats Between 1978 and 1981	214
12.3:	Changes in Majorities in Mixed City Seats, 1978 to 1981	217

New Zealand Politics and Social Patterns

		Page
12.4:	Changes in Percentage Shares of Valid Votes between 1978 and 1981 in East Coast Bays and Pakuranga	221
12.5:	Change in Majorities in the Northern, Central and Western North Island Region, 1978 to 1981	222
13.1:	General Seat and Maori Seat Electors' Support for Social Credit, 1954-1984	235
13.2:	Maori Seat and General Seat Support for Social Credit Expressed as Shares of the non-Labour Voting Sector, 1954-1984	236
13.3:	Maori Seat Voting Changes between 1981 and 1984	252

Figures

2.1:	Classified and Equal Societies: West Europe and New Zealand	81
7.1:	The Left with and without the Democratic Soldier Labour Party	145
7.2:	The Left 1928-1960: Candidates' Average in Each Class of Seat	151
7.3:	The Shares Won by the Left, 1928-1960, in Maori and European Constituencies	158
10.1:	Party Percentages of All Stable Voters, 1969-1975	178
10.2:	The Parties and the Vote Changers, 1975	184
13.1:	Fifty Years of Maori Voting	227
18.1:	Structure of the Broadcasting Council and the Corporations	311

Part One

Society and Politics

I

Fiction and the Social Pattern: Some Implications of Recent New Zealand Writing

It seemed to be quite widely held at the Writers' Conference in May of 1951 that criticism of the novel and short story in New Zealand is played out. There were not thought to be enough works to sustain examination more than once in, say, twenty years. We had E. H. McCormick's *Letters and Art in New Zealand,* published in 1940, and a chapter of seventeen pages in *Creative Writing in New Zealand* by J. C. Reid on fiction from the Great War to 1946. So on this reasoning the market is saturated, presumably, for the next fifteen years. Yet, quite apart from the need to explore the standpoint of sociological criticism, to which the present writer referred in a note in *Landfall* on the Writers' Conference, the attitude that any more criticism is uncalled for overlooks the quantity of considerable fiction produced since the works of E. H. McCormick and J. C. Reid.

Any list of 'considerable' fiction is bound to be arbitrary; but it is necessary to give some consideration to what has been produced and when in order to see whither New Zealand fiction has travelled. Before E. H. McCormick wrote what is clearly still the outstanding critical conspectus of New Zealand writing Katherine Mansfield had produced all her work and Frank Sargeson his two collections of short stories, *Conversation With My Uncle* and *A Man and His Wife.* Thus the two major subjects for criticism yet to be raised here were at least open for discussion. McCormick deals also with four novels of Satchell, four of Jane Mander's, two of C. R. Allen's, four of Robin Hyde's, short stories by Alice Webb and B. E. Baughan, *Children of the Poor* by John A. Lee, and, last and best of these, John Mulgan's *Man Alone* which appeared in 1939. The first collection of Roderick Finlayson's short stories, *Brown Man's Burden,* had also been published, in 1938.

Between 1940 and the appearance of J. C. Reid's survey (1946) three novels were brought out together with the same number of collections of short stories.[1] The four issues of *New Zealand New Writing* (1943-5)

[This chapter, written in February 1952, is an extended version of an address delivered to the NZ University Students' Association Congress in January 1952. It was first published in *Landfall,* Vol. 7, No. 1 (1953). Ed.]

introduced among others, as short story writers, D. M. Anderson, David Ballantyne, John Cole, Maurice Duggan, A. P. Gaskell, W. H. Pearson, Helen Shaw and Greville Texidor, and printed Finlayson, Gilbert and Sargeson. Since 1946 there have been ten novels and three collections of short stories[2], as well as twenty issues of *Landfall* with an average of two short stories or short story length extracts from novels in each issue. *Landfall* has added or established new writers, including three who appear more than once there, Bruce Mason, P. J. Wilson and O. E. Middleton, and thirteen who have contributed just once. Also, the ninth issue of *Book*, in 1947, was a short story number.

Thus, possibly it is not too much to say that the bulk of considerable fiction produced here (leaving aside Katherine Mansfield) has been printed since 1946, and undoubtedly has been printed since 1940 when E. H. McCormick produced our most weighty criticism so far.

This impression that we have enough extended criticism partly arises from the sheer bulk of recent occasional criticism over the radio, at the back of magazines and in school journals; an occasional criticism which has room at times for the pregnant remark but which tends to repetition of what can be grasped and stated quickly. But a less obvious part of the explanation for the impression of a surfeit of criticism proper may be that in the search for good writing produced by New Zealanders about New Zealand the poets were the first to strike oil. E. H. McCormick regards Eileen Duggan's poetry as the close of one chapter with Ursula Bethell, J. C. Beaglehole and the Phoenix poets, Fairburn, Mason, Curnow and Glover, as the start of the next. This places the poetic strike at the beginning of the decade which closed with Mulgan's *Man Alone* (1939) and Sargeson's *A Man and His Wife* (1940). The relative gusher of prose came later—on the whole, nearly ten years later—the strength of the earlier poetic achievement perhaps acting to obscure the timing of the later development and, in particular, to obscure the fact that criticism came much nearer in time to the beginning of the developments in fiction than to those in poetry. Whether this did obscure the rapid and recent development of prose or not, some investigation of the sources of the phenomenon and of its significant features seems justified.

It is fairly patent that we have to thank the depression for the original impetus. McCormick, who missed very little, said 'The "Great Depression" disorganised New Zealand's economy ...; it led to political changes more radical than those of the nineties; it effected a reorientation in outlook of major importance to New Zealand's literature and not without some influence on its art ... it can be said with certainty that a continuation of the comfortable pre-depression conditions could not have led to the New Zealand of 1940 with its signs, few but positive, of adult nationhood.'³ The overturn in social conditions broke up the crust of complacency, allowing artists to see into what lay beneath. At the same time the disturbed conditions upset the pattern of normal lives and made some men, who might otherwise have taken a more usual course, into artists or apprentice artists forced to look below that broken crust.

This process took time. *Phoenix Miscellany*. 1 of September 1933, which was also the first collection of Allen Curnow's poems, has as first line 'Strange times have taken hold on me', but the 'strange times' were personal, the volume was concerned with the poet's relation to God. By 1939, in Curnow's *Not In Narrow Seas*, The Wind, which blew the emigrants to New Zealand and 'serves still to remind the patriot that the fight for liberty continues', reflects:

> The flag rides rattling at the hoist
> At prison and at madhouse door;
> I swell'd their sails and what's the end?
> The poor insane and the insane poor.⁴

The *Phoenix* of the Auckland students of 1932 duly re-arose as Ronald Holloway's Unicorn Press of Auckland and the Caxton Press of Christchurch. Here, and particularly in the poetry of the second half of the thirties published by Denis Glover at the Caxton, the development proceeded. Prose was largely taken up by direct political statement in the columns of *Tomorrow* from 1934 onwards. The Unicorn Press brought out the twenty-nine pages of *Conversation with My Uncle* in 1936 and Roderick Finlayson's *Brown Man's Burden* in 1938. By 1940 Sargeson, Mulgan and Finlayson, with four appearances between them, stood alongside a variety of significant poetry. But the presses and the precedents were established for the war period when a further major disturbance of the social pattern, coming at a time when the impulse of the depression was subsiding, carried the development on.

Political prose, *Tomorrow*, and those interested in writing by the depression and the sequent Labour Government supported the four 'progressive' bookshops. The bookshops brought forth the Progressive Publishing Society and the Progressive Publishing Society produced *New Zealand New Writing*, edited by Professor Ian Gordon. Here was an opportunity to publish for those whose routine of existence had been thoroughly disoriented and who saw New Zealand and New Zealanders in the services in the illuminating glare of the war years. The poets had put writing on the map and at considerable personal cost given writing a rough direction and some prestige.

Reinforcing and possibly outweighing this was the example of *Penguin New Writing* which had been coming out since late in 1940. Here was a continuing model of the short story of record, a model slab-of-life form into which could be put the slab-of-life experiences which, heightened by the vital-seeming quality of wartime, were felt so sharply by those shaken out of their civil rut. Moreover, the New Zealand short story writer Frank Sargeson, who had made the biggest stir and whose short novel *That Summer* was published in a sequence of three numbers of *Penguin New Writing* in 1943, used this same form either for presenting an exactly composed incident or for a clothes line of incident like *That Summer* itself.

Those who took the opportunity and were printed first in *New Zealand New Writing* include, as the list earlier in this article shows, many who were to persevere until, in the second half of the forties, they produced novels, short story collections and provided the basis of *Landfall* fiction; in brief, wrote the material whose sources have been sought.

Many, however, wrote once and wrote no more. Twenty-five made a single appearance in *New Zealand New Writing* or *Speaking For Ourselves* or *Book Nine* for the twelve who have continued on into *Landfall* or into books of their own. The major reason for this steady execution is obvious enough on reading the short stories. Briefly, it was not found possible to produce works of art without using art. The slab-of-life form was deceptive in its apparent simplicity. It appeared to be plotless and a mere matter of reportage and description. It was easy to miss at first the selection and arrangement of incident and detail which revealed, in those stories which were successful, an attitude to the matter handled. To lack such an attitude was to fail to invest the event or situation recorded with a significance in relationship to anything outside the event or situation; it was to lack a standpoint to shape art from occurrence. Many were tempted by what seemed a new path in writing open to any who had been roused to walk by stirring events, but of the crowd few persisted until they had learned 'the trick of standing upright' there.

The subtitle to one short story in *New Zealand New Writing* describes itself and many of its neighbours as 'Fragment of an autobiography which is extremely unlikely ever to be written'.[5] Unlikely because the writing of even the first short story hinted ever more loudly at difficulties that previously had been unseen and now, for want of the aptitudes and techniques, must be largely ignored. Unlikely also because the finished products revealed their formlessness which arose from their authors' lack of the minimum of a consistent attitude to their experience on which to ring each coin of incident before deciding its place. The greatest want—the novice writers' want of a position in relation to their world which might have conferred a function and consequently some structure on their stories—was the widest spread and the most telling in its effects.

Indeed, if the same matter is approached from the opposite end it is noticeable that the survivors had certain common characteristics. They remained loyal, on the whole, to what is very loosely called the realistic school, allied therefore to the major school presented in *Penguin New Writing*, and inclined, in retrospect and justification rather than in preparation, towards the American literary descendants of Dreiser and, remotely, of Mark Twain. To see with J. C. Reid 'the indebtedness of many of the prose contributors [to *New Zealand New Writing*] to Ernest Hemingway, Gertrude Stein, William Saroyan, Sherwood Anderson, Leslie Halward, James Hanley and even Gerald Kersh'[6] is to see altogether too much and yet too little: too much influence and too little of other factors bringing about a common technique and approach.

One of the main difficulties, for example, which confines the approaches possible to those who write and set their fiction in New Zealand is the absence here of widely recognized psychological stereotypes. The squire, the parson, the cultured aristocrat, the Birmingham businessman, the clerk with white collar and umbrella, the spiv or the Cockney, just have not got established local equivalents. This has many effects. It makes it difficult, if not impossible, to use the ordinary lending-library-romance technique of sketching in a few of the outlines of an attractive or villainous stereotype and allowing the reader to do the rest with his emotionally positive stock picture. Those who have had to do with the writing of New Zealand students of any age or have read the women's weeklies will have noticed how overseas stereotypes from English romances or Hollywood are borrowed at any cost to congruity in order to fill what is felt but not recognized as a gap.

Stereotypes are not wholly wrong but rather the highest common factor of general observation in a stable pattern. Where the pattern has not been stable for long enough nor been sufficiently stratified and geographically various to provide a variety of stereotypes, the consequence for the serious writer is that he cannot touch in any of his characters lightly or make them begin to live by showing one or two exactly observed departures from the expected norm. Each character must be handwrought; the author cannot take character roughcast from the mould and file to taste.

So each author is driven to be his own sociologist, patiently observing the unrecognized majority pattern as well as the minor variations of which there will be all too few. For the New Zealand pattern is of a piece. Place New Zealand society behind the hierarchical time-cut fretwork of English society and its lower middle class would nearly cover all our variety with some allowance for the middle class (our upper few) and the exceptional, the man alone, the unfortunates who have fallen through the New Zealand pattern. Even the vivid colours of destitution in *The Witch's Thorn* do not hide the grey lower middle class ideas beneath. And if the fiction here sounds like a report it may be that the reader's mind selects out what there is in it of report because that report has not been made elsewhere and is needed.

Again, where the fiction seems to derive from the realists of the American Middle West, in particular from Sherwood Anderson's *Winesburg, Ohio*, it may be because the American writers were tackling the same kind of problem in very similar territory. The answers given and the form of the answers would then be likely to look the same in both areas if there had been no literary influence at all. And this also suggests an answer to the problem of why New Zealand writers are so remarkably alike in their technical methods and in their subject matter considering their numbers and considering that, apart from a very real regard for Sargeson's work and his precedents, there is so little contact between writers and hardly any of the basis of a literary school.

As well as presenting the problem of exploring the pattern, this type of homogeneous society had no acknowledged place for authors, that is, it had ready no paradoxically-named 'déclassé' division of the middle class. Also there is no separate class which is, as a matter of habit, an informed audience. Thus the difficulties imposed by smallness of population are increased. If the writer without a place was to be like other exceptions here he would drop through the scaffolding of the pattern into the basement of national life. In fact, so homogeneous and hence so insistently demanding was the pattern that in order to see it, in order to write about it, it was necessary to escape outside and often away from it.

The first and truest escapees—those who exported themselves overseas—may not, as has often been said, have been escaping an exile here and going to values at their source, but instead have been escaping *into* an exile, an exile in England. For the new generation who are writing now, the depression or the war shook them outside the pattern and made a temporary place for them on the outside. It was no longer imperative to go to England and stay there, though many were removed and returned by the war as appropriately as if it had been prescribed.

The temporary place on the outside has been retained by working at other jobs and accepting the fact that writing here must be virtually unpaid, be for a small audience, and carry few perquisites of recognition and prestige. But there the writers are on the outside, like men clinging to the net which encloses a balloon, unable to live in the gas-filled interior, but in a fine though precarious position to see where the balloon is going and to tell from the whiffs of escaping gas how things are in the interior.

And what do they report of the interior? What do they say of the course of the balloon? What is the attitude of the New Zealand writer to his society?

To deal with these questions I do not propose to follow the writers into that technique which I have called elsewhere comment by indirection, a technique indicated, if not imposed, by the nature of the artistic problem in this country. When my review of Sargeson's *That Summer* was written in 1947 (*Landfall 3*)[7] it seemed to me then, and reviewing and reading other New Zealand fiction has confirmed me in the impression, that the writer here must as a first step achieve the illusion of realism; must detect and present what would be taken for a photograph of reality by an audience which has neither an album nor so much as a snap. But it is, after all, a composed engraving which must pass for a photograph of reality, for the details cannot be included in their temporal proportions. Joyce's *Ulysses* could hardly hold one day of Bloom's Dublin. In making the necessary excisions a passive comment can then be inserted by leaving out not only what would be fussy for the design but also what is not held to be significant in illustrating the writer's attitude. It is enough of comment, without a statement of the place in our community of illicit sexual information, to snap first Arnold and then Henry, in *I Saw in My Dream*, with an eye at the bathroom keyhole.

The comment, then, is in the inclusions and the omissions. Art and imagination, too, lie not in fresh creation after the imaginative uncovering of reality, but lie in the selection from this reality. This is one of the reasons why the technique of presentation chosen is so often the participating 'I' who tells his experience—and incidentally serves as a hero—without benefit of comment or chorus. The writer can select experiences for this 'I' who does not fully understand what affects him and tells us his view from an angle of vision the constriction of which is in itself informative but negatively so. For a New Zealand writer to choose the technique of omniscient narration from a platform outside the action would disperse the emotional force engendered by participation and constriction while letting the writer in for the whole task of drawing the social diagram.

To make the participating 'I' the hero in the formal sense also fits the increasingly autobiographical tendency of the modern novel in most countries. This tendency is encouraged by the 'amateur' standing of serious writing here and, increasingly, elsewhere; for the amateur is tied by his job to a certain place and to certain people and will tend to write best about what he knows and about his own life in particular. The technique of the participating 'I' also draws on the homogeneity of experience in New Zealand in solving the problem of drawing in the reader, who will have felt with the 'I', thus allowing identification with the hero to occur when there are otherwise few heroic stereotypes available. The very painstaking construction of character, which involves making a stereotype and then distinguishing a personality out of the stereotype, which is the writer's extra task here, is made to serve the further function of building the hero and the comment.

To achieve his story, his hero, and his comment, the author may winnow his experience with intuitive taste like Sargeson, or, like Ballantyne, by a direct emotional blast out of a vividly remembered childhood. And it should be noted here that, far from feeling alien in New Zealand, writers of prose have gained much of their force from memories of a childhood identified with the community, which Helen Gardner has emphasized as being vital to creative writing.[8] The writer in New Zealand meets his childhood with adult rebellion, not with the knife of indifference. To cut away the past by indifference to it would constitute a real alienation for the writer, for whom childhood is the period of fullest union with his community.

However the writer goes about it, if he selects the right phenomena for his hero to experience in the action he will touch the nerve ends of life in this society. Were he to add analysis and explanation, to point out how he sees society and explain what cause and effect he illuminates by emphasising this or that event, he would be writing sociology or history or both.

But the critic is at liberty and it is his function to give an analysis of cause and effect and thus to tie up the phenomena selected by one or several authors. So the critic provides a background for the stories which he has to examine and makes it possible for the bold relief of the stories to be set against his sketch map of the society. What follows does not pretend to have been arrived at with the help of the full apparatus of the academic sociologies. The surveys, the tests, the records where they exist, and the money are not available; the fifty or a hundred years of time and the dozens of men have not yet been expended.[9] But the artist must work in the territory before the trigs are put up and he knows anyway that the inconstant magnetic variations of society will only allow the sociological surveys to come some points nearer the absolute than he.

II

This sketch, then, begins at the point where the outlook of New Zealanders was imported. For the New Zealand pattern, as should be obvious, was not a fresh growth but grew up from the trunk of the British social pattern. The visual analogy is of a Y, one of the arms of which is our pattern, the trunk reaching up in time to early and mid-Victorian England. The continual reference to a 'young' country, 'adolescent' culture and the rest by our commentators can become an annoying semantic fallacy diverting them from the facts. For it is important to grasp that the pattern came ready-made from a given tradition and circumstance. It was as old as Great Britain when it arrived.

It is also worth emphasising that it took its central features from the type of immigrant who first came in considerable numbers. Without entering any controversy about the 'ultimate' importance to New Zealand's founding of the Wakefield gentleman-pioneer, it is fairly apparent that the three thousand one hundred men, women and children 'of the labouring class' sent by the New Zealand Company to Nelson would do more to determine the beliefs and outlook of their area than the 'eighty owners'[10] who eventually arrived—however loudly money talked.

And so it went on. The key years for the import of the pattern were those between 1861 and 1881. In 1853—after all the Wakefield-style colonies were begun—the population was 28,000. In 1861 the European population was 99,000; in 1871, 256,000; in 1881, 490,000 and in 1901 it was 773,000;[11] which gives a rough ratio at those dates of 1:4:10:20:31. The sudden and great surge was felt between 1861 and 1881, the depression thereafter tapering down the increase. The population multiplied five times in the sixties and seventies but rose by only a half in the eighties and nineties. Gold was discovered in Otago in 1861 and in Westland in 1865. The Maori Wars of the sixties necessitated soldier settlement in the North Island and food production wherever possible. Then, as the magnet of gold lost power from 1870 on, the Vogel public loans and assisted immigration took up the burden. However they came 'these builders of New Zealand were agricultural labourers, town craftsmen and domestic servants'[12] or, as Mrs Elsie Locke put it in entitling a pamphlet to show 'Canterbury without Laurels', these archetypical builders were 'The Shepherd and the Scullery-Maid'.[13]

The Britain of the working-class immigrants of the sixties and seventies was the Britain of the industrial revolution, in fact, of the nadir of that revolution, of its most cramping, bitter and hardest phases in which the immigrants' childhood was passed. And though the extreme lengths of *laissez-faire* had been shortened somewhat since the forties the great cities were still rapidly gathering in more lives to strain and begrime. The sudden overturn of expectations established in better circumstances, the narrowing hopes, the misery and disorientation spread evangelicalism in religion and produced Chartism in politics, and of the two the former is much the more important both in the British and the New Zealand social picture. 'Enthusiasm', Methodism, nonconformity the puritan outlook and Calvinist rigours gave hope and direction in the social storm to the children from the deserted village.

Indeed, if it was the middle class which carried this puritan and nonconformist outlook in the revolutions of the seventeenth century, in the revolution of the nineteenth millions of the expanding lower middle class and working class joined them. Halévy, the great historian of British society in the nineteenth century and of its religion, writes: 'the lower middle class which was everywhere nonconformist, pietist and puritan'[14] and 'during the nineteenth century Evangelical religion was the moral cement of English society. It was the influence of the evangelicals which ... placed over the proletariate a select body of workmen enamoured of virtue and capable of self-restraint. Evangelicalism was thus the conservative force which restored in England the balance momentarily destroyed by the explosion of the revolutionary forces [of 1832 and earlier].'[15]

G. D. H. Cole concurs. Of unionist developments he states that 'together with Radical dissenting ministers they [the Anglican Christian Socialists] were responsible for preventing that hostility between the organized working class and organized religion which became universal on the Continent.'[16] The wide spread of evangelicalism and its socially active, if ultimately quietening, effect, can also be seen in the fact that 'The promoters of the Factory Bill of 1833, Oastler, Sadler and Lord Ashley, were all three Evangelicals and all three Tories.'[17] Halévy sums up by saying: 'We shall witness Methodism bring under its influence, first the dissenting sects, then the establishment, finally secular opinion.'[18]

By the sixties and seventies, then, religious enthusiasm had become widespread, fully institutionalized and properly respectable. The preacher in the tin chapel of the slums had succeeded for the lower classes to Wesley circuit-riding and preaching in the fields. In Scotland the 'Free Church', which had in its origins tended to attract 'Evangelical'[19] elements grew after the secession of 1843 into a denomination able to send with renewed Calvinist enthusiasm a strong if dour message with the crofter and the mill-operative to New Zealand. The Irish Catholics, too, though they would have no part of Methodism, were possessed of a poor man's Church with its priest living amongst and near to the peasantry who voluntarily supplied their priests' entire livelihood. The Irish of O'Connell's day had their revival in a mixed political and religious form and they insisted that no government money or English-organized help for the hierarchy should come between them and their priests.[20]

The message evangelicalism preached to the poor fitted the situation it answered. It emphasized grace and sin. The Hammonds have pointed out how Wilberforce and his active Anglicans at the end of the eighteenth century began 'a Society for the Reformation of Manners, which aimed at enforcing the observance of Sunday, forbidding any kind of social dissipation, and repressing freedom of speech and of thought wherever they refused to conform to the superstitions of the morose religion that was then in fashion.'[21] Wilberforce and his fellows coerced the English poor (though not the rich), but the poor ended by coercing themselves.

The poor built on the foundations of Wesley and Wilberforce and on the advice of Hannah More. Another course—unfortunately available on the face of it only to the less rapidly and far less totally industrialized French—is indicated by the Hammonds when they write: 'The spirit of common gaiety, killed in England by Puritanism and by the destruction of the natural and easy-going relations of the village community, survived in France through all the tribulations of poverty and famine.'[22]

In the face of the industrial revolution the doctrine of work was elaborated and the sins of the flesh extended to encompass all the pleasures which might divert the energies from the arid struggle to survive and—that faint but driving hope—to escape up into the classes that did not face an end in Potter's Field. Sex and drink and ease-taking led to terrestrial and eternal damnation both. In the overcrowded squalid conditions where much moral backsliding was accompanied by much grinding failure there was a high rate of emotional acceptance of the proposition which connected immorality and failure as cause and effect. The Old Testament virtues, product of a patriarchal tribal society, were burnt, to the accompaniment of much flickering of hellfire, into our immigrants by the acid emotions of life in slum and factory and unemployment. For those many who failed or resisted or were broken there was no alternative morality. Even Chartism and unionism, which offered more of an explanation than guilt and sin, were linked with the prevailing outlook rather than constituting an outright opposition to it.

The outlook and the moral scheme were not lost in the cabins and holds of the emigrant ships coming to New Zealand. They travelled better in the habits and attitudes of the immigrants than the Churches could with their buildings, halls, schools, hospitals and vicarages. The Churches which had been associated with the elaboration of the puritan pattern tended increasingly over the decades to be left out. The denominations might move in fresh directions, their theological emphases might alter, but they were no longer in sufficiently vital contact with enough New Zealanders to alter the design of the pattern. Somewhere about the turn of the century or possibly later (though the failure of the Church sponsored attempt to introduce nation-wide Prohibition seems to indicate the first decade of the new century at the latest) the pattern can be considered a thing in itself. It was by then unconsciously assumed and beyond the redirection of changing Churches which might have supervised and readjusted it in happier circumstances.

The Churches, in fact, had not been essential to confirm the pattern as it was brought off the ships. For the puritan morality received a more obvious sanction. In the new land and with the new tasks it fitted, it worked. 'Work, deny yourself and you will be prosperous and saved' presided as a motto over the cracking of the spine of the bush. The sober, upright, industrious man who abhorred the flesh had opportunity to show his fibre as shepherd or gold miner or settler in the North Island backblocks. The shopkeeper and mechanic with slight capital could thriftily build on this clear field where at 'Home' they could not have begun.

Out of nothing came something and the promise of success which should crown effort was realized and the Victorian proposition became an axiom. The institutions of patriarchy were there also, son learning from father by sharing in his tasks, the girl from the mother, their isolated life dominated by a male figure of command. In reality as in the model situations of injunction, fairy tale, Bible and manly talk the scene was set around the central figure of the father who directed and brought the family to a better future. Many, if not most, prospered only to a minor degree and some not at all, but the proportion of success was infinitely greater than in the lands they left and more than enough for the myth.

But this was not all that the new circumstances had to say in the matter. They were now to contradict their earlier confirmation of the puritan cultural pattern. The essence of the contradiction lay in the fact that conditions now grew easier, yet this had the effect of making hard work less efficacious since opportunities for the great majority were more and more restricted. Shopkeepers and tradesmen found that there was a low limit on expansion in a small country, patchily settled by a low density of population, and having no neighbouring territories. New Zealand became a land of the small shopkeeper, safe from overbearing competition, but confined to his modest competence. The great wool and wheat estates began to break up in the nineties, pressed by legislation and red ink. The advent of refrigeration and the separator drove the New Zealand farmer towards the small family-farm which allowed him, except by the occasional grace of the overseas market, the same kind of limited competence as his town counterpart obtained.

In comparison with Europe New Zealand was a land of milk and honey, a lucky historical accident favoured by a temperate climate, by untapped soil, by a defence from the British Navy that was not paid for in heavy debt, and by a technology, developed elsewhere, which was ready to bring all to fruition at the right time. But the outlook, the morality that the immigrants had imported, had not been evolved for a land—relatively—of milk and honey; especially when the milk and honey were evenly distributed.

Now, only the very exceptional and the very lucky man could go to the edge of settlement and break his way into greater rewards. Overall, it is probably true to say that the immigrants in thirty years had risen by a step in the English ladder and that, as a whole, New Zealanders had arrived securely at the economic equivalent of the English lower middle class. Their economic circumstances, moreover, while not allowing New Zealanders much more than lower middle class standards, were yet easy enough to free most of them from that nagging fear[23] of dropping back into the lower class which underlay the lives of the immigrants' new equivalents in England.[24]

Conditions were easier in New Zealand, the competence was soon come to, but the ceiling on the ambitions of the majority made itself felt at the centre of things by limiting and changing the role played by the husband. No longer could he raise the family a visible, respectworthy notch by undeviating hard work and abstemious living. Once out of his time at a trade or plugging away at the mortgage on shop or farm he was almost as well off at twenty-five as at fifty. Regular opportunities for overtime were the exception in town, and, as rising land values took up the slack of good times, there was a limit to what the farmer could mortgage himself into in settled districts.

Mother now stepped into her own. The exact grade the family would occupy was fixed increasingly by mother's skill in spending to the greatest advantage a nearly fixed income. Mother 'managing' the household succeeded to father 'making a home'. An interesting parallel can be drawn here with an examination by E. H. McCormick of the evolution in Katherine Mansfield's characters. 'Andreas Binzer, that caricature of the domineering, egotistical male, begins to take on human form, frail though not villainous, as Stanley Burnell; the wife and the grandmother are no longer depressed drudges, but the more plausible managers and diplomats of a middle-class home.'[25]

It is noteworthy also, that Mr McCormick suggests that Katherine Mansfield's earlier phase, when she saw family conflict as being between 'sensitive wife and domineering husband', is 'one that links Katherine Mansfield with the novelists of the nineties and may, in part, be derived from their pioneer or near-pioneer background.'[26] Katherine Mansfield reflected, then, a change of attitude some thirty years after the facts on which the attitudes were based had changed—a not uncommon lapse of time.

Katherine Mansfield thus passed approvingly from the first version of the basic New Zealand sentimentality—that women are good and men are brutes—a first version which rendered the male as an uncouth active brute, to the next version which pictures the male as an ineffective, insufficient, unhelpful brute who has to be humoured and is 'really rather like a child at times'. That Katherine Mansfield does so with consummate art and by exactly registering her early milieu does not absolve her from an involvement in the sentiment nor release her altogether from its confinement.[27]

And agreement with the results of the changing role of the husband, and therefore of the male, did indeed prove to be a confining and distorting act. For though the circumstances which had originally confirmed the puritan pattern and morality were reversed, and the churches which had elaborated it were left on one side, the pattern itself did not depart, and that pattern was patriarchal at base and demanded of the male a role, an achievement, and a life which went clean contrary to the new facts.

Father—increasingly a townsman[28]—was a figure who departed for work in train or tram and returned at his children's bed-time. No longer did he teach the son by example in the bush or at the counter. The children went to school and the mother pointed to undone homework if much of the old participation was asked. Only in a depression and only on the farms did the family really return to that joint effort directed by father in his own sphere that had been a pioneering characteristic. Mother now had the children on her hands and in the home, which was her sphere, where she directed, and where her work and management, so central to the family's position, could be observed and absorbed by the children, girl and boy.

The pattern enjoined work and promised reward and respect for it. Mother had learned and believed in the morality of work and her role, unlike father's, continued to demand and to reward it, as specified by the pattern. Here in New Zealand it was possible with the aid of machine-produced copies, scraping, and much effort to imitate in a bungalow elements of that High Victorian display of the upper middle class which the immigrant domestic may have seen and envied back in England. Certainly a 'neat and tidy' house with an overfurnished unused 'drawing room' became social essentials.[29] Thrift and duty would 'do wonders', and, with the new vote that was contemporaneous with woman's new position it might even be possible by Prohibition to enforce abstinence on the husband and add to the family's funds while taming the remainder of his outbursts.

And under all these puritan virtues of work, thrift, abstinence of all kinds, and duty there slipped in a simple materialism combined with self-complacency. This complacency would only have been hypocritical had it been realised that only when the virtues were necessary expressions of a living faith and a genuinely religious attitude were they properly virtues, and that they were not virtues when pursued for themselves and the goods and social standing their practise purchased. That so many ministers of every denomination should not have noticed the substitution of the means for the end, but, instead, have encouraged this elementary materialism because of its formal virtuousness, is something of a tragedy. Instead of being re-examined, the pattern, the code and the morality were aided to carry on, as rigid as the law, like the hypertrophied superego as pictured by Freud and just as unconscious.

Unconscious, too, was the father's adaptation to the change. Driven from the bridge, he occupied himself in the fo'c's'le 'with the boys'. The mechanics' institutes which dated from pioneering times were followed by the sports clubs[30], the R.S.A.s, bowling clubs for the older men, Masonic Lodges, Rotary, Savage, and Creditmen's Clubs, and, of course, 'the pub'. In the scouts and the primary school team, through serious football and the races, on yachts or at the servicemen's smoke concert, men need never lack an equalitarian comradely substitute for singular, hierarchical, patriarchal family life.

A. P. Gaskell's collection of short stories, *The Big Game*, ranks as our leading treatise on this aspect of New Zealand society. Whether he is dealing with a football player's tension within himself and with his teammates during the week before a deciding game, or evoking the subtleties of concealed values in a morning's gossip among Home Guardsmen, Mr Gaskell never ceases to display the variety, importance, and vitality of links between men in this community.

An amusing diagram of the sexually polarized society can be examined in the typical New Zealand dance hall; the men with the men in a clump at the door, the women with the women ranged, usually, along one side of the hall. And this extends in the upper income brackets even to separate entertaining and in homes at most levels to separate subjects of conversation and separate groupings of men and women at private parties.

For the solitary man or the husband who must needs do his *quid* for his wife's energetic and pointed *quo* there always remains the garden. John Cole in his story 'A Touch of the Old Trouble'[31] manages this situation precisely and brings out with insight and skill the implications of lonely frustration for the excluded father and unsatisfied husband. Out of Jack's huge burlesque excavation in the back garden Frank Sargeson makes a biting symbol for all the bitterness involved in his story 'The Hole That Jack Dug'.[32] The hole is deep enough to bury half the house and its animosities and, by its very purposelessness, constitutes for Jack a vivid silent gesture against waste of effort and waste of spirit.

The male institutions, as well as providing a substitute for a fuller family life, serve as a setting for the reassertion by men of their idea of themselves as men, as active, 'manly', commanding personalities, willing to take risks, displaying skill, courage and ability for valued recognition. The pattern has continued to insist on these attributes though the pattern's central institutions, the family and the job, no longer provide an arena for these attributes and an audience for them. Guthrie Wilson in his novel *Brave Company* has emphasized the supreme opportunity provided by war for this reassertion, and, as perhaps the most competent writer among the many New Zealand authors of war diaries who remain inside the pattern and share its values, Mr Wilson unconsciously demonstrates the function of war as a release from frustration and a reaffirmation of the New Zealand man's picture of himself in the face of social contradictions in civilian life.

This reaffirmation takes the form, in Mr Wilson's novel, of an insistence on the value of war as a test. His hero, Private Peter 'Lawyer' Considine, remembers with approval in the heat of a charge[33] an aphorism which he later repeats almost exactly: 'But no. Two things are of the greatest moment to men—women and war. And the greater, because of its demands upon fortitude, because of its nightmare quality, is war' (p.265). 'Lawyer' thinks that war 'is not wholly vile' when it 'gives men like our commander and our corporal the opportunity to dominate us who are of a weaker mould in all that is inherently (perhaps primitively) manly' (p.51). 'Lawyer' also reflects that 'Men do not create heroes of their fellow men, but Hadfield is as near being a hero to me as any other man I have known. By that, I mean that he is a very good soldier.' (p. 247). And as 'Lawyer' feels less than his heroes so he, with Hadfield, feels more than the 'pail of water, civilian water' in which the returned servicemen will be 'but a drop of red blood' (p. 36). Similarly 'Lawyer' admires above his own learning the virtues of the playing field (p. 43) symbolically transferred in the figure of Major Cadman to the battlefield.[34]

It should be unnecessary to add that so much concentration in the pattern of living on the provision of a male environment from playground to bowling green makes for a fair degree of latent homosexuality. It is not unnatural that this passes unrecognized by the mass of men except in the inverted form of much bar-room humour at the expense of 'queens' and a very strong aversion from certain physical traits imagined to be feminine. Many New Zealand authors indicate their perception of the unconscious signs of this strain in the national character both in novels and short stories.

It has been treated fairly directly in P. J. Wilson's 'End of the River'[35] and in Bill Pearson's 'Uncle 52'.[36] A. P. Gaskell in the masterly story 'The Fire of Life'[37] sketches a skittish schoolteacher confronted with the possibility of marrying a solid manly woman. Dan Davin examines the reaction of New Zealanders another way, by introducing a homosexual character—an Englishman—in his novel of the New Zealand Division *For the Rest of Our Lives*. But it is Frank Sargeson who, in the novels *That Summer* and *I Saw in My Dream*, has followed, with the most subtle observation of nuance and gradation, the implications as far as they go, still more or less latent, but touching the surface in the lives of lonely and overstrained men like his backblocks farm labourer.

This element of latent homosexuality, encouraged by too intensive and lifelong separation of the sexes, is to some extent attributable to the disorientation of the boy growing up in a home where formally, and by all the injunctions of the pattern, the man should command, but where, in observable fact, he does not. The boy cannot learn the role he is verbally instructed is his by the essential learning process of watching the father perform and fulfil that role. Insofar as it is the mother who directs and initiates, when the morality, the code, and the pattern proclaim her happy submission, it is the children who are confused.

A confusion in learning the respective roles of male and female makes adjustment in marriage harder. When to that is added an institutional superstructure of the partially segregated type, and to that is superadded a conviction that abstinence from the pleasures of sex, or at least from most of them, is probably the better part of morality, then indeed are the difficulties of marriage, and hence of family life, greatly multiplied. I cannot call to mind one significant New Zealand novel where the European father is treated as the dominating figure in the home or where a fair degree of tension between parents is not recorded. Among the short stories only Gaskell's tale, 'The Pig and Whistle',[38] of nineteenth century Little Akaloa is exceptional in this regard and then the date of the setting is some explanation. Whether partly in agreement with the values of the pattern, like Courage in his *The Fifth Child*, or not at all, like Dan Davin in his *Cliffs of Fall,* our fiction focusses, as between the parents, on the mother, and shows the children making what sense they can of the situation.

That the children make too little sense of it is seen in their strong reaction to the situation as soon as reaction becomes possible—when they start to earn between fifteen and eighteen. This reaction takes the form of a rebellion, which seems, but only seems, to be a rebellion against the pattern. Actually, to strike out against parental authority, to loosen or cut most of the remaining threads of communication with the parents, to assert or experiment with other values and practises than those lauded in and associated with the home, this is the normal course over the ten years between seventeen and twenty-seven. A period of adolescent and post-adolescent *Sturm und Drang* seems to be an inherent part of cultural patterns deriving ultimately from the European complex; though not being a part, apparently, of all cultural patterns.[39] However general this period of adolescent strain may be it is still worth looking at the form it takes here and at the manner in which this planned detour helps to bring young New Zealanders with all the more force back onto the straight and narrow path for the remainder of their lives.

This period of rebellion and experiment, as it seems to the participants, is perhaps the key period in the tightening of the pattern round the individual. Its forerunner, the period roughly between twelve and seventeen, a period of doubt in the parents and discovery of adolescent identity, without, however, the possibility of taking action and of being more than a spectator, is the period which has provided Ballantyne in *The Cunninghams*, Finlayson in *Tidal Creek*, and Bruce Mason in 'Summer's End',[40] with a standpoint for their heroes. The key period itself is treated by Davin in *Cliffs of Fall* and *Roads From Home*, by Sargeson in sections of *I Saw in My Dream*, and by many in short stories.

The break with the parents in New Zealand is aided and accentuated by the lack of communication between generations. Possibly the gap between parents and children arises from the methods of discipline employed, with father as the last physical resort, and with mother using a variety of emotional pressures which decline in effectiveness with use and with the increasing age of the children. With increasing age the child's emotional insight grows sufficiently to allow the child to understand and thus be less vulnerable to the psychological mechanisms of the pressures consciously employed by the mother. Again, the difficulty of accounting for, or more frequently of ignoring, the differences between enjoined fiction and observable fact about family relations imports confusion into parent-child communication. This confusion may play a considerable part in widening the gap.

Had the parents not rebelled themselves and been drawn back to an adherence to those fictions by what they took to be 'the facts of life' they might not be so keen to protect children from rebellion or deviation by insisting on the fictions. Insisting on the fictions removes the need for the parents to dig into their own well-buried difficulties, regarded now as past failure and felt as present discontent. So to protect themselves, and, as they hope, their children, parents continue to insist on what will prevent examination and discussion. They confine themselves, usually, to worry and to one of the many variations on the theme summed up in the phrase 'you'll learn.'[41]

Dan Davin in *Cliffs of Fall* puts the problem in this soliloquy of Mark, his university student hero. 'As for confiding in her [the mother], what sort of intimate confidence could exist between one generation and the next? His mother was too garrulous to be trusted and too given to needless worrying, even if he had had the slightest impulse to confide in her, which he had not. She could give him no advice which he would be likely to take. He was divided from his parents by education as well as by age, by difference in temperament as well as by the fact that they were now static in their outlook while his was still shifting and developing. What use would advice be, given from the standpoint of one set of values and standards of conduct, when, had he subscribed in the least to these values and standards, the situation would never have arisen? ... His father had remained silent. Mark could tell by the noise of his shifting and stirring in the bed that he was embarrassed. He felt sure that as absolute a silence had prevailed hitherto between his mother and father on the subject of their children and sex as between parents and children.'[42]

Mark launched his rebellion, in his first independence as a lodger, by absorbing the spread of other ideas provided by the university and by attacking through Bohemian party-going and some promiscuous experiment with sex 'the manners and morals their grandparents had brought with them from Scotland'.[43] For the non-university majority the weekly dance, party-going, and occasional sexual experiment are accompanied by less theory and hardly any chance that a theory may lead on to understanding which might emancipate them from the compulsion of patterned action and reaction.

The young man's image of an attractive companion is variously compounded. On one hand there is the element derived from the mother-image and the mother's advice revolving round the 'treat her as you would a sister' motif. On the other hand there is a combination of the inaccuracies of the shelter-shed, the daring and idealized reiterations of films and radio, and hope. This bifocal view of women is partially incorporated in the stereotypes of the 'decent girl' and the 'good thing'. It is also partly met, as all such mixed demands must be met, by a mixed response on the part of the girl. 'Petting' at parties is some sort of compromise, in one individual's action, between 'bad' and 'good' behaviour, between approved and disapproved courses of action.

The girl, too, has contradictory demands. Earning for herself, with the background of home equipment provided and taken for granted, she has more money to spend with less responsibility than she will ever have again. Mother's doctrine of work and saving hardly fits the girl's circumstances, containing, as it does, an unattractive picture of life. So mother's example falls temporarily into the discard. Along with the doctrine and the example there is a tendency to reject also the home picture of relations between women and men as unsatisfying, and, with regard to sex, predominantly unpleasant. This picture mother passes on to daughter with much more emotional freedom than the mother would feel with her sons, though, as far as can be gathered, it is conveyed with no more explicit detail than the son receives. Mother's picture does not fit the exciting dance and party-going entanglements which are new, irresponsible, fleeting, and altogether different in background to the economic setting of the mother's frustrations.

The excitement and the economic elbow-room combine in the girl's case to lend amplitude to the hope of a Prince Charming conveyed by film, magazine, and the corner lending-library novel. This hope is a natural romantic answer to the doctrine that 'a woman's work is never done'. The consequence, however, is that the eventual disappointment will be all the greater and be concerned with both budget and bed. For the girl does not lose her subconscious assumption that her mate should act his secondary role, as her father had done, while she adds now a demand that the mate bring economic ease and act in a commanding, sophisticated way which is unlikely under the circumstances of the pattern.

In fact the girl demands those very 'manly' attributes which the young man hopes to assert and which he has been taught (though family life contradicts them) he should possess. The demand and the hope coincide and produce a spurious conviction in the young couple that they have escaped being like mother and father. The young man can even act the economic Prince Charming until marriage forces him to face all his psychological debits and financial shortcomings at one time.[44]

The period of rebellion containing, as it does, the maximum of strain and, for the individual, an assumption that he is on his own uncharted course, is, as it were, the shock-absorber of the whole system. Here, if anywhere, the pattern itself is most vulnerable and is subject to the greatest likelihood of change. Enough individuals striking out on their own detour from the usual detour may carve out a new route. It is certainly possible that the period of rebellion may henceforth start earlier. The developed U.S. film version of the romantic myth of Prince Charming had a foothold ready in our pattern. And the re-emphasis on the 'good provider' has a corollary in Prince Charming's younger brother, the well equipped and sophisticated youth, the successful 'dater' of the American high school.

It is no very unlikely step to an extension of adolescent experiment back in the normal life-history to the early post-primary school years on the American model. To shift the emphasis unconsciously from the sexual aspect to the respect of competitive display of attractive boy by attractive girl and vice versa[45] fits the simple competitive materialism, if not the more limited financial resources, of New Zealand parents. A 'golden age' prior to an adult life of undeviating work beginning in the mid-twenties would be a considerable but not impossible change for the New Zealand pattern to undergo under the unremitting influence of the U.S. cultural pattern. Such a change—though the only foreseeable one—would hardly alter the basic tenets of life here, or meet the real, if implicit, criticism of artists and the thousands they speak for.

Whether the route of the detour is permanently changed in this way or not, many fail to take the corners in this stretch of the life-history engendered by the pattern. It is here that, in the general strain of parentally unguided adjustment, some extra shock may prove too much for the individual as it does for the heroes of *I Saw in My Dream* and *Cliffs Of Fall.* Then, as with Sargeson's story, one arrives at the point of departure for that New Zealand odd man out, the New Zealand bachelor,[46] the social stray, the 'Man Alone'. The lessons of male companionship, the dominant mother, the emphases of latent homosexuality and family conflict all join to produce for many an insuperable barrier to companionship with women and to marriage.

The 1936 Census gave the percentage of those over sixteen who had 'never married' as, European male, 39%; European female, 33%; and 'married' as 56% and 56.5% respectively. Those legally separated, widowed, and divorced made up the remainder.[47] The number of married women of childbearing age (between fifteen and forty-five), expressed as a percentage of all women in that age group, works out at 63.5% married for 1878, 52.1% for 1921, 50.4% for 1936, and 56.9% for 1945.[48] So for all those above twenty considerably more than a third of the males are unmarried and about one-third of the females. A majority of unmarried adults naturally make a more or less usual adjustment, but for many the period of rebellion and single experiment is unconscionably prolonged.[49] This provides those exceptions whose existence our writers of prose fiction have emphasized and we must return later to an examination of the artistic use made of those exceptions.

The normal termination of the period of rebellion, however, is marriage. Marriage occurs in New Zealand at the average ages of thirty for men and twenty-six for women,[50] and, if first marriages alone are considered, at twenty-seven and a half for bachelors and twenty-four and a half for spinsters.[51] Long engagements are fairly common, being connected, particularly in the more comfortably-off brackets, with the girl's desire to keep up, not 'with the Joneses', but with her mother's style and standard of living. A certain amount of cohabitation by engaged couples seems to be almost expected by an unexpressed convention and produces, owing, as A. R. D. Fairburn remarked, to the loyalty of the young men who marry the mothers, a high proportion of seven-month babies.[52]

How high a proportion is uncertain, but such pre-marital experiment certainly carries no guarantee of a corresponding adjustment. Though intercourse between those engaged probably accounts for the greater proportion of pre-marital experience, because the partnership is likely to be more continuous and embody more trust, yet the opportunities even for this are not very numerous in a land without the roadhouse, the anonymous large hotel, the motel and the tourist cabin. Moreover, the lessons of such experience are bound to be confusing since it is never possible to eliminate either the extraneous excitement or the difficulties of situation.

Most couples come to the honeymoon, symbolically regarded by New Zealanders as slightly ridiculous or humorous, and often occupied by an exhausting tour of the country, with years of romantic excitement behind them but without having solved in any way the fundamental difficulty inherent in the conflicting images of the roles of man and woman. They then have precious little time left to solve them before the first baby. In 1948 41% of first babies were born to marriages of under one year's duration, and 34 % to marriages of under two but over one years' duration. So over three-quarters of all first babies are 'on the way' inside fifteen months of marriage.[53]

The newly married man, about to become a father all too soon, and faced already with the difficulties of setting up a home, must suspend his efforts to reconcile the several model men he ought to be and suspend, also, the tasks of filling in the considerable omissions in his own knowledge of love-making and of adjusting his own bifocal view of women.

The expectant mother feels ill-prepared for a baby without an elaborate layette. To receive seventeen matinee jackets is only too normal and, with mother's assistance, the gifts emphasise the work that remains to be done 'to be ready for the baby'. The pre-natal fears of the expectant mother are in no way diminished by the beliefs of the average New Zealand expectant grandmother. The clinics, such as those of the St Helens system, spend a great deal of time laying the most elementary spectres of ignorance. The slow headway made by the Grantly Dick Read method of natal care is some measure of the tension felt and expected, with all the attendant repercussions between man and wife.

When the baby arrives the mother displays it to her circle of friends; and works. The 'Father of One' who wrote to the newspaper[54] complaining in none too stable terms that the baby had ousted him and that he was now 'a bill payer to a neurotic nurse' provoked a revealing outburst of patterned injunctions to accept the situation and make the best of it by working hard to help the mother, for 'after all, we the mothers have to go through the ordeal'.[55] 'Mother of Two' thought husbands often to blame for 'devoting most of their leisure hours to the pursuit of selfish pleasures—golf, fishing, shooting, etc.'[56] Some parent correspondents suspected that 'Father of One' was a 'spoilt boy'[57] who hankered after the attention he had received from his own mother, while most advocated more work about the home and sharing in the concentration on children. Everything from 'God's will'[58] to 'maturity'[59] was invoked as laying down to 'Father of One' the duty of submergence in and acceptance of a situation the basic outline of which was not denied.

The new mother is tired. She is discovering that on the family's income 'what with the baby and everything else', she must do a great deal. It is not true except in terms of the pattern that the baby needs to be displayed or have his elaborate rig-out or that the house needs carpets, or an oak bedroom suite, or a bow-fronted china cabinet. But such are the unexamined assumptions that now catch up with the young mother. Her own mother and her similarly placed and minded women friends, who are her psychological mainstays, do not disillusion her because they agree. The woman who placed a wall-to-wall carpet and a dining room suite in a tent at an Auckland motor-camp for the two years she had to live there was asserting, rather colourfully, the New Zealand scheme of the elementary decencies. To achieve or 'make do' for these necessities which are not necessary personal relations are sacrificed to work in the name of 'facing facts' which are not facts.

If the wife is tired and inclined more and more to feel that what mother told her is now shown to be true by experience she is also fearful. Contraception has just failed for the couple in the case of the first 'accident'. It does not need a Mass Observation Group to discover that the timing of the arrival of children is usually accidental or that married people are profoundly unsure of their knowledge of contraception. Marriage guidance workers and overseas visitors have expressed to the writer their surprise at how insufficient and difficult of access are the facilities of trained help in this matter compared with what is known and available both in England and America.

Under what is felt to be the necessity of preventing another child ruining the prospect of making a 'decent home', the knowledge that illegal abortion may be the only recourse for another mistake in contraception gives sordid substance to the wife's fears. Of those dying from sepsis following abortion during the years 1931-5 62% were married women.[60] The Department of Health advertises that 'the latest figures indicate that in New Zealand there are 4,600 unlawful abortions a year. For every 100 births there are 7 natural abortions (miscarriages) and 13 *induced abortions.*'[61]

Fear and weariness do not make a good background for the delayed attempt to reconcile the already considerable distortion of relations between man and woman inherent in the pattern. The solution is all too frequently found in a severe limitation of intercourse summed up in a phrase that a woman medical practitioner described to the writer as characteristic of the consulting-room report: 'My husband is a good chap, he doesn't bother me much.' Another medical practitioner said that the greatest problem he found among young married women was the sudden onset of frigidity shortly after marriage. The domestic tragedy does not lie in this alone but also in the extension of the lack of adjusted relationships from one field of potential common interest to the next.

This blighting process is aided by the earliest memories of both husband and wife as to the realities of married life and by the construction of social institutions which provide a refuge for the husband outside the home. The son, now married, follows the father's example out of the home because 'reality' has set in.[62]

In truth the pattern has simply reasserted its main constituents. The conclusion that this was only to be expected since life is like that covers and explains the failure for the participants. The wife reasserts her idea of herself and of her value by imitating mother's pattern more closely, creating the husk of respectability and respect-worthy success around the kernel of marital defeat.[63]

The woman who cannot conform, who continues with a romantic picture of escape, has occupied our fiction writers less. Possibly this is because most of our writers are men; possibly it is because women, having a more clearly defined consistent role which has an avenue of satisfaction in the children, attempt to escape their working destiny less often—anyway until it is too late to try, when the double reckoning of children leaving home and menopause arrives. This last situation frequently produces crisis and a 'nervous breakdown' as a conclusion to years of lonely striving.[64]

It is the subject of a novel by James Courage, *The Fifth Child*, which shares in the New Zealand woman's formalised and sentimental picture of herself. The conclusion confirms the pattern when the farmer husband is compelled to say: 'I daresay the world's not going to end because I arrange to stay in my own bed in future' ... 'Our youth, our day's over,' he said after a minute. 'Barbara and Ronald and the others, they're the generation now. Let them take this passing-on-of-life business as theirs. They can have it.' He cleared his throat and drew in a long breath. 'You and I will get along as we are. After all, there's a good deal left between us ...' The wife concludes this passage on the homeopathic cure by adding 'Come and sit down now, dear, and don't fidget.'[65]

The women who break early, who insist on seeking an alternative fate, yield to the romantic promise they first met as young people. Its pathetic essence is expressed by Greville Texidor's character, a returned serviceman, in the story *Anyone Home?*

'Everything's going to be different from now on. We're going to please ourselves. We're both young. We'll go away to Auckland or to a beach somewhere.'[66] Almost the same expressions occur to Helen, the mother, in D. W. Ballantyne's *The Cunninghams*. 'Suddenly the idea came that perhaps she and Fred [her lover] could go to the city, start another life together, forget all the worries of Gladston.' (p. 133.) The tubercular and hysterical Queenie in Ruth Park's *The Witch's Thorn* thinks 'I don't owe the old woman anything. I don't owe the kid anything! I'm going to Auckland and I'll get a job and I'll get well and then ... I'll have a lotta fun!' (p.7).

But if the pattern pinches in family life there is no escape outside it. Dan Davin's character Elsie in *Roads From Home* dies in a car crash, but not before thinking 'But they'd be after her now, the whole pack of them. They wouldn't let her get away with a thing like that. Her only hope was to clear out of the country altogether, if she didn't come home to him. She'd have to make Andy take her to Australia. A place like Woodlands, or Invercargill for that matter, doesn't forgive. But would Andy be prepared to take it on? Probably not. He'd rat on her sooner or later.' (p. 231.)

Economic opportunity and the pattern make no Prince Charmings among the lovers any more than among the husbands. Andy puts the dilemma to Elsie exactly. 'Suppose we do go off together. What happens? Sooner or later you start wanting to settle down ... Only natural for you, I mean. But it isn't for me. And then you'd be wanting me to turn into something different. Well, suppose I did and, mind you, I'm not saying I would, where'd you be then? You'd be just where you were last week only a darned sight worse off. Because, believe me, if I did settle down I wouldn't be as good at it as that John of yours.' (p. 223.) Elsie concludes that she must try, 'love or no love, to build a life for him [her husband] and for Michael [her son].' (p. 225).

The result of defeated aspiration in the regular pattern of marriage is not as stark as this. But the resultant underlying and powerful frustration, loneliness, and lack of love[67] is a reservoir for bitterness and hatred which provides the sour discordant ground-tone recorded in New Zealand fiction. Young people in their early thirties look back upon their period of revolt and see false and foolish adolescent hope. They feel that they were trying to 'kick against the pricks' and that facts have taught them better. Failure to succeed in bucking the system precedes quiescent assent on the part of young married people and breeds a conviction, shared by their parents in their day, that the children should be protected by being thoroughly ingrained with those values that time has 'proven'. Failure for one generation's young people thus helps to ensure that they will create the conditions for the failure of the next.

If New Zealand often seems a conservative arid country, and its politics, for one example, are frequently so,[68] this relapse into convinced conformity, with its undercover motivation of unsatisfied bitterness, may be part of the explanation. It may also help to explain the short creative lives of many who hope to become writers, and, more generally, what sometimes appears to be a frequent failure of promising men in their twenties to make a contribution equal to their talents during the next twenty years of their lives.

This convinced and self-protective conformity bears also on the whole question of the reception of New Zealand writing by New Zealanders. New Zealand writing is conspicuously plain and straightforward. The very few experimental writers in another vein than the realistic, such as those in the magazines *Hilltop* and *Arachne*, have obviously suffered from a lack of solid beams from which to spin their insubstantial webs. Without the establishment of a local Trollope or a Dickens a local Firbank or Waugh cannot fly far. The number of experiments is, then, tiny and the bulk of New Zealand fiction has had nothing of the esoteric or cryptic about it. Yet it is ignored by the public or resisted quite as much as if it had been thrown down from the highest of ivory towers.

The reason is obvious enough. The more clearly the writer produces the illusion of reality, the more exactly he probes for the nerve ends of life here, the less likely he is to be read as long as a great many of his potential public are trying to forget, to ignore, to cover their defeats. Against the intensity of the creative writer's exposure of what lies beneath the crust of everyday is pitted the full conservative strength of the pattern. Where it is not ignored the clinical report of the writer on the state of his patient is answered by the charge that the writer is perverse and unhealthy in mind for having noticed anything amiss.[69]

From making this charge it is but a step to laying a further charge— that to portray, however responsibly, the failures of society is in itself contributing to cause those failures.[70] The artist has probably been saved from becoming a scapegoat so far by the smallness of his audience. He may yet need, like Anatole France, to make 'the principal business of his life doing up dynamite in bonbon wrappers'.[71] The artist should certainly heed the discharge of frustration and bitterness on the heads of more numerous but equally isolated groups in the community which has, in the past, been spectacularly out of proportion to any 'crime' committed, even including the crime of difference.

The excessive strength of public feeling about the laziness and good-for-nothing qualities of government white-collar workers in the twenties, the unemployed in the thirties, wharf-labourers in the forties and 'townies' widely in country areas, is partly a measure of the brackish pools of emotion, fed by the pattern, which must find an outlet. If the writers must risk this emotion being directed at them they can also take it as a confirmation that their underlying analysis does not lack in substance.

If, in fact, this feeling of purposelessness, of frustration and bitterness arises in the way that has been suggested and implied by our writers then the family as it is in this pattern is serving as a centre of constrained conformity instead of willing cohesion, of discontent instead of content. Those who look to the integrated family as the basic institution of any successful variant of Western European culture—and it appears self-evidently to be so—have a duty to face the problem if our basic institution is not functioning properly. Clichés about the value of ideal family life do not meet the problem if family life is far from ideal and the question of how to improve it is raised. Rebellion against the failures of our pattern is too frequently dismissed, in advance, as rebellion against an idealised statement of how each institution ought to work. That is, the rebel is accused of rebelling against what he agrees with because he points out and rebels against the fact that institutions are working in a different direction and in a worse fashion. The continuing rebel is our rarest product, for the reasons outlined earlier, and his news from outside, presented as art, is worth intelligent consideration.

Certainly the writers who continue to write continue to rebel. They concern themselves, moreover, with figures of rebellion, with men alone, with the occasional violent outbursts of individuals striking blindly against the symbols of authority, with the young coming to awareness and taking sides against their surroundings, with the lost or venturesome few against the many. Not only *Man Alone* but also de Mauny's *The Huntsman in His Career* and the none too successful *Outlaw's Progress* of R. M. Burdon were novels directly concerned with the theme of contorted solitary life exploding into nearly-meaningless, violent crime. The subsequent implacable hunt by monolithic authority contains something of a parable about the solid pressure of society upon the individual. Violence, homicidal or suicidal, in Davin's *Cliffs of Fall* and *Roads From Home*, in Ruth Park's *Witch's Thorn* and in Gaskell's 'All Part of the Game'[72] is directly related to collapse under pressure from society which cannot be met. This pressure also underlies the distorted personality of the murderer in Frank Sargeson's most powerful short story 'A Great Day'[73] and of Henry in Gaskell's 'You Can't Go Three Days'.[74] The man alone appears again, farming by himself or as a farm-labourer, in Roderick Finlayson's *Tidal Creek*, in Sargeson's *I Saw in My Dream* and *That Summer* and short stories like Sargeson's 'Making of a New Zealander',[75] Gaskell's 'Holiday'[76] and Phillip Wilson's 'A Change of Heart'.[77]

This concern with the isolated individual, isolated in every sense, who may or may not explode into violent gestures under the distorting weight of a pattern he does not understand, is the writers' way of examining the society they depict. The mismade character structure is not without pattern any more than the normal character structure. The forces which the social milling machine exerts to mould and trim its sound citizen coins out of the child's malleable alloy may be more accurately gauged from the bad bent pennies that result when the alloy fails under pressure. The writer cannot dismantle the whole milling machine but he can exhibit the bent pennies and help his society to draw its own conclusions about how sound coins as well as unsound coins are made and at what cost.

The depiction of the gestures of violence produced in the society also raises the question of the values from which the artist works and his answers to the question how far society works well or ill. It is plain that faced with the problem of acting by giving whole-hearted uncompromising approval to the attitudes of the pattern, the New Zealand writer stops short. When, like the boy of John Kelly's story 'For Ever and Ever',[78] artists must act alongside society, must shoot the hawk which attacks from the necessities of its nature, they, like the boy, do not participate fully.

Bill Pearson's gripping story of the profound uneasiness of soldiers shooting the thief in their midst[79] clearly raises this question of participating with society against the anti-social crime. So does Erik de Mauny's novel which ends with his hero, Villiers, a journalist become soldier, killing a character obviously based on Graham.[80] This crime remains for Villiers something of a criticism of society since society is shown to be directly involved in making the criminal capable of the crime. Villiers concludes thus on whether he should shoot to kill: 'If it should be the act of another, I should have to consent to it, because I should have no power over it. But by making it my own, I make the responsibility mine: *and I do not consent.*'[81]

The writer takes the responsibility of his real share in what he feels are the best of the community values and in their name acts but does not consent by making a criticism of the discrepancies, the contradictions, and the shortcomings of the pattern of life by showing individuals caught up in it or distorted by it. To the simple materialism, shielded and confirmed by the puritan moralities, the artist opposes the results of that attitude and demonstrates the insufficiency of it when confronted by crisis.

The facts of death and failure and violence, as has been exemplified, are often juxtaposed by New Zealand writers with the framework of the pattern grown insufficient to support the crises it produces. The young man whose mistress has just died of an abortion in Dan Davin's 'The Quiet One' is helpless. '"So that's how it is," he said. "She's dead." I didn't say anything. I just stood there, wishing I was anywhere else in the world. "If only I'd known," he said. "Christ, man, I'd have married her a hundred times, kid and all." He stopped. His mind must have been going over and over this ground for days. He gave a laugh suddenly, such a queer, savage sort of a laugh that I jumped. "If it'd been twins, even," he said.'[82]

At its quietest, in James Courage's intense and fine-drawn short story, 'After the Earthquake', the death of an old and invalid woman, and the daughter, Annie, who has nursed her, thereupon taking a lover, produces in the Blakiston family who visit Annie only an inquisitive comment from the Blakistons' son which is answered by a symbolic 'Shut up about it, that's all.'[83] The incapacity of the Blakistons to express real sympathy and the doubt raised as to their sensitivity to most aspects of the situation are movingly real, as are Annie's bemused reactions. A. P. Gaskell sums up the whole failure of the patterned attitude to deal with tragedy in his story of the girl enduring a beer and singsong party at which all know her fiance has just been killed overseas.[84]

In the name of what selection of elements in the national scene do the writers point to deficiencies and condemn? When Mr J. C. Reid says of John Mulgan's hero in *Man Alone* that 'There is no room for things of the spirit in Johnson and his like, nor in the sort of society they would build'[85] it would seem that Mr Reid has mistaken the writer's report of symptoms and his diagnosis for the writer's prescription. At even a first reading of Frank Sargeson's *That Summer* or John Mulgan's *Man Alone* one cannot but be struck by the writers' attitude of unjudging pity for their driven and socially damned characters.[86] That pity proceeds from the writers' sense of the deprivation of things of the spirit in their characters' lives, if Mr Reid wishes it put in those terms, things of the spirit such as charity, humanity, and joy. The lack of these qualities or their distortion by the social pattern is what makes victims instead of whole people out of the subjects of the writers.

In the search for these qualities a few writers have indicated a belief in 'natural man'. Roderick Finlayson in his pamphlet *Our Life in This Land*[87] has adopted a belief, à la Jean-Jacques Rousseau, in the simple life of the soil. With this is linked Mr Finlayson's great admiration for the Maoris, which stands out in all his books. Frank Sargeson's equivocal end to *I Saw in My Dream* suggests a catastrophic finish to the persistence here of mismade civilization, and the character of Cedric, who walks out of his parents' shack and almost out of society after a boyhood of friendship with Maori children, is an erratic warning sporadically making an appearance throughout the story. Ruth Park makes her Maori character, Georgie Wi, into the best Catholic in the district, a successful patriarchal father, sole protector to the European waif-heroine, and a happy man. Professor Beaglehole adds some substance to the dream by pointing out that 'The Maori rate of psychosis is about one-third of that of the non-Maori population'[88] and he suggests the possibility that tribal support and security in the trials of 'the competitive aggressive world of the Pakeha' may help to account for the difference.[89]

It is remarkable, in view of the public's attitude to the Maori outlook, that that outlook should have been held up at all in literature, or that stories including Maori characters should be disproportionately numerous. But this does not imply that most writers stand with an appropriately localized version of the noble savage. The superiority of the Maori in certain adjustments has been mainly used for contrast. With the exception of Roderick Finlayson, the writers' true platform of values must be sought for elsewhere.

Those values can be descried easily enough. They are the values of humanitarian liberalism, values which have always been present in New Zealand, though less often dominantly so than many critics of those values assert. The writers speak largely on the basis of those elements which do not stem mainly from the puritan tradition imported and incongruously set down in a land fit for human ease and companionship. They would brick off the blind alleys of work to no purpose, that is, to no purpose save socially respectable accumulation. The stereotypes of men's and women's roles which no longer fit the facts they would like to see adjusted in the knowledge of a reality exposed to the light and air of public recognition and discussion.

If the writers were professional sociologists or professionally concerned to see that the family—the central institution in the creation and enjoyment of our values—ran smoothly, then they might advise, without inconsistency, that personal crises which do occur should be met, not with fear and shame, but with greatly extended psychological services to supplement the physical welfare services existing. The social burdens of women are many: in a world of scarce bungalows there is no substitute for the assistance once provided by the three-generation unit; ever more rapidly changing circumstances to which the children must be educated also unfortunately diminish the aid which the elderly can provide; and this more complicated life must be lived without readily available help in family planning and guidance and allied matters, and without crèches, kindergartens and home aides, which the mother often does not know to ask for even where they do exist. All these burdens could be lightened. There would be more than a possibility, the writers imply, that this much release from avoidable strain and distortion of all kinds would produce people capable of squarely confronting the unavoidable crises of life with a more Christian understanding of their implications.

For our writers work in the light cast by liberal humanitarianism, which is as strongly embedded in Christianity and western values generally as the elements in our society that the writers attack by exposing their effects. If humanitarianism is, as is frequently said, not enough and démodé, let philosophers, theologians and sociologists explore the ground and find in sizable, usable quantities, within our society, the ore of something that can be cast into an alternative to our present and to the future which the writers imply might be achieved on the basis of that present.

Meanwhile the attitude which the New Zealand writer takes to his society, and which informs his work, will continue to be based on the possibility here of a truly human ease and depth of living and on an attack on the distortions produced by an irrelevant puritanism of misplaced demands and guilts. The artist must sound his trumpet of insight until the walls of Jericho—the pattern as it is—fall down.

Notes

1 Between McCormick and Reid:
 Novels:—
 Sargeson, *That Summer* (1943)
 Sargeson, *When the Wind Blows* (1945)
 Davin, *Cliffs of Fall* (1945)

 Collections of short stories:—
 Gilbert, *Free to Laugh and Dance* (1943)
 Finlayson, *Sweet Beulah Land* (1944)
 Speaking for Ourselves (ed. Sargeson, 1945)

2 Since Reid:
 Novels:—
 Davin, *For the Rest of our Lives* (1947)
 Courage, *The Fifth Child* (1948)
 Ballantyne, *The Cunninghams* (1948)
 Finlayson, *Tidal Creek* (1948)
 Sargeson, *I Saw in my Dream* (1949)
 Davin, *Roads from Home* (1949)
 de Mauny, *The Huntsman in his Career* (1949)
 Courage, *Desire without Content* (1950)
 G. Wilson, *Brave Company* (1951)
 Park, *The Witch's Thorn* (1951)

 Collections of short stories:—
 Gaskell, *The Big Game* (1947)
 Davin, *The Gorse Blooms Pale* (1947)
 Cole, *It Was So Late* (1949)

3 E. H. McCormick, *Letters and Art in New Zealand* (Wellington, 1940), pp. 169-70.
4 Allen Curnow, *Not In Narrow Seas* (Christchurch, 1939), poem 9.
5 *New Zealand New Writing*, No. 1, p. 39.
6 J. C. Reid, *Creative Writing In New Zealand* (Auckland, 1946), p. 58.
7 [Review, *That Summer and Other Stories* by Frank Sargeson, *Landfall*, Vol. 1, No. 3 (1947), pp. 218-22. Ed.]
8 Helen Gardner, *François Mauriac: A Woman of the Pharisees* in *The Penguin New Writing* 31, p. 101. See also O. Von Nostitz, *Georges Bernanos: His Life and Work* in *The Dublin Review*, No. 452, Second Quarter, 1951, p. 75. 'Thus he [Bernanos] was able to say of his books that all the good things in them came from a very great distance, from "the deep sources of childhood" and that his vocation consisted precisely in striking the notes that he had once heard many years ago.' The same

search in a more dissonant, flatter, less sonorous scene is apparent in Sargeson, in Ballantyne and in Bruce Mason, to name a few.

9 Three valuable sociological reports are in, however, H. C. D. Somerset's *Littledene* (Wellington, 1938); Ernest and Pearl Beaglehole's *Some Modern Maoris* (Christchurch, 1946) and T. H. Scott's *From Emigrant to Native* in *Landfall* 4 and 6.
10 W. B. Sutch, *The Quest For Security In New Zealand* (Penguin, 1942), p. 21.
11 Population figures from W. M. Hamilton, 'The Farming Industries', in H. Belshaw (ed.), *New Zealand* (Berkeley, 1947), pp. 137-9.
12 Sutch, *The Quest For Security In New Zealand*, p. 9.
13 E. Locke, *The Shepherd and the Scullery-Maid* (Christchurch, 1950).
14 E. Halévy, *A History of the English People*, Vol. III (London, 1927), p. 200.
15 Halévy, *A History of the English People*, Vol. III, p. 166.
16 G. D. H. Cole and R. Postgate, *The Common People*, 1746-1946 (London, 1946), p. 323. And compare also Graham Wallas's remarks in his Introduction to Halévy's Vol. I (London, 1924), pp. vi and vii.
17 Halévy, *A History of the English People*, Vol. III, p. 165.
18 Halévy, *A History of the English People*, Vol. I, p. 339.
19 A. N. Prior, *Disruption* in *Landfall* 5, p. 13, and for emphasis compare Halévy, *A History of the English People*, Vol. III, p. 214.
20 Cf. Halévy, *A History of the English People*, Vol. I, pp. 408-11 and 418-23; Vol. III, Chapter III.
21 J. L. and B. Hammond, *The Village Labourer* (London, 1948), Vol. II, p. 23.
22 Hammond, *The Village Labourer*, p. 24.
23 H. G. Wells both in his *Autobiography* and in his novel *The History of Mr Polly* shows the form and the power of this sapping fear.
24 Cf. W. T. Doig, *Rich and Poor in New Zealand* (Christchurch, n.d.). Mr Doig in his pamphlet makes some interesting points on the basis of 'the analysis of Social Security Declarations made by the Government Census and Statistics Department' in 1939 for the tax year 1937/38. Of 350,000 returns covered those of men over twenty numbered 323,822. 38% of these received under £208 a year, 55% received between £208 and £520, 5% between £520 and £1000, and 2% above £1000 (p. 6). The percentage of men in each occupation receiving *more* than £10 a week were: doctors, 72%; employer-accountants, 57%; dentists, 50%; architects, 46%; managers, 44%; sheep-farmers, 30%; employers of labour, 28%; and dairy-farmers, 14%. Apart from the unemployed, the poorest section were farm-labourers, of whom 69% received under £3 a week in cash and 91% under £4 a week in cash.

Of 50,273 wharf-workers, coal miners, quartz gold miners, fitters, motor mechanics, mechanics, construction and general labourers, and drivers, precisely 80 made over £10 a week, or 0.015% of them (figures based on pp. 8 and 9). The size and composition of the lowest income group, including as it must a high proportion of unemployed and farm-labourers—and therefore, possibly, of bachelors—is an interesting confirmation of the New Zealand writers' implicit view of the importance and character of this group. The 2% above £1000 a year make as minor a mark in the statistics as they do in our literature. There is a surprising percentage of those in what one might have assumed would constitute an upper middle class of professions and occupations falling at this time below £10 in weekly earnings. The tax year 1937/38 was neither a boom nor a depression year. It is perhaps too prosperous a year, but about the right period to furnish a background for the writing this article is concerned with.

Fiction and the Social Pattern 53

Professor H. Belshaw in *Standards of Living, Wages and Prices* (Wellington, 1941), provides (p. 19) figures for the 1938/39 tax year (a less typical year for our purposes). He gives the percentage of male income receivers over sixteen in various income groups which may be used as some sort of check. 16.4% received under £200; 58.3% received between £200 and £499; 15.0% received between £500 and £999; and 10.7% received £1000 or more. The brackets are not quite the same but it can be seen that the two upper groups are very considerably greater and the lowest group diminished by these figures, though inflationary changes would offset this to some extent. Despite the variation, generalizations about 'a modest competence' for 'the great majority' still appear to be justified.

25 McCormick, *Letters and Art in New Zealand*, p. 137.
26 *Letters and Art in New Zealand*, p. 136.
27 A reminiscence of the first version of this sentimentality can be noticed lingering on, in infectious spots, in James Courage's novel *The Fifth Child*. Something of a shift to the second version occurs in his *Desire Without Content*. Cf. a review by the present writer in *Landfall* 20.
28 The majority of the population resided in the counties at the census of 1906. By the time of the census of 1911 the majority resided in the boroughs. See *New Zealand Official Year-Book* (1918), p. 88.
29 E. A. Plishke in *Design and Living* (Wellington, 1947), comments on this type of display, particularly from pp. 34-7, but he does not mention the function that the accumulation of inefficient and labour-making objects of bad taste serves in constituting a visible record of work done and patterned attitudes upheld.
30 'To the stranger the most amazing feature of New Zealand sport is the completeness of its organization. Every little town has its tribe of clubs.' Historical Branch of the Department of Internal Affairs, *Introduction to New Zealand* (Wellington, 1945), p. 234.
31 Included in his collection *It Was So Late* (Christchurch, 1949).
32 Included in Frank Sargeson (ed.), *Speaking For Ourselves* (Auckland, 1945).
33 G. Wilson, *Brave Company* (London, 1951), p. 162.
34 The present writer is not of the opinion that most New Zealand servicemen carry to the full the outlook of 'Lawyer'. But the very heavy sales of *Brave Company*, heavy for a New Zealand novel in New Zealand, show that the views are not felt to be basically untypical or offensive. Certainly, too, the literary merit of the descriptions of action is considerable. An unfortunate corollary of the assertion by 'Lawyer' of the 'manly' virtues is the depreciation of others. Moral courage is held to be composed of 'a thick skin ... a distended egotism and a platform speaker's love of an audience' (p. 72). Admiration of Hadfield's 'invulnerable armour of ... fatalism, a dry, mocking acceptance of things' (p. 265) and of the similar Cadman (pp. 184 and 285) is accompanied by a hatred of those behind the lines with other tasks employing other qualities. This produces a dangerously over-simplified view of history and politics. 'Chiefly I hate all self-important people who love the public platform, who rise by bombast, whose inadequacy to their responsibilities causes wars that they do not fight.' (pp. 10 and 11). It is not without significance that when the minor Italian heroine says Mussolini was wrong because he failed, 'Lawyer' adds only the thought that the Italian men failed Mussolini (p. 60). The dual view of women on pp. 1, 218, 64-9, 73, 101 and 206 strikingly reveals the many demands and the contradictory allocations of approval and disapproval which accompanies 'Lawyer's' other attitudes.
35 *Landfall*, 16.
36 *Book Nine*.

37 Book Nine.
38 Included in *The Big Game and Other Stories*.
39 Cf. Margaret Mead, *The American Character* (Penguin, 1944), pp. 85-7. Margaret Mead here suggests that adolescent tension is a necessary price paid for the valuable acquisition of conscience and its attendant private guilt. Adolescence is the difficult phase in which—though the parents themselves are rejected—the child's introjected image of the parent as good and punishing and rewarding becomes generalized into adult standards of good and right conduct imposed internally and not by public shame. For discussion of examples of adolescence in other cultures see also Ruth Benedict, *Patterns of Culture* (New York, 1934); A. Kardiner (ed.), *The Psychological Frontiers of Society* (New York, 1945); and Margaret Mead, *Growing Up In New Guinea* (New York, 1930).
40 *Landfall* 9 and 10.
41 It would be interesting to enquire how far the New Zealand emphasis on the merit of being older arises from a need to compensate for lack of other distinctions in a homogeneous and unstratified society, with, accordingly, too little monetary or other reward for the penalties of aging. Mr Coates was regarded as 'having youth on his side' at fifty *(N.Z. Herald*, Supplement, 8 Dec. 1928, p. 5) and Labour Cabinets have been even older than those of Reform and National. Professor [Leslie] Lipson in *The Politics of Equality* (Chicago, 1948), (pp. 466-8) remarks on the New Zealand Public Service demand for promotion by seniority with as many as possible of everyman getting two or three years at the headship before retirement. The multiplication of local bodies like Rabbit Boards may serve by multiplying local dignitaries. New Zealand had the huge total of 680 local bodies in 1942 (E. B. Dalmer and H. S. Southern, *Counties at the Crossroads* (Christchurch, 1948), p. l3). The growing hagiography of pioneering probably over-emphasizes the work-virtue of those now old, at the same time, paradoxically, as the age benefits are allowed to stand at an unlivably low level.
42 Dan Davin, *Cliffs of Fall* (London, 1945), p. 13.
43 See Davin, *Cliffs of Fall*, p. 90. Mr Davin also remarks there 'The reactionaries were heartened and strengthened by a powerful nucleus of Scottish Presbyterians ... Peasant virtues ruled business. Business ruled the country and the towns.'
44 A recent advertisement in the January 1952 *Here and Now* is to this point. 'A message for young men. Now that your heart's set on marriage you'll be hard stretched to save that one thousand pounds by Easter. You definitely can't afford a car—and you can't ride a bicycle? Then read ...' (p. 31). The car, which completes the Prince Charming outfit, must be sacrificed just when it becomes really vital to ease the hard work of early marriage and parenthood.
45 On the morphology of the American 'dating' system see Margaret Mead, *Male and Female*.
46 Not all or most bachelors by any means. But as Mr Allan Nixon pointed out in the second of his 1951 radio talks on the family, the bachelor's social position, whether as cause or effect of bachelordom, is worse in most respects. Using the Government Statistician's Report on the 1936 Census as a basis it was shown that in 1936, among the men over 35, 1 in 24 of the married were unemployed but 1 in 10 of the single, and 1 in 6 of the married were employers of labour but only 1 in 13 of the single. Mr Nixon added: 'The bachelor, compared with the married man of the same age, suffers more sickness, is less often in steady employment, enjoys less than his share of the national income' and 'the prison population includes *twice* as many single men as married men ... and the same division of the sheep from the goats is reflected in our hospital populations and in our mental hospital

Fiction and the Social Pattern 55

populations, too.' Mr Nixon warned his listeners against ignoring age-constitution of institutional populations as they affect these figures and against taking the position as being always the effect and never the cause of bachelordom *or* vice versa; but the figures do, as he said, illustrate something of a 'disordered condition'. It certainly bears out the relevance of much New Zealand writing.

47 Quoted by E. Beaglehole, *Some Modern Maoris* (Christchurch, 1946), p. 48.
48 Based on figures at p. 55 of the *New Zealand Official Year-Book (N.Z.O.Y.B.)*, (1950). On the basis of figures at p. 79 of the *N.Z.O.Y.B.* (1918), I have calculated the number of unmarried males *over* twenty expressed as a percentage of the total of all married males plus unmarried males *over* twenty. This is very nearly the percentage of unmarried men in the adult male population at the following census years: 1891, 46.3% unmarried. 1901, 43.9% unmarried. 1911, 46.6% unmarried. 1916 (a war year), 37.0% unmarried.
49 It should be noted that, to judge from the statistics of the marriage rate, New Zealand is not unusual. Our marriage rate for 1948 was 9.9; that for Denmark, 9.4; Canada, 9.6; Australia, 9.7; Austria, 10.0; Israel, 10.8; and the U.S.A., 12.3. *Vide N.Z.O.Y.B.*, 1950, p. 101.
50 This is two years later on the averages than the figure given by the British Registrar-General of 24 in 1945 and quoted in the *British Medical Journal*, 15 July 1950, p. 123.
51 *N.Z.O.Y.B.*, 1950, p. 70.
52 A. R. D. Fairburn, *We New Zealanders* (Wellington, n.d.), p. 35. Mr Fairburn undoubtedly expresses a common opinion among doctors and nurses but figures cannot be found in the *Year Book*. Illegitimate births total 4% of all births annually, on an average, though they rose to 6% in 1944, the year after the Americans were here in their greatest numbers and young New Zealand men were absent in their greatest numbers.
53 *N.Z.O.Y.B.*, 1950, p.61.
54 *New Zealand Herald*, 22 March 1951.
55 *New Zealand Herald*, 26 March 1951, 'Mother of Three'.
56 *New Zealand Herald*, 27 March 1951.
57 *New Zealand Herald*, 30 March 1951, 'Father of Three'. Cf. 26 March, 28 March, and 3 April.
58 *New Zealand Herald,*. 27 March 1951, 'Partner, Not Servant'.
59 *New Zealand Herald*, 3 April 1951, 'Understanding Mother'.
60 E. Beaglehole, *Mental Health in New Zealand* (Wellington, 1950), p. 96.
61 Department of Health advertisement No. 4a in the series 'For a Healthier Nation'. Dr Keith Simpson in *The Lancet*, 8 January 1949, p. 47, quotes figures for England and Wales from the Interdepartmental Committee on Abortion, 1939. These 'conservative' figures show between 44,000 and 60,000 'unlawfully induced' abortions a year; so that the New Zealand rate would appear to be about double the English rate, though doubtless the conservatism of the English figures and the low (on Dr Davis's calculation) proportion of all English abortions held to be unlawfully induced would account for much of the difference. Dr Albert Davis gives a clinical survey of 2,665 abortions in the *British Medical Journal*, 15 July 1950, pp. l23-30. The average age of the patients was 29, but this is explained by the fact that abortion is much commoner among married women, and that the average age of marriage is fairly high—24. 'In rural communities and in the purlieus of wealthy districts, the proportion of single girls is higher.' One-seventh of Dr Davis's cases in a 'working-class suburb' were single, Roesle (1929) gave one-sixth as single, McIlroy (1929) reported the married 'most frequent' but Richelt 'found

that 65% of his large series were unmarried'. Dr Davis points to the influence of 'convention' and it appears that abortion rates vary markedly according to class attitudes. Thus English analyses tend to confirm the analysis of New Zealand conditions presented here. 'Severe complications' were 14% of single cases and 6% of married cases, probably because of 'the inexperience of these single girls, their isolation, and the desperate nature of their predicament'. If the single figures for severe complications are also higher in New Zealand, for similar reasons, then the figures for deaths from sepsis following abortion would not yield the true proportion of single and married in the total number of abortions, but instead, would exaggerate the proportion of the single. So a figure higher than 62% will probably represent the true proportion of all abortions here which are abortions of the married.

62 Not only does the husband assert his picture of himself and find companionship in a male social environment outside the home, he may also find excitement there that he does not find with his wife. Skill and capacity for personal relationships are not pre-requisites for the 'thrill' of gambling and the excitement is joined to a hope that a 'lucky break' may propel the investor through his normal income's dreary ceiling. This applies also to many a wife. On horse racing alone in 1950 £25 million were bet through the totalizator. The Government kept 9.1% of this and the racing clubs 8.2 % (*N.Z.O.Y.B.*, 1950, p. 495). This can be compared with the figure of £345 million for 'personal consumption' in 1949/50, representing 'consumption goods and services purchased by individuals and non-profit-making bodies' but not 'goods and services received free from Government social services' (*N.Z.O.Y.B.,* 1950, p. 1082).

63 The success of the New Zealand marriage as a working partnership and the variety of diversion by attainment of material goods may be judged from the comparison which follows of U.S. figures of non-relief farm families (from the *U.S. Department of Agriculture Year-book*, 1940) with figures (from W. T. Doig's study *A Survey of Standards of Life of New Zealand Dairy Farmers*, Wellington, 1940) on equivalent New Zealand possessions. The comparison is quoted by Hamilton, 'The Farming Industries', in Belshaw (ed.), *New Zealand*, p. 158. The figures, which are percentages, relate to 1936.

Facilities	N.Z.	U.S. (income $1000-$1249)	U.S. (income $2500-$2999)
Running water	94	16	43
H. and C. water in kitchen and bathroom	69	8	30
Electric light	80	19	44
Telephone	63	29	52
Car	78	71	80
Radio	82	54	81
Electric refrigerator	4	4	20

64 'For twenty years she had been living, without knowing it, in despair. Despair may become an unconscious state of mind ... Only the presence of the boy Andrès had made it possible for her to live up to that resolution. He was right. She *had* made use of him: *had* lived on his life.' François Mauriac, *The Dark Angels* (London, 1951) pp. 229 and 228. The effects of puritanism on family life have been dealt with by three French masters, Mauriac, Bernanos, and Gide. Cf. criticism cited

earlier and the critical article on Gide's *Et Nunc Manet in Te, suivi de Journal Intime* by Peter Quennell in *The New Statesman and Nation*, 29 December 1951. There is no group in English or American writing which could teach so much to our writers on their chosen subject.

65 James Courage. *The Fifth Child* (London, 1948), pp. 212 and 213.
66 Included in *Speaking For Ourselves*. Quotation at p. 94.
67 There is an illuminating chapter which I have discovered runs parallel, but in broader terms, to the general thesis advanced here, on the relation between mental disease and New Zealand's 'organization of social and economic life', in *Mental Health In New Zealand* (Chapter XII) by Professor Ernest Beaglehole. He adverts there to Karen Horney. The present writer found Dr Horney's general picture of the relation of lovelessness and lack of affection to neuroticism in, for example, *The Neurotic Personality Of Our Time* (London, 1936), and also Erich Fromm's *The Fear Of Freedom* (London, 1942), stimulating reading in expanding his thesis from reviews. The thesis could be linked, too, with the concept of *anomy* dealt with in a recent article (to be continued) in *Political Science*, Vol. 3, No. 2, by R. H. Brookes.
68 The belief, beloved of schoolbooks and orators, that New Zealand is or was a laboratory of political experiment rests largely on the work accomplished in two brief periods of active legislation, roughly 1891-8 and 1935-8 Prior to each of these eruptions the New Zealand voter had first to experience depression then an attempt to revamp conservatism by spending proposals (Vogel in 1881 and Ward in 1928), then a further period of negative conservatism, before the risk was run.
69 There were some notable examples of this at the Writers' Conference held at Christchurch in 1951.
70 Edmund Wilson in *Classics and Commercials* (London, 1951), first chapter entitled 'Archibald MacLeish and the Word', does a wonderful wrecking job on MacLeish's arguments laying just such a charge.
71 Quoted by Edmund Wilson, *Classics and Commercials*, p. 473.
72 *Landfall* 13.
73 Included in *A Man and His Wife*, Wellington, 1940.
74 Included in *The Big Game*.
75 Included in *A Man and His Wife*.
76 Included in *The Big Game* .
77 *Landfall* 19.
78 *Landfall* 9.
79 'Social Catharsis' in *Landfall* 4.
80 Stanley Graham, a married West Coast farmer, aged 40 and with two children had his cowshed condemned by the Health Department and was in financial difficulties. After threatening a neighbour, and later a policeman, he shot and killed four policemen who came to his home. During the subsequent search involving hundreds, he left the edge of the bush to return to his home three times, the first time killing two young men guarding his home. He was killed on 20 October 1941, after a twelve day manhunt.
81 *The Huntsman in His Career* (London, 1949), p. 259. There is more than a hint of elementary existentialism in this soliloquy; but de Mauny's italics pick out the key sentence and the simpler truth.
82 *Landfall* 11, p. 239.
83 *Landfall* 8, p. 307.
84 In *New Zealand New Writing*, No. 4. and included in *The Big Game*.
85 Reid, *Creative Writing In New Zealand* , p. 60.

86 Cf. the present writer's review in *Landfall* 3, p. 221.
87 R. Finlayson, *Our Life In This Land*, Auckland, 1940.
88 Beaglehole, *Mental Health In New Zealand*, p. 28. This is the more notable since in other institutional populations Maoris are present in more than even proportion to population.
89 *Mental Health In New Zealand*, p. 93.

2

Great Expectations:
New Zealand Since the War

It is a commonplace in the history of science that an advance in measurement leads to the discovery of anomalies hitherto hidden in the inaccuracy and that these in turn lead to discovery of new scientific laws.

J. D. Bernal, F.R.S., in *Penguin Science Survey 1961*

The soil grows castes; the machine makes classes.

Michael Young in *The Rise of the Meritocracy*

In surveying political and social developments in New Zealand since the war let me first disclaim, as is customary, expertise in so general and extensive a subject. An expert is a man who gets his head above the crowd by standing on a pile of other people's books and, in this case, the books are just not there. What I do know rather more about than is usual is how New Zealand electors judged policies and politicians thus setting limits, by those judgements, on the choices made by their masters *pro tem*. It is a knowledge many people are sure they share while parties and Cabinets, being by trade sharebrokers of opinion, are certain they not only understand the past and present views of the electorate, they are even confident they know how to shape their future—until they go out. For myself I claim only the safe past.

Yet the most obvious feature of New Zealand's postwar politics, the similarity of the two main parties, appears to negate the link between electoral opinion and party policy. For despite the likeness of the parties, the bulk of electoral opinion is certainly divided deeply and divided on an enduring basis. I have argued elsewhere that New Zealand consistently votes as two nations, the countryside and the city, though the city in turn is also divided against itself. But the two parties, each resting in the main on one section, since 1946 have agreed on social and economic policy to a marked degree.

In the first place they both accepted the structure of the welfare state much as it was created in 1938. One might have cut down a means test

---

[This chapter is the substance of an address delivered to the NZ University Students' Association Congress in January 1962. It was first published in *Landfall*, Vol. 16, No. 3 (1962). Ed.]

here or equalized pensions and superannuation benefits there but both were agreed that the system must go on dispensing security and mildly redistributing income come what may. Both parties emphasized that they achieved full employment in their terms of office, or overfull employment as its critics called it. Both parties promoted low cost housing, each fresh encouragement, whether purchase of State houses or three per cent loans or capitalization of the family benefit, being adopted by the other party. Both parties agreed in conducting heavy programmes of State investment in primary and secondary education, in roading and electric power, not to mention farmland development, the telephone system, freight railway equipment, aviation and aerodromes and so on. Above all, both parties concurred in leaving the major portion of the economy to the operations of private capital, checked and in part controlled by the State, but neither comprehensively planned nor threatened with expropriation.

The control of capital issues was almost entirely removed by Mr Nordmeyer, not by Mr Watts.[1] Food subsidies were cut by a National Government, but what tells is their continuance. When Mr Nordmeyer set taxes at 31.7 per cent of the national income in 1958/59 he did not quite reach the 32.1 per cent taken in 1951/52. When the tax bite decreased to 28.8 per cent in 1959/60 it was neither more nor less than the 29 per cent usually levied by his Nationalist predecessors. Labour might prefer to build and rent State houses but it ended by loaning money cheaply so couples could build for themselves. National did prefer to allocate foreign exchange to importers or to work more indirectly again by squeezing overdrafts. Faced, however, with an overseas funds emergency in 1961 like that confronting Labour in 1958, Mr Marshall and Mr Lake operated the machinery of import selection left by Mr Nash and Mr Nordmeyer.[2] Thus whether he was listening to the late Sir Sidney Holland on the worth of moderate, arbitration unionism or to Mr Nash on the value of the South-East Asia Treaty Organisation; to the late Mr Skinner on the need to break down agricultural protectionism in wealthy markets overseas or to Mr Holyoake on the healthy increase in factory production within New Zealand, the voter could with reason have entertained doubts about the party colours of the speaker.[3]

Even after allowance is made for the capacity of men to oppose one another fiercely over minor matters of emphasis and after taking into account their emotional attachment to party images constructed from past victories and present catchcries it would still be surprising if no alternatives had arisen to the tacit agreement of Labour and National. Like the poor, of course, we have always with us some Independents. Over the six elections since the war an average of six[4] have put up each time in the non-Maori seats and received, in their total of 38 contests, an average of 2.04 per cent of the franchises of those qualified to vote for them. Just three times candidates have secured significant shares, in every instance because they had once been prominent in the winning party thereabouts.[5] Without inflation from these three sources the average obtained by the other 35 Independents collapses to 1.15 per cent. In our postwar politics salvation has not been sought outside the parties.

Nor has it been sought in the Communist party. To the left of Labour lies impossibility, as Table 2:1 makes plain. As the Cold War froze over and hardened into relative permanence the average Communist vote shrank ever smaller. The two big efforts were made when Labour was going out, in 1949 and 1960. Despite the demonstrable discontent of Labour stalwarts and despite the advantage to the Communist party of choosing their contests, the Communist candidates saw most of the ex-Labour votes shift past them into National or non-voting. Communist intervention affected not one result while, in its second or 1960 push, the party discovered that its previously paper-thin support had been further shorn in half. Indeed, to appreciate the unimportance of Communists and Independents in the New Zealand result as a whole, it should be realized that their shares, taken together, amount to considerably less than the share contributed by spoiled ballots in five elections out of the six.

Table 2.1: The Portion Voting Communist Amongst All Qualified to Vote

Election	1946	1949	1951	1954	1957	1960
No. of Candidates	3	16	4	8	5	19
Ave. % of seats contested	2.77	1.57	1.04	0.92	0.85	0.75
% share in N.Z. total	0.10	0.30	0.05	0.09	0.06	0.18

The alternative to the major parties in fact arose to the right of Labour and, on balance, to the right of National as well. Social Credit is a curiously old-fashioned party. Pledged to untying a Gordian knot which was cut through twenty years ago, they preach the doctrines of Major Douglas, a figure from the days of harsh deflation and mass unemployment. But they preach amidst an era of bouncing inflation and jobs for all. The more attractive of the party leadership are reminiscent of the Single Taxers of the nineteen-hundreds in their earnest dogmatic idealism. In the cottages and baches of the pensioners in Auckland's East Coast Bays, Waiheke or French Bay, for example, the party's vote is more than twice the city's norm. California's Ham N'Eggers of the nineteen thirties would recognize the mood. After all, what but a politico-financial revolution could convert a bare sufficiency to ample comfort so late in a man's life history? And more antique again, yet also more modern, is the Poujadist aspect of Social Credit—the one-man businessman's detestation of the taxes which fuel the contemporary state, his resentment of the controlling paperwork which overwhelms him and his suspicion of the unionists whose highest ranks rival him in status while their lower ranks assert standards for paid help which he cannot meet.

Here we have the link with the *bêtes noires* of the countryside—taxes, controls and high-cost labour—for the farmer, too, is a one-man businessman. Here also is the reason why the well-to-do city suburbs do not support this heresy from the National party while their traditional partners in the rural and farmer seats do. The professionals, executives and city employers are inured to the characteristics of the mid-twentieth century. With the exception of the trusty band of Adam Smithites in the Constitutional Society they have come to terms with the omnicompetent state and live by, with and even from it. They prompt the concessions which the National party must make to add sufficient suburban and town seats to its country strongholds so as to arrive at power. Once there, it is the city component which recognizes the shapes imposed on a government by awkward reality while it is the more numerous country back-benchers who caucus against cotton mills.[6]

Like their parliamentary representatives, the farmers are only half-reconciled to the times. In the conduct of their farms and the co-operative business of processing and marketing their products the New Zealand farmers have few if any peers in general flexibility and readiness to adopt fresh techniques. Yet, paradoxically, in their politics they hanker after the days when all the cost figures were smaller though individually farmers were then usually small and struggling themselves. Social Credit is made to measure for nostalgic men of a few fixed ideas concerning public affairs. The party would do away with internal controls, drastically lower taxes and rates, increase benefits, get rid of foreign exchange allocation and import selection, while in addition, staying the cramping hand of the banker-cum-civil servant trying to adjust overdrafts. Social Credit as a faith is in essence the belief that simply by adding to the economy the device of 'debt-free credit creation' all modern excrescences on untrammelled private ownership would fall away, leaving conditions for the small man of capital even better than they were for grandfather.

A minority of North Island farmers sought abundant rural credit through the Country party in the nineteen-twenties, just as their fathers in the Farmers' Union of the nineteen-hundreds had demanded the other side of the coin: 'freehold, free trade and free contract'. In the thirties, the Douglas Social Credit movement in the Waikato and Northland led the dairy farmers into their one brief flirtation with a Labour party pledged to control the creation of credit. Slowly through seventy years of co-operation the farmer has extruded the suspect 'middleman' until the bankers, the stock and station agents and the taxgatherers are left. Thus Social Credit's basic attitudes are in no way new to the political scene. Now the North Island farmers, for whom Labour is an unacceptable amalgam of all they distrust, have in the Social Credit party somewhere to turn when they weary of National's likeness to other governments and long instead to journey back towards the promised land. Where the Social Credit electors' hopes are not pitched so high, at least they enjoy the chance to vote against a National Government without thereby voting for Labour, just as rural protest utilized the vehicle of the Liberals in the nineteen-twenties in order to punish Reform in safety. Either way there is no chance that they are casting a ballot for change in the grand outline of the *status quo*—except, of course, inadvertently.

For the common factor among the three parties which collect votes and the divided people who give them, is conservatism. The majority approve in general of things as they are while the dissident minority approve of them as they were in some halcyon age. Naturally everyone can suggest a minor improvement to suit his or her case. Social Credit has, as we have seen, gone so far as to offer one large amendment, but it is an amendment guaranteed not to alter but to bring out the true nature of the existing system. A few pensioners appear to constitute the only group ready for radical alteration.

This should occasion no surprise, though for those brought up on the tale of Seddon and Savage and of radical experimental New Zealand it takes patient reconsideration to grasp the current facts.[7] It seems worthwhile to reiterate that: 'The belief, beloved of schoolbooks and orators, that New Zealand is or was a laboratory of political experiment rests largely on the work accomplished in two brief periods of active legislation, roughly 1891-8 and 1935-8. Prior to each of these eruptions the New Zealand voter had first to experience depression, then an attempt to revamp conservatism by spending proposals (Vogel in 1884 and Ward in 1928), then a further period of negative conservatism, before the risk was run.'[8] Conservatism is the usual state of unchallenged people everywhere, especially when a historical fluke grants them prosperity in addition. Turning from the people who are not ordinarily interested in politics to the parties which are, one encounters less reason again to be puzzled by the prevailing conservatism.

The preservation and administration of the *status quo* is, of course, the very function of the National party. As for Labour, it had not really blown its brains out in 1940 when Lee went, but it had expelled, or quietened the noisy men of new ideas and had given absolute predominance to the administrators and consolidators of past achievement.[9] Until 1958 it publicly owned not a concept beyond the hope of return with more of the same old 1938 formula: a lot of welfare, a little insulation and as much price and wage stability as the merchants and unions would endure. The defeat of the militant unions in 1951 showed that industrial radicalism, an independent radicalism outside the parties, could no more survive the temper of good times than the cry of 'radicalism put down' could summon up a crusade of Labour members of Parliament. For indubitably it was the Labour Government which had conducted the dress rehearsal for 1951 when it broke the Auckland Carpenters in 1949.

In 1951 the conduct of the Labour leadership revealed their certainty that the country at large had use for nought but Labour's embarrassed silence. They knew the voters' mood was conservative for there they were in the wilderness. To the wilderness they had gone in a beautifully even glissade, notwithstanding all their shrewd compromises, their patient caretaking, and the balanced slaps and pats administered to each sectional interest in turn, their own groups included. The only question left was: is the mood deepening?

It can be seen from the graph [omitted] that the Labour vote—the heavy black line at the top—continued evenly on down in 1949 and 1951. To a considerable degree the fall was slowed in 1954. Nevertheless, this was the fifth successive general election to reveal a decrease in Labour support. Then at last, nineteen years after Labour's peak there was a rebound upwards in 1957. Unfortunately for the party, the recovery did not even restore it to the 1946 level at the tail end of the first Labour Government. By the conclusion of the fifties the party's situation was worse than ever. The 1960 election marked the unkindest cut of all and Labour leaves the graph at a point nearly 9 per cent lower than where it entered. It is therefore clear that, so far as Labour—the alternative conservative party with the reputation for radicalism—is concerned, increasing prosperity has meant almost constant subtraction of voters.

One might expect that the voters in their deepening conservatism would simply be transferring to National as the party fitted by fortune and design to suit the age. And it must be remembered here that Labour had so successfully moulded and suited the previous era that when Labour appears on our graph it has come down from the heights of acceptance by more than 50 per cent of all New Zealanders entitled to vote. Did the National party, then, put on weight with prosperity as Labour had initially borrowed strength from economic adversity?

The answer is 'no' according to the facts displayed on the graph [omitted]. National's best year was 1949 when it secured 48.17 per cent of the available franchises. That was the year the party first got into power. At the next election in 1951, despite the Korean War wool boom and the made-to-order issue of the strike, National's share of the potential vote actually declined slightly. Labour suffered its usual three and a half per cent slide but, instead of the discontented joining National, they simply stayed at home as is indicated by the unusually sharp increase in non-voting. Sir Sidney Holland's men collected an extra four seats and the result was hailed as a conclusive vindication of Nationalist policy, but in truth the party was being rewarded with seats, not for gaining recruits, but for descending more slowly than Labour.

In 1954, with the appearance of Social Credit on the right, the five-year-old National Government received the most sudden and stinging rebuke administered to any government of the day since George Forbes's Coalition was dismissed in 1935. Since at the same time non-voting and Labour support also decreased (by Non Vote -2.53 and Labour -0.53 per cent respectively) Sir Sidney Holland's numerous lost supporters cannot have gone there. They must have deserted to the new party.

It is worth observing carefully the likely ingredients of the new party's voting strength. National was down seven and a half to Labour's half per cent, which suggests a Social Credit capture of 15 National: 1 Labour. This ratio, however, ignores the contingent of one-time non voters—two and a half per cent—who came back on to the market in 1954 to shop for a change along with the ex-Nationalists. The great bulk of those taking a spell from voting in 1951 were ex-Labour. It seems possible, then, that as many as four in every five of those returning to the ballot in 1954 could have been Labour in 1949. Calculated in units of half a per cent, the overall situation consequently looks like this:

Table 2.2: The Possible Sources of Social Credit Support in 1954

	From National	From Labour
Fresh losses in 1954	15	1
Non-voting in 1951	1	4
	16	5

Having made a generous allowance for ex-Labour participation via the route of non-voting in 1951, the ex-Nationalist share of Social Credit's membership still adds up to rather more than three-quarters of the whole.

The new party was, as observation of its composition and aims suggest, a Nationalist heresy.

The graph [omitted] shows dramatically where this withdrawal of confidence landed the Nationalists. Over the whole of New Zealand, with twelve hundred thousand votes available, the party in power had a lead of one and a half thousand over Labour. Aggregating National's lead over its nearest competitor in all electorates—and in Hobson a Social Crediter came second—that margin was 710 votes. If ever one might have looked with confidence for an evenly-divided House it was in 1954. In fact, however, such a House was not returned until 1957 when Labour held a lead over National not of 1,548 votes but of 47,397. In 1954 the Nationalists obtained a comfortable margin of ten seats in a House of eighty, or 12.50 per cent in return for their surplus over Labour of 0.06 per cent of those qualified to vote. As for Social Credit, in terms of the voting public's preferences that party has held the balance of power ever since its creation without once securing a seat, let alone swaying a government. It may be concluded that the New Zealand electoral system has a bit of a lean on.

Table 2.3: Party Membership of Parliament, 1946-1960, under Proportional Representation and in Fact

		1946	1949	1951	1954	1957	1960
Labour	P.R.	41	38	37	35	39	35
	Fact	42	34	30	35	41	34
	Diff.	+ 1	- 4	- 7	0	+ 2	- 1
National	P.R.	39	42	43	36	35	38
	Fact	38	46	50	45	39	46
	Diff.	- 1	+ 4	+ 7	+ 9	+ 4	+ 8
Social Credit	P.R.				9	6	7
	Fact				0	0	0
	Diff.				- 9	- 6	- 7

To accept for a moment the proportional representation enthusiasts' premise and take as perfectly representative the consideration of validly-cast votes alone, we can see plainly that bias existed in the system before Social Credit appeared to confirm that first-past-the-post voting strikes heavily at third parties. Indeed the system has three biases: against third parties; for whichever party is the government; and, largely because of our method of drawing electorates, a bias against Labour and for National. If one sets up a like table for the 76 non-Maori electorates only, the distortion is seen to be worse again. Fate has called in the old New Zealanders to redress in part the balance of the new. Nevertheless my point is not to underline the deficiencies of our method of representation but rather it is to show up the falsity of the connection between a party's superiority in seats and its presumed success with public opinion. In 1954 a conservative party of government in a time for conservatives was knocked down surely enough. It was, however, counted back in.

There are two concluding observations to make on National's erratic course as the natural vehicle for conservatives. Firstly, despite the widespread impression that the government must have lost supporters because it went out in 1957, in fact the National party at that election gained nearly one per cent more votes. It achieved this rise despite the attractions of the much-denounced 'Walter's Hundred Quid', possibly because the party was flourishing its own '25 per cent rebate'.[10] The groups which were emptying out were the previous non-voters (down 1.74 per cent) and the Social Credit 'oncers' (down 3.39 per cent), a ratio of 1:2. Even if we suppose that all Labour's 1957 acquisitions from the non-voting group amounted to no more than finding young substitutes for, or re-enlisting, the remaining old-Labourites who ceased voting back in 1951, we are still confronted with the realization that two-thirds of the new strength which put Labour back on the Treasury benches was originally shaken loose from National in 1954 and, after trying Social Credit first, came to Labour in 1957.

Had these voters transferred to Labour directly in 1954 there would have been a change of government at a period when export prices were much better than those Labour did in fact encounter. This in turn would have altered considerably the kind of impression Labour made on its return although, as will later be argued on general grounds, it is hard to believe an eviction in 1960 could have been avoided. In any event, the ironic conclusion remains that in 1954 National was the beneficiary and Labour the victim of a Nationalist heresy.

It is observable, secondly, that the heavy rejection of the second Labour Government in 1960 was not accompanied by a corresponding gain for National. Over half the rejectors moved to non-voting (3.08 per cent), where they now hang ready to rally to an attractive Labour programme as in the past. Considering the favourable circumstances and its adroit campaign National acquired a surprisingly minor share (1.64 per cent) while Social Credit did well to survive and pick up 1.03 per cent on an inconsiderable outlay of men and money. The Rt Hon. Walter Nash's lost supporters in 1960, less numerous than Sir Sidney Holland's in 1954 but equally disenchanted, responded by retiring from the vote in high dudgeon instead of transferring their allegiance.

It is not just that the workings of the electoral system allow National's inflated majorities in the House to give it a spurious air of triumph and widespread agreement. It is not only that a third choice for conservatives has horned in, initially at the expense of Labour though in the longer run to National's cost. What is notable is the proof of discontent with both major parties. Labour has diminished in a prosperous age and this might have been expected. Less predictably, National is discovered to have fared little better. At the end of the decade the annoyed Labourites mainly withdrew from the poll though two further choices in National and Social Credit were offered them. More telling again is the early instance of 1951. Discontent with both parties was reflected then, strong in respect to Labour, very mild towards National, yet its mere existence a cause of surprise as a verdict on a new government, two years on its way in high old times. The 1954 readiness of the ex Nationalists to try anything rather than go Labour or stay National argues in the same direction. The Social Credit candidates, after all, might well have suffered the treatment accorded to Communists and Independents, namely, a derisory indifference. Only once in the fifties was the major movement at an election towards either of the major parties and that was the 1957 surge towards Labour, already deferred for three years and destined to subside at the very first opportunity.

I would hazard that a clue to this even-handed ingratitude on the part of voters can be derived from considering the relation between what was available for the electors to enjoy and the occurrence of elections.[11] First it should be recalled just how spartan the good old days really were. In 1939 the index of goods stood at 73, that is, 73 per cent of what was available to New Zealanders in 1957. With war's wholesale diversion of men and materials the index dropped to 70, 69, 64, 62 and 58 in successive years. The Labour movement lost support in 1943—a great deal of support if the Democratic Soldier Labour party is separated out. In the last year of the war the index stood at 53, a little over half what New Zealanders had at hand twelve years later. There was a reviving bounce to 64 in 1946 but by then the Labour Government was well and truly identified with scarcities, while the exodus of its supporters proceeded.

Labour should have gained as the pre-war standard was approached (1947, 71) and exceeded (1948, 82). Alas for the party, the index dropped five points to 77 in the crucial election year of 1949. The first Labour Government was loaded down with memories of the ration books, permits and licences with which it had shared out the diminished stocks of war. Probably it was bound to sink below its unencumbered rival. The additional weight of the 1949 setback can hardly have helped.

The great issue in 1949, so far as National candidates could make it, was inflation. This was often just a code word for the costliness of what one could not yet afford besides summing up the disappointment caused when the same old regular purchases absorbed nearly all one's suddenly numerous postwar pounds. It is true that the pound depreciated during and after the war. But the fairly severe inflation commenced when bank credit began its outpour in 1949. This grew to a torrent in the next two years at the same time as wool prices attained the highest figure New Zealand has ever known and receipts rained down on some. The index of goods available rose to 87, then 90 in 1951 in the midst of an inflation which also bore unequally upon the income earners beneath. The result of the 1951 election was as paradoxical as the factors in it were contradictory. Labour was punished for the strike and for not being associated with prosperity nor, indeed, with anything positive. On the other side, the current inflation seems to have outweighed the real rise in total goods available, while National's proclaimed virtue in smashing the watersiders went unrewarded by lovers of order.

Picking up our cycle again after this confused interruption, the trend in the index and its political accompaniments can be summarized thus:

Table 2.4: Goods Available and Election Results, 1954-1960

(1957=100)	Volume of Goods Available per Head	Election
1952, 101 (+11); 1953, 84 (-17); 1954, 90 (+6).		1954, very heavy Govt. loss in support.
1955, 106 (+16); 1956, 102 (-4); 1957, 100 (-2).		1957, Oppsn. gains strongly, Govt. goes out
(1949/50=100; 1957= 107)	Real National Income Per Head	
1958, 108 (+1); 1959, 107 (-1); 1960, 111 (+4).		1960, voters abstain, Govt. goes out.

The first moral to be drawn is that it does not pay at the polls for a government to have even one poor year to be remembered by, particularly if the memory is heightened by some colourful policy such as squeezing credit or taxing the consumer. The second moral is that, whatever a party's long-term record in supplying materials for materialism, it cannot expect to satisfy the New Zealand elector in his present mood. The elector is for the *status quo* in principle, yet against the way it treats him personally. To compare the early nineteen-forties with the fifties is to compare dearth with plenty, yet the voter has acted as though he thought plenty not enough, anticipated more and resented anything less. Postwar New Zealand politics have been peppered with great expectations.

Our political leaders have grasped this well enough. They understood it sufficiently, for example, to set up a charmingly irresponsible countercycle of splurging on imports in each election year, starting with 1951.[12] The countercycle has consequences, of course. One partisan advantage of the countercycle in its recent form is that it leaves to the incoming party the headaches of restoring the balances, thus spoiling its future reputation before it can begin. But this makes it all much more a matter of deliberate planning than in fact it is. The countercycle arises out of trying, particularly hard in an election year, to feed the insatiable Kiwi. Next year worms have to be rationed.

The National party holds the distinction of being the only party to do this to itself. The 1951-52 spree brought on the foreign funds crisis of 1952-53, met by the allocation of external exchange. It was a poor eighteen months all round and in 1954 National supporters said so, as we have seen. The after-effects of the 1954-55 bracer was dealt with by means of the credit squeeze which struck the small businessman and the homebuilder a much heavier blow than its hypothetical victims, the possessors of big overdrafts and lengthy import invoices. In return the National Government stayed down and went out. But not before leaving behind it the largest import crisis so far recorded.

To meet it Mr Nordmeyer produced the Budget of 1958 and import selection. He also faced one of the root causes of the symptom of exchange crises, the problem of markets and manufactures. Alas for good resolutions, there was a fourth import rush, followed by the usual defeat of the government, followed this time (under National) not by stern measures and recuperation, but by ignoring advice and by 'steady does it'—though what was being done positively about the perilous level of overseas funds was difficult to detect. In the midst of this, Britain applied to join the E.E.C. and suddenly every corrective, applied or neglected, looked inadequate. Gazing back at 'the seven fat years' it should be remembered that if the funds spent on *half* the private cars and their petrol which came in during the fifties had been invested in manufacturing plant instead, while the citizens continued to use buses, then we could face the sixties with some assurance after a steady decade of healthy growth. The

Jaguars and the 'State house bombs' alike have something to answer for.

The very basis of the prosperity which has proved so insufficient is at present threatening to contract if not to shrivel up altogether. Before it leaves us, however, we should review our conclusions about the effects of prosperity. On the one hand, it conservatises, it is narcotic. On the other hand, it does not satisfy and shares with narcotics the characteristic of creating a craving for ever bigger doses. Prosperity leaves the electorate both 'for'—the electorate demands and votes for three kinds of conservative party—and it leaves the electorate 'against'—there are sharp swings of opinion against successive governments. No administration has proved able to win over and hold even its own side amongst New Zealand's organized and articulate economic groupings and certainly no government has delivered enough for everyman.

Something of this kind of situation appears to be developing now in Great Britain with the Liberals serving as an urban, genteel and sophisticated equivalent for Social Credit here. The addition of a discontented searching about to the original adoption of *status quo* politics has come a decade later in Great Britain than it did in New Zealand. If we look elsewhere for parallels they are remote. In the United States of the fifties there has been alternation in the major party colours of the presidents, but the balance of parties and power in Congress has proved remarkably stable. Perhaps we might liken the special restlessness of New Zealand conservatism throughout the fifties to the mood of the Canadian electorate in 1958 when it turned out the Liberals. The Canadians were, nevertheless, turning towards a major party and there could be no close similarity to a scene dominated by the realities of heavy unemployment. As for Australia, its long quiescence under Menzies offers no guide.[13] Both National and Labour in New Zealand have been thrown out for committing half the offence which Menzies has lately managed to survive.

There would appear to be something singular in the way prosperity has failed to satisfy the born egalitarians of New Zealand. It is as though our electorate has picked up a truth about this era, that under the guise of nothing happening some major quality of New Zealand life, some characteristic tone, is being lost. The unique feature of New Zealand life consists in the fact that our fragment of European civilization has not developed European-style classes but possesses instead a loosely-graded society, an equal society. It is this which is quietly corroding away so that year by year New Zealand becomes more normal, more like the rest of the West.[14]

In order to understand why our situation is now trending towards normality, we must see why it was ever abnormal. For it is obvious that the first ships, simply by bringing British migrants, brought also the western type of thrust for prestige, place and power and imported the objective of social differentiation for the successful, to be marked and buttressed by separate education, employment and entertainment. The pressures toward western normality, in short, were coeval with colonization. Dr Young's aphorism, 'the soil grows castes; the machine makes classes', focusses the problem. Since New Zealand began and long continued as predominantly a farmers' country, why did the owners or the active farmers not become the cream of a classified society, on their way, fancifully, to becoming a caste? Our history is contained in the answer to this question just as our recent history lies in the fact that the answer is ceasing to apply.

The first check on the elaboration of classes was imposed by the time it takes colonists to get established. The few Wakefield gentlemen were the obvious candidates to found an upper class and Wakefield endeavoured to give them a running start towards this goal. This potential gentry did not become an actual gentry because few came and fewer still mastered how to make the land pay. By drawing on sixty years of colonial experience Australian sheepmen and bonanza wheat companies later turned the trick only to be wiped out in the Long Depression of the eighties or reduced to a minority too tiny to define the shape of a society. They were kept on short commons or foreclosed by the distant owners, the lenders of British money in the land companies and behind banks and agencies. The problem for individuals of paying off or meeting the terms of external capital regularly lengthens the time it takes to stabilize family fortunes and lay the foundations of class in developing areas. In the sense that New Zealand land did return dividends to the homeland it could also be said to have helped support an upper class from the beginning, but it supported that class in England and left New Zealand society all the more in flux.

Thus the first Wakefieldian group was scanty and initially incompetent for their task; the second Australian group were much reduced by economic contraction and dependence. This reprieve for equality was protracted by the demands of technological change. Refrigeration, cheap sea freights and the separator made small meat and dairy farms ideal at a time when politico-economic miscalculations from Wakefield to Vogel had overcrowded the labour market. Given the franchise, these men and their wives voted themselves the opportunity to succeed sheep as the principal inhabitants, of New Zealand. They were too numerous, however, for all to become leading citizens and they were at first too few, too grateful and too unorganized to seek power on their own, an objective reached only in 1912.[15]

Meanwhile in urban New Zealand machines and manufactures had arrived, to the point where cheap labour was sweated in the eighties and incipient classes could be descried in the towns. Yet in the thirty-five years from the end of the Long Depression to the start of the Great Depression the businessmen and the urban owners did not manage to graduate from being an aggregation of the better-off to constituting an articulated, differentiated upper class. Representative businessmen entered the Liberal party and Cabinet and helped to arrest the Liberals' zeal for change. Later they contributed more to the direction of Reform policies than was warranted by the electoral strength they could muster. Nevertheless, this was an unco-ordinated seeding, not the sturdy growth of a class.

In the first place, any urban wealth was recent while the habit of having large numbers of children, who had then to find mates on an unclassified and ill-regulated marriage market, made for the early dispersion of family gains. The small size of New Zealand set narrow limits round commercial and manufacturing opportunities. Continued competition amongst a horde of little concerns cut down rising families at a time when competition was diminishing or being combined away entirely in larger countries. The only big institution in New Zealand was the State which hindered the process of class formation by deliberately equalizing men's chances within its machinery when it promoted on long service or talent instead of on inherited capital, social connections and private education. Moreover, the means to political action remained in the hands of New Zealand's potential lower orders. They had supported wealth-distributing techniques in the nineties when an economic breakdown had occurred. State credit, education and pensions carried on the blurring of group dividing lines. State arbitration, too, sustained a much wider and stronger unionism than New Zealand would otherwise have possessed, even if arbitration also hobbled what it fed.

New Zealand's large towns, some almost cities, thus had machines but they were not yet manufacturing classes. The net effect of urban New Zealand was rather to act as a check on the farmers who reached power with Massey in 1912. A second brake on their social elevation was the continued smallness of the economic unit in dairy, meat and mixed farming. It required far more than the scattered sheep stations of Canterbury, the Wairarapa and Hawkes Bay to sketch in the outline of a squattocracy. Moreover, farming was at times distinctly unprofitable. There was a third brake in reserve—the farmers could lose political power in a prolonged economic crisis.

All these brakes were applied at one time or another in the period prior to the Second World War. The cities tended to slow down or even contradict the process of class formation, possibly throughout the period and certainly after the handsome profit-taking and low real wages of the

First World War. From 1921 onwards farming became a hard, chancy business of over-capitalized land values, wavering prices and glutted markets. Then in 1935 the farmers' government was decisively defeated.

One hundred years after its founding, the New Zealand I grew up in thus remained notably equalitarian, and, when one remembers that this was so for the whole of a sovereign entity, it was uniquely equal. This was not the result of ingenious planning by a few nor the reward of successful watchfulness by the many guarding a valued state of affairs. Undoubtedly the radical devices of the few, such as Ballance and Reeves, did help disproportionately.[16] It is also true that the electorally-approved role played by the active State was as much a prime factor as, say, the limited size of the country. But the overall situation was a gift from all of our history, not something specifically designed and achieved. The equalitarian society was something nobody could have counted on, in that it was given by one combination of factors and preserved by another. By the same token, it was subject to change without notice should the brakes on social and economic differentiation be released. In brief, that is precisely what has happened in the last twenty years.

Of prime importance is the revival and concentration of the farming community. After the pit of the Great Depression there was nowhere to go but up. In 1935 the guaranteed price scheme had the effect of building a protective floor under land values. Next, the onset of war meant that after 1940 farming became very profitable indeed, especially for those who had got in while farm prices were at rock bottom and had possessed the stamina to hold on. Mechanization was possible and necessary to replace farm labour called away to the war and it continued rapidly in peace because labour was scarce and deemed overly expensive. The proportion of New Zealanders working on farms had been declining for decades before the early thirties. Now this trend was resumed and steadily accelerated.

Rehabilitation after the Second World War was a controlled and measured process compared with the self-defeating, disorderly rush promoted by Reform after 1918. The Labour Government's scheme demanded knowledge of farm life or training, with the consequence that the new element introduced was smaller and land values did not suffer collapse after jumping to illusory heights. When land sales control was at last removed, the process of concentration could go quietly forward, sorting farm owners into the well-to-do and 'the tinpots', as one observer called them.

The old road to ownership through labouring, farm management and sharemilking is now longer and rougher than ever before. During National's first regime there were even some complaints from farm sons about the prohibitively high cost of going on the land. As yet there is no sign of a break in the psychological identification which binds together wealthy and hard-pressed members of the rural community against Labour and the city. However, the appearance of Social Credit offers, among other things, a vent for the feelings of those left behind by prosperity in the countryside. This outlet should be increasingly used whether social differentiation proceeds further or whether it ceases because markets and prices deteriorate and all are prompted to seek round for some political solution.

Whatever the sixties bring—and reverses or a levelling-off seem probable—the forties and fifties witnessed a significant relative narrowing of the section of New Zealand families owning farms and an unprecedentedly rapid rise in their economic status. Times would have to be very bad before mechanization fell off, while the optimum economic unit has got larger in the interim. Therefore there is little chance, short of political intervention, that the farm-owning sector will widen again in a recession. So an appropriate social status should be accorded to successful ownership in due course, even if it is diminished and deferred by future economic reductions.

At several points in this rise of some, though not all, farmers, it was of importance that another brake on class formation was gradually released. The farmers and the better-off in the city and town came back to political power by instalments. The exhaustion of the militant impulse and the weakness of the militant remainder in the Labour movement were revealed at the time of the expulsion of Mr J. A. Lee in 1940 and emphasized by the awkward situation and meagre showing of the Democratic Soldier Labour party in 1943. It was of more effect, however, that the manipulation of the economy, necessitated by the war effort and in consonance with Labour's busy State, should have returned influence and sometimes power to economic associations like the Federated Farmers, the Manufacturers, Chambers of Commerce and so on through a tribe of federations, guilds and lesser pressure groups. Some organized body had to be consulted to keep the economy on an even keel and get production moving, with the result that whatever was was king.

The considerable weight of Mr F. P. Walsh and the Federation of Labour was thrown behind a continuation of this situation after the war. Mr Walsh became the key figure on the Stabilization Commission. Price control and stabilization policies protected the ordinary citizen against adverse movements in the cost of living. But the policies could only be administered by continuously consulting the interested associations. All the forces of growth released after the war promoted those lucky enough to be part of the *status quo* when it was first stabilized, while the function of the associations was, naturally, to see that there were no changes detrimental to those included by the system. Finally, of course, the National Government was returned just when those who had got on their feet since the Depression were standing steady enough to contemplate with equanimity the disappearance of supporting controls. Prices, importing and land sales were released and the primary producers were subsequently given the major voice in their marketing organizations. Now, when overseas funds fall or Labour succeeds to office, the worst that threatens is a return to wartime stabilization *with* representation, so that political power is never wholly lost by these groups.

We must not neglect the third brake which has been 'off' for the last two decades, for it may be most important of all that the machine appears at last to be manufacturing classes. The drive towards local manufacture followed from the first Labour Government's preoccupation with putting men back to work, 'developing the nation' and 'insulation'. At first the factories were comically tiny backyard components of what was tagged 'the milk bar economy'. Some operations, like housing and public works, nevertheless reached a new scale because of mass operations arising from State policies. War continued the forced growth and put a premium on the going concern by funnelling orders, materials and labour to existing firms which could best use them. With returning peace came returned men. A fringe were assisted into business on their own, mostly in retailing. The fresh encouragement to local manufactures afforded by import allocations or licensing was most helpful to the sturdy, whose financial arrangement also best withstood the credit squeezes. Penrose is full of factories whose real beginnings lie in some shed of about 1936.

National's last phase and Labour's second term were golden years for manufacturing. Meanwhile the scale of operations was again getting larger and concentration was speeding up. Foreign firms entered the field and whole industries, like pulp and paper, demanded big corporations and major investment to begin with. The new doctrine of 'manufacture in depth', adopted while the second Labour Government was in office, has intensified the process just as budgetary provisions have encouraged takeover bids and the concentration of business.

State interference, far from harming the privacy of private enterprise, has introduced an executive element of considerable intelligence to assist the local business leadership which has been, hitherto, seriously undertrained and subject to dilution by the practice of executive inheritance characteristic of tiny firms. Underneath, supporting the whole structure, rests the mass of compulsory trade unionists. They were given social security and jollied peacefully through the war by the Labour Government. Then their militants were quietened by the defeats of 1949 and 1951. And in the fifties their well-marshalled majority has been pacified by the necessity of overtime and the demands of time payment. The manufacturers of, say, New Jersey might well sigh for such bureaucratic interference, such a Federation of Labour, and such a low rate of man-hours lost in strikes.

Reviewing the factors which formerly rendered the cities impotent to assist in class formation, we find them now neutralized or reversed. Population growth, a welfare standard of living, greater capitalization and concentration of control, have all contrived to let manufacture overcome the limit of New Zealand's size. State action and arbitration unionism have been positively helping the process along Lastly, more decades have elapsed in which the accumulations of time could add to the quota of well-established business and professional families.

The new men of prosperity have gathered on the crests of Auckland's eastern ridges not in dozens but in some thousands. Whereas the wealthy of the 1890's built in little clusters and those who arrived in the tens and twenties built by streets, in the 1950's whole self-consistent suburbs have gone up in five years. The hills behind Kohimarama and the slopes of Meadowbank bear a load of modernistic, 'executive homes' where grass greeted the National Government. Nor is the phenomenon confined to Auckland, though it is parodied and topped off by the patch of outsize, ranch-style bungalows built for the American executives of a North Island timber town.

Ironically, it was the first Labour Government which inaugurated the great leap forward towards residential segregation by building State houses not here and there or in a mixture of sizes but in great uniform tracts. The Housing Division did use up some scattered Crown sections and it tried to vary the number of bedrooms within its boxy plans. But the seductive economies of scale obtained by mass building and the Labour Government's own intentness upon the single, narrow aim of 'housing the worker', perverted the intended effect. Individually the houses were a help towards an easier future for each family unit. Built street on featureless street, however, the State settlements and many of their Nationalist group successors had unexpected social side-effects and potentially defined their inhabitants as different from, for instance, the inhabitants of equally definable Kohimarama. The old-fashioned intermixtures of Dunedin or Wellington, where the character of any quarter-mile is qualified by scores of exceptional dwellings, creates a healthy variety which a Taita or a Wesley cannot show.

Even marked differences of wealth, the appearance of a substantial moneyed group and the advance of residential segregation do not suffice to establish true classes. For different economic grades to be transformed into social classes it is necessary that separate patterns of life be elaborated for each class. Nobody, contemplating New Zealand in the fifties, could accuse the upper grades of neglecting to try; nor could an observer accuse the lower grades of failing to imitate what they could. In a land without servants this has been a busy decade for 'upper' wives, turning from the dishmaster to shuttling the children to the private preparatory school and hurrying back to preparation for entertaining. Item by expensive item the equipment in the roomier homes of the prosperous has drawn ahead. The acquisition—while young—of a permanent holiday house at certain resorts sets a more obvious barrier. Travel overseas after marriage, regular dining in restaurants, expense account living and frequent holidays are all signs of differentiation.

But the substance will lie in a combination and perpetuation of these and other things; a nearly exclusive course from cradle to grave which can incorporate talented outsiders but cannot be duplicated outside. Accordingly it is significant that private preparatory and secondary schools are multiplying, at least in the north, existing facilities are being extended and the staffing brought up to State standards where it lagged. Certain notable old State grammar schools, drawing on 'the better areas', are being pressed in to serve the trend and Roman Catholic colleges are by no means immune.

Nevertheless the gaps in class formation are as obvious as the achievements. The English style of club is rare and the more appropriate American country club is a thing of the future. No widespread merger between the well-to-do of the city and country has been effected. Education is still, on balance, definitely an equalizing force, though an undue prolongation of secondary schooling and a juggling with bursaries and university fees could alter that balance. Marriage, always an acid test, seems to have retained much of its random colonial sweep. What we are confronted with is a suddenly-enlarged pile of pieces—some of them interlocked—for the jigsaw puzzle of class society. Mercifully we do not yet have to gaze at the assembled picture.

Gazing at the pieces in isolation has been enough to unsettle the electorate however. The fifties have been ten years of trying to keep up with fresh 'necessities', new gadgets, new luxuries, new standards of expenditure and of aspiration. The race after goods has not been notably competitive. It is simply that it keeps on going. New prizes keep appearing and there is no end in sight. Full employment did not suffice so the forty-hour week was swamped in overtime, eagerly sought and willingly supplied. Wives went to work at every level, but most assiduously where their contribution constituted the difference between buying and making do. Adolescents encountered high wages, married earlier and attempted to begin where their parents left off.

The consequence was often punishing personal strain, some envy, considerable anxiety and constant vulnerability to economic fluctuation. Prosperity did not satisfy and the voters reacted as if a poor year was a disaster. When overtime disappeared or a wife lost that spare-time job or an overdraft was cut down, then with it went the vital margin for dressing better, enjoying more and owning the latest. In the scheme of values current in the fifties it *was* a disaster, and it shows up as such on the electoral seismograph.

To put it paradoxically, easy times banished the easy life. Formerly the women struggled towards a decent, widely-agreed standard within the home while the men soon bumped their heads against the ceiling of the socially and economically possible, which was at much the same height for everyone they knew. Surviving could be hard work at times, but there was an achievable end to effort except in a real depression. Moreover, so many desirable things were at everyone's hand or easily available through family and friends. A farm holiday or a spell at the beach, casual entertainment, dances or a boat for the boy. In the fifties such pleasures were increasingly translated into money terms, elaborated, graded and reduced to alternative expenditures. The sensation that over in X or Y there were plenty of people who 'could have the lot without busting themselves' was an additional irritant.

If uneven prosperity disappointed the expectations it aroused, what is the outlook if prosperity goes? For the kind of change in society and attitudes that New Zealand has undergone since the war is scarcely reversible. No one can answer such questions but they are worth raising and a few conclusions stand out.

The cures New Zealand has been offered for its existing exchange difficulties and its future difficulties with insufficient markets and a surplus labour force all involve more manufacturing, either to process the products of 'naturally strong' primary industries and/or to make our imports go further by manufacturing 'in depth'. In both cases the trend towards bigger business and the formation of classes will continue unless consciously checked by vigorous redistributive taxation, intelligent educational policies and the taking of such a grip on town planning and housing that it necessitates total reform of local bodies and perhaps of urban land holding. Failing this it would be richly ironic if National and Labour, hand in hand, blindly led businessmen, farmers and the rest into a future of classes, class conflict and root and branch radicalism.

There is an allied problem and that is how to import enough capital without our development turning into a support for the rich overseas. Plainly we will have to negotiate our terms carefully and keep to them.

And if Britain is excluded from the Common Market while insisting on Commonwealth quotas, then it will be really hard to argue our case for developing competitive manufactures instead of resigning ourselves to the fate of exchanging primary for secondary products. Given some workable U.K.-E.E.C. compromise, however, there is a good prospect that New Zealand could import its capital on a bank-to-government or government-to-government basis and have the State distribute it by means of an Advances Corporation as it once spread State-raised capital to the farmers. Such a process would keep most of the control within the country and much reduce the outflow of profit. Monopolies and privileged sectors of the market will have to be conceded if the manufacture of limited-run products is to be attracted. On the other hand, such contracts need not run for ever, and if monopoly or near-monopoly must be permanent, eventual nationalization could be provided for from the start.

The primary problem raised in and by the postwar era up to now remains, to my mind, how to prevent the disappearance of that most interesting exception in the Western world, equalitarian New Zealand. Drift and failure to cope will not save it. Uncontrolled and undirected manufacturing development will kill it. The Labour party, which has a traditional interest in equality and lives by assuaging and reducing group difference, may yet be driven towards more social planning, more competitive State corporations and more socialism of a limited anti-monopoly type, simply in order to avoid that final hardening into classes.

Should the Labour party fear to act and muff its chances when in power there is little prospect of an answer, because the National party has no perceptible interest in countering the process of class formation and less than no taste for the kind of measures necessary. If no answer is found in time, however, the fate before us is perhaps not so horrid as might have been expected even twenty years ago. In Western Europe, including the United Kingdom, true classes have existed for centuries. The concentration of control and ownership progresses on an international scale but nowadays there is sufficient wealth present to prevent the levels bumping one another as they once did. This situation seems likely to persist providing there is a continuous widening and intensification of markets and providing war continues to threaten without occurring. Welfare policies in Europe plus economic union plus the third industrial revolution plus the second agricultural revolution have combined to bend the phenomena of class away towards a more neutral zone of feeling. The facts and the inequalities of class persist but their effect is softened and padded in such a way as to remove the desire for or the possibility of meaningful conflict.

New Zealand, on the other hand, is proceeding from an unlike, classless position, thus:

Figure 2.1 Classified and Equal Societies: West Europe and New Zealand

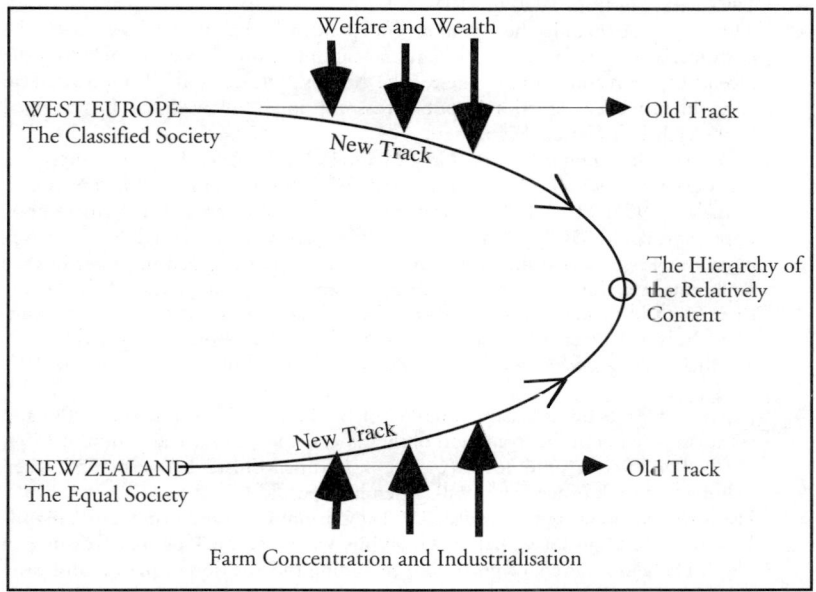

Because of the personal and heedless nature of the pursuit of property and in the absence of political leadership, the country may experience unease but will have no effective consciousness of class-inducing pressures. They will persist unless most strongly and deliberately opposed and New Zealand will travel on down the track it has taken since the war until it meets the E.E.C. countries at the same social point within the next ten to fifteen years.

Notes

1 [Arnold Nordmeyer was Minister of Finance in the 1957-1960 Labour Government led by Walter Nash. He was Leader of the Labour Party between 1963 and 1965. John Watts was Minister of Finance between 1954 and 1957. National governed between 1949 and 1957. Ed.]

2 [John Marshall was Deputy Prime Minister and also held the portfolios of Industries and Commerce, Customs, and Overseas Trade between 1960 and 1963, the first term of the 1960-1972 National Government. The Prime Minister was Keith Holyoake. Harry Lake was Minister of Finance between 1960 and 1963. Ed.]

3   [Sydney Holland was Prime Minister between 1949 and 1957; Clarence Skinner was Deputy Prime Minister and Minister of Agriculture in the 1957-1960 Labour Government; and Keith Holyoake was Prime Minister in the last few months of 1957 and then from 1960 until 1972. Ed.]
4   This does not include the nominal 'Independent' who in 1954 served all the customarily forlorn purposes of National candidate for Westland, including the receipt of the regular vote in the regular booths. The party itself nominated no contender. In these statistics the public's assumption is followed: that he was equal to the eightieth National candidate.
5   J. A. Lee, Democratic Labour, Grey Lynn, 1949: 18.76%. Hon. F. Langstone, Independent Labour, Roskill, 1949: 7.16%. W. R. Vallance, Independent National, Marsden, 1954: 11.31%. Only Vallance's vote, if all given to the winner's chief opponent, could have upset the result in the electorate concerned. Such a cross-party transfer by a personal following, in this election engaged in protesting the replacement of one National choice by another, seems highly unlikely. So the three 'significant shares' do not possess the real significance of altering any result.
6   [The Nelson Cotton Mill. See 'A Case Study: The Nelson Cotton Mill' in A. Mitchell, *People and Politics in New Zealand* (Christchurch, 1969), pp. 67-102. Ed.]
7   [Richard John Seddon became Premier of the Liberal Government in 1893 and was instrumental in the formation of the Liberal and Labour Federation in 1899. He died in office in 1906. Joseph Savage was Prime Minister between 1935, when Labour first took office, and 1940, when he died. Ed.]
8   From a lecture delivered in January 1952 at Curious Cove and printed in *Landfall*, March 1953, p. 53 [See Chapter 1]. [Julius Vogel became Colonial Treasurer in 1869. He held a variety of portfolios, including the position of premier for brief periods, between 1869 and 1876. He became an MP and minister again between 1884 and 1887. Sir Joseph Ward, Liberal and then United, held ministerial posts at various times between 1891 and 1930. As Leader of the United Party he helped win the 1928 election with a promise to borrow £70,000,000. See Chapter 6 in this volume. Ed.]
9   [John A. Lee, MP between 1922 and 1928 and again between 1931 and 1943, became a dissident in the first Labour Government and was expelled from the Party in 1940. He formed the Democratic Soldier Labour Party. Ed.]
10 [Walter Nash, Leader of the Labour Party between 1951 and 1963, in response to the shift from taxing past incomes to present ones, promised to rebate the first £100 due in February 1958. The new scheme was to begin in March 1958. National offered a 25 per cent rebate. See Robert Chapman, 'From Labour To National', in W. H. Oliver with B. R. Williams (eds.), *The Oxford History of New Zealand* (Oxford and Wellington, 1981), p. 363. Ed.]
11 The Index employed for what was available is an index of volume of goods per head prepared for the Industrial Development Conference of 1960. This takes us from 1939 to 1957 on the base, 1957=100; but for the last three years, 1958-60, some indication of the direction of movement has been gleaned from the 1961 *Economic Survey's* index for real national income, a different measure on the base, 1949-50=100.
12 I have explored this, and certain other topics touched on here, at full length and in proper detail in a joint work, *New Zealand Politics in Action*, which should appear soon. [See R. M. Chapman, W. K. Jackson and A. V. Mitchell, *New Zealand Politics in Action. The 1960 General Election* (London, 1962). Chapman's chapters

are: 'The Scene is Set: 1957-1960', pp. 30-73; 'The Unusual Electorates', pp. 203-34; and 'The General Result', pp. 235-96. Ed]

13 [Sir Robert Menzies, a Liberal Party leader, was Prime Minister of Australia between 1939 and 1941 and between 1949 and 1966. Ed.]

14 I would not wish to be taken as having argued that New Zealand society is or was markedly unlike every part of every other society. Sociological accounts of small town and rural life in the Middle West and Northwest of the United States portray almost the same situation which we know. Western Australia and South Australia in the middle fifties struck me as much like home. These examples are, however, regions of larger entities which have long contained big cities, true urban proletariats and considerable upper classes living a life with a distinctly different pattern from what is possible or customary below. New Zealand did not have these features and was thus far unique.

15 [In 1912 the Reform Party led by William Massey won the general election. Reform attracted the support of many farmers. Ed.].

16 [John Ballance held a variety of portfolios, becoming Premier in 1891 when he formed the first Liberal government. He died in 1893. William Pember Reeves was a minister between 1891 and 1896. Ed.]

3

No Land is an Island:
Twentieth Century Politics

Whether New Zealand is isolated because it is geographically remote, what remoteness and isolation involve, are questions which particularly concerned those who were very young men at the beginning of the Second World War and who began to enter the cultural life of this country during the war and at its end. I can remember discussing these topics in the immediate post-war years with Harry Scott, Kendrick Smithyman, Keith Sinclair and the men whose works really decided the matter, like Rex Fairburn and Allen Curnow. And I know from Harry Scott that the argument went on in the South. These questions were our staple of discussion partly because to answer them was to understand whether one could be a New Zealander; not so much to answer the expatriates' question: whether this country was a place worth spending one's life in; but rather to explore the probability that New Zealand was a positive community, already able to command and use for life the best one could give. They were very much young men's discussions for we neglected the element of necessity which dogged the expatriates of the previous generation and made them constantly turn from their life overseas to thoughts of New Zealand and the special relevance that living in one's own community alone can confer.

As is often the case with questions, we asked them partly because we were so sure of the answers. New Zealand was a community and a good one. Life here was no endless second best at the periphery of other peoples' culture but a life led at the centre of a new variant of Western civilisation, small but growing. It felt natural, sensible and worthwhile to be here and we wanted to proclaim the fact.

Proclaim it, moreover, in the face of a different and provocative verdict rendered in a pioneering series of essays by M. H. Holcroft. His conception of the New Zealanders was that they were doubly alien: cut off out here from valid participation in the high culture of Europe and alien to the forbidding landscape and to a mysterious otherness which

---

[This chapter was first published in Keith Sinclair (ed.), *Distance Looks Our Way: The Effects of Remoteness on New Zealand* (Hamilton, 1961). All the chapters were first delivered in the 1960 University of Auckland Winter Lectures. The lectures were organised by Dr Harry Scott, Head of the Psychology Department. Harry Scott died in a climbing accident in 1960. Ed.]

he found in the New Zealand scene. This struck us as a mystification. It was no less an inflation of the loneliness of the backblocks and a distortion of the impressive shadows cast by our mountains for having been embodied in a few of the best poems of the forties. We felt at home here, at ease in our environment and we were certain that the real message of our poets and short story writers was the same. The writing of the generation of Glover and Sargeson, Fairburn and Curnow proved what we felt in our bones: there was a national consciousness, and a national life very much worth living.

Some years spent examining New Zealand writing, first our prose, then our poetry, have only confirmed me in the view that the expression of this national consciousness followed straight on from the depression of the nineteen thirties, in which profound and general experience our community appears to have recognised itself truly for the first time. I was interested to see that Dr J. C. Beaglehole, in the twelfth volume of the *New Cambridge Modern History* published this year, adopts the same dating for the same fact. And that fact of national consciousness, looked at in another way, means that we have created something of our own, a life and an outlook that is a little different.

But not very different. For our variant pattern was made in despite of constant communication with the world outside. It was created out of the same types of social institution, the identical intellectual counters, and a selection of the same economic facts as Australians, Americans or British deployed. I can recall a conversation in a long hut on the North Shore held in either 1948 or 1949. A composer, some short story writers and two poets were arguing about the isolation of New Zealand. My brief contribution was to insist that any isolation would be eroded in the torrent of books, films, magazines, music and even concert artists flowing into the country. The discussion moved on to agreement that writers here missed less than musicians, musicians missed less than painters, and that probably dramatists were the only group heavily affected by being confined to transmitted culture, the occasional trip and local experience.

In short, New Zealanders, despite their physical remoteness from New York, London and Paris, are part of the world-wide dialogue of European civilisation. Our most sensitive intelligences have devoted themselves to articulating authentically New Zealand attitudes, a national pattern which all have shared in creating and feeling. But we live in an age when national differences constitute no more than regional variations on international modes of living. We are different; but not very.

Yet it did not occur to me to see if this was true of our politics. I sought about for the origins of our difference in our history, but not for the expression of that difference in our state. It certainly did not occur to me to ask if the difference as shown in politics was sufficiently great to need an explanation and, if so, whether that explanation lay in our remoteness. Now I have been asked to think about these matters I begin by wondering why I did not enquire earlier.

First of all, I think, like most people I was interested in whether this was a good state, not in whether ours was unlike other states. Secondly, I suppose I assumed that there were more fruitful places to look for the expression of national differences. I looked at the creative products of the time for signs of the true consciousness of self, place and people. It is the overall pattern which is likely to be different, not the threads nor yet the colours taken one by one. This pattern is best discovered by the synoptic view of the artist and most clearly displayed in his works. Politics are after all only one set of institutions and habits among a people, a fraction not the whole of their lives. It would be perfectly possible for those institutions to be nearly the same as elsewhere while the overall pattern was rather different. The more politics becomes a matter of collective techniques and impersonal organisation, the more it develops into a choice of instruments for putting into effect characteristic values— instead of a way of setting the values themselves—then the more we can afford *not* to look there for the origin of values and the demonstration of differences. A work of art, such as a novel, tells you more about the person and the people who created it than an event in the community like a wedding. A wedding tells you more about the culture than would a knowledge of the bridegroom's political party colours.

So when I looked for difference in national attitudes and for the explanation of difference I looked where probably they were most visible and found with my generation that difference existed, that it mattered a lot, but it was not very great. Looking at our politics I think the same can be said *diminuendo*: that our politics differ slightly, the overall difference matters, but it is composed of dozens of small variations on themes borrowed without any impediment from remoteness whatever.

To set our politics over the last seventy years alongside those of the other three colonial countries of British descent, the United States, Canada and Australia, reveals what a concert of wind instruments they play. Add into the comparison Great Britain itself—like New Zealand, a unitary state—and one has the political equivalent of the phenomenon of simultaneous invention and cross-fertilisation which, Lewis Mumford points out, is an enlarging characteristic of modern science and technology. The general structure of politics is the same in all five countries; two fairly similar parties alternating in power, prodded and embarrassed at times by a party of change and protest on the flank. We share in the great moods and phases of politics, such as the last dozen years of deepening conservatism. The acts we pass are usually suggested elsewhere while a version is frequently to be found already on some country's statute books, as for example our compulsory Industrial Conciliation and Arbitration Act[1] which followed New South Wales's voluntary measure. Occasionally we develop something important by giving a new twist to an old course of action, like permitting the capitalisation of the family benefit for housing.[2] Family benefits are as old as Australia's baby bonus of 1912 and there was state aid for low cost housing by 1933 even in the United States. Occasionally what is new is the fact of action itself. The farmers' cry for cheap credit had resounded across the United States, Canada and Australia for a full quarter of a century before New Zealand did something about it with the State Advances Act of 1894. Such instances of New Zealand novelties are not common, however, and what is striking is their indebtedness to a stock of ideas and precedents held overseas.

To turn now to the general structure of politics in these countries. There is one considerable cleavage. The United States and Canada have not in this period of seventy years experienced a party coming up on the left of their more liberal party and replacing that liberal party; Great Britain and New Zealand have. The Australian experience is instructively betwixt and between. Whatever the explanation offered for this contrast it can hardly be remoteness. In Great Britain the Labour Party caught up with the Liberals in 1924; half a world away they were equalled in New Zealand in 1925. Across a common border the traditional two parties of Canada and the United States repelled the Patrons and the Populists in the early nineties, the Progressives in both countries in the twenties, and met and contained the challenges from hostile grain farmers and radical union labour in the thirties. This parallelism occurred although the two federations are differently balanced in respect of the powers of the centre and the states, and despite one being parliamentary and the other presidential in form.

Perhaps then, it is not proximity or distance which causes the split into two groups, but whether the constitution is unitary or federal. Australia is worth a look in this connection. Before 1901 it was a continent containing six separate states. In each state Labour was formed or forming by 1891, for trade unionism was stronger in Australia generally than in New Zealand or Great Britain, and far stronger than in Canada or the United States. The Labour movement in the Australian states was able to hurry liberal state governments into moderate social change in the nineties and establish itself as a series of third parties in the process.

The making of the Australian Commonwealth cut across this process, just as Canadian federation and the onset of the American civil war had cut across and reset political development there, so bequeathing to the present the Liberals and Conservatives, and the Republicans and Democrats, respectively. Likewise in Australia, by the time the first Australian federal Parliament met, the situation was already in essence what it was to remain. There were two poles present which have persisted, Labour and the rest. In this the situation was of the federal type.

On the other hand, there were so many non-Labour representatives for the first nine years in the Commonwealth Parliament that they could afford to split and carry on the kind of politics they were used to in the old unitary states—the group in power giving concessions to Labour in exchange for support, or 'giving a little milk to the young tiger' as it was termed. This was a more developed version of the contemporary relations between the Liberals and the Labour movement both in New Zealand and Great Britain. By 1910, however, the underlying situation in the Commonwealth was clarified as a majority Labour government at one pole and a fused party of opposition at the other. Australia was federal in having two great parties, really from the time of the federation. It was unitary in having experienced the replacement of concessionary liberalism by a party drawing its support from the lower economic strata right across the economy.

Australia mixes the two experiences because it is at once federal in constitution and yet basically unitary in its economy. For beneath the constitutional complex of federalism in Canada and the United States there lies a complex of economies. Both Canada and the United States are large and varied enough to contain several sharply differentiated economies each with its own appropriate politics of protest. When the wheat farmers agitated in the Far West of the United States in the early eighteen-nineties their radicalism and their proposals raised no echo among the corn and hog farmers of the Middle West, or skilled industrial labour in the Eastern States. When the grain farmers of Canada rose up at the start of the nineteen twenties their movement captured the prairie legislatures but made no impression on the more numerous East. Radicalism in these truly continental lands tends to persuade its own economy but fails to carry the others. The great national parties accordingly persist, for they represent two estimates of the highest common factor of agreement between several economies.

The one-economy countries, and on balance I must include Australia, do not have this built-in protection against radicalism appealing to disaffected groups spread throughout the country. And, of course, the United States and Canada enjoy this protection less and less as the network of urbanisation and industrialism advances west and south.

The significance for a country's politics of having the more liberal of the two old parties replaced by a party of the left can also be exaggerated.

For parties originating on the left drive steadily towards the centre to get power and drive even closer to the centre to keep it. The dispute between radicals and moderates in the ex-Socialist parties about whether to abandon further nationalisation was run through in New Zealand in the forties, Australia in the middle fifties and Great Britain in the late fifties. It would be fair to conclude that the Liberals of 1900 in all three countries have been replaced as major national parties by liberals. There is a four- to five-year period of bustling legislation and reform before the party of change becomes just one more party of administration. When all the scurry is over, though, it is the party of the left that has lost its basic shape and purpose, not the *status quo* it was going to overthrow.

The American system achieves somewhat the same result in one of two ways. After the Populists suggested numerous reforms in the eighteen-nineties and the forces of Progressivism set up a clamour for change in the nineteen-hundreds, both the Republicans and the Democrats tried to capture the protest vote by putting through reform in moderate instalments. Third parties in the United States do not replace the two great parties, they cause one or both to veer off course into some limited change. Alternatively, a crisis may cause the slightly more liberal party, the Democratic Party, to become very much more liberal and inaugurate extensive changes of its own will and motion. This happened between 1933 and 1937. The changes were only partly successful and you will have noticed that reforming zeal lasted five years, after which the Democrats resumed their role as a party of administration.

As to the general structure of politics in each of the five countries, we can sum up, then, by saying that they are alike. Such difference as exists between them is not due to any one country's remoteness from any other, but is due partly to the complicating and deadening operation of a federal constitution in three instances, but even more, to the presence in two cases of a complex of economies which must be drawn together by traditional parties of compromise. Even then the two systems work out to the same result more frequently than patriots assume. The remoteness of New Zealand in this respect can have had little effect.

This brings me to the likeness in what I have called the great moods or phases of politics. At first it is not close but the likeness increases with time. In New Zealand the really vigorous era of Liberal legislation runs from 1891 to 1894 with a coda in 1898, while the party itself stayed in power until 1912. There was limited co-operation with the Labour movement, some social legislation, a vigorous push for development and help for the small farmer. In Victoria, New South Wales, South Australia and Queensland, the same sorts of things were being done in the same decade of the nineties. On the Australian federal level an equivalent policy was carried through under Barton and Deakin until the succession of a majority Labour government speeded the programme further. That Labour predominance ended in 1916. Canada's Liberals got into federal power in 1896 and stayed there, doing as little as they could as colourfully as possible until 1911. In the United States the Progressives got the upper hand in the Republican government about 1902. Their principles can still be seen at work until the Democrats, also temporarily 'captured' by Progressivism in 1912, tired of reforms in 1916. Britain did not enjoy its Liberal surge till 1906. The concessions were over by 1911. Asquith and the party struggled on until they, too, became war casualties in 1916. The age between 1890 and the First World War would justify the label, an age of limited reform, most intense in New Zealand and Australia, least so in Canada.

The commencement of the age of limited reform is somewhat uneven even if its end is not. So perhaps this handicap start indicates a valid difference, an instance of remoteness affecting, well, three of our examples. The explanation concerns the previous era. A great deflation had stretched from 1873 to the early nineties, and this hit our five countries most unequally. In the United States and Great Britain it satisfied the urban industrial populations by increasing the purchasing power of their wages. It did make them mutinous in their impoverishment when they fell into unemployment, which they often did. Yet there was sufficient real wage rise, where industry ruled, to allow reform to be delayed until an era of more stable prosperity in the nineteen-hundreds gave governments extra room to manoeuvre, more substance to concede. Where agriculture predominated the great deflation meant diving prices and dragging depression for all, ameliorated only where increased production could shore up the sagging returns. Of agricultural countries, Canada came best out of it economically, and did least politically. In Australia and New Zealand, where depression was deep, the concessionary Liberals were driven into action five or ten years before this agricultural slump lifted. Reform in the South Pacific was therefore begun early, in the nineties, and was aimed at rebuilding prosperity up from the foundations. Reform in the United States and Britain began a decade later and was aimed to pass a little of prosperity down to the ground floor.

This age of limited reform ended in a queer twilight of violence and conflict before the lights went out all over Europe with the First World War. Dangerfield's book, *The Strange Death of Liberal England*, records the dockers', miners' and Irish strikes; upper middle class suffragettes chaining themselves to the rails of Parliament and being force-fed in prison, and strangest of all, the 1914 mutiny of British army officers in Ulster. During 1910 in Canada the Liberal hold on Quebec was loosened when fanatic opposition developed against aiding Britain by building a Canadian naval squadron. The French Catholic Nationalists, under the rabble-rousing Bourassa, helped the Conservatives throw out the Liberals the next year. Even Australia enjoyed the excitements of a double dissolution of both House and Senate, while New Zealand underwent the embittering Waihi strike of 1912 and the socially divisive waterfront struggle of 1913. In the United States, 1912 was the peak year for the Socialist Party and the I.W.W. It was also the year when ex-President Theodore Roosevelt split the Republicans and, as his followers sang 'Onward Christian Soldiers', T.R. declared, 'We stand at Armageddon and we battle for the Lord'. He was a little previous. The horrible eruption of war made these anticipatory spouts of tension look minuscule.

The war was an era of its own. It maimed and eventually killed the Liberals in the unitary states, it drove the more liberal of the traditional parties in the federations into divisions and stark conservatism. Here in New Zealand Ward led his Liberals into coalition with the conservatives in 1915.[3] Then by helping to force through conscription and allowing prices to rocket he got his party such a name in the cities that it spent the last dozen years of its life as an alternative conservative party of the countryside. In Great Britain a coalition of the orthodox eventually made Labour the one choice of the disaffected. In 1916 Lloyd George severed the body of British Liberalism in order to lead his private following and the mass of Conservatives. And Billy Hughes in Australia did the same thing in the identical month. They make, indeed, a remarkable pair, alike in powers, rôle and personality. Hughes demanded conscription and smashed his party to get it. Labour in the Commonwealth took the whole of the twenties to recover from that blow. The conscription issue also split Liberalism in Canada.

Only in the United States, where war came late, were there no coalitions and divisions. The Americans paid the price in an end to reform and by a fulfilment of President Wilson's fears. 'Once lead this people into war and they'll forget there ever was such a thing as tolerance. To fight you must be brutal and ruthless, and the spirit of ruthless brutality will enter into every fibre of our national life, infecting Congress, the courts, the policeman on the beat, the man in the street. Conformity will be the only virtue and every man who refuses to conform will have to pay the penalty.'

The Democrats lost their *raison d'être* in 1916, their hold on Congress in 1918 and the Presidency in 1920. They did not offer any more than an alternative and unsuccessful conservatism until the transformation of 1933. The twenties were, in fact, an age of alternative conservatisms, unsteady prices and ideological exhaustion and bankruptcy.

The 1921 slump put King's Liberals into power in Canada and very nearly had a like result in New Zealand in 1922. That year the high Tories reasserted themselves in England by replacing the distrusted Lloyd George. In grave harmony, the Country division of the Australian conservatives ejected Hughes from his Prime Ministership in 1923. In the United States Harding had the decency to die of scandal that year and let Coolidge in. It was said of Coolidge that 'every time he opened his mouth a moth flew out', and so it was with them all. Looking back, they seem imprisoned in antique ideas and declining circumstances, unable to cope or do more than hold off the protests of farmers and unionists as puzzled as themselves. The depression thirties opened with no solution in sight even to the erratic twenties. It was an era which had produced questions but not answers.

With one possible exception those answers had to be evolved and accepted by parties and electorates during the Great Depression itself. The new framework of public institutions and popular thinking which was then run up has served to this day as the basic structure of our social and economic policy. War strengthened the main girders of the system by forcing on economic control, training civil services equal to managing the economies, ensuring general acceptance of planning and income redistribution, and employing and feeding the bottom third of the population at a standard they will not peacefully surrender. Last, but not least, the cold war and the garrison state have continued to underwrite wartime full employment and have solved the problem of what to do with the surplus ten per cent of production. Welfare came by warfare out of depression.

The possible exception I mentioned earlier to my generalisation, that the depression fell upon parties with their minds still vacant, is the New Zealand Labour Party. In an article published in 1929 Mr Nash forecast roughly what he in fact did from 1935 onwards.[4] But the condition of knowing something radical to do was a disqualification for being allowed to do it, at least until the old parties had left no worn stone unturned.

Quite probably we get a better idea of what would have happened in New Zealand if Labour had won the 1928 election from the fate of the two more thoughtless, more respectable and more popular Labour parties, which accordingly did have the bad luck to win in 1929. The Treasurer of the Australian Labour government, who presumed to suggest innovations, was outmanoeuvred and ousted by the rigidly orthodox within the Cabinet. The new Treasurer, who favoured cutting expenditures to the bone and tightening belts, led a breakaway from the Labour Party and ended up as Prime Minister in the conservative government which followed his successful treason. In Great Britain it was the Labour Prime

Minister himself and his Chancellor of the Exchequer who headed the deserters and the subsequent conservative administration. As a result, the inauguration of modern times was delayed in Australia until 1941, when Labour came to power just before the Japanese crisis; while the welfare state in Britain had to creep in under the wing of the wartime coalition and then wait to stand upright until 1945.

Lest our New Zealand government seem too unusually advanced it is worth noting that they had the benefit of their predecessors' mistakes and occasional worthwhile experiments. They had three years of the American New Deal to contemplate whilst Keynes's theories had, by 1935, put an academic gloss on what came naturally to desperate men. The contrast with J. A. Lee quoting Keynes is the unfortunate Forbes being instructed by an official of the Bank of England, Sir Otto Niemeyer. As Rex Fairburn put it:

> The heart is gold, the name is Otto,
> 'Women and children first' the motto.

In the United States it had not been the women and children who had gone overboard first, but the millionaires. Wags enquired of prospective dwellers in top storey apartments, 'for renting, sir, or jumping?' Down with them went the reputation of the economic system of which they were the finest flowers. Franklin Roosevelt was therefore less bound by popular precedents and preconceptions, more urgently pressed for action, than any American since Lincoln. He chose to reconstruct, not on any one plan, but by trying dozens of schemes, usually several at a time. But the main lines of action he pursued: public works, the short work week, relief, crop guarantees, trade protection and insulation, encouragement of trade unions, home loans, cheaper credit and more government spending on social services; these were the lines followed in New Zealand under Savage and Nash after 1935, and in Canada half-heartedly under Bennett from 1931 to 1935, wholeheartedly under King thenceforth. New Zealand did not hesitate and stumble half way as did the U.S.A. but we all were headed in the same direction at the end of the depression, whether we had walked into it looking backwards or forwards.

The parallelism with which post-war welfare and prosperity in the five countries led on to conservatism is so marked that newspaper editors have noticed it. Sunday journalists advise Labour parties to give up the dogmas of radicalism now that they have given up its practice. It is true that there was no need to throw Labour out in Australia and New Zealand in 1949 and Great Britain in 1951, nor to refuse a Democrat the Presidency in 1952 or eject the Canadian Liberals in 1958. By then they meant no harm to the *status quo*, and the one alternative conservative party readmitted to power—New Zealand Labour—has done none. We are again in an age of alternative conservatisms, much more stable economically than the last, and with its problems stacked away outside, in the armouries; beyond partisan debate.

So much for the great moods or phases of politics in the five nations. New Zealand shared in the era of limited reform, the twilight of violence and the wartime illiberalism. The alternative conservatisms filled our nineteen twenties too, and if our participation in depression and the welfare reformation was thorough, so has our political sleep of the last ten years been sound, unbroken by the nightmare foreign policies of our time. If New Zealand is remote and isolated it is from the realities of the last defence, not from the political experience of the previous seventy years.

In tackling the questions of the general structure of politics and the successive phases of politics I have, I believe, been dealing with the hard part of establishing that New Zealand politics is not unusual. Had I examined the origins of specific institutions and ideas it would have been simpler again to demonstrate exchanges, borrowings and parallels. That, however, might have amounted only to showing that in a bungalow and a mansion the bricks may be the same shape. Instead, I trust I have shown that, however far New Zealand may be from Britain, however tiny our building and large the American, they are all state houses on the same general plan, simply painted according to taste.

Therefore I shall skip over the American, British and Australian ideas, institutions and practices which are represented here in New Zealand and give instead two illustrations. The first represents the ethos of the eighteen nineties and comes from Australia and the 1905 Budget speech of Mr (later Lord) Forrest. 'What is the use of Parliament', he asked, 'unless it exercises all the powers of the State in order to carry out great works of public utility and advantage for the improvement of the public estate and of the condition of the people?' The second of my quotations is a Canadian's comment from 1917. It applies also in Australia and New Zealand from the eighteen-nineties to the nineteen-thirties and even beyond. 'Consult the annals of Canada', said Paul Lamarche, 'for the past fifty years at random and whatever party may be in power, what do you find? The Government is building a railway, selling a railway, or blocking a railway'.

Does remoteness, then, affect our politics in any way at all? The answer seems to be, not a direct, but an indirect affirmative. For the nineteenth century title of economics, political economy, expresses a continuing truth. Politics is to economics as a tightrope walker is to his wire. If remoteness affects our economy it will then be mediated through to our political life where the politicians will struggle to balance out and moderate its effects. That happens; and the last fortnight's Industrial Conference[5] amounted to the politicians asking the experts how to tighten the wire and what sized shivers were likely to run through it in the near future.

Every New Zealander knows that we live well by sending meat, butter and wool 12,000 miles, and get four-fifths of our returns in raw or partly-finished materials and one-fifth in finished goods. Obviously those 12,000 miles are a factor; a remoteness factor. What is worth pinning down is that the 12,000 miles are only one factor in an equation, and not even a fixed factor. The distance our goods travel matters, first, because we send and receive such a proportion of all we produce and consume; second, because what we send is bulky, heavy and costly to move; third, because there are still limits to the technology of transportation.

The steamship dropped the cost and speeded the delivery of our goods in the last third of the nineteenth century. In the eighteen-nineties new fleets of refrigerated ships were the precondition of new exports. Chilling changed the meat trade again, while in the nineteen twenties and thirties freight rates dropped further and speed increased. Dehydration, boning of meat and so on can help shrink the cost and the effects of those 12,000 miles, while air freight could now cut the time factor to a fifteenth and should eventually match or lower the cost of shipping meat and, possibly, dairy products. The economic effects of remoteness are inversely proportional to the techniques of transport. As the techniques have improved the miles have shrunk.

We do not choose to produce heavy, bulky goods because of remoteness, but because of our resources. We began with two and a half resources. They were the climate, which will not grow the Swiss watches of the food trade, like oranges or coffee, but will grow wool. Then there was our market, the parent state, Great Britain. In a world too poor or too protectionist to buy, it was our fortune that it was England—at our antipodes—which was both free trading and our metropolitan country. The half resource is represented by the soil, which we exhausted and have since had to spend fifty years in rebuilding from the subsoil up.

Some of our resources were missing, either at the start or permanently. For to suppose the impossible for a new colony, had we had the plant and the skills in 1840 or 1900 we might have manufactured delicate, light luxuries and components for other peoples' heavy industrial civilisation. Switzerland has no resources except the training and experience of its inhabitants and their stock of capital. In the late nineteen-thirties and early nineteen-forties a New Zealand designer of genius managed to produce power implements in the Mackenzie Country and sold them overseas against the competition of Caterpillar and

International Harvester. But, of course, colonies get few already-successful, skilled men. Education, like charity, has to begin at home. As for capital, that takes generations to lure out and to fructify. Meanwhile New Zealand had gradually found the pastoral staples it could produce and designed its institutions around them.

As for heavy industry, New Zealand had the resources of heat and power but not the store of high-grade metals. Had we possessed them we would then have run into the barrier of distance. The five great industrial complexes of the world: North-eastern America, England, North-western Europe, Russia and Japan all lie alongside or in the midst of customers by the hundred million. Australia does produce good steel more cheaply than anywhere else, but that in isolation will not reproduce America.

It goes part of the way, however, which brings me to why we are great traders. Australia's basic market for industry is itself and New Zealand. This market is just large enough, apparently, to permit one or two firms in each line to grow sufficiently big to be efficient, always providing the raw materials are Australian. New Zealand has not the materials for the Australian scale of heavy industry. Therefore it has not the by-products of heavy industry to support a full range of light industries. Nor has it, because of its size, the local market to allow a complete range of light industries to grow to efficiency. The result is that we cannot live comfortably unto ourselves by balancing primary with a full secondary industry and resting tertiary services on top. Such secondary industry as ought to be increased depends on processing raw materials—wood, wool, fish, scenery and such—which are plentiful here. Much of the product of this type of secondary industry has to be sent overseas in the same way as primary produce. So we must continue as great traders and bear with the effects of remoteness as that factor enters into the complex equation which shapes our economy and underlies our politics.

Distance thus helps determine how we make a living but our resources have more voice in this. They dictate that we trade, which, in turn, ties us and our fortunes the more firmly to those parallel states overseas: Britain and the U.S.A., Australia and Canada. The New Zealand community, pulled by and pushing its politicians, has made a real heavy industry out of wool, meat and butter; one more big firm with a total work force one-fifth larger than the General Motors Corporation employs. Our ideas and techniques, like those of the G.M.C., came out of laboratories and studies. They travel light in books or come as men by plane. And depression reaches General Motors no faster than it does us, for slumps transmit by ticker tape and cable and radio-picture.

But the final ruin which can now be transmitted at once and universally is nuclear war. And war is simply a political measure which has technically outgrown itself. Once upon a time the protection offered by our remoteness appeared absolute. In 1938 Mr McIntosh and Dr Sutch could write: 'In the event of a war there are many other ports, focal points and streams of trade, which would attract an enemy attack and would provide greater results than any that could be achieved in New Zealand waters. The amount of shipping involved is relatively low and can be directed over such widely divergent oceanic routes as to make attacks on it improbable.'[6] As for New Zealand itself, that was generally thought of as a place from which troops came, not to which they went.

Our real protection in those days was the weakness of potential enemies and the strength of the Royal Navy. New Zealand spent the nineteenth century under the aegis of the greatest naval power on earth. That was its protection then; not distance. That was why we could accumulate the means of production at the rate we did. Britain was paying our defence costs, and navies used to be relatively cheap. Had we been paying for the armies of a Serbia our society might have been more Balkan in tone. When the age of mass struggle did arrive, of course, we were emotionally prepared to send fighting men. We sent a contingent to the Boer War; then lost more proportionately than Belgium in the first Great War, or than any ally, except Soviet Russia, in the second. The men might go and die; nevertheless the New Zealand homeland, like the Australian, American and Canadian, remained untouched.

It did not remain unmenaced. The aegis of Britain was gone. It could be seen beginning to move off in 1902. The Anglo-Japanese Treaty and the implicit agreement to Japanese predominance in the North-west Pacific was a clear sign that British trade extended to more areas than Britain could protect alone at any one time. Within sixty years her grip had equally gone from India's 400,000,000 and Somaliland's 400,000. The Japanese reached the Equator by 1914.

What determined the changed problem of defence was now the factor of size. Australia and New Zealand were not big enough to protect themselves and not remote enough to be safe. So Singapore was built for a British fleet which could not be spared when the time for it came. New Zealand military men anticipated as much. Asked in 1939 what would happen if Singapore should fall, a British staff officer replied, 'Take to the Waitomo Caves'. By then the Cabinet knew where to seek profitably for strength. Step by step through 1940 and 1941 the Roosevelt administration edged from diplomatic to economic to total conflict with Japan, while New Zealand did everything a small state could to encourage and co-operate with the process.

It was not, however, until December 1941 that the New Zealand people got an inkling of how Poles feel about Germans or Yugoslavs feel about Italians. New Zealanders missed becoming victims, but they lost that spectator feeling. The one human, widespread effect of remoteness in this field, the popular illusion of automatic safety, had been removed.

This has had clarifying and bemusing effects. The people are now conscious of the last war. They remember that, remote or not, we were so small we had to be saved by a power mighty enough to operate in our area. It is generally understood that, amid large events, small states will be swept along behind their protectors, just able to hold a course in the eddies by elaborating their own diplomatic service and their own self-contained, armed forces. New Zealand's Fraser manoeuvred at Dumbarton Oaks and San Francisco to enlarge the role of the little states in framing policy at the new United Nations.[7] What he hoped for was an international version of the long familiar Commonwealth consultation—the small power's right to an occasional hearing for a minor modification.

He was also struggling to make the U.N. as much as possible like the reformed League of Nations which New Zealand had proposed in 1936. Those New Zealand Labour government proposals included the automatic enforcement of sanctions involving the risk of war against an aggressor and the waging of war if necessary. Collective security was the highest stage of idealist thinking about foreign policy in an earlier technological and diplomatic age. It was a small-power solution to the competition of a ring of great states, some of them discontented. It presumed the overwhelming preponderance of one side, the right side, which would be an *ad hoc* alliance of several great states and a horde of little ones against one or two aggressive powers. Moreover, it presumed the possibility of that old-fashioned happening—a victory.

In 1945 and since, despite the emerging super-state ranking of the United States and the Soviet Union, we have argued as we did in 1936. Despite the atomic bomb, the outmoded concepts like victory, strategic positions, bases and wars against aggressors are still thought of as rational possibilities, indeed worthwhile practicalities. Despite the bipolarisation of diplomacy and the end of any possible preponderance for either side, the United Nations is deemed to be an improved League and the high moral tone of the upholders of collective sanctions is still to be heard. Somehow, they assume, security is feasible.

Official action and pronouncements on foreign policies contain something from all three safeguards of the past: the British attachment, the moralities of collective security, and dependence on the United States. But it is the last to which the other two are uneasily adjusted. We join, we sign, we train, we co-operate, and we do not rock the boat, as we dared to rock the Commonwealth boat with our 1936 proposals.

The people, the officials and the parties grasped that our immunity from attack disappeared in 1941, along with our remoteness. But what disappeared in 1945 was far greater. We lost our remoteness from total destruction. We thought we had understood the lesson of our size, so we therefore picked our defender and fell silent, just when defence became a contradiction in terms and at the very time when fresh principles, initiatives and ideas became more urgent than ever before. The superstates are obsessed with their delusions of defence and prestige, spheres and competition. The world can hardly look to them for the way out. Instead it is the medium and small states—conscious that nowadays no land is an island—that offer the most hope, if only they would be active, vocal and troublesome.

However, as I have said, our politics do not differ very much from those of the leaders in our camp. The minor effects of geographical distance or remoteness were never more inconsiderable. We share an age of alternative conservatisms, internally satisfactory, externally desperate. We should cherish and express every alternative concept our small differences can give rise to.

Notes

1 [1894. Ed.]
2 [Capitalisation of the family benefit to help house purchases was introduced in 1958 by the 1957-1960 Labour Government. Ed.]
3 [Sir Joseph Ward. See Chapter 6. Ed.]
4 [Walter Nash was a Labour MP between 1929 and 1968, a minister between 1935 and 1949 and Prime Minister between 1957 and 1960. Ed.]
5 [The Industrial Development Conference was held in Wellington, 13-17 June, 1960. Ed.]
6 [Alister Donald McIntosh and William Ball Sutch. Source unknown. Ed.]
7 [Peter Fraser was Prime Minister between 1940 and 1949. He died in 1950. Ed.]

4

Patronage in a Changing World

It has been properly said that the most effective technique of the British aristocrat is never to explain and never to express regret. Being neither an aristocrat nor English, I would like to do both by asking you to consider the plight of the speaker at this low point of the day in the uneasy middle of a conference that wishes to get down to work. The speaker has been anticipated on where the arts are about to go in the seventies, the way the arts are organised now has been described, the politically most forceful motives for giving some real help in the future have already been canvassed, while the New Zealand artist's Holy Grail, a defined national identity, has been held up to the light of the arts that matter most among the generation of the seventies. There goes the future and the present, the stick and the carrot, so that all that is left is the past, with any mumbled lessons it may have to proffer to the swinging mini-skirts of relevance. Indeed, one finds oneself here to talk about patronage to a Conference which is thinking about Arts Council disbursement of tax-raised assistance and the two things are not the same thing. So perhaps there is something to be learned by turning aside at this point and considering what patronage was and is and how it relates to Arts Council assistance.

Historically patronage has meant what patrons gave, namely a knowledgeable and lasting support to individual creative artists. The archetypical patron was the Renaissance despot who was expected not only to make his way to power by his own vigour and intelligence but also to maintain public respect for his court by the intelligence with which he spent public resources on the right artists and the impressive arts. Patronage was a transaction between men of taste, the despots, and men of talent, the creators of works of art. It had little to do with performers—though bands of players might be given the prince's benevolent protection—and even less to do with the creation of audiences, for the people were part of the pageantry of life not the consumers of works of art.

The victory of the state as a form of political organisation in the late fifteenth and sixteenth centuries tended to thin out the ranks of the great patrons and aggregate too much patronage and power over taste

---

[This chapter is the text of a speech delivered to the Arts Conference in Wellington, April 1970. The topic of the Conference was the policy of the Arts Council. Ed.]

and therefore over artists into the hands of monarchs. Even so, a fair number of these sovereign patrons were men or women of discrimination. Beneath them their aristocrats also diverted far more wealth than they could safely afford to status-seeking patronage of their own. It was a terrifyingly hit-or-miss business. Yet for three centuries it covered Europe with a fabric of fine buildings, sculptures, paintings and furniture which our era has yet to equal with tens of times the resources. No petty Italian principality or German electorate of three millions of miserable peasants would have so little in the way of fine buildings and interiors to show for any of their centuries as has, say, New Zealand for its last hundred years.

In many ways it was the English aristocracy of the eighteenth century—an intermarriage of daughters of commerce and the sons of land—who began the era of collecting and ended the age of the patron. The London season for plays and displays developed along with the art market and judgment by consensus among buyers instead of judgment by the personal choice of the patron. The East India nabobs of the late eighteenth century were followed in the nineteenth century by the cotton and cutlery millionaires, the ironmasters and the railway kings. These men discovered what they ought to buy from fashion and through dealers. Dealers and buyers made up the impersonal market and the impersonal market supported the creative artist. The age of the public auction, the public concert and the public gallery had begun.

Sir George Beaumont who died in 1827 has been called the last of the patrons. By passing his paintings not to a nephew but to the nation he helped found Britain's National Gallery. Thus ended an era when artists, to be known, had first to find or be discovered by patrons who would commission them and thereafter display their works within a great house visited by other men of rank who might also form a good opinion of the artist.

In Britain as in the United States the upper middle classes passed steadily from imitation of their gentlemanly and neo-classical betters to an all-too explicable preference for the detailed, the realistic, the anecdotal and the grandiose. They began without taste but ended with strong preferences from programme music to turreted houses. Successful artists, composers and performers did very well indeed as had the buyers they depended on. The unsuccessful, for their part, were free to starve in the garret of their choice.

For the time being a stable situation had been achieved with great art being produced, yet with hardly any patronage as such. Patronage had made mistakes in plenty about what and who would last among the creative. The impersonal market fuelled by the upper classes of the nineteenth century made more errors again. Nevertheless it worked.

There had been, moreover, a notable enlargement of the audience. The 400 families of eighteenth century England were now joined by tens of thousands of old and new rich and the upper-middle classes had been decisively added to the gentry and the aristocracy. The audience for the arts was still only a very small proportion of the whole, yet to complain that the mass of men were excluded from an appreciation of the highest things of their civilisation would be quite anachronistic. They always had been excluded, even in fifteenth century Florence. But with the grinding industrialisation of Britain came a further impoverishment of every other aspect of life from the dismal buildings the mass had to live amongst down to the disappearance of holy days, festivals, shows and pomp. The majority of folk had been left with no time even for their own culture. Meanwhile high culture flourished precisely because—such is the unfairness of the world—society's resources were concentrated in the hands of a few tens of thousands who by then had a good deal more than enough leisure and money to maintain the impersonal market for art.

Two government policies struck at this equilibrium. Free trade brought cheap American wheat flooding into Britain and the consequent decline in British agriculture forced the land-owners, the distinguished occupants of the stately houses, to begin emptying out their galleries. Cheap wheat came one way and expensive pictures went the other. It was income tax and death duties, however, that spread the rot. Then the Great War, with its consequent collapses of empires, privileges and currencies, finally exhausted the capacity of Europe's nineteenth century network of upper classes to sustain the arts through the public market.

The European rich had once made it a perquisite of power that their ballet, their theatre, their opera, should receive assistance from the public exchequer. That, however, was really gilding the lily. They could and largely did maintain the performing arts until 1918. Thereafter the new middle class regimes could occasionally be persuaded to subsidise an opera house here or a state theatre there, from considerations of political prestige or national identity or as tourist lures. But these subsidies were now the lifeblood of what remained. The creative artist could look in vain for the lush European market of the 1900s. The rich themselves had been, with frequent ingenious exceptions, taxed back into the middle classes. What the Ministers of Finance had taken away only they could now restore. Meanwhile the middle classes were being seduced from the high arts—which were only marginally theirs in the first place—by phonograph, by film and radio, and by the never-ending pursuit of the Joneses.

The contrast with the American experience is an instructive one for those interested in patronage. Before the Civil War the moderate fortunes of the young republic were devoted to genre and landscape painting with a vaguely patriotic and democratic flavour. After the Civil War the simply enormous accumulations of wealth made during the industrialisation of America went uncontrolled by any taste on the part of the arriviste tycoons who now made their fortunes. The super rich were so wealthy that they could have revolutionised the arts of their time had they known how to patronise them. Unable themselves to know and to encourage art by collecting artists they instead collected dealers and the dealers sold them the past of art, specifically the European past of painting, sculpture and decoration. This accomplished the last notable relocation of the world's major art treasures. It far exceeded the transfers Napoleon achieved with his loot, and matched the onetime accomplishments of the kings and gentlemen of England. Indeed only monarchs and governments, both tax-supported, could still stand against the American super rich when it came to competing for Old Masters.

Sophistication, too, grew apace, if not always among the multimillionaires, then among their agents. Dealers began to seek out and to follow scholars. Collectors combined with public galleries and later universities to develop connoisseurship into scholarship about the arts. Genuine scholarship began to correct and then to transform or supplant the old tastemakers on the reviews and in the salesrooms. The academics invaded the other arts and gradually there emerged the possibility that these institutions, each in its own way, could nearly produce the effects of true patronage, that is, the effect of informed taste giving continuing support to individual creative artists and even to small groups of performing artists.

In America this development of arts scholarship rested on the same enormous fund of wealth in the hands of a few. There was not even an income tax to trouble them until 1913. The Great War only made them richer and the nineteen twenties were a heyday of business combination conducted with the encouragement of a Republican administration. At first they were persuaded to contribute to or found universities, museums, and philanthropic foundations. Their wives, as they learned, favoured opera, ballets, and symphonies. The ultimate way to cash in one's art collection for prestige became the presentation of enough paintings to fill an entire gallery already given to city or nation. This had a happy secondary consequence for art dealers by removing yesterday's fashionable purchase from tomorrow's auction, so sustaining prices for all that remained on the market.

Next came the twist to the story. Depression added the last element needed to form contemporary American patronage. The Roosevelt Democrats, trying out all manner of relief measures, paid hordes of young artists to paint murals in post offices, play Shakespeare to High Schools or dance in the boondocks. The standards were wildly uneven at the start, wherever there were any, but they did not remain so. When recovery came at the beginning of the forties a huge fund of released artistic energy and ambition stood ready to be further supported by the still surviving wealth of the super rich operating either directly or more often through institutional channels. The foundations and the universities, the theatre trusts and opera companies, the galleries and symphonies were ready to provide patronage and market for a gigantic efflorescence of high art and low, new art and old. The focus of contemporary painting, the novel, poetry, perhaps modern dance, wavered across the Atlantic. Whether it was experimental film, electronic music or giant metal sculpture, somewhere there was support for it over and beyond the quick verdict of the salesroom and the ticket office.

It has been said that the arts are unevenly spread geographically through the United States and socially through its classes. Doubtless this is partially true, though envy may exaggerate. And Heaven forfend that we pay all the prices in social distortion that have gone into constructing this American phenomenon. What I do want to point out is that one of the major artistic explosions of any age was here accompanied by the evolution of new forms of patronage. This patronage was given by institutional patrons it is true, but they were and are various and individual in their financing and in their judgments, capable of responding locally and in a thousand ways to the full, rich idiosyncracy of growing art.

Meanwhile back at the former centre of things in old Europe, quite different impulses were at work, more collective, equalitarian and given to working through government. The crisis of the Second World War for Britain was a social crisis as well as a military one. Everything that was best in Britain seems to have been galvanised into activity. Those to whom the arts meant most felt impelled to bring them to an embattled people who deserved to know something more of the civilisation they were struggling to protect. The wartime Council for Education in Music and the Arts was the predecessor of the present Arts Council in Britain and therefore the ancestor of our Arts Council. It is significant that the Education Act of 1944, the Beveridge plan for social security and the Arts Council idea were all born together. The conclusions in respect to education, welfare and art were the same. What could no longer be done on a partial or individualistic or private-purchase basis would have to be done together as a public, universalistic effort.

How to do it was clear enough but it was perhaps less clear what should be done, at least in regard to bestowing the arts on all. By contrast, social security's outlines almost designed themselves. But which arts at what level ought to have their faltering free market restored to working order by government subsidies? Considering the tiny resources made available to the arts, whether absolutely or when compared with the resources poured into education and welfare, it is surprising in retrospect how little debate there was on such questions of priorities.

The matter of standards was promptly settled in favour of the highest attainable. This has meant in effect depth against breadth, the professionals as against the amateurs, a focussing on the standard-setting company or the major exemplars of an art as against scattering the bread all over the waters. This is, of course, the same judgment as one might expect of scholars and connoisseur-collectors, the tastemakers who had prevailed at the end of the previous era of the upper middle class market.

Let me make plain that I am not complaining about the decision, but trying to analyse not simply the assumptions which triumphed but also those which went under, the alternatives which never were. For choosing the few and the highest has many advantages. Recipients are much easier to defend against the critics and reviewers. Their evident qualities will impress restive MPs who might prefer to subsidise eggs rather than eggheads. Then, of course, there are fewer of the best to maintain. Moreover, if one uses expert and participant panels for each art, as the Arts Council does, then the most likely way to panel or committee consensus is to invite agreement on excellence, long proven or at least demonstrated early and clearly. When, in addition, a country has an old and glorious tradition to maintain in a given art, as Britain has in, say, drama or poetry, then the highest standard attainable may be very exclusive indeed but quite inevitable as the aim of a national body.

That, however, is not quite the way true patronage worked. For persons are more whimsical than panels, and patrons more given to playing hunches, favourites and the peculiarities of their own taste. Indeed one important function of the patron was the support he could give to the young artist in the making, or to old ones out of the mainstream or positively fighting the currents of the time. It is in fact hard to see how any one body such as a Council, precisely because it is intelligently officered, responsibly advised and carefully steered to joint conclusions, can reproduce the effects of a variety of patrons with their many standards, and conflicting views. Perhaps this is a further penalty of a collective, relentlessly intercommunicating and depersonalised age.

There yet may be ways of producing some of the effects of patronage as contrasted with the collective encouragement of the highest standards attainable. One important method the Arts Council has increasingly employed is to devolve and delegate by working through regional arts associations. Such bodies by their very number break up uniformities of view and judgment. By their closeness to the seeds of new growth they are bound to provide a little unstandardised cover and distribute some of that warm mulch of local and personal enthusiasm which protects the spindly stage of art and artists. And in the end there is little ultimate risk to the highest standards in all of this. The hard wind of metropolitan criticism will blow soon enough around anything which grows.

The Arts Council has also endeavoured to attract local bodies, companies and trusts into the encouragement of the arts. Insofar as they simply enlarge the market for established artists and performers this is a good thing but it is hardly bestowing patronage except in the vulgar sense of buying tickets. Local bodies have proved slow learners where it comes to using their powers of rating for cultural purposes under the 1948 British Act and this seems to me fairly inevitable given the habit councillors have of seeking concrete, measurable results for every penny spent. Moreover, councillors, like other politicians, are in constant need of publicity so that the expression of hostile views on 'what has been done with our rates' has become a recognised gambit all over the Western world. If Arts Council experts are called in to do the choosing this negates the independence of the patronage being given. If they are not, there is little protection from that simple arrogance which considers artists as just pipers to be paid but examined closely by a sub-committee on their choice of tunes.

Fortunately there are many exceptions and I would instance in this country the largely favourable treatment of its Art Gallery by the Auckland City Council. Nevertheless it would seem that the most suitable and attractive role for local bodies to play in the encouragement of the arts is by helping to house them. Art centres, galleries, concert halls and theatres are satisfyingly concrete manifestations of civic effort and there is certainly enough to be done in the provision and maintenance of well planned, handsome buildings for the arts to busy local bodies for many decades to come.

Similar constraints apply to encouragement of the arts by companies. Shareholders and particularly boards of directors want to see a return to the company while the nature of real patronage does not lend itself to quantifiable or immediate returns. Subsidising employee attendance at cultural events, running store displays or buying contemporary art for the boardroom is some encouragement to the arts, no doubt, but it is acceptable because a version of these functions has to be undertaken in any event. The search for prestige advertising has led firms to commission works of art, underwrite losses on seasons of this and that and, more frequently, to run competitions. The problem is, of course, to convince the querulous on the board that the firm's name is sufficiently prominent, that the 'free' publicity is worth its weight in prize money each and every year the event is promoted, and that whatever has been chosen is worthwhile and will do public credit to the company seeking prestige. All this is hard to achieve and, as with local bodies, one either protects the promotion by bringing in the Council, which adds no new judgments, or one risks the development of instant critics in unexpected places.

And when all is said and totted up this still leaves aside the problem of providing real patronage. In the United States it has not been the corporation which has been the patron, Mr Paepcke and the Container Corporation of America notwithstanding.[1] The creative sabbaticals, the scholarships, the collections, and the sustaining grants came from institutions created by individuals whose money was completely theirs to distribute.

This thinness of corporation patronage for the arts is the more noticeable when one compares it with the attitudes of science- and technology-based industry towards science. There the money does flow towards the ideas and towards the men who will subsequently sustain the industry. In this country governmental decision rightly linked the support of our symphony to the revenues of radio, which uses music—of all sorts—as its principal raw material. Now that those revenues have been cut into by television and are about to be cut into by licensed private radio, we shall see what we shall hear. Nor is there any sign that the principle involved will be extended by having N.Z.B.C.-T.V. plow back into film schools, film libraries, film-making, and the theatre at large a comparable share of its revenue.

I have looked at several ways the British Arts Council has sought to increase variety in the encouragement of the arts and the final one deserving mention is co-operation with universities. In North Wales, for example, finance is being given for a theatre on a site provided by the University which will use the theatre when a company supported by the Arts Council is away touring. This building in common will strengthen the development of drama within that University as well as in that community generally. Now this points to a possibility for patronage proper. Because in Britain, as in the United States, the universities are not one body of judgment but many, they can constitute a class of patron. University developments and departments vary from place to place though they range always within an acceptable scale of standards. This scale is much wider in the United States where roughly three times the British proportion of the population get the chance of tertiary education. Nevertheless the differences of view and taste and judgment among British or New Zealand universities remain adequate to the task of constituting independent centres of patronage. Indeed, the whole trend for creative artists to move into, or be generated within the wider universities of our time strengthens the role of universities as patrons. The largely spurious dichotomy between creation and analysis is dissolving so that careers which move from training to creation and out to performance and back to criticism and instruction are becoming common in the fine arts, drama, literature, film and music.

The problem outside the U.S.A. is not to get this evolution to occur but to speed it to the point where the community enjoys the invigorating effect of a multiplicity of origins for cultural growth. We must do with taxes what the great private fortunes accomplished in America. Moreover, it will have to be done against the organisational nature of the government which raises the taxes. Like large-scale business and industry, government tends always to bureaucratic centralism in itself and in its creatures. The British Arts Council has shown awareness of this tendency and its dangers by looking outside itself for allies like the universities and the great urban local bodies and by commencing to delegate to regional arts associations. In New Zealand the problem is harder again. The University tradition is so much shorter and so much more exposed to myopic demands that it should yield short-term training instead of long-term education and cultural depth for the community. The urban local bodies are divided and small while the regional arts associations are as yet only hopes and propositions. And there are virtually no very rich and absolutely no super rich to help. So the New Zealand prospect for patronage is bleak.

Nor would developed patronage in New Zealand, nor perhaps in Britain, seem likely to have chosen to distribute their resources as amongst the arts in the same way as the Arts Council machinery has chosen to do in both countries—the patterns of expenditure in both showing a remarkable family resemblance. For the patron when he has existed has always exercised a taste formed in his city or country, among his contemporaries and their interests, and according to those arts and artists awaiting his cultivation. The Italian despot had his stable of sculptors, painters and litterateurs; the German elector supported his composer/conductor, chamber orchestra or string quartet; the Russian Grand Duke might favour certain dancers or keep a poet or some actors. But everywhere patronage was governed by place and time and flowed with cultural developments rather than endeavouring to dictate what should develop or be developed and in what ideal proportions.

Not, I fancy, that the British Arts Council began with a clear scheme in which expenditure on ballet and opera had to rank first; symphonies, concerts, and the theatre next; then fine arts and some poetry, tailing away to literature in general. This order of priorities is what has developed given several factors. First comes the size of the performing unit in a given art. If an opera house, an opera company, directors, stage designers, an orchestra and so on are required for a performing unit in that art then their cost is the minimum which has to be subsidised if that art is to be presented at all. Poetry, by contrast, may seem supported for the price of a podium for a night and an occasional award. It follows that, if every art can develop some pressure to be encouraged, then each of them will first be given what appears to be the minimum necessary for its own survival even if this produces extraordinary disparities between the allocations to the various arts—as it has. Unless the overall grant from the state is thereafter sharply increased, the time may never arrive when a second round of assistance above the minimum is shared out on some other basis than survival.

The second factor relates to the first. When an expensive art with a big performing unit shows signs of collapse—as did symphonic music in London at one stage—then aid and advice must be rushed to the disaster area where so many are visibly foundering. This aid-to-the-stricken-giant approach is facilitated by union reinforcements who add a persuasive common touch of practicality and honest livelihoods endangered to the embarrassment of divas and directors.

The third factor contributing to present priorities is the orientation towards the performing arts and towards audiences. This orientation arose from what the original Council for Education in Music and the Arts existed to do, namely to bring art to the people. It arose also from the attractiveness to politicians of the concept of state-supported distribution of good things to numerous recipients, whether welfare benefits to voters or performances to audiences. The corollary to this is, of course, that if you know what it is that ought to be distributed, and audiences are regrettably sparse for it, then additional resources will be needed to sustain the performers until the audiences learn or can be taught what they are missing.

The fourth factor is the need of the national organisation to compete in all fields. To précis one member of the British Arts Council: 'if there were an Arts Olympics, Britain would gain many gold medals'; and, I would add, they would not have been amateurs that won but professionals specially trained up for these events by the Arts Council. Nor is this attitude without its own shrewdness and logic. With hundreds of millions of tourist dollars winging their way to a large choice of European destinations, London's swinging must be reinforced with a full roundabout of the best opera, ballet, theatre and concert.

The fifth and final factor is the tendency of any national institution to accrete round itself an establishment for its field and an establishment view. Necessarily it gives more weight to the tried, traditional and the prestigious. It will get round to the new in time and will certainly risk a ration of the experimental but its main role is maintenance. This should help to account for an interesting contrast in contemporaneity. Within each established art what the British artists and performers are assisted to do is very much of our day and age. But the emphasis and the balance which the Arts Council maintains as between the arts evokes an older taste. Indeed, the proportions would have been admired in the Paris of Edward VII.

Turning to New Zealand we must add a sixth factor: the operation of respectful imitation. It takes us a century to get things cultural going; one-third of that century for frank imitation, one-third for confusion of models, and one-third for provincial assertiveness. Then we are off. In the matter of the encouragement of the arts and in respect to the ratios of subsidy to be given we appear to be in the first third of our century of preparation. Regardless of the difference between fifty and two and three quarter millions of people; regardless of the fact that we are not moored opposite a continent brimming with opportunities to tour, to exchange, to compare, to recruit; regardless of how different are our native preferences, frailties, and strengths; we have reproduced here the proportions evolved by our British exemplar. We struggle to maintain one of everything: an opera company; a symphony, a ballet, a theatre, a true Noah's Ark of the arts. Let us hope that the tourists from America when they come are charmed rather than indignant to have found at the costly ends of the Pacific a very mini-Britain.

How, given the nature of patronage, might New Zealand patrons have supplemented the efforts of our Arts Council and even chosen fresh directions for themselves? Being of this given time and this place they would not have missed the particular strengths of the arts in New Zealand as they had developed unassisted. The number of worthwhile poets, short-story writers and novelists would have struck them as justifying real support. Nor would the inadequate subventions of the State Literary Fund, so often going to publisher rather than writer, have stood in their way. The rapid burgeoning of painting and sculpture would have brought forth scholarships and fellowships in quantities sufficient to consolidate the potential gains. Perhaps some Croesus could have found the tens of thousands of dollars necessary to insure and tour, say, three exhibitions a year of the masters that will never now hang permanently in this country.

The New Zealand patrons would be quick to scent and follow up the recent development in the writing of plays, the making of films, and the genuine native strength of the lesser arts and crafts such as pottery. The patron might think more of housing and improving the amateur drama which exists and about the founding of university theatres and the endowment of department of drama and film. They would certainly not neglect the few theatres that have established themselves—all of them. In music it would be characteristic for them to reinforce successes like the chamber music circuit, the Cambridge School and resident groups of performers at the universities. But here our New Zealand patrons, if only they existed, would be on the border of territory which the Arts Council has made its own. The patrons' interest and emphasis would still differ in being directed first and foremost at supporting the composer or choreographer, the creative artist working in a medium for which there was already a public interest, a self-sustaining audience even though a small one.

Such patronage is not altogether imaginary. There have been one or two true patrons such as Dr Charles Brasch whose intelligently exercised encouragement has had a disproportionately fructifying effect.[2] Our universities are experimenting more whenever they can squeeze a little extra from their grant. Further businesses may be lured into the experiment of giving travelling fellowships or commissions on which an artist may live for a time. Local bodies may be led to do more towards housing the arts and the proprietors of the mass media may be directed to do more to feed the arts that sustain them.

Nevertheless, New Zealand patrons are likely to go on being few and far to seek. So one is positively driven to urge on our Arts Council a certain schizophrenia: that it assist other institutions to act the patron; that it delegate and divide choice; and that it add to its chosen field of encouragement for the performing arts more of the emphasis which patronage places on the creative artist and the developing, living arts of this place and this time.

Notes

1   [At the time this was written the Paepcke Corporation was publishing a series of full page coloured reproductions of their odd selection of contemporary American artists in a number of magazines. Ed.]

2   [Dr Charles Brasch was founder and editor of *Landfall* for many years from December 1947. Ed.]

Part Two

Town, City and Country

5

Psephology

Psephology is a newish name for a middle-aged art: the study of elections. The practice was elaborated by Americans; the Greek name was awarded by Oxford which, mainly within Nuffield College, possesses an active body of psephologists. When the present Master of Pembroke College, R. B. McCallum, coined 'psephology', he referred to the Greeks' custom of dropping a pebble *(psephos)* into an urn at their elections. The new name contains no scientific claims and, for traditionalists, may serve as it were to disinfect the study and help on its acceptance. Unfortunately, however, it does suggest that what is being studied is as old as Athens. Certainly choice between candidates is ancient but choice by a mass electorate running into the millions is not, and it is the nature and habits of the mass electorate with which the psephologist is principally concerned.

The study is, indeed, the natural fruit of the growth of multiparty representative systems resting on a broad franchise. The fact that the vote was possessed by nearly every adult male in the United States as early as the eighteen-thirties is undoubtedly connected with the early establishment of departments of Political Science in that country around the turn of the century and even before. While these departments duly considered constitutional law and political philosophy, they began also to take an interest in what was happening around them. President Woodrow Wilson's first fame as an American academic, for instance, came from a book on the existing structure of United States government, the book's more profound thoughts being borrowed from that superb British journalist, Walter Bagehot.

The study of the history of a country where an election might exceed a colonial war in significance likewise focussed attention on the electoral process as it had been. A dozen years ago I was given the volume which won the prize of the American Historical Association in 1912.[1] It contains seven coloured double-page maps (a formidably expensive inclusion) showing the percentages won by the parties in every county of the Southern States between 1836 and 1852. From these the author, A. C. Cole, is able to locate movements in sentiment—'the largest Democratic gains (between 1840 and 1844) were made in the regions where negro slaves were in a minority'—and measure their political weight—'The

[This chapter was published in the *University of Auckland Gazette*, Vol. 5 (1963). Ed.]

percentage of Democratic gain in those regions was double that in the black belt except in the case of North Carolina'. Cole can then go on to discuss the issues which were before the electorate and might account for this kind of result and its specific distribution and then proceed to connect the sorting agent—in this case the campaign to annex Texas—with the post-electoral actions of the new members and their parties.

The third contribution to psephology, which followed the academic consideration of elections as one element in the contemporary structure of politics and followed, also, the study of elections as major historical events in democratic societies, was made incidentally to the commercial pursuit of information about the mass market. In the nineteen-twenties extensive interviewing was begun in the United States to find what all levels and conditions of men thought of specific products. Those interviewed were more and more accurately selected so that as a sample they should correspond to the characteristics of the whole population they represented. During the thirties, Elmo Roper and Doctor George Gallup applied this technique to political subjects, partly to provide feature articles for newspapers and partly to check the results of their methods against the hard facts of opinion as registered at the ballot box.

The correspondence was so good for the presidential election of 1936 that this established the reputation of opinion polling, particularly when the *Literary Digest's* old-fashioned enquiry by means of millions of postcards collapsed ignominiously. The *Digest's* postcards went to telephone and car owners who naturally 'elected' the Republican while the worse-off were giving victory to Roosevelt. Twelve years later Gallup himself stumbled badly when he suspended interviewing in September, 1948, convinced that Dewey would win. The 'Don't Knows' and last minute changers plumped for Truman in hundreds of thousands and, by upsetting Gallup's forecast, forced him to improve both his timing and his sampling so that subsequent error has been nearly confined within two per cent and is usually even less. In 1960, for example, despite the expressed convictions of many commentators who had toured with the candidates, seen the crowds and expected a Kennedy landslide, Roper announced, 'This is the most volatile election we have ever tried to measure and it could go either way.' The election was, of course, won by 112,881 votes or one-tenth of one per cent of the whole.

The case of Kennedy's win by a hairbreadth brings out the fact that in an age of closely balanced followings the margin of victory is frequently within opinion polling's margin of error. No doubt this is distressing to candidates but for psephologists it is less dire since they want to know about a whole range of opinions, the vast mass of them being precisely enough delineated when error is a possible two per cent, or when it is five for that matter. If one recalls the shifts to which editors were once reduced—'thinking Englishmen believe'; or historians—'the conscience of France was pricked'—one can only be thankful for the existence of an index which tells us to within a point or two the proportions rallying to the Eden government after Suez or what electors thought of Macmillan's handling of defence after the Polaris agreement.

By using the same techniques the university psephologist, at some expense, can amplify and supplement the information he gets *gratis* from his newspaper. He can explore such questions as when voters make up their mind; what kinds of message about politics voters attend to; whether they put issues or leaders first; what kind of picture of major parties the voters carry round in their heads; and so on. This usually requires more than one interview because memory plays ego-building tricks like the strange increase a year or two after an election in the number claiming to have voted for the winner.

By such investigations psephologists are learning more about the way mass opinion is formed in our society and how it persists, knowledge which, in addition, lights up whole stretches of our past. There are those who deplore such knowledge, however, because they both presume that it is already very extensive and precise and that politicians will use it either to mislead electors or, paradoxically, to follow them sheepishly. This is akin to the extreme attitude which begins by idealizing the electors as wholly rational beings and ends in disappointment by imagining the kind of voter sketched by Michael Frayn: 'Do not make the mistake of over-estimating me. Take me as being for all practical purposes lazy, unintelligent, bigoted and self-absorbed.'

Naturally voters do not correspond to these creatures respectively of hope and of fear, nor are politicians usually foolish sheep or villainous bell-wethers. The sound and fury as well as the sense proceed from the fact that the things which political action can decide do matter to people, passionately on occasion. Therefore, as Theodore White put it in *The Making of the President*,[2] 'politics is the slow, public application of reason to the governing of mass emotion'. Now and again one could reverse that quotation it is true, but Goebbels did not need a psephologist to instruct him how to rouse feeling against order. Instead, it is the application of reason which is more likely to benefit from the accurate diagnosis of existing opinion while constructive leadership is more to be looked for when its quiver of persuasions is full, the range is known and the scoring of bullseyes in the past is properly recorded.

Since 1945 David Butler, H. G. Nicholas and Richard Rose have recorded and dissected each British election as and after it occurred. Successive postwar elections in the United States have brought forth such fascinating accounts as White on Kennedy's road to power and such impressive analyses as Angus Campbell's *The Voter Decides* on the Eisenhower-Stevenson contest of 1952.[3] This accumulating record of the performance of the mass electorate is cheering rather than depressing. For it is in the long run and on the basis of experience that the elector shows wisdom. Thus, even if past elections were not important historical events in themselves, they would still be well worth studying simply to lengthen the span of performance on which our collective and occasional master can be assessed. And each insight from the psephology of the present renders it easier to make sense of old elections and, in return, to demonstrate precedents, connections and development.

Until 1960 it was this psephology of the past, arising from investigations into the history of New Zealand's politics, which was especially pursued at the University of Auckland. The first masterate thesis on this subject, done under the supervision of Professor Willis Airey and completed in 1948,[4] was followed by a series of theses on a particular election or two, and then by a series charting the movement of votes since the turn of the century at every polling booth in the Auckland metropolitan area, the Waikato and Taranaki. Response at the grass roots is thus known in a way which is not possible in, say, the United Kingdom where the statistical unit is the constituency. As the *Guardian* recently put it, reviewing a book analysing the 1960 election, 'In New Zealand things are more helpfully ordered ... [and] trends can thus be noted over very small areas of population, and general conclusions more positively advanced.'

Not too positively, one hastens to add, for, as with most studies dependent on the judgment of humans and numbers, one is soon at the limits of what can be proven. To borrow from Lord Keynes's essay on Jevons: 'The significance of his method may be expressed by saying that he approached the complex economic facts of the real world, both literally[5] and metaphorically as meteorologists.... The simplified abstractions of pure theory ... did not blind him to the fact that the material to be handled is shifting and complicated, and will only yield up its answer if it is arranged, compared and analysed for the discovery of uniformities and tendencies.... He would spend hours arranging his charts, plotting them, sifting them, tinting them neatly with delicate pale colours like the slides of the anatomist, and all the time poring over them to discover their secret'. Keynes ends with a warning which is as applicable to psephology as to 'the black arts of inductive economics': 'the scientific flair which can safely read the shifting sands of economic statistics is no commoner than it was'.

Notes

1 [A. C. Cole, *The Whig Party in the South* (Washington and London, 1919). Ed.]
2 [T. H. White, *The Making of the President, 1960* (London, 1962). Ed.]
3 [A. Campbell, G. Gurin and W. E. Miller, *The Voter Decides* (Evanston, Ill., 1954). Ed.]
4 [Robert Chapman is referring to his M.A. thesis entitled 'The Significance of the 1928 General Election: A Study in Certain Trends in New Zealand Politics During the Nineteen-twenties' (Auckland, 1948). Ed.]
5 Jevons spent five years in Sydney and in 1859 published *Some Data concerning the climate of Australia and New Zealand.*

6

The Sad, Slow End of the Twenties

The 1928 Results

When the votes were counted everyone was astounded by the wonder Ward had worked, United having shot up from 12 to 28 seats, and by the collapse of the Coates majority from 56 seats to 29. It felt as though New Zealand had taken a real decision and ended a political era. The truth was, however, that the United escape route led only backwards, not only in personalities and policies but also in electoral loyalties and in the distribution of the vote. New Zealand had not even escaped from the politics of the twenties, for Ward had contrived merely to restore roughly the voting balance between the parties that obtained in 1919: Reform 31% in 1919, 32% in 1928; Liberal/United 29% in 1919, 29% in 1928; Labour 19% in 1919, 23% in 1928.

The main facts had not been altered. The three-party system which see-sawed its way back to 1919, and in a sense back to 1911, was still there. An indecisive electoral result, needing Parliamentary recombination to produce a government, had appeared once more in 1928 as it had in 1911, 1914 and 1922. Labour remained what it had been in 1919, a minority party of change confronting an overwhelming majority of conservative New Zealanders who preferred to believe that the concept of the nineties, country developmentalism and primary exports for the British market, was the right response to a later age.

The result in seats, of course, was not the same as that in 1919; but the degree to which 1928 was a restoration of 1919 voting, even within the sections, is really rather remarkable:-

---

[This is the last chapter of *The Political Scene, 1919-1931* published in 1969. In the preceding pages, Robert Chapman analysed the parties and the policies of the 1920s, including the general elections of 1919, 1922, and 1925. The Reform Party, led by Gordon Coates, won a sweeping victory in 1925 against the National Party (formerly the Liberals) led by George Forbes. Reform won 56 seats, National won 12, and Labour, led by Harry Holland, won 12. In 1927 the United Party was formed from Forbes' MPs, some dissident Reformers, and some former Liberals. Their Leader was Sir Joseph Ward (aged 73) who had represented Invercargill from 1925. During the election campaign of 1928, Ward, misreading his notes, promised to borrow 70 million pounds to be used to develop New Zealand and thus, in this period of a depressed economy, provide employment. Ed.]

Table 6.1: Parties, Voting and Sectionalism, 1919 and 1928

	Town 1919	Town 1928	Country 1919	Country 1928	City 1919	City 1928
Lib/United	32	30	30	29	26	26
Reform	27	35	37	38	25	25
Independent	—	—	1	4	—	—
Country	—	—	—	3	—	—
Labour	19	23	12	14	29	35
Informal	1	1	1	1	1	1
Non-Voting	21	11	19	11	19	13
	100%	100%	100%	100%	100%	100%

The Cities

The dramatic quality of 1928 in the fate of United and Reform lay in the contrast with the immediate past of the 1925 result. The greatest voting change lay in the cities. Here United more than doubled its vote, going from 12% up to 26%, and took 7 seats where it had but 2 in 1925. Contrariwise, Reform's seats were halved from 12 to 6 and its vote dropped by twelve points from 37% to 25% United scored best where it had an air of freshness as a contender returning to the fray after an absence of an election or two. This was particularly true in Auckland, where 5 of its gains were made.

The clue to the nature of United's city victory, however, lay in the kind of constituency they took. Before the Great War the Liberals had been the proprietors of the working men's seats while obtaining much the lesser share of the well-to-do and middling electorates. Now in 1928 they emerged briefly as an alternative conservative party of the city with a strong appeal to the middle levels of small business, shopkeepers, tradesmen and skilled workers. Worried by growing unemployment beneath them and hoping against hope that good times could be recovered in the only way they knew—by loans and works—they turned from Coates to Ward. Labour was still not a party for which the 'respectable' could easily vote. However, there had been no recent frightening strikes to make a switch away from Reform seem perilous, while the disenchantment with Coates was profound and there was nowhere else to go but to United.

The result was that United captured 4 seats of this sort and retained the 2 they already held. Reform lost Eden, Roskill and Parnell to United and Labour contributed Auckland East which John A. Lee had held on a split vote in 1925. Reform kept an equal number of these middling and better-off electorates (6) but the Reform candidates' loss of votes was large in all of them. Indeed the reaction against Reform was so powerful that in Wellington North and Wellington East, where United failed to stand and was thus not there to catch the windfall, Labour managed to scrape in.

In the core of the cities Labour held on in 9 seats, took a new seat which had been produced by a redrawing of the electorates, and re-took Dunedin North from Reform. Nevertheless, there must have been a sizeable fringe of city working people moving across from Labour to United, for Labour was generally down about six points in its own seats and it actually lost Grey Lynn to United. Doubtless the glint of Ward's millions drew them and also the possibility that Ward might lead a government and carry out his plans, whereas Labour seemed fated never to come near power regardless of how loyally trade unionists supported the Party. The great majority in core areas, however, continued to cling to the working men's party.

So the overall result in the cities was that Labour (13) kept their strongholds in the heart of the cities while the suburban constituencies were divided between United (7) and Reform (6).

The Towns

The towns presented a milder version of the city movement of opinion. Reform lost 10%. United picked up 7%, non-voting rose 2%, and Labour added 1%. As an important result, the three parties were now closer together (Reform 35%, United 30%, Labour 23%) than they had ever been before and, partly in consequence, the division of seats proved to be more representative of the spread of votes. No party's lead was enough to give it a huge bonus like that of Reform in 1925 nor was any party so far behind that it elected no town MPs like Labour in 1919 and 1925.

This evening-out was partly the result of United and Labour each failing to run candidates in two seats. Had Labour run in Nelson and Invercargill, United would in all likelihood have kept both seats anyway. It had no difficulty in holding Wanganui where Labour appeared, nor was the retaking of New Plymouth from Reform impeded by the presence of a third, Labour choice. On the other hand, both Labour's captures from Reform, Napier and Timaru, were close enough to have been difficult to predict had United run. The absence of Ward candidates in these two towns is a good illustration of how generally unexpected were the Liberal revival and the slaughter of 'the Coates Majority'.

The Countryside

In the countryside the one common factor in the results was the rush away from Reform which, here too, lost 10%. Poor prices and the dairy control muddle, the arbitration impasse and the failure of rural credit to improve matters, unemployment in rural areas and, above all, the reaction against finding that Coates equalled slump instead of prosperity, these combined to drive voters helter-skelter out of the Reform camp. It should be stressed that the ex-Reformers were not very particular about where they went except that they were most reluctant to enter the Labour fold. In the 7 constituencies where Labour was a possible choice but there was no United candidate, Labour's vote rose but it captured nothing and simply retained Buller and Raglan, both seats influenced by mining votes.

Where United candidates appeared it is plain that ex-Reformers preferred Ward's men with their traditional aura and golden glitter to either the Country Party or anti-Coates Independents.[1] United took Waikato against Reform and the Country Party and captured Rotorua against both parties and Labour as well. In the 4 cases where United appeared against a combination of Independents, Labour and Reform, the Independents came a poor fourth in all instances. Yet where arrangements had been made with United to give the Country Party a clear run or where United simply did not stand against an Independent, then the voters proved ready to elect a Country or Independent MP in 4 cases out of 6. United's absence thus helped the Country Party into the Bay of Islands and assisted Independents into Stratford, Egmont and Rangitikei. It is thus apparent that the 1928 vote in the countryside was first of all a vote of 'No-Confidence in Coates'. Secondarily, the dislodged and discontented vote preferred to move towards an organised, familiar and positive conservative alternative, although it would accept any rural conservative alternative if that was all that was presented. Lastly, Labour was not yet an acceptable party in the countryside proper.

Then did all Labour's heart-searching over its rural programme produce no effect whatever? In 1925 Labour ran 21 candidates and received 13% of the vote; in 1928 it ran 23 candidates and received 14%. Labour did manage to regain two seats, paradoxically from United. Labour won back Westland with a gain of 1% and re-took Waimarino on a three-way split. These were mining and timber electorates, however, and their recovery was no indication of rising popularity in the countryside generally as the overall figures show. The conspicuously moderate, Liberal-style land planks had not been enough to decontaminate Labour which was still regarded by country people as the party of the city, of trade unionism, and of dangerous, radical experiment.

Despite this inability to turn Reform's misfortunes into farmer-Labour MPs, the resolve to keep on running Labour candidates in some rural areas in 1928 had an important effect on the eventual balance of parties in the House. Where Labour did not run, 11 United, Country or Independent MPs emerged, compared to 6 Reform MPs. Where Labour did run, 7 United men won, but so did 7 Reformers. Plainly, the presence of Labour candidates attracted enough anti-Government votes to materially reduce the chances of ousting Reformers. Without a Labour man in a given country seat the odds favouring an anti-Reform victory were almost 2:1; with a Labour candidate present they fell to 1:1. Labour thus helped to prevent the surge against Reform from turning into an overwhelming victory in the countryside for United and its allies. Labour's true interest was to stop both United and Reform as far from a majority as possible. The largely accidental pattern of running Labour candidates in some country areas but not in others happened to assist this result.

The Difficult Three-Party Situation

As it was, the 1928 election did leave Reform and United almost equally distant from possessing the magical number of 41 MPs which permitted a party to elect a Speaker and govern on its own. Reform had 29; United had 28 and the probable help of 1 Country and 3 Independent MPs. The 1928 verdict had confirmed the three-party situation in its most difficult form. It had kept Labour in confinement, reduced Reform to a minority party, rejected Coates, yet withheld a majority from Ward. Ward's consolation prize was that Labour's 19 MPs could not govern by themselves nor ignore the way New Zealand had spurned Coates. Labour would have to give Ward his chance to govern. Labour's consolation prize was that either they held the balance of power between separate United and Reform parties or, if United and Reform somehow coalesced, then Labour would at last be left as the only alternative to a single conservative coalition.

Strategically it would have been wise for Labour to have employed its balance of power to bring about the coalition of its enemies as rapidly as that could be managed. Only with United and Reform in alliance could Labour expect to recruit all the disillusioned voters instead of having to watch them dodge past Labour on their way back and forth from Reform to Liberal to Reform to United. A party confident of its own power to attract support and sure that its opponents had nothing to offer would have wanted those opponents combined and on their way to discrediting themselves as fast as possible. Had Labour demanded a high price for its support or been ready and quick to withdraw it, then United might have been compelled to turn towards Coates much earlier than it did.

Long years of deferred hope, however, had sapped the confidence of the Parliamentary Labour Party. They were impressed by the miraculous Ward revival, and by the reception his schemes had received among potential Labour supporters. 'Labour' said the *New Zealand Worker*, 'had everything to gain by allowing Sir Joseph the opportunity to implement his policy.' Holland re-emphasized this view in the House and on 10 December 1928, at a special session of Parliament called by Coates, the Reform Government was defeated by 50 to 28, United and Labour voting together. Ward then took office. Holland outlined the legislation Labour would like to see, but he made no conditions and Ward accepted none. The Labour Executive went so far as to describe United as 'a Government with a varied programme much of which the Party can support.' Underneath, however, Holland recognised, as many Labour MPs did not, that Ward would not prove better than Coates nor essentially different. 'I wonder', he wrote, 'whether when they have kicked Sir Joseph as they kicked Coates they will run after some other golden calf.' There was, in fact, one more conservative alternative for New Zealanders to try before the politics of the twenties was exhausted—the Coalition of United and Reform formed in September 1931 and given a mandate at the election of December 1931.

Ward Disappoints and Delays

Time and adversity had first of all to wear away the gilt from the Wardian calf before the shaggy crossbred of Coalition would be led up from the back paddock. Ward started from weakness. Apart from himself, only Wilford and Ngata had ministerial experience. Ward was driven to include four in his Cabinet who had not even served in Parliament before. He chose to overload himself with portfolios, thus adding to the strain on his already failing constitution and reinforcing the tendency for everything to turn on his decision. His first statement killed some hopes. There was £3 million backlog of loan applications which Ward proposed to work through before Government interest rates dropped from five and three-quarter to four and three-quarter per cent as advertised. He gave a sop to Labour by raising the rate of wages on public works but New Zealand was waiting for the chink of the £70 million and renewed prosperity.

Having looked into the finances, Ward announced that 'an important London transaction' barred his way. What this was did not become clear, though press and later Parliamentary discussion settled to the view that it must have concerned the conversion of the £20 millions of debt maturing in 1929. It seems to have been something between an excuse and a muddle. Ward later accused Stewart, the Reform Finance Minister, of committing his successor not to borrow in London for a further two years if he got a loan to cover the £20 million conversion. Later again, Ward admitted he had been mistaken about Stewart's negotiations. Then on 20 December 1928 Sir Joseph put paid to the hopeful electors. 'I wish to make it quite clear that at no time have I suggested that seventy millions was to be borrowed in one year.... Obviously such a proposal was out of the question, as it would so disturb the country, and no responsible man would make such a suggestion.' After riding to power on the suggestion, this was unconsciously ironic. But Ward then added that the £6-8 millions he would borrow per year 'is no new system, it was put into operation by me thirty-four years ago' and concluded with the much neglected truth that such borrowings 'would not amount per annum to the average amount the country has borrowed during the last three years.' 'The Wizard of Finance' had whisked the cause of his preferment into oblivion.

Thereafter inaction followed. In March and April two Reform railway projects, the Palmerston North deviation and the Rotorua-Taupo line, were stopped and a United railway project at Parnassus in the South Island was recommenced. Instead of huge land settlement projects, a very few estates were bought for subdivision. Before Parliament met in June, Ward made much of a small Budget deficit and his ministers began to speak of 'retrenchment'. He extended the Rent Restriction Act—which cost the Government nothing—to keep Labour quiescent, and he doubled the primage duty to raise revenue and please the manufacturers. Labour was opposed to higher indirect taxes which hit the lower incomes disproportionately. But the Party found itself powerless to act because it was too poor to risk another election so soon after the last and its fear of Reform was greater than its frustration with the inactivity and the occasional ill-will of United. Unless Labour would move against him, Ward was safe except from his own party and his health.

United Begins to Break Up
Both now began to fail. United's one member from a poorer Auckland city seat, J.S. Fletcher, threatened to leave United unless something were done to tackle unemployment. Ward was ill and absent for a week. Then on his return he suddenly promised that 'within the next five weeks there will be no unemployment in New Zealand of men capable of going to work.' Holland pledged the support of Labour to the policy while Ward made ready to juggle loan funds to put the unemployed to work on land settlement, irrigation, forestry and local body projects. Unfortunately Ward did not realise the size of the problem. Official figures said 2,466. Trade unions knew of 5,226 not counting youths and women. Ward called for unemployed men to register and discovered 6,000 before the

figures were for a time suppressed. By mid-November nearly 6,000 were employed on Ward's schemes, and yet 3,000 more remained. The problems were now beyond cure by the old remedies.

At the beginning of October 1929 Ward fell ill once more and thenceforth did not reappear in the House. He managed affairs as well as he could from his Parliamentary rooms, then from his Heretaunga home, and then from hospital in Rotorua. The same month there was trouble with A.E. Davy, United's National Chairman, who complained of Labour's influence. The ex-Reform wing of United resented being 'a minority Government' and fancied another election might remove their apparent dependence. Fletcher, at the other end of the Party, now voted against the Government to express his different discontents.

The possibility that an election might help was tested when Wilford became High Commissioner in London and his United seat was speedily filled by Labour at a by-election. But the real test of United's nature and of its Liberalism was the fate of a Bill to levy additional land tax on 1,450 of the largest landowners. Because Reform fought the Bill bitterly, United turned round and gutted its own measure by widening the hardship escape clauses. Then, when Labour subsequently moved to increase the pay of the lower ranks in the Public Service, Reform supported United in throwing out the motion. Even this conservative co-operation did not silence Davy who in January publicly complained about Ward's habit of one-man leadership and opposition to Reform. Davy now wanted a coalition. Jenkins, an ex-Reformer and member for Parnell, who agreed with Davy, left the United Party and resigned his seat which was captured comfortably by Reform. Davy was dismissed and with him went four of United's principal organisers. To round out this picture of disintegration, Fletcher, for opposite reasons, chose this juncture to sit as an Independent.

Forbes, Cuts and Coalition

Ward and his lieutenant, Forbes, retained command of the ship but the vessel was obviously motionless and down by the bows. At the end of May 1930 Sir Joseph felt compelled to resign. He died six weeks later, taking with him, the only commanding reputation in the Party. Ngata was a distinguished and able man but one preoccupied with Maori affairs. Otherwise United possessed no-one to challenge Coates and Downie Stewart on the Reform side nor Holland, Savage, Fraser and Nash on the Labour benches. Forbes succeeded Ward as Prime Minister but he was undoubtedly the least impressive occupant of that office New Zealand has seen in the twentieth century. Not only was United poorly led, it was uncertain even of its traditional policies. Its caution now amounted to paralysis of thought and will while its focus, Sir Joseph Ward, had departed without leaving behind a single instalment of his advertised policies.

In the form in which those policies became known in 1928 they were the product of accident and impossible to fulfil. It is a bitter comment on the politics of the twenties that they made Ward Prime Minister. But as a scholar of this period, R.G. Habershon, has pointed out, times were not so hard in 1929 that some of the large design could not have been executed.[2] The truth was that Ward and his United following proved to be in many ways more orthodox and rigid than Coates and Reform. The differences between the alternative conservative parties, never large, were now indistinguishable and their colourful rallying cries—'Coates and Confidence', 'Ward and the £70 million loan'—were exploded slogans of the past. There was nothing for it but to combine if a new face was to be turned to the electors.

Even this process took sixteen further months to achieve—nearly as long as Sir Joseph had governed. The problem was that most Reform and United politicians and their backers believed their policies to be significantly different from one another because they had such a restricted view of what was possible in the way of reshaping the economy of New Zealand to meet the growing crisis. To both Reform and United what Labour represented was not a reasonable alternative but another world, a topsy-turvy world which overturned what was obvious and certain in the twenties. Since Labour was quite out of court, the 'respectable' parties would have to go on struggling about how best to cope and about who would best cope. United and Reform knew the old Liberal way to run New Zealand as a 'distant farm' of Britain and how to apply State borrowing from overseas to enlarge its production. If this ceased to work, both parties were at a loss and could think only of economising until somehow the conventional solution began to work once more. Reform had made this response in 1921-22—and come back to win. Ward had begun to prune in 1929. Then in May 1930 Forbes commenced his prime ministry by forecasting a Budget deficit of £3 millions which would be met by cutting expenses and raising customs and petrol taxes. At once Reform opposed the choice of taxes, preferring more cuts in expenditure. Leading Reformers like Coates and Bell were contemptuous of 'the incompetence of most of the present gang in administration'. They considered them 'an extravagant, useless crew whom Reform would not combine with'. To Reform the odour of the £70 million proposal still hung over United while Labour's continued support added a positively radical taint.

Coates was used to fighting about such differences. He was a product of the three-party system, possessed a fierce loyalty to his own party and had seen Reform rebound into power before. Perhaps it could be done again if only United could be forced to accept responsibility and the unpopularity of the necessary economising or as Coates put it, 'your responsibility to balance your Budget'. Three further by-elections provided mixed indications. Reform's vote improved in Invercargill, but United then won in Waipawa, only to be dismayed in turn when they very nearly lost Southern Maori to the Ratana candidate. The Massey strand in Reform thinking was represented by Downie Stewart who had believed since 1914 that the moderate parties should combine to provide stable government as being the first priority. The issue came into the open in November 1930, but although export prices were now disastrous and registered unemployment reached 12,000 by Christmas, Coates contented himself with issuing a seven-point plan for economies as the Reform terms for considering fusion.

Nothing could be done until Forbes came back from Great Britain and the Imperial Conference. A London Banker, Sir Otto Niemeyer, had meanwhile reported in favour of rigid economy to the United Government. British opinion concurred. Forbes returned in January 1931 full of determination to retrench heavily and convinced that any unemployment insurance schemes which paid sustenance allowances without extracting work at the same time would weaken the moral fibre of the nation. He put a stop to just such a scheme enacted by his party at the end of the previous year and prepared to cut in real earnest by reducing wages on relief works, putting the railways under a board which would stop remaining construction, and amending the arbitration system so the Court could reduce the awards. This was the end of Forbes' uncertainty. He now knew with stubborn strength how he ought to proceed. It was also the bitter end of developmentalism and of the Liberal solution. In the consequent struggle to defend the basic wage the Labour Party was compelled to fight the Forbes measures while Reform supported them, at first without commitment to eventual fusion.

Thus the politics of the twenties ended in March 1931 for United and for Labour. The uncertainty and lack of confidence which had hamstrung the Parliamentary Labour Party for over two years disappeared in the struggle. Labour was now the opposition, the alternative government. It represented a new set of answers to immediate problems of depression and to the future of New Zealand. Those answers would gain in clarity and substance over the next 5 years. Yet it would be wrong to underestimate how much Labour owed to the past and to the lessons of the twenties.

The vague outlines of guaranteed prices, a free medical scheme, a housing programme, the family benefit, comprehensive pensions and provision for unemployment had all appeared in their writings and speeches by 1928. The party stood for the promotion of manufacturing as well as of primary industries. Labour had learned the value of moderation and of arbitration. It had adjusted its land policies to the fact of family-sized farms and contracted and transformed its proposals for nationalization into the intention to exercise overall direction of credit and the economy. Above all, the twenties had begun to drive home what became Labour's deepest conviction, that securing full employment came first. On the other hand, the twenties had brought Labour only minority support spread unevenly over the sections. Ward's unexpected revival threw Labour into tactical confusion and produced two years of hesitation and groping after principle. This suggests that the twenties did not leave Labour with the necessary confidence in their own policies to take up the task of government without further arduous experience.

For Coates and Reform the end of the twenties arrived in September 1931 when Coates concluded that he could no longer avoid coalition. He put off the sacrifice of independence until the last moment and was finally forced into it by Forbes's grim determination not to carry on at all unless a common front was arranged. Coates and Stewart got the key posts controlling finance and employment while Forbes remained Prime Minister of a small Cabinet of five from each party. Outside Parliament the struggle between the party stalwarts went on surreptitiously. Though 'Coalition' labels were handed out to sitting members for use at the general elections, they did not suffice to protect many Coalition United MPs from having to face Independent Reformers nor prevent several Coalition Reformers encountering 'United' or 'Liberal' opponents.

By grouping on the one side 'Coalition United' and those taking 'United' and 'Liberal' designations, and, on the other, 'Coalition Reform', 'Independent Reform' and similar variations, it is possible to see how at the election of November 1931 the balance had changed between those loosely-connected and mutually distrustful camps. Over all 76 European seats, when compared with 1928, United went down nine points to 20%. Reform fared less poorly by dropping five points to 27%. Labour climbed six points to 29%, Independents went from 2% up to 4%, and the Country Party moved from 1% to 2%. Next to Labour, the greatest gainer was non-voting—from 12% to 17%. The political uncertainty and withdrawal marked by high non-voting, which had introduced the period in 1919, were back by 1931. Through the gauze of Coalition, however, it was still possible to pick out elements of the same three parties and note that, though their relative sizes had altered, the location of their sectional support remained much the same.

It is apparent that the coming of the Great Depression had not yet worked a major change in the outlook and party attitudes of the voters.

That change would come as the Coalition Government settled in and the Depression dragged on. But, until an effective proportion of the voters had changed their assumptions and their allegiances, the era had not concluded. In this sense, 1931 was the last election in the politics of the twenties. The electors had spent the elections of the twenties endeavouring to avoid altering their assumptions while they turned from this alternative conservative party to that in search of secure prosperity. It was not to be found on the voters' terms. The three-party structure which expressed their lack of satisfaction and their oscillating indecision goes back in some aspects to 1911 and beyond. In the twenties this three-legged structure stood complete, creaking but firmly founded on sectional divisions, braced by familiar party loyalties and the Parliamentarians' desire for office. The onset of the Depression remorselessly pressed on this structure until slowly it was overthrown piece by piece. Finally only its foundations in the assumptions and preferences of the voters remained.

Notes

1 [The Country Party was formed in 1924. Earlier in *The Political Scene 1919-1931* Chapman traces the development of this party. Ed.]
2 [R. G. Habershon, *A Study in Politics, 1928-31*, MA Thesis (University of Auckland, 1958). Ed.]

7

The Response to Labour and the Question of Parallelism of Opinion, 1928-1960

This article has a dual purpose. It is designed, firstly, to measure Labour's nation-wide acceptance in the nineteen-thirties, to delineate the electoral passage of the first and second Labour governments into and out of power, and to examine that general reorientation of voter opinion which turned the three-party system into a two-party struggle with one sustained and several temporary irruptions from Right and Left. The aim is thus to illuminate the political history of our recent past by taking those closer measurements which have become familiar in contemporary psephology and so to reduce and define what historians of politics must explain. This task is attempted by carrying back in time analytical methods worked out at length in a study of the latest New Zealand election, *New Zealand Politics in Action*.[1]

Secondly, since public opinion as recorded at elections is the cadaver on the bench, the dissection should answer some questions of political science. Of first importance among them is the question of parallelism in opinion. Did changes of political preference in the various sections into which this analysis divides the body politic happen at the same time and did they take the same general direction? Or did an alteration in one section tend to cancel out an opposite movement in another so that trends deduced from national totals represent no more than resultants of a confusion of opposing tendencies? Was there, in other words, any kind of national judgment reflected in the New Zealand elections of the last 32 years? Where opposed and mutually cancelling tendencies appear were they, seen in the light of time and subsequent elections, simply the epiphenomena of lasting sectional conflicts, forever at odds in their movements; or were they the consecutive expressions of a slow-growing nation-wide opinion which took effect rapidly in one section, more haltingly in another, but eventually everywhere? If this last possibility seems to have been the case, how many elections—two, three or more—were required for the process to work itself out? Do these New Zealand

[This chapter is Robert Chapman's contribution to the book he co-edited with Keith Sinclair to honour the retirement of Willis Airey, Professor of History at the University of Auckland. *Studies of a Small Democracy* was published in 1963 by the University of Auckland. The introduction, 'Willis Thomas Goodwin Airey', was written by Chapman and Sinclair. Ed.]

electoral results, then, constitute a case of conflict or of concurrence, immediate or deferred?

Several questions depend from the problem of whether or not there was parallelism of opinion. To take the lesser ones first, there is the matter of public opinion polling. If a considerable measure of concurrence can be shown to have existed right through New Zealand's change from a three-party to a two-party system and over several decades, then politicians and students of the political process will have to pay correspondingly close attention to the results of contemporary questionnaires on party standing since the design of the social sample used could be quite poor yet still, according to the three decades of experience, yield the correct answer which would be roughly the same whichever sections of the body politic were asked to give an opinion. Historians of this country's politics will also need to be rather more interested in the results of past by-elections, for, if national parallelism did exist, it is less likely that any given trial of strength in mid-term reflected no more than trends peculiar to the sectional nature of the electorate fought over. Providing some method can be found to correct distortions arising from absenteeism—that notable characteristic of by-elections—then the historian will be presented with a scattering of approximate tests of national opinion where he once contemplated a series of local events and a regrettable absence of general information.

A finding that national trends amounted merely to the swirling where sectional cross-currents meet would teach no more than that those politicians were right who sought their party's salvation in the assembling and balancing of programmes of concessions to this group and favours to that. Party leaders placing power first would then seem to have no rational recourse but to choose their allies among the sectionalisms according to the number of their parliamentary seats and promise away.

On the other hand, a finding that a moderate or even high degree of parallelism existed, would have more encouraging implications in an age of unitary economies and planning on a national scale. For a record of sustained parallelism would indicate that government acts and opposition programmes had regularly made an overall impression, attaching or detaching a fraction of voters in every section. The stricter the parallelism, the less attractive would appear the technique of shaping policies or platforms to enlist some one section and not others, because the desired separate response in the target section would represent a problematical gain, difficult to achieve and not worth the attendant repercussions. Indeed, it might be argued that substantial parallelism could constitute a measure of maturity in a party political system, indicating that the electorate, though sectionally diversified and equipped with an elaborated range of group attitudes and institutions, was yet capable of responding electorally on a nation-wide scale to political stimuli administered—by force of contemporary social and economic integration—at the same national level.

This argument cannot be pressed too far, however, nor can total correspondence be expected. Absolute parallelism is improbable because, for one thing, in order that a party may lose 10 per cent of the total vote in each of two sections, the party must have held the same initial percentage of the vote in both sections or else must lose votes at two different but precisely related rates. Suppose the Labour Party in a poor city area took first 60 per cent, then 50 per cent of the vote. The loss would be 10 per cent of the whole and one-sixth or 16.67 per cent of the Labour vote. If, in the farming section, Labour obtained 30 per cent, then 20 per cent, again the Labour loss would be 10 per cent of the whole but in this case Labour would have lost one-third or 33.33 per cent of its own vote. Given that the electoral process begins with each section holding a different estimate of the parties, then an identical response among all the voters of every section—say the movement of one-tenth in each—would produce as many different rates of change for the particular parties affected as there were sections.

This mechanical fact alters in its meaning for a party according to whether it is rising or falling in favour. A party which has been in power and been popular will have a record affecting all sections and will already possess a sizeable proportion of each section from which voters can move. Assuming that something like a nation-wide judgment does occur, then the rates at which the party of government declines in the various sections should keep more nearly parallel than would, say, the rates of increase for a new third party which has only the short reach of its recently announced programme to stir up a common movement of votes in all sections. Such a new party would climb twice as rapidly in one section where it drew perhaps four per cent as in another where it took a two per cent share, yet the difference of two per cent of the whole would be in itself minor.

It should be borne in mind, then, that examination is unlikely to reveal perfect or absolute parallelism in New Zealand since that would require eight sectional first cousins of 'the national will', all at least in touch by telepathy and presumably equipped with a common computer. Condemned to fall short of such perfection as the findings will be, it is nevertheless worth putting these questions to the facts of the last third of a century. Is there evidence that a national judgment is passed at elections? And is this judgment sufficiently uniform to make certain variations significant?

Table 7.1: Sectional Differences in Reception of the Left

	1928	1931	1935	1938	1943	1946	1949	1951	1954	1957	1960	Ave. of unstarred	Ave. of all 11
Poorer City %	43.55	49.09	60.26	63.42	59.14	58.46	54.54	50.76	50.53	56.17	48.83	54.07	54.07
Percentage Points Below Poorer City:													
Special Country	5.75	9.58	5.65	5.29	5.84	4.29	4.76	5.43	3.06	5.58	5.15	5.49	5.49
Large Town	16.10*	14.01*	15.95*	7.77	6.77	9.35	8.81	8.94	9.60	10.20	7.55	8.62	10.46
Marginal City	15.70*	17.48*	15.07*	10.48	11.09	10.80	10.75	9.94	12.22	9.56	6.53	10.17	11.78
Rural	33.32*	30.44*	18.58	16.64	16.90	17.65	17.17	16.72	19.34	21.25	19.15	18.16	20.65
Richer City	26.14*	25.42*	26.48*	19.94	19.28	22.55	22.74	21.25	19.17	21.72	18.48	20.64	22.11
Farmer	32.95*	39.97*	24.28	20.41	23.21	22.90	23.55	23.16	23.08	24.73	23.35	23.19	25.60

* See page 146

An answer is set out in Table 7.1. Omitting the Maori vote for reasons which will be discussed later, the other seven sections were arranged according to the average height of their vote for the Left[2] over the 11 elections covered. Each of the six sectional results below the top line of results for the poorer city districts was then subtracted for the successive elections from whatever was the poorer city percentage. Thus the table presents the *difference* in Leftness between each of the sections and that exemplar of Left enthusiasm, the city strongholds. As support for the Left first rose and then fell in the poorer city districts, it will be seen that enthusiasm must have flowed and ebbed likewise in every other section since the sectional distancing—the difference between each of six sections and the poorer city areas—remained remarkably constant.

When it is remembered that around one million voters were thus making up their minds so consistently for three decades and that tens of thousands in every type of electorate and all over the country must have chosen ten times to alter allegiance together irrespective of native sectional predisposition, the table pays a rather wonderful tribute to the unity of changing decision within the continuing sectional diversity of national opinion.

For this appears to be the central paradox of New Zealand voting: the sections remain rigidly at odds in their party preferences and yet they move nearly as one in judging the performance of governments, whether governments of the Left or of the Right. Each section has a different and continuing image of the Left and of how favourable to its basic interests the Left will be or has already proved to be. Yet, instead of these sectional expectations being realised in party action by the parties formulating or executing policies which the sections would adjudge blatantly favourable to some and plainly inimical to others, past acts and present programmes produce agreement that all sections have been affected much alike, certainly to the point of causing a like proportion of voters to change sides in each section. No such conclusion, however, can have been fed back into the sectional system from successive elections. Having acted alike and produced almost the same share of defectors everywhere, the voters of the various sections do not go on to revise their images of the Left until there is only one blended, common image. The sections do not draw together. They continue broadly as favourable or as hostile to the Left as they began.

If it be legitimate to apply twentieth-century data from one end of the world to a nineteenth-century debate at the other end, then one can recognise how this New Zealand paradox would at once support and upset the European analysts of class conflict and the proponents of a national identity. On the one hand, those political philosophers who looked to class struggle to energise history might profess some satisfaction at the way sections have confronted one another through the decades even within the peaceable New Zealand microcosm. Such satisfaction would hardly survive the evidence that the sections do not struggle; their electoral verdicts concur instead of contending. On the other hand, seekers after the nation united could take pleasure in sectional correspondence at elections only as they were pained by the obstinately dissimilar orientations of those lesser nations, the sections.

These sections must now be described briefly since they are not all quite the same as those defined in *New Zealand Politics in Action* for the analysis of the 1960 election. The city constituencies are here divided exactly as there into safe National (found to be richer); safe Labour (found to be poorer); and marginal; the last being either mixed or middling in social composition and marginal in party allegiance. The 'large town' class of seat also remains as before. But in the countryside the dividing line between the farmer and the rural sections has been lowered from 50 to 40 per cent of the population resident in small boroughs and town districts.[3] This alteration was made in order to bring into sharp focus just how electorates with a clear majority of the population living on farms responded. A glance at Table 7.1 will show that 'farmer' seats were only 4.95 per cent more opposed to the Left over the whole period than the 'rural' seats with an admixture of from 40 to 80 per cent of small townsmen. So the basic sectionalism of the whole countryside and its service centres on the one side, against city and large town on the other, is not much affected by the classificatory refinement. Some further clarification was secured by extracting from among the farmer and rural classes of seat those few electorates—containing a total of 67,762 voters at the maximum and 56,321 at the minimum—where mining or the timber industry seriously distorted the normal occupational and conceptual pattern of the countryside. These electorates became the 'special country' class and were found to rank second only to the poorer city areas in their enthusiasm for Labour.

To begin with, the analytical divisions were based on observation of where parties had captured seats since 1908. By a pragmatic process the definitions of the sections were refined as the twin axes of separation became ever more apparent: rural/urban; wealthier/poorer. So striking were the voting regularities uncovered by this analysis, however, that they threw into prominence the question of how each party's following could have been behaving to produce such general harmony. First thoughts suggested that in a section where the Left was weak and there were few Labourites to annoy—areas where voting Labour was a private assertion of dissidence from prevailing attitudes—in such a section even a strong national movement away from the Left could shift but a small proportion of the entire voting population. The Labour Party itself might even lose at the same rate as elsewhere but this would appear as the response of a small proportion of the whole. Correspondingly, in the poorer city electorates, a defection from Labour ought to have appeared as a landslide by comparison with the effects of the same defection in the farming section. Yet the outstanding feature of the results summarised in Table 7.1 was the likeness of the proportions of the whole who were moved to act in every section. Thus first thoughts stood contradicted. Patently the rate of gain or loss to and from the Left's own following would bear investigation.

A measure of this is provided by Table 7.2. Ideally the voting population in all sections should have been held constant in numbers and kept within the same constituency boundaries for a third of a century. Then one could, for example, have taken the 93,318 Labour voters in rural electorates in 1946, noted that there were 4,625 fewer votes for Labour in 1949, and expressed the 4,625 as a percentage of the 93,318 to show the rate of Labour loss. In actuality, the steady growth of the number voting at each election forbids such a proceeding, since the overall numbers involved by the calculation increase each time, thus falsifying the subtraction process. Resort was had, therefore, to the percentage shares of the whole achieved at succeeding elections because these percentage shares remain true irrespective of the enlarging number contributing to them. In the instance just mentioned, Labour took 40.81 per cent of the whole qualified rural vote in 1946 and 37.37 per cent in 1949, a loss of 3.44 percentage points. Looking solely at Labour, the party share in 1949 was less by 8.43 per cent of the share it had possessed in 1946, and this ratio is here termed the rate of loss (or gain). Table 7.2 sets out the rates at which the Left rose and fell between 1928 and 1960.

It will be noticed, firstly, that there are roughly four orders of rate of change for the Left: the exceptional, as in 1931-35; the large (1928-31, 1935-38, 1954-57, 1957-60); the moderate (1938-43, 1946-49, 1949-51) and the small (1943-46, 1951-54). On three out of the four occasions when change within a section 'went the wrong way' the national change was small in degree and the pattern was weakly delineated. Secondly it will be seen that a definite pattern emerges most clearly at times of moderate change when third party effects are also absent or minimal (1938-43, 1946-49, 1949-51). The basic pattern in these three columns is simple; rate of change tends to increase going from top to bottom, which is to proceed from the section most favourable to the Left down to the least Left section. When, thirdly, one reads the whole table with this pattern in mind, it stands out that this pattern is really a particularly clear sight of a general rule, just as equal change and therefore even distancing is the general rule for Table 7.1. The distortions are magnified in Table 7.2, yet there is an order to it.

Table 7.2: Rates of Gain/Loss for the Left, 1928-1960

	1928-31	1931-35	1935-38	1938-43	1943-46	1946-49	1949-51	1951-54	1954-57	1957-60
Poorer City	+12.72	+22.75	+5.24	-6.75	-1.15	-6.71	-6.93	-0.45	+11.16	-13.07
Special Country	+4.52	+38.22	+6.45	-8.31	+1.63*	-8.10	-8.94	+4.72*	+6.57	-13.66
Large Town	+27.80	+26.31	+25.59	-5.89	-6.22	-6.88	-8.55	-2.13	+12.31	-10.20
Marginal City	+13.50	+42.96	+17.15	-9.24	-0.81	-8.12	-6.78	-6.15	+21.67	-9.25
Rural	+82.31	+123.49	+12.24	-9.70	-3.39	-8.43	-8.91	-8.37	+11.96	-15.01
Richer City	+35.96	+42.71	+28.72	-8.33	-9.91	-11.45	-7.20	+1.85*	+9.85	-11.90
Farmer	-13.96*	+294.52	+19.54	-16.46	-1.03	-12.85	-10.94	-0.54	+14.54	-18.96
All 76 European Electorates	+16.45	+58.10	+15.57	-8.36	-2.24	-8.29	-8.07	-1.33	+12.72	-13.05
	large	exceptional	large	moderate	small	moderate	moderate	small	large	large

* Marks instance where sections were moving against the national trend

Taking up the hint that the pattern would emerge most strongly over the unadorned two-party period, Table 7.3 was prepared. The left-hand column shows the percentage share of votes cast by the whole voting population which was lost by the Left over the 13 years from 1938 to 1951. This can be compared with the right-hand column which gives the percentage rate of loss from the ranks of the Left alone during the same term.

In this table the pattern is more explicit again than in the clearest previous instance, that for 1946-49. The shares of the vote lost by the Left are notably even, the result for all but the farmer section clustering close to the national figure of 12.88 per cent, while the farmer seats are within easy reach. By contrast, the rate of loss increases markedly from 19.96 to 35.83 per cent. Again the rate of loss is inverse to the basic strength of the Left; the rate enlarges very regularly with the shrinkage of the proportion normally preferring the Left.

Table 7.3: Loss of Votes by the Left, 1938 to 1951

	Share of all Votes Lost by Left	Rate of Loss from Left
Poorer City	-12.66	-19.96
Special Country	-12.80	-22.02
Large Town	-13.83	-24.85
Marginal City	-12.12	-22.89
Rural	-12.74	-27.23
Richer City	-13.97	-32.13
Farmer	-15.41	-35.83
All 76 European Electorates	-12.88	-24.47

Before coming to a conclusion, another check was made. The clear instances on Tables 7.2 and 7.3 were drawn from situations undisturbed by lasting three-party conflict, let alone by the fluctuations of party-building. All were examples—even the thirteen-year jump from 1938 to 1951 was an example—of Labour decline. Would the rule hold when increases in party following were considered equally with decreases and when third parties were permitted to take up their independent pull? Table 7.4 makes two such inclusive comparisons. The two columns on the left give the averages for the ten changes, regardless of whether the Left went up or down, between 1928 and 1960. Because the richer city constituencies, being city seats when Labour was very largely a city party, started out in 1928 with the Left considerably higher in favour than it then was in rural and farmer seats, the richer city rate of change was not exaggerated, as were the farmer and rural rates, by the process of rapid reorientation in 1931 and upbuilding of the Left in 1935. Hence the one noteworthy irregularity in the second column and hence, also, the reason for setting out the third and fourth columns which omit the first three elections and show the position for the 1938-60 period which still includes a lengthy sag for the Left, a recovery and another drop, besides a two- and a three-party situation.

Table 7.4 offers firm evidence that the pattern indeed corresponds to the general rule. What holds constant is the share won or lost. For this to be so, on average, a progressively larger percentage of the Left's following must be added or detached in proportion as that following constitutes a smaller part of a section's entire voting strength. When the possibilities were reviewed earlier in this article, the improbability of absolute parallelism was stressed precisely because it would involve such different but such exactly related rates of change among party supporters in the various sections. Measured over the long term, and even over certain three-year periods, the required seven ratios are found to be related and related with a considerable degree of exactitude.

Table 7.4: The Left and its Shares of the Whole Vote, 1928-1960 and 1938-1960

	1928-1960		1938-1960	
	Ave. Share of whole vote gained or lost by the Left in 10 changes	Ave. Rate of gain or loss to or from Left in 10 changes	Ave. Share of whole vote gained or lost by the Left in 7 changes	Ave. Rate of gain or loss to or from Left in 7 changes
Poorer City	4.57	8.69	3.70	6.60
Special Country	4.70	10.11	3.82	7.42
Large Town	5.27	13.19	3.49	7.45
Marginal City	5.23	13.56	3.89	8.86
Rural	6.11	28.38	3.51	9.40
Richer City	4.91	17.23	3.29	9.27
Farmer	6.09	40.33	3.64	10.76
All 76 European Electorates	5.21	14.42	3.45	7.72

The picture of decision-taking which emerges retains that element of paradox already noted. The political situation at an election has one impact on every section: the Left loses Y per cent of the whole or gains Z in all sections alike. It is as though all the voters, forgetting their assumptions about the parties, were considering the same features of the political situation, and it undoubtedly happens that, whatever the local balance of parties, Y moves out or Z moves in. It seems that the parties cannot single out their own supporters to appeal to and to activate. Within each section there are not as many separate juries as there are parties; 'the twelve good men and true' comprise all the electors in a section. And, as between sections, the juries in all deliver like verdicts. This likeness implies that the features which all sections are considering have been visible for a lengthy period so that they can become equally notable or notorious in all quarters. This fits the generalisation, now well established in the study of politics, that the time of decision for electors lies months and even years before election day. By the same token, an election must be principally a judgment on the past, a response to the widely known and widely felt record of the party of government. It may—very rarely—be active approval as in 1938, or it may be passive disapprobation as in 1954 or 1960, or it may amount to headlong flight from the unfortunate as in 1935. Whatever the verdict, *experientia docet*.

Besides lending support to these major conclusions, a knowledge of the rule is useful when isolating and assessing divergencies. In the author's examination of the 1960 election, for example, a high rate of loss from Labour was noted among the farmers, 'a greater *rate* of loss than in any other class of seat including the Maori.'[4] The argument there, despite this seemingly significant divergence in the rate of loss, was rested squarely on the absolute shares of the whole vote lost in each section, and they pointed to reaction among strongly Labour sections—poorer city, special country and Maori—as the prime cause of the débâcle. An acquaintance with the rule that the highest rate of loss or gain will be found in the sections where the party is weakest, confirms that the emphasis was laid on what was indeed abnormal. The 1938 to 1951 Labour loss among farmers was 46 per cent higher than the rate of loss for all European electorates. The 1957 to 1960 Labour loss among farmers was 45 per cent higher. By contrast the poorer city rate for 1938-51 was 18 per cent lower than the national rate whereas in 1957-60 it was virtually identical (13.07 for poorer city compared to 13.05 for the seventy-six electorates).

On past performance the farmer rate for 1957-60 ought to have been as high as it was; the poorer city rate should have been much lower. The signal deviation lay in the over-large share which departed from Labour in poorer city districts (-7.34 per cent, as against -5.77 per cent for all European constituencies). The displaced rate of loss was merely a companion phenomenon. Contrariwise, the farmer share lost (-5.96 per cent) was close to the national figure (-5.7 per cent) while the farmer rate of loss, far from warranting or contributing to explanation, was not unduly high but quite as normally positioned as the share itself. The finding that rate of change rises as party following diminishes is no more than the enunciation of a corollary which inevitably follows if the fundamental generalisation is true: that the share of the whole voting population of a section won or lost will tend to be equal to the shares won or lost in the other sections and thus parallelism as between the sections will be preserved. In turn this means that the prime indicator of meaningful sectional variation at an election continues to be inequality in the shares obtained.

The two questions posed at the outset have now been answered. There was a national judgment passed at these New Zealand elections; and it was sufficiently uniform to make sectional variations significant. These conclusions in turn point to the importance of reviewing the main causes of departure from the norm of parallelism. Four ways in which variation can arise stand out as worthy of close attention: third party effects; the number of candidates put up; party appeals directed at or happening to hit particular sections; and social changes which gradually modify the political view in a section.

On the face of it, the introduction of a third party reproducing the positive appeal of an existing major party, whether of Left or Right, seems improbable because needless and because it could offer only inexperienced as against experienced representatives of sectional principles and interests. Therefore new parties might be expected to put forward programmes with an unfamiliar combination of ideas and offers aimed at disrupting the existing pattern of sectional responses by drawing some sections more than others, or even at the expense of losing all attraction for others. The Country Party of 1925-35, which appeared in and appealed only to rural and farmer electorates, is a nice example of this. Sectional variation and distortion of the mirror images of the party of the Right and of the Left are then at a maximum, for any given size of third party, because interference is localised and concentrated.

This is to neglect, however, a major function of third parties, their negative role as receivers of dissidents and registrars of discontent. Again and again in the period under review the party of government found itself confronted by an animated simulacrum of itself, brandishing rather the same formulas, jigging up and down on nearly the same ground while vociferously complaining either that the Government had not carried through its principles or that it had not administered them successfully. The grey economic aftermath of Coates's rosy campaign of 1925 set the United Party on its way to the triumph of 1928.[5] The onset of the Great Depression brought forth dozens of unendorsed Reform,

United and plain unofficial Coalition candidates in 1931—a ragtag protestant company without even a different name to conceal their identity with the official Right they were opposing.[6] The prolongation of the Great Depression and the continued lack of success for the ideas of the party of the Right produced the Democrats, who shared those ideas and fitfully cried for them in their utmost purity.[7] So it was with 1954 and the arrival of Social Credit; it was the import cuts and the setback of 1952-53, not Social Credit's theoretical conundrums, which procured this heresy on the part of Nationalist supporters.[8] Each time when success for the government of the Right has gone glimmering, protest has not taken the form of a party with a fresh approach and new appeals, but has assumed instead the thin disguise of an alternative conservatism. As summed up, this is not altogether true of the appearance of Social Credit. This party did proclaim a dogmatic difference, but on the other hand it received votes from ex-Nationalists for alternative conservative reasons and very much in proportion to Nationalist strength in each section, only the richer city section yielding less than its due.

Labour's case differs. As the party of government it suffered only once from division and this is significant in itself. In predominantly conservative New Zealand it is the Right which can half-afford to split and which does support alternatives. Moreover, the Democratic Soldier Labour Party could hardly charge the parent party with lack of success but did accuse it of weariness in well-doing and timidity over principle.[9]

However, for our purposes the important likeness among the revolts of Left and Right is that the New Zealand third parties, which in this period expressed dissidence and recruited protestants, were broadly similar in appeal to the parties from which they derived. Therefore they cut into their own side instead of carving out an irregular central strip from both Right and Left. Consequently tables like 7.1 and 7.2, which show the Left by itself and therefore pick up conservative third party effects only where they eat into the Left, reveal surprisingly little distortion since the effects of such third parties tend to be confined to their own side. Even there, the alternative conservative offshoots, being broadly similar in sectional appeal to their major party, reduce the percentages that the major party secures in each section without deeply affecting its sectional composition and distancing. That this holds for Left revolts also can be seen from the following figure. On the left side a sequence of elections, 1938-1943-1946, is shown in terms of sectional percentages for the Left with which is included the Democratic Soldier Labour vote in 1943. The right side gives the sequence when the D.S.L. votes are subtracted. The overall picture is changed from a decelerating descent into a sharp fall and moderate recovery, but the sectional distancing is not greatly affected.

Figure 7.1: The Left with and without the Democratic Soldier Labour Party

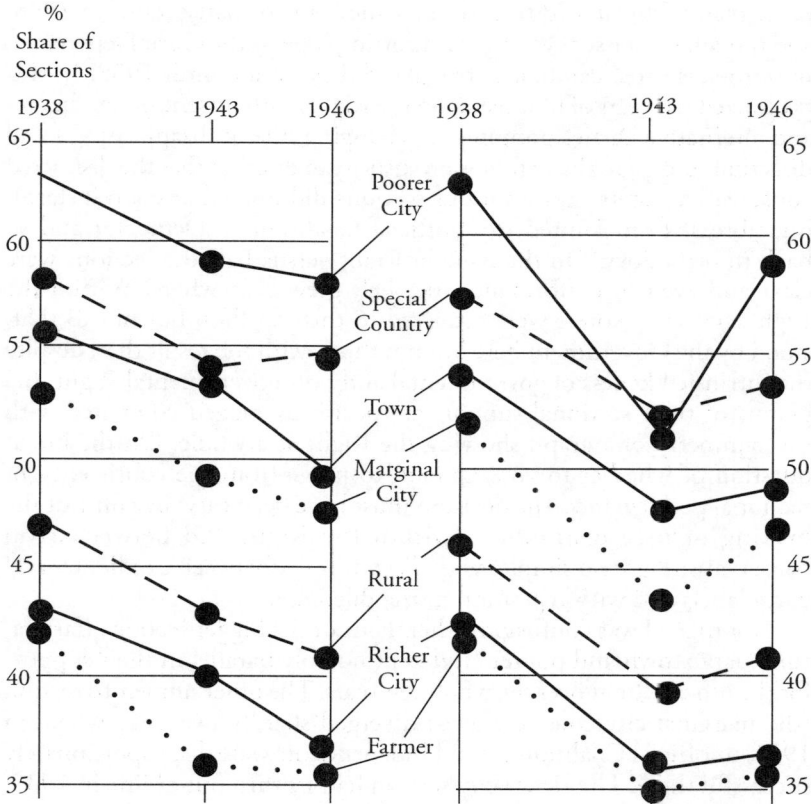

The one displacement of order is caused by the failure of the third party to appeal to or to compete in all special country electorates.[10] The fortunes of the Left, when taken as a whole, were nearly parallel in poorer city and special country electorates. But the D.S.L. did better and, conversely, official Labour was harder hit, in urban areas. Either way, the mirror image of the Right was not distorted by divisions internal to the Left.

Some points of interest and qualification should be added to this explanation of parallelism's relative imperviousness to third parties. Firstly, the situation up to 1938—essentially a three-party system breaking down—is not quite the same as the situation thereafter. The nineteen-twenties saw a major conservative party (Reform) and a minor one (Liberal/National/United) in competition with one minor radical party

(Labour). This three-party system proved remarkably resistant to being rendered down into a simple, two-party, Right versus Left system. Though the Coalition arrived in time for the 1931 election, though the radical party plainly threatened to and did achieve major party status in 1935, and though most issues were given a cutting edge by the Great Depression, nevertheless three-candidate struggles did not cease until 1938. In this protracted ten years of indecision on the Right, with dissenting candidates and alternative parties popping up, changing hue or disappearing in all directions except to the Left, it is no surprise to discover that the distracted conservative voters in the various sections did not achieve a transfer in line abreast from United to unofficial Coalition to Democrat and so back to orthodoxy. On the issue of Right versus Left the sections were clear and even in performance; the Left grew everywhere. Within the Right, however, voters were attracted to this rebellion but not to that, stood by the Government here but not there, with the result that, despite the intrinsic likeness of governmental and non-governmental Right, the graphs of their sectional support are positively ragged compared with the symmetry of a graph showing the Right as a whole. On the broad question of whether to vote Labour, to judge from the consistency of sectional performance, the decision must have been easy; by contrast the making of nice distinctions within the Right and between rival conservatisms got no simpler with discontinuity between candidates and party labels and with repetition of the dilemma.

Not that all was confusion either. Four of the bigger sections (farmer, rural, large town and poorer city) kept notably parallel in their support for the official Right over the whole ten years. The other numerous section (the marginal city constituencies) diverged sharply just once when, in 1931, unofficial Coalitionists and Independents were disproportionately successful there. The richer city section had its turn out of line in 1935. Only the special country electorates were disoriented twice, because the endorsed Coalitionists did so well in 1931 and the Democrats and oddments fared extra badly in 1935. Four definite displacements out of the twenty-one possibilities offering is not a record of anarchy in opinion, although doubtless the surcease from picking and choosing was welcome when it came.

When it did arrive, the sectional balance between Left and Right had been adjusted. Reference back to Table 7.1 will illustrate that, up till 1938, though the distancing of sections is not in disorder, there are some inversions and the starred figures are larger than the unstarred. Either in 1935 or in 1938 the sections take up the distancing which is thereafter almost constant in degree as well as in order. Two country sections (farmer and rural) shifted to the Left in 1935 by 13.27 and 13.72 percentage points as measured from the old to the new average. The three remaining urban sections (richer city, marginal city, large town) all shifted in 1938, by 5.37, 5.91 and 6.73 percentage points respectively.

What this means in party terms is that the Nationalists did not succeed to the entire share of the vote once marshalled under the banners of Reform and United. Labour permanently narrowed the gap between the most Left and the least Left sections. The result in 1935 was by no means so decisive as the enormous Labour victory in seats made it appear.[11] There was still a structural alteration to come in 1938 when the other urban sections moved closer to the poorer city section; and not until then was the new two-party system fully established.

Since 1954 a persisting three-party situation has reappeared. It is a nice paradox that the less Social Credit has made of its ideological distinctness—and with each election the party's leaders have increasingly urged candidates away from financial abstractions—the more the voters have singled that party out as having an unusual, a third appeal. Social Credit continues to be most seductive to the Right, yet it has not remained a sectional replica of the National Party. Table 7.5 sets out this process. The left-hand column for each election gives National's percentage share in each section. The middle column presents scaled-up index figures[12] of what the Social Credit share in each section would have been if Social Credit had been as strong a party over all seventy-six European electorates as National in fact was.

Beginning as a party drawing votes where National drew them, Social Credit is becoming proportionately less and less popular in the city and more attractive in the country. In 1954 its alternative conservative charms proved insufficient only in the richer city seats, whose business and

Table 7.5: The Sectional Profiles of National and Social Credit

	1954			1957			1960		
	Nat.	S.C.	diff.	Nat.	S.C.	diff.	Nat.	S.C.	diff.
Richer City	50	32	-18	54	27	-27	55	22	-33
Farmer	49	52	+3	50	61	+11	52	65	+13
Rural	48	47	-1	48	54	+6	50	61	+11
Marginal City	44	35	-9	43	24	-19	44	22	-22
Large Town	41	43	+2	42	40	-2	43	40	-3
Special Country	36	29	-7	35	44	+9	38	48	+10
Poorer City	30	36	+6	31	34	+3	33	34	+1

professional voters were apparently diverted from the pleasures of protest by the repulsion of unorthodox finance. This repulsion grew among them in 1957, when the mixed and middling marginal city voters also disproportionately withdrew their support from Social Credit. In 1960 both sections were even less drawn to the now familiar third party. Meanwhile the reverse process occurred in farmer and rural constituencies and, what is more impressive, also showed up in Labour's only extra-urban stamping grounds, the special country seats, where farmers mix with miners and timber workers.

In the course of three elections, therefore, Social Credit's support has changed profile from the likeness of one of National's immediate family in temporary revolt to the independent outline of a second cousin with set and separate purposes. As one result, the pattern of sectional support for the major party of the Right is slightly disturbed (a crossover shift of 4.39 per cent as between 1951 and 1960) in that the richer city seats replace the farmer section as the outstanding champions of the National Party. Though farmers continue to be the greatest partisans of the Right, in and after 1954 their effort is more divided than that of the richer city constituents. On the mirror figure of support for the Left, farmers remain at the bottom, since the division among the farmers remains internal to the Right. The only sign of Social Credit's irruption is that the rural section's line of support for the Left sinks fractionally below that of the richer city constituencies,[13] a possible indication that Social Credit and National added together are a trifle more attractive in the countryside than National solo would have been. In short, though a protest party has appeared on the Right, become established and evolved some individuality of appeal, third party distortion of the parallelism of either the Right or the Left remains indisputably minor, and movements of electoral opinion retain their nation-wide character.

We must turn now to investigate and estimate the effects of another potential distorter of parallelism: the number of candidates put forward by a party. The party's share, particularly the share of a fresh third party, may be small in some one section because that party runs fewer candidates than there are seats with voters ready to support the newcomer. Indeed, this reason was advanced as a possible explanation of Democratic Soldier Labour's weakness in special country electorates. To find whether this is widely true or important it is necessary to work out the individual constituency results; then, for each party in turn, select those constituencies where it stood candidates; average the percentages its candidates achieved; and compare that average with the percentage share the party obtained in all seats whether it contested them or not.

Table 7.6: Country and Independent Country Candidates

	1928	1931	1935
Number putting up	5	6	4
Average in seats contested	25.94	28.54	32.79
Share in farmer and rural sections	3.71	4.98	3.99
Share in 76 European seats	1.42	1.91	1.55

Obviously the difference between the share in all and the average in the contested seats will be most dramatic where a party runs just a few candidates in picked constituencies. As an extreme example, here is the record of one of the two special appeal third parties in this period. The importance which this party possessed within its chosen context was from fifteen to twenty times as great as its general significance and, though we cannot make even a rough estimate of what seventy-six Country candidates would have achieved, we can be certain that one result of a full slate would have been a drastic lowering of the average percentage. For in order to make a show of running everywhere, or even widely, the party would not only have had to fight entrenched members and unfavourable electorates, but would also have had to modify its particular appeals in order to spread.[14]

Other third parties, save the Communist Party, have done so and therefore a better idea of 'normal' distortion from this cause is to be had from considering the fate of a party which contested most (53) but not all (76) European seats (see Table 7.7). Here the averages do little to change the original picture of a small, notably urban party, strongest within the cities and towns wherever Labour was strongest, but undesired in the countryside even where Labour was lodged.

Table 7.7: Democratic Soldier Labour—Shares and Averages (1943)

Section	% Share	Ave. % in Contested Seats
Poorer City	7.85	7.66
Town	5.78	6.54
Marginal City	4.76	5.26
Richer City	4.32	4.57
Rural	2.77	3.78
Farmer	1.35	3.95
Special Country	1.30	3.63
76 European	4.46	5.66

The Country and D.S.L. examples bring out the unlikelihood that major trends in opinion will lie concealed from history by a third party's decision to limit the numbers of its candidates. If they are severely limited this is a guarantee that the significance of the trend will be minor, in all probability even within sections most welcoming to the party. Moreover, a small band of candidates constitutes an admission by the party that it recognises the favouring trend will prove localised and in general weak and therefore the party is shaping itself accordingly. If the limitation is mild, most of the gaps will occur where the party simply cannot find candidates because not even the eternal spring of hope in the breast of the amateur politician is able to wash away the high odds against a creditable local showing. Had candidates arisen for unpromising areas they would indeed have been smitten hip and thigh, and the sign of this is that the wider-spread parties have small spans between their averages in contested seats and their share in all, while rapidly diminishing returns are their reward in marginal sections.

Instead of a paucity of candidates especially obscuring and twisting the destiny of little parties, it seems that the record of large and established parties is more prone to upset in this way. The United revivalists of 1928 superimposed a fresh character upon a party with a traditional role, thereby investing it with a remarkably catholic if temporary magnetism. The power of this magnetism was the surprise of the election, so it is less wonder that it was under-estimated beforehand by potential candidates. Instead of seventy-six seats, fifty-seven were fought by the party, including one where two 'United' men were in contest. There is no reason to suppose that above two or three of the 'missing' candidates could have been elected; but a full slate would have brought United's 26.57 per cent share of all votes considerably nearer its 35.25 per cent average in seats contested, thus cutting a noticeable further slice from Reform and taking a sliver from Labour. This likelihood posits some indirect effect on the Left and, since the Left itself was under-manned in 1928 and 1931, it would be advisable to enquire into the direct result of this factor there.

Lumping together Labour and a fringe of Left-of-centre contestants as before, and then finding the average percentage the Left obtained in each section, we get the position illustrated by Figure 7.2. A glance confirms that taking candidates' averages instead of shares leaves unaffected the major thesis of parallelism in opinion. After a little jostling at the lower end, the sections sort themselves out in 1931 and away moves the spectrum of national opinion. One can see the farmer and the rural constituencies shift up towards the poorer city line between 1931 and 1935, and also detect the structural adjustment between 1935 and

The Response to Labour 151

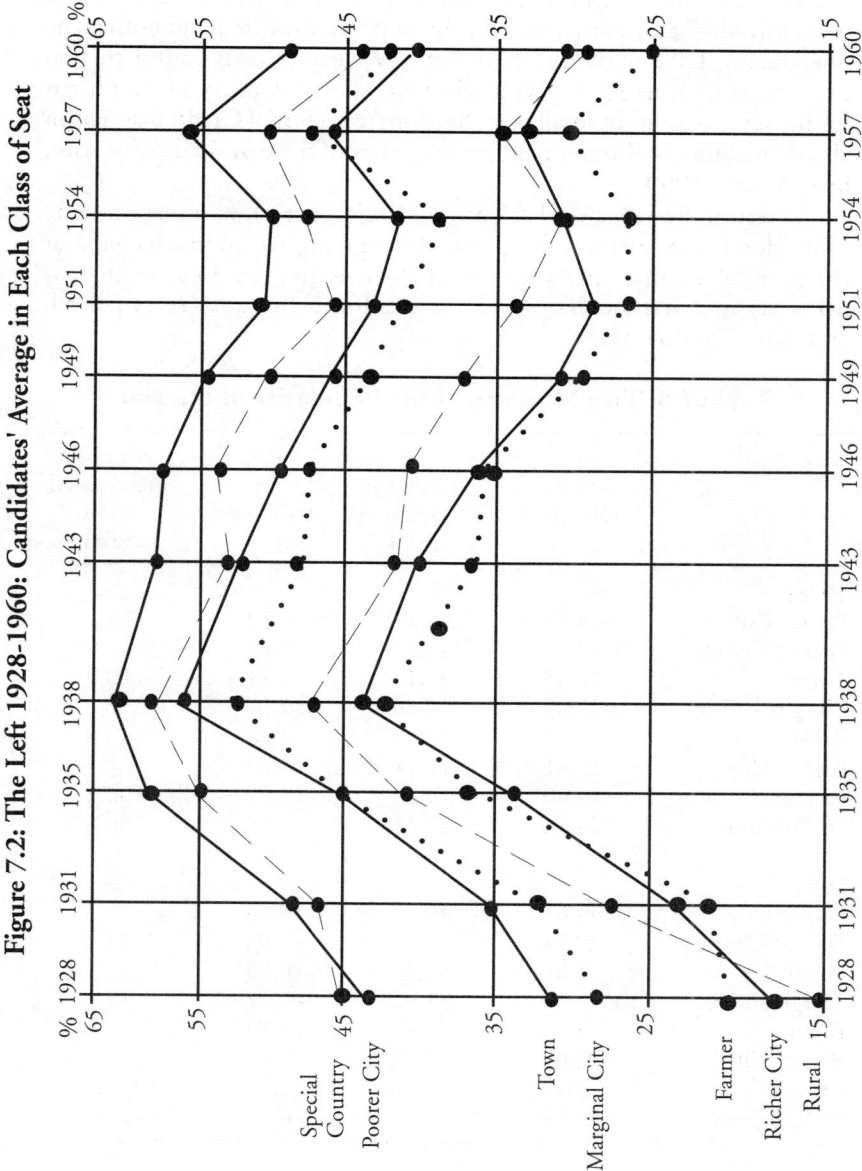

Figure 7.2: The Left 1928-1960: Candidates' Average in Each Class of Seat

1938 when large town, marginal city and richer city narrow the distance to the Labour enthusiasts at the top. The downward pull exercised by Social Credit attraction for rural and farmer electorates is visible at the bottom right-hand corner where, by contrast with its neighbours, the line tracing Labour voting in richer city electorates is found to bob upwards as early as 1954, a year when the special country section lifted for the same reason. In small part, freedom from Social Credit distraction also contributes to the comparative buoyancy of the marginal city section in 1957 and 1960.

To return, however, to the topic of candidates run, we must examine more closely the least satisfying end of the graph, its commencement at the peak of the three-party system of the twenties. To do so easily it is necessary to juxtapose shares and averages for the unsatisfactory period, and Table 7.8 does this.

Table 7.8: Two Measures of the Popularity of the Left

Section	Share Obtained	Average in Contested Seats	Difference	Number Uncontested: Total Seats
1928:				
Poorer City	43.55	43.43	−0.12	
Special Country	37.80	44.97	+7.17	1:6
Town	27.45	31.19	+3.74	1:10
Marginal City	27.85	28.09	+0.24	
Rural	10.23	15.41	+5.18	4:12
Richer City	17.41	17.11	−0.30	
Farmer	10.60	19.69	+9.09	10:22
76 European	24.74	29.62	+4.88	16:76
1931:				
Poorer City	49.09	49.12	+0.03	
Special Country	39.51	46.57	+7.06	1:6
Town	35.08	35.36	+0.28	
Marginal City	31.61	31.92	+0.31	
Rural	18.65	27.49	+8.84	4:12
Richer City	23.67	23.22	−0.45	
Farmer	9.12	21.40	+11.71	13:22
76 European	28.81	35.24	+6.43	18:76

At once an explanation is offered by the average column for certain oddities and inversions in the share column which interfere also with the regularities on Table 7.1. Instead of the farmers actually cutting their share for the Left between 1928 and 1931, according to the successive averages the popularity of the Left edged up. The very low rural and farmer share figures for both elections are revised upwards in the averages, as are the town and special country results also, so evening-up the sectional gradient from top to bottom and anticipating the harmonious gradients to come. Unfortunately, though, a simple acceptance of the averages would be unjustified and this can be shown best from the details of the special country section.

Motueka was the electorate which Labour left uncontested both times and to judge by the 1935 result, when all six special country seats were fought, it was the hardest of the class for Labour to fight. To accept the averages of the easier five seats as also representative for Motueka would, therefore, be fallacious. It would be better to recognise the 1935 performance of the constituency and work back from there.[15] By doing so, one arrives at adjusted sectional averages of 42.96 per cent for 1928 and 44.56 per cent for 1931. These percentages are no matter of revealed truth, they are products of hypothesis and may still be inflated by as much as half a per cent. But they take into account the Left's difficulties in Motueka, instead of ignoring them. All seats in farmer and rural sections were hard for the Left to fight at this time, but some were doubtless more 'impossible' than others and we must presume that, on balance, they were the seats candidates more often declined to fight. So again, the averages of those sections would come down in any realistic assessment of the sectional popularity of the Left.

Allowing for avoidance of very difficult seats thus reduces somewhat further the importance of distortions caused by failure to run candidates, even among large parties where this factor is of general moment. The figure for the potential popularity of a full slate of 76 Left candidates lies between the share and the average and, in 1928, was probably around 28 per cent and in 1931, 32 per cent, so distortion arising from the deficiency of candidates was of the order of 3 per cent in both cases.

As far as sectional parallelism is concerned, the net result of a reasonable adjustment for absent candidates would be to anticipate in 1931 precisely the order and nearly the distancing which applied in and after 1935. The 1928 adjusted result would likewise come near to all the later ones though the richer city constituencies would remain further to the Left than rural seats for the last time. Parallelism, in short, would be almost perfect, so we may conclude that one of the principal factors, if not the greatest factor in delaying the arrival of the exact political proportions of the latest era was the natural difficulty faced by Labour in finding candidates to fight hopeless battles in order to let a minority express its real preference and so enhance their party's prestige.

The third suggested way in which variation might arise, namely, through party appeals directed at or happening to hit particular sections, was the cause of nothing so striking as the interference occasioned by absent candidates. Moreover, it is not so independent a factor as to have escaped discussion already—in connection with special appeals made by third parties. When one contemplates the time and energy lavished upon designing party programmes and doing administrative favours to persuade 'the floating voter' or interest 'the farmer' or 'the unions', it is ironic that there is so little evidence of major party success in isolating and capturing these elusive beasts. 'The floating voter' escapes because, though reputed deadly, he is in truth a mythical animal, a misleading name for a quite usual voter who happens to reside in an evenly balanced seat. Perhaps this real quarry goes free because the hunters do not know where to look for or how to trap the kingly marginal in his town and suburban haunts. Probably, however, major parties suspect that too free a display of baits and nets for wild outsiders will alarm their own domesticated sections and this inhibits their hunting and renders its results so meagre.

Undoubtedly the best examples of the parties particularly affecting certain sections are recent, minor and, I fancy, not quite, if at all, what the parties intended. Figure 7.2 shows Labour leading home the town and marginal city voters in 1957. Family benefits, housing loans and the form of Labour's tax rebate cast a spell over these electors just when the economic conditions and inhibitions prevailing under the National Government were judged most trying for the urban man of the middle sort. In 1960, of course, the performance of poorer city and special country constituencies was upset when the follow through from austerity struck these sections a much resented blow.

The strike election of 1951 produced an unflattering and unequal reaction of a different sort. The figure shows Left support in the 'Labour' sections (poorer city, special country and town) descending more steeply than it did in the remaining 'National' sections. Either the Rt Hon. Sidney Holland, the champion of order, was having more effect on his opponents than on his friends, or Labour sections were uncommonly disgusted with their own party.[16] It would seem from the following table that the latter was the case. Everywhere movement went into non-voting; but Mr Nash's erstwhile supporters supplied the mass of that movement within their own sections, whereas, in the sections of the Right, between one-quarter and one-half was furnished from the conservative column, a veritable yawn in the face of the National Party's anti-militant rectitude.

Table 7.9: Origins of Non-Voters in the 1951 Strike Election

	Informal	Right*	Left‡	Non-Voting
Special Country	-0.31	-0.51	-5.01	+5.83
Poorer City	-0.33	+0.04	-4.61	+4.90
Town	-0.25	-0.12	-3.99	+4.36
Farmer	-0.21	-2.06	-3.39	+5.66
Richer City	-0.45	-2.43	-2.29	+5.17
Rural	-0.31	-1.13	-3.33	+4.77
Marginal City	-0.29	-1.14	-3.06	+4.49

* Right here includes Independent and National voters.
‡ Left here includes Communist with Labour voters.

Already this analysis of the effects of special programme appeals is turning into the measurement of specific irritations, irritations affecting so much of the general electorate that the search for the causes of variation is trenching on the main trends themselves. Before these are finally isolated there remains a last question to discuss: do departures from parallelism arise as the consequence of social change gradually altering the attitudes of sections?

When the European electorates alone are considered, the brief answer is 'not recently'. The economic and social pressures of the Great Depression bore with inexorable force upon the two conservative-one radical party system, especially in the rural and farmer sections where for decades real choices had been reduced in prevailing attitudes to two, both conservative. Between 1931 and 1935 an exceptionally rapid, not a gradual alteration of attitude drove up the line of Labour acceptance in the countryside. The Left advanced from being out of the question into the realms of imminent possibility, if not of respectability, and, as has been noted earlier, the lasting displacement amounted to between thirteen and fourteen percentage points.

Perhaps this countryman's lurch towards the Left should be taken as a fair gauge of just how considerably parallelism can be affected when social dislocations fracture set attitudes. For the multi-party situation had not yet collapsed nor had alternative conservatism been erased at the time this radical twist took place. The 1938 shift of five to six percentage points on the part of town, marginal city and richer city sections, on the other hand, did accompany the elimination of the third party. Here is an instance of the manifold and inextricably blended action of the depression in discrediting and discouraging third parties, in rendering Labour's programme relevant and in compelling electors to rethink their personal position and revise their favourite views.

Thenceforth, strongly sustained parallelism bears witness that the effects of recovery, war, boom, and the uneasy surgings of unprecedented affluence have made a fundamentally similar political impact on all sections. In a recent article, I have argued that deep social change is occurring and has been reflected in the successive rejections which governments have suffered from 1954 onwards.[17] But those rejections were the joint gestures of every section.

That generalisation is not without some truth even in respect to the eighth section, the Maori voters, for it was in 1954 that their electoral performance came haltingly and erratically into phase with the rest, for the first time since 1928. During the first three decades of the twentieth century, Maori electors had followed in the wake of European trends. To judge by results, the fact that a party held power constituted the greatest single recommendation for its candidates at subsequent elections. Personal standing—the *mana* and connections of a leader like Sir Apirana Ngata—could survive the customary withdrawal of support from M.P.s tied to the 'Outs', while calculation of tribal feeling undoubtedly assisted at the choice of candidates by parties and voters. Nevertheless, a party such as Reform, which offered less than nothing to any Maori who was not an immediate assimilationist, eventually found itself holding three out of the four Maori seats. Indeed, Reform twice retained power by courtesy of Maori Reform members, though there was no sign of their grasping and making use of the fact.[18]

It is this pattern of increasing support for 'the powers that be'—once they stood revealed by European decision—that can be found again in the thirties. The pattern is not precisely repeated because the Ratana Party (related to an intrinsically Maori church, but not bounded by it) anticipated the downfall of the Coalition and broke through the nominally European labels and fabric of the party system in Maori seats. Their first victory came at a 1932 by-election and the Ratana member, E. T. Tirikatene, in non-Maori matters spoke and caucussed with Labour. Two Ratana representatives were elected in 1935 and when the new Labour Government was established, they duly supported it. In this way instead of having to build for itself from scratch, Labour in 1938 could present and elect three Labour men.

So far the process is reminiscent of past swings towards the government of the day. Trends in the European sections have been followed, but at a distance and in a semi-detached and authentically Maori fashion. In fact, when one reflects on Ratana's innovations, the following after European trends was accomplished in a more positively Maori fashion than ever before. From that point, however, the plot is rewritten and political action, social change and alteration of political attitudes cause and reinforce one another.

In fairness to the first Labour Government one must stress that it had an overwhelming majority in the House when the two Ratana members were formally recruited to the Labour Party by agreement in 1936. Moreover, though a Labour Maori organisation dated only from 1932, Labour Maori policy was much older and was coloured by Harry Holland's enthusiastic idealism.[19] The Labour Government in its first term transformed the Maori scene when, among other such actions, it included Maoris as equal beneficiaries of welfare legislation and found money for intensified land development and Maori education. Political action therefore accompanied the final adhesion of Ratana members but preceded conclusive alteration of Maori voters' allegiance. Social change, however, was already at work. The Maori birthrate had begun to soar previously at the end of the twenties. Then the depression, by rendering rural labouring jobs desperately scarce and ill-paid, made it impossible for the old life to go on unaltered, unassisted and unconsidered.

From 1938, instead of levelling off at three Labour members comfortably returned, Labour's Maori voting strength climbed up and up. Figure 7.3 presents the comparison between the Left's share of the franchises of all Europeans qualified to vote and the equivalent Maori figures. The latter unfortunately must embody estimates for non-voters until the 1957 election when Maori voting from a roll began.[20] As some check, the Left's shares of European and Maori valid votes are supplied, their disadvantage being their inherent exaggeration of support and their distorted presentation of any trend connected with non-voting.

On the showing either of valid or of all qualified votes it is patent that Maori differed completely from European in what they did and intended at the four elections between 1938 and 1954. Furthermore, to trace the Maori figures is to see succinctly demonstrated the near-reversal of Maori voting habits themselves. If superimposed on the graph of all sections, the Maori line rises through and away from its farmer and rural associates and crosses all the other tracks until it competes with and surpasses the poorer city line in support for the Left. Likewise the Maori population during this period set out on their trek from country to city and began their transfer from rural labouring to industrial jobs.

This is not to assert that Maori voters are now urban or have grown to share the political attitudes of the city worker. What can be affirmed is that Maori voting now is at least consonant with Maori economic interests and standing, when measured by European responses. In the fifties, for example, a National Government was no more followed by the election

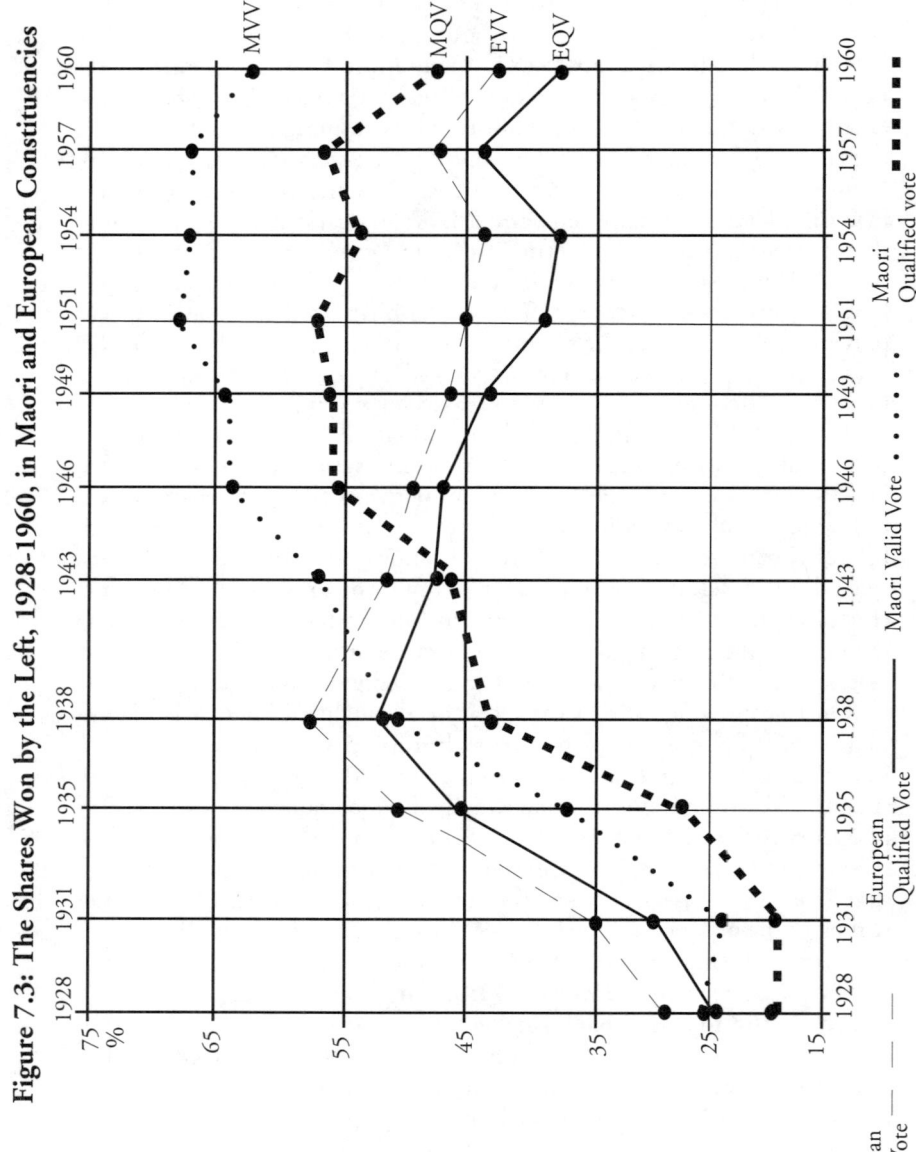

Figure 7.3: The Shares Won by the Left, 1928-1960, in Maori and European Constituencies

of Maori National members than it was followed by Nationalist victories in poorer city seats. On the other hand, Maori reactions still differ. National's onset was greeted with extra Maori votes for Labour, whereas in other sections, Labour support sank. In 1957 Labour rose comparatively slowly in Maori seats and Social Credit went up six times as fast there, instead of declining as elsewhere. The Maori rebuff to Labour in 1960 certainly accompanied a poorer city rebellion but, again, the two were quite dissimilar in cause and consequence.

Meanwhile, beneath the rough correspondences, a further contrast was manifesting itself. The gap between the number of Maori adults and the number voting has widened rapidly in recent years, nor has the new roll registered anywhere near all the Maori adults, although enrolment is compulsory. It would appear that a primary political habit of most New Zealanders is just not being taught to nor acquired by young Maoris as they move into the disorienting urban environment.[21]

Altogether, one can say that in this period the Maori voting pattern has been revolutionised and a more European style of voting by economic interest has been adopted. Yet this style continues to be modified by Maori issues, like the All Black Tour controversy; by strong Maori loyalty to benefactors, whether they be political organisations or men; and by Maori concerns, such as the Ratana concept of 'holding the four corners' (the four seats) and making the Treaty of Waitangi an organic part of New Zealand's constitutional law. The Maori voter is now meaningfully related to other New Zealand electors whom he more closely resembles in political motivation. Yet he retains his independence, his cultural possessions show in his voting, and so does the social stress to which he has been subjected. In consequence his section participates only sporadically and partially in the parallelism of the other New Zealand electors.

That parallelism of opinion is the outstanding feature of the years 1928-60. In setting it out, analysing its features and considering singularities and distortions, the electoral response to the Left and to Labour has been measured from a variety of angles. It was a nationwide response which by 1938 had, except in the Maori seats, crystallised into lasting sectional judgments which have persisted down to the most recent election through Labour's survival and defeat, recovery and rejection.

Parallelism of opinion about the Left was weaker when the full-scale three-party system of the twenties was in dissolution, when social pressures were fierce and countrymen were changing their attitudes about the Left and while Labour could not field a complete team of candidates. The last factor, in the 'difficult' country sections where seats went uncontested, depressed the Left's share by an estimated 3 to 5 per cent. An allowance for this leaves the underlying concurrence of sections all the more patent. Since the depression and Labour's social security programme of 1938, this concurrence has flourished despite challenges on Left and Right. Social Credit's slow acquisition of a particular appeal in the country has modified the distancing of the sections to a minor degree but fortunately in an explicable way. For it is precisely in terms of the regularity of sectional distancing that we are enabled to assess a government's special appeals and the localised irritations it causes. The diagnostic alarm is sounded when the share won or lost by a party in one section differs markedly from the shares won or lost elsewhere. The norm is equal movement, and the observer can concentrate on this, knowing also, however, that the rate of loss from the party's own ranks will vary inversely with the strength of that party in a given section.

Whether these characteristics hold true elsewhere is for others to test. Undoubtedly New Zealand, in the period under review, provides a remarkable example of a stable party system, which is to say, a matured organisation of political opinions capable by parallelism of repeatedly arriving at national and nearly unanimous judgments of governmental performance, while expressing in sectional distancing the varied assessment of parties held by the various kinds of electorates.

Notes

1   R. M. Chapman, W. K. Jackson and A. V. Mitchell, *New Zealand Politics in Action, The 1960 General Election,* London, 1962, especially pp. 235-64 where the method and its rationale are set out. In two senses the method has come full circle, for a sectional analysis of elections on rural/urban lines was first employed by the writer to deal with the period 1908-35, in a thesis done under the supervision of Professor Willis Airey in 1947-48.

2   'The Left' for the purposes of all graphs and tables, except Table 7.9 includes official New Zealand Labour Party candidates; 'Independent Labour'; 'unofficial Labour'; in 1928, 'Liberal-Labour'; and in 1935, Ratana candidates. Besides these, more disputable inclusions are five who ran without Labour competition: three Independents, Harry Atmore in Nelson throughout, David McDougall in Mataura for 1935 and 1938, W. Grounds in Kaipara for 1935; and two Country men for 1935 only, one Independent with Country leanings, A. C. A. Sexton in Franklin, and one Country Party man, Captain H. M. Rushworth in Bay of Islands. The Lee-ite party of 1943, Democratic Soldier Labour, is included in tables except where specifically subtracted. Two nominal Independents, C. G. Scrimgeour in Wellington Central and W. E. Barnard in Napier are classified where their known sympathies lay—as D.S.L. Reports, lists and advertisements in the *New Zealand Herald* and *Auckland Star* were the initial sources for party allegiance, checked where needed against local papers, and modified to take account of past allegiance since the voters' view, not the party's, was made primary. Raw voting figures were

drawn from AJHR [*Appendices to the Journals of the House of Representatives*], papers H-33 and H-33A in 1929, vol. 3; 1932, vol. 3; 1936, vol. 3; 1939, vol. 3; 1944, vol. 2; 1947, vol. 4; 1950, vol. 3; 1952, vol. 3; 1955, vol. 3; 1958, vol. 4; 1961, vol. 4. Percentages for 1943 are only as exact as the data for a wartime election. The qualified voters' figure taken was the sum of enrolled civilians and Armed Forces valid and invalid voters. On this see AJHR, 1944, vol. 2, H-33C. To eliminate avoidable distortion, figures were interpolated for non-vote, informal and winner for the 1931 unopposed Coalitionist victories in Pahiatua, rural; Oroua and Waitomo, farmer. For 1943 the same items plus a notional Labour candidate were interpolated in Mataura, rural; and Awarua, farmer. Interpolation was by means of projecting sectional trends forward from the 1938 electorate figures and backward from the 1946 electorate figures and taking the median point.

3 The urban percentage in the countryside was found by taking the whole population of boroughs, independent and incorporated town districts for census years (except for 1946 when an adjustment was made to adult population to conform to the then basis of representation) as shown in the *New Zealand Official Year-Books* for 1927, 1937, 1946, 1951 and 1957. These were allocated to electorates on the basis of the Representation Commissions' Reports in AJHR, 1927, vol. 3, H-45; 1937-38, vol. 3, H-45; 1946, vol. 5, H-46; 1952, vol. 4, H-46; 1957, vol. 4, H-46. Then each electorate was classified by percentage of urban to the whole population as given in the Reports, the classes being 0-39.99%, farmer; 40.00%-79.99%, rural; 80%+, either town or city.

4 Chapman, Jackson, Mitchell, p. 270.

5 R. M. Chapman, 'The Significance of the 1928 General Election' (unpublished thesis, University of Auckland), 1948, pp. 39-42, 46.

6 R. G. Habershon, 'A Study in Politics, 1928-31' (unpublished thesis, University of Auckland), 1958, pp. 100-1, 122-39, and E. P. Malone, 'The Rural Vote: Voting Trends in the Waikato, 1922-1935' (unpublished thesis, University of Auckland), 1958, pp. 153, 156-60.

7 S. Wigglesworth, 'The Depression and the Election of 1935' (unpublished thesis, University of Auckland), 1954, pp. 145-9, and G. Fraser, *Ungrateful People*, Auckland, 1952, pp. 66-7.

8 Chapman, Jackson, Mitchell, pp. 272-3.

9 J. M. Orbell, 'Politics of Prosperity. A Study of Political Opinion in Auckland City and Surrounds, 1938-1957' (unpublished thesis, University of Auckland), 1960, pp. 17-31, and F. L. W. Wood, *The New Zealand People At War, Political and External Affairs*, Wellington, 1958, pp. 129-30, 264-5.

10 As an alternative investigation, the D.S.L. percentages were ranked and correlated with 1943 official Labour, where the two competed, to see if both did well in the same places and conversely—the two correlated weakly at .218. But a moderate correlation of .464 was obtained when strength for Labour in 1938 was correlated with strength for the D.S.L. in 1943. The graph, by sorting out types of electorates, is the better analytical tool in 1943.

11 The Left as defined here elected 58 supporters in a House of 80 and there were 53 official Labour men. To do it, the Left mustered 50.25% of the New Zealand valid vote and 45.01% of those qualified to vote.

12 The Social Credit index figures simply represent the product of finding the ratio between National's vote in all European seats and Social Credit's vote there, for each election in turn, and then multiplying the relevant sectional Social Credit percentages by this fixed figure.

13 See the 1954 and 1960 columns of Table 7.1 where this graph is presented numerically.
14 Cf. pp. 184-5 of Dr B. D. Graham's article above. [The reference is to Graham's article 'The Country Party Idea in New Zealand Politics, 1901-1935' in Robert Chapman and Keith Sinclair (eds.), *Studies of a Small Democracy: Essays in Honour of Willis Airey* (Auckland, 1963), pp. 175-200. Ed.]
15 Taking the 1935 Labour percentage and subtracting sectional trends yields a notional Motueka figure of 34.52% in 1931 and 32.92% in 1928, slightly below, then above Thames, its nearest parallel in composition. Adding the notional figure to the other five in each case gives the adjusted average of 44.56% and 42.96% respectively for the section.
16 M. E. R. Bassett, 'The 1951 Waterfront Dispute' (unpublished thesis, University of Auckland), 1961, pp. 80-9, 219-32.
17 R. M. Chapman, 'New Zealand Since the War, Politics and Society' in *Landfall*, vol. 16, no. 3, September 1962, pp. 252-77. [Reprinted here as Chapter 2, 'Great Expectations: New Zealand Since the War'. Ed.]
18 S. E. McClean, 'Maori Representation, 1905 to 1948' (unpublished thesis, University of Auckland), 1952, pp. 85-91, 114, 127-8. See also Bruce Brown, *The Rise of New Zealand Labour*, Wellington, 1962, pp. 176-8, 185 n., on relations between Ratana and Labour.
19 [Harry Holland was Leader of the Labour Party from 1919 until his death in 1933. He was succeeded by Michael Joseph Savage. Ed.]
20 Maori adult population figures, either census or inter-censal estimates, were taken from *New Zealand Official Year-Books* for 1928, 1929, 1938, 1946, 1947-49, 1950, 1957, 1959 and 1960. A chain of election year estimates was formed and from these were subtracted the totals voting at each election, thus measuring the 'gap', two-thirds of which was taken to be non-voting and added to make up qualified voters, yielding this sequence of percentages for non-voting: 1928, 18.19; 1931, 21.66; 1935, 20.28; 1938, 14.90; 1943, 15.99; 1946, 10.62; 1949, 10.77; 1951, 14.47; 1954, 16.84. Officially registered non-voting for 1957 and 1960 was 14.45 and 22.91. My 1928-54 estimates may be a little low, but the official 1957-60 figures are more so. On my method, 1957 Maori non-voting was 23.13%, not 14.45%, and the 1960 discrepancy will be wider.
21 The differences between Maori valid voters and the estimated adult population: 1946, 8.3 thousand; 1949, 8.6; 1951, 11.7; 1954, 15.4; 1957, 21.8. The discrepancy between officially qualified voters in 1957 and the estimated population was 14.7 thousand, a remarkable number of unregistered voters. They should interest both the Electoral Department and parties in need of supporters.

8

The 'No Change' Election: 1963

As last night's announcer read for the 78th time that dry description 'No Change', he summed up and named the election for us all: the 'No Change Election'. Looking over the results, section by section, it is positively uncanny how, yesterday, the voters of New Zealand went out and repeated themselves. They simply conducted the 1960 election over again with about the same amount of non-voting and a total net movement of just one-fiftieth of the roll numbers. Comparing election night figures for 1960 and 1963: National is down by one-tenth of one per cent of the valid vote and has lost a seat, Labour is up by one-third of one per cent and has captured Manurewa, while the Liberals are plus what Social Credit is minus, roughly one in a hundred of all voters. Mr. Cracknell was being prophetic when he said last night that Social Credit had something in common with the Liberals.[1] They have; it is that one per cent.

No matter how undramatic this result may appear—and at first glance it does seem to be a poetically just answer to an undramatic campaign—the very sameness of the results for two elections, three years apart, is in itself startling. Such a thing is very rare indeed. I cannot recall any New Zealand election in this century which so exactly reproduced its forerunner though there was not much movement in general opinion between 1911 and 1914.

So far as parallels in the history of individual parties go, there was also almost no change for Labour between 1951 and 1954. Down to that time, at every election it had been steadily falling from its peak in 1938. Thereafter it rose and fell and now stands checked. National's popularity, on the other hand, has been much steadier, with one exception. This was the precipitous drop in 1954 when Social Credit appeared. Thereafter, even though they lost the Treasury benches in 1957, National's percentage of votes rose a little, and then a little more in 1960; so last night's fractional drop leaves them very much where they have been for the last three elections.

The familiarity of the fate of both major parties suggests that we are still in the same post-war political era that began around 1947 and which is so like the post-war nineteen-twenties, a predominantly conservative

---

[The text of this article stands as it was delivered over the N.Z.B.C. in *Point of View* on 1 December, 1963. It was published in *Comment*, Vol. 5, No. 2, January 1964. Ed.]

age, uncertain in its prosperity. There is a difference, however. Throughout the nineteen-twenties prices went up and down and government majorities went up and down with them. Throughout the fifties credit and import cuts have come on and gone off and each time the electors have struck at the party they deemed responsible. It seems to confirm the reasoning that in the absence of dramatic credit squeezes and new controls the electorate has responded in kind. The traffic light has been neither 'Stop' nor 'Go' but 'Amber'. Steady has indeed done it.

This seemingly neutral result is in fact a notable victory for the National Party, indeed much more of a victory than 1960. Then it was not so much National who won the election as it was Labour who lost it. This time the Holyoake Cabinet have prevented what the past has led us to expect—a falling off in support just so soon as a government has had a chance to show its hand. Any real falling off would have been fatal, for a general shift of anything over two per cent would have knocked the marginal seats over like ninepins. There was no general shift and the marginals are as they were.

It is all rather reminiscent of Colonel Ross's conversation with Sherlock Holmes. Ross asked 'Is there any other point to which you would wish to draw my attention?' And Holmes replied 'To the curious incident of the dog in the night-time.' 'But the dog did nothing in the night-time.' 'That was the curious incident.'

Actually last night there were two dogs that did not bark. I have discussed the absence of protest in the absence of anything immediate and notable to protest about. The other thing which was notable for its absence was any marked change in non-voting or in the total for third parties. By comparing the vote cast with the enrolled voters at each of the last three elections and then measuring the movement from one election to another it is possible to get some idea of how non-voting has varied. Unless there is some extraordinary variation in the number of special envelope votes they are counting now, which would upset my estimate, the indications are that non-voting has gone up by not quite half a per cent and that should mean an 89.5 per cent final poll. Less than half a per cent is not much more non-voting and it could prove smaller; but what *is* surprising is that neither Labour nor National, Social Credit nor Liberal have been able to lure the abstainers of 1960 out again to the polls. Normally any rise in non-voting is followed by a fall three years later in which at least half the abstainers return.

This is linked with the failure of the new Liberal party to make any real impact on the election. When Social Credit appeared in 1954 it scored eleven per cent of the valid vote. The Liberals took but 0.86 per cent. This is less than was obtained by the now forgotten Real Democracy

Movement during the Second World War. It is in fact more the sort of performance that might be expected from a number of Independents. In 38 individual attempts since the War, Independents have averaged a shade over two per cent of the votes in the seats they have contested. In the seats which the Liberal Party contested yesterday they averaged exactly three per cent. It will take a power of faith to keep the Liberals on the electoral scene after such a greeting.[2]

The communists for their part have done one-third as well as the Liberals. In the seats they fought they averaged less than one per cent— 0.9 per cent of the available vote to be precise—instead of the 0.8 of last time. Even those who fear the party most will lose no sleep over its showing at this poll nor, for that matter, at any previous New Zealand election.

If it were not for Hobson, 1963 would have been a year of little cheer for Social Credit. They were as energetic as ever. They had a personable leader. But they still sank one and a fifth per cent. Some of the slippage must naturally be attributed to the four missing candidates who neglected to get themselves nominated. However, if we drop those four seats right out of the reckoning for all parties, this only brings Social Credit's share in the remaining 76 seats to 7.96, which is a drop of 0.8.

Hobson's choice, of course, is yet to be discovered.[3] Between the early and the final result in 1957 the Social Credit percentage rose slightly. But that was when there were far fewer Social Crediters. They came second to National in Hobson in 1954 and did so again in 1960, and that year was when the large part of Mr. Cracknell's ascent was accomplished. In 1963 he has taken in another five per cent of the enrolled from Labour and one more per cent from National. It is significant that between early and final results in 1960 Mr. Cracknell's percentage was lowered a little and Mr. Sloane gained 496 envelope votes as against a Social Credit addition of 317. The past suggests a margin of perhaps 150 for Sloane but it will be, as the Duke of Wellington observed, 'a damned close run thing' in which a couple of amended booth results could reverse the whole.

Either way, Social Credit has again become more of a Country party and notably lessened its share in Maori seats. The Maori seats have again seen the most active voting movement of the whole election. Non-voting there has dropped a point, though an ever rising part of Maori abstention is hidden in failure to enrol in the first place. The nation-wide attention focussed on Eastern and Northern Maori, however, was suitably rewarded there by a four and a six point drop in non-voting and in those two seats both major parties gained in their share of all enrolled voters—the principal loser in both cases being Social Credit. Labour's sag in Maori votes has been reversed and National looks like a respectable contender in the Maori electorates for the first time since 1938.

To talk of Labour's upturn in the Maori constituencies or of National's gains there is, nevertheless, a diversion from the main point of the election. By dint of vigorous organisation and publicity on National's part and because of a number of major events that did *not* take place (by fortune, as with Britain's entry to the E.E.C.—or by design, as with the 'Steady Does It' Policy) because of all these things, nothing new happened at the elections.

I could recite the trends in all the various sections and there is a faint pattern to them, as there is when light airs strike a squadron of becalmed yachts, turning some one way and some another. In the absence of stronger forces, for instance, being sitting members who attend to their correspondence did assist candidates a little. Examining the trends for sitting members, regardless of party, there is, over the whole country, a shift by 0.9 per cent of the voters from being against to being in favour of their representative. Small as this movement may be, it was *above* average in 1963.

The waves and troughs of recent years have been reduced to microscopic and contradictory cross-currents affecting individual electorates and there they may safely be left for the entertainment of the specialist.

Those who thought that empty halls and departed audiences meant a measure of content with the status quo were correct. New Zealand's great debate about economic growth and how best to secure it—the contemporary theme first in the U.S.A., then in Britain, now in New Zealand and Australia—has had to be squeezed through television tubes and out of loud speakers. Fortunately, at least the M.P.s were listening to their opponents and we may all yet benefit indirectly from the liberal economic education some of them dispensed.

But I do not feel it was future growth or future taxes which stayed the hands of the electors yesterday. If such a maestro of the art of politics as Sir Robert Menzies chose right now as a good time for governments in the South Pacific, he had his reasons and we have seen them displayed here and over there.[4]

Notes

1 [Vernon Cracknell led the Social Credit Party through three general elections, 1963, 1966 and 1969. He was MP for Hobson between 1966 and 1969. The Liberals were a 'new fringe, ultra-conservative' party. See Chapman, 'From Labour to National', in W. H. Oliver, (ed.), *The Oxford History of New Zealand* (Oxford and Wellington, 1981), p. 365. Ed.]

2   [By 1966 the Liberals were 'defunct'. Austin Mitchell, *People and Politics in New Zealand* (Christchurch 1969), p. 163. Ed.]
3   [Vernon Cracknell failed to secure Hobson in 1963, losing to the National incumbent, Logan Sloane. Ed.]
4   [Sir Robert Menzies, Leader of the Australian Liberal Party, was federal Prime Minister of the Liberal/Country (now National) coalition government between 1949 and his retirement in 1966. Ed.]

9

The 1969 Election

Two points should be made clear at the outset of this analysis. First, all the comparisons are made on the basis of election-night figures for 1966 and 1969—a procedure I have followed in broadcasting about elections since the 1950s. Thus the changes are properly comparable and every 1966 figure has also been adjusted to allow for the boundary changes which took place between the two elections. Secondly, the percentages I use are based on the total roll so that everyone is allowed for, both voters and non-voters alike. The common practice is to base percentages only on those who actually cast a valid vote. This inflates the popularity of parties and obscures the true movement of the vote which, as a net movement, can often go into, or come out of, non-voting and so affect the result as it did yesterday. Yesterday the non-vote dropped 2.0 per cent. At the same time Social Credit dropped twice as fast, providing a further 4.2 per cent of the roll to go elsewhere. And the accurate measure of Social Credit's decline is that it went from 11.5 per cent of the roll in 1966 to 7.3 per cent in 1969. Thus Social Credit lost well over a third of all the support that it once possessed. Between them, the two victors of the 1966 protest election, the Social Credit League and the Non-Vote party, have both suffered a defeat this time. Meanwhile Labour and National have both gained as has the Independent vote, in the ratio of three Labour to two National to one Independent.

For some time I have been studying this tendency for the two main parties to move in tandem, and I do not think it has previously been commented upon. It is a very important characteristic of our politics. One should not think of a swing between the major parties so much as expecting them mostly to climb or fall together but at different speeds, while third parties and Non-voting do the same thing but in the opposite direction. During the 1950s and 1960s it has been particularly associated with the appearance of Social Credit as a party which thrives on local discontent and temporary protest. This is not to suggest that Social Credit's candidates and stalwarts do not have very firm beliefs to uphold, for they do. Rather, it is to point out that many of those who voted for the League in 1954 and in 1966 —its two bumper years—have gone in

---

[This chapter is the text of Robert Chapman's analysis of the 1969 election results, broadcast the night after the election. It was subsequently published in *Comment*, Vol. 10, No. 4 (April 1970). Ed.]

at one election and come out at the next. The Party has thus proved to be more of a revolving door than the entry for a new Parliamentary force.

The defeat of Mr Cracknell on Saturday is likely to prove a mortal wound to the party's hopes for it reveals how little the League has achieved in and out of Parliament in 15 years of effort.[1] Its general decline in its favourite rural seats, which amounted to a loss of 4.2 per cent, also disposes of the helpful prophecy that the Party was bound to grow and was therefore worth supporting. This loss among the farmers was only exceeded by Social Credit's 4.9 per cent drop in the secondary centres in New Zealand, the towns like Wanganui, Hamilton and Nelson which exist partly to service the farmers. There was a sense in which Social Credit was hoping to serve partly as a country party. That hope has now dissolved and the votes so released have flowed back towards the main parties and, in particular, towards Labour.

This flow is not absolutely even all over New Zealand because Social Credit had been differently composed in the various electorates, comprising more ex-Labour voters here and more ex-Nationalists there. Moreover, when they came out of Social Credit they did not always return to their former party homes. But overall, it is clear that Labour gained more than National from the process and stands to profit further in 1972 if the process continues now that Social Credit has lost its toehold in Parliament and is seen to be in general decline. For 15 years the unintended effect of Social Credit has been to muffle and absorb the impulses towards movement between the major parties. Originally very strong impulses, such as that against National in 1954 or towards Labour in 1957, have been damped down into no real change in Parliamentary strength or a weak majority of one. Since the equally strong rejection of Labour in 1960 there has been very little electoral change either in 1963 or in 1966. This time the quite drastic shifts in the towns in 1969 are portents of what could happen once Social Credit is no longer numerous enough to absorb all the action out of New Zealand politics. It is one of the ironies of our time that Social Credit's demand for new men and new policies has had the effect of retaining the same men and the same policies in power.

The Prime Minister, however, can justly claim great credit for the fact that the Cabinet he leads has gathered in enough of Social Credit's departed following to keep him and his Party in office.[2] Taken overall, the 60s have been prosperous. Yet they contained enough economic ups and downs to have unseated a less seasoned and flexible rider. Above all, National has held on in the cities where price rises, housing costs, and the growing strains on the education, health and welfare systems might have been expected to tell against the Government. In the 22 poorer city seats of New Zealand, which remain Labour strongholds, National nevertheless went up 3.1 per cent while Labour rose only 2.6 per cent. Even more vital for National's survival last night was the fact that, in the 11 marginal city seats, National rose 3.1 per cent to Labour's 1.9 per cent rise. It is, therefore, appropriate that in the four richer city seats this tendency reached its climax with National rising 4.1 per cent compared to a 1.5 per cent Labour rise. In all classes of city seats National did better than Labour out of the declining Social Credit and Non-Vote, but the more well-to-do the seat was, the more this was true. Apparently National's division of the fruits of affluence contented more people than it discontented.

By the same token, Labour, which in my opinion had just too much new policy for any party to put over, has obviously failed to put all that policy over, even to its own supporters in the cities. This was the old-fashioned aspect of Labour's effort, arising naturally as it does from Labour's huge accumulation of policy points which are added to annually by their Conference. On the other hand, Labour did gain absolutely if not relatively in the cities, and it did gain a new stature for its leader. The polls reveal the rapid rise of Mr Kirk and computerised factor analysis suggests that, while only a few points of Labour's policy did much to sort the voters out, Mr Kirk himself was a prime factor in the gains scored by his party.[3] The arena of television and the vigour of Labour's advertising made this possible. We might well look back on 1969 as the real opening of the age of television politics, as it was of public opinion polling and of public questioning and confrontation brought into the living room. All these fresh technical aids to democratic participation have arrived in time to offset the increasing de-personalisation of a mass urban age. Both parties will need to match the quality of their candidates to the opportunities and dangers which these developments bring with them. The victory of the Government suggests that its team, taken together, in the end overcame the impression created by Mr Kirk, helped by some among his associates.

So much then for city New Zealand—probably contented on balance and possibly fearful of demonstrations and industrial trouble on their door-steps. When the election results are analysed, however, there stands revealed another New Zealand, a discontented New Zealand. It is the New Zealand of the regional centres, of the countryside, of the South Island, and of the Maoris. Taking the last first, everybody in the Maori seats except the Independents made their contributions to Labour. Maori non-voting dropped 3 per cent, Social Credit went down 1.3 per cent and National declined 1 per cent. Just as Social Credit's rise was delayed for three years among Maori voters from 1954 to 1957, so its full decline seems to have been delayed this time. What is more notable is that only in the Maori seats did National join Social Credit in going down. The issue which has been very much alive in all the Maori constituencies has been the Maori Affairs Amendment Act of 1967.[4] Labour's opposition to it and its pledge to alter that Act have been duly rewarded. Despite some able National candidates and despite the Government's pledge to contemplate revision of their own Act, the National vote has suffered.

Turning to the 14 towns such as Napier and Hastings we find a 4.1 per cent Labour rise and only a 1.9 per cent rise for National. Whereas, formerly, National was 2.8 per cent ahead of Labour, it is now only 0.6 per cent ahead in these seats, and this despite the outpour of Social Credit votes in Wanganui towards National. It seems likely that the secondary towns are registering a deep unease about whether they have been left out of the development of New Zealand. Labour's emphasis on decentralisation of industry, on secondary centres, and its particular attention on regionalism in local government, on technical institutes and community colleges for the secondary centres and its particular attention to campaigning and to candidates for these towns have garnered votes. Had the party possessed a similar kind of specialised appeal for the marginal city seats it might well have turned out the Government. Indeed, the first marginal city finals to come through, such as St Albans in the South Island, suggested that this might be the case. However, Auckland and Wellington in the North Island soon put a stop to such speculation.

The analysis of the way the trends differ in the North Island from those in the South Island also shows the real discontent of the South Island at being, in its opinion, left out of the rush towards development. In the North Island as a whole, Labour gained 2.7 per cent to National's 2.6 per cent. In the South Island, Labour gained 3.7 per cent to 0.9 per cent for National. It is plain here again that Labour shaped its policies and campaigned assiduously to obtain this result. Even Mr Holyoake's hint that the South Island might expect some new cabinet ministers was unable to erase the impression that Labour's programme offered a change from which the South Island would benefit.

In the countryside, where National has always been the strongest party and from which most of its cabinet ministers come, Labour gained at four times the rate of the Government. With National now standing at 40.6 per cent of the roll and Labour at 27.6 per cent, National need not fear to be dispossessed in its heartland. Just the same, National will have to heed the warning that there is not much pleasure being taken in the way things are going for the farmer.

There is a special division of this discontented rural New Zealand, Northland. In this election much the same motivation produced three quite different results. In Hobson itself the desire to get something done and to have effective representation moved the voters to replace Mr Cracknell by Mr Sloane. Social Credit was down 5.8 points, Labour was up 3.9 points, and National up 1.6. Voters in reply to a questionnaire stressed their need for better communications of every sort, better education and more development. In the Marsden electorate, which contains Whangarei, Labour collected 8.9 points in nearly equal shares from Social Credit, National and Non-Vote. In displaying this trend, Whangarei was representative of regional centres elsewhere in the Dominion. The last of the trio is Rodney, and here all that was achieved was a stand-still. Northland in general simply underlines that the return of the Government has been accompanied by due notice of discontent from the New Zealand outside the cities and below Cook Strait.

As another expression of this dissension some 2.2 per cent of the Rural vote went to Independents of one kind or another. This was the largest effect produced in any section of the New Zealand electorate as a result of this year's super-abundance of Independent candidates. Altogether Independents drew 19,347 votes which was 1.3 per cent of the total roll. The five members of the Women's Independent Party picked up 742 as justification for their television time.[5] The W.I.P.s averaged 0.8 per cent of the roll in the seats they contested. The Independent left took 1.0 per cent in its seats; the Independent right, 0.7; and the 15 Country Party candidates averaged 2.9 per cent.

Only Mr Dallas of Westland and Mr Ryan in Grey Lynn had any effect and that effect was to lower Labour majorities in overwhelmingly safe seats. Probably it was the very safety of these seats which led the voters to consider that they could afford to register discontent with their situation. In Westland, National dropped 8.3 points, Labour 7.8 and Social Credit 7.7, all contributing evenly towards the 27.1 per cent scored by Mr Dallas. In Grey Lynn, Social Credit was down 4.4 and Labour 9.6 to help bring Mr Ryan up to exactly equal J. A. Lee's percentage in the same seat 20 years before. The Independents, of course, are exceptions by definition.

What has more meaning is the socially significant trend which can sometimes be detected. In the 1969 election one such development helps to account for one of the election's real surprises—Labour's loss of Waitemata. The trends here are strikingly parallel to the trends in Tamaki and in Pakuranga. In Waitemata, a young and energetic Labour candidate saw his vote drop 0.8 per cent while National gained 8.6, largely at the expense of Social Credit. In Tamaki, Labour was down 4.3 while National rose 7.9. In Pakuranga Labour's shadow Minister of Finance, Mr Tizard, gained 0.1, National rose 6.4, and Social Credit dropped 3.8 per cent. In each case National had a strong candidate. But strong National candidates elsewhere did not profit so heavily.

The cause more probably lies in the fact that these three electorates contain the busiest builders of 'executive homes' in Auckland. Labour, it should be noted, had already obtained its three new strongholds on the outskirts of Auckland and Wellington as a political by-product of low-cost housing. The strengthening of Tamaki, Labour's loss of Waitemata, and the shakiness of Pakuranga are the other side of the same coin. National can benefit from the more expensive housing. In those three electorates National gained 7.2 per cent overall and Labour dropped 1.4. In the remainder of Auckland, National only gained 3.4 per cent and Labour gained 1.0.

It is still true to say, however, that Auckland did not maintain the rise in Labour sympathies which it had registered in 1966. It may be significant that the scene of the noisiest demonstrations at public meetings and the home port of most of the strike-bound Union Company vessels was also the city which contained one of Labour's losses and was the scene of its most tightly-fought marginal battle. Some of the demonstrators no doubt regard the victory of either party as irrelevant. Probably many of the seamen and the numerous other workers who took industrial action during the campaign are quite indifferent to its effects on the fortunes of the Labour Party. The only indications that we have of an adverse effect is the different response to Labour and National registered in Auckland from the response found elsewhere in the country.

Interestingly enough, this also neatly accounts for the difference in the findings of the two kinds of poll taken by the National Research Bureau. The country-wide poll in November corresponds remarkably well with their findings of gains for both major parties, a 3 per cent rise for Labour, the parties 'level pegging', the fall for Social Credit, and the drop in the non-vote. In the country as a whole these all came true. The check poll of 500 in Auckland showed the situation there to be distinctly more favourable to National. Though it was a little over-estimated, substantially that, too, was realised. Moreover, the publication of polls earlier in the year showing a quite different situation did not have a bandwagon effect which prevented the trends from changing.

In conclusion, it can be seen that Mr Holyoake has won his fourth term with an encouraging overall rise of 2 per cent which yet conceals some warnings that there is a New Zealand outside the cities which wants the attention of his Government. National has been confirmed and the politics of the sixties are to go on into the early seventies At the same time Mr Kirk and certain of Labour's programmes have received a rather stronger endorsement than was accorded to National. Labour can see that what was modern in its approach succeeded and that what was not, did not. The deflation of Social Credit has opened up the possibility of a very different kind of politics after 1972. It may not come about. But the verdict of 1969 was an open one. It holds the promise of decisions which will produce political activity and change instead of the muffled compromises of voting intention characteristic of three-party systems.

Notes

1 [Vernon Cracknell, the Social Credit Leader, held Hobson between 1966 and 1969. Ed.]
2 [The Prime Minister was Keith Holyoake, Leader of the National Party between 1957 and 1972. Ed.]
3 [Norman Kirk was Leader of the Labour Party between 1966 and his death in 1974. He was Prime Minister between 1972 and 1974. Ed.]
4 [This Act 'gave the Maori Trustee compulsory power to purchase "uneconomic" interests in Maori land of under £50 .... [and] decreed that Maori land held by fewer than four owners lost its designation as Maori land and had to be registered in the Land Transfer Office in the same status as European land.' Ranginui Walker, *Ka Whawhai Tonu Matou. Struggle Without End* (Auckland, 1990), p. 139. Ed.]
5 [The Women's Independent Party campaigned on issues concerning women's rights. It did not reappear in later elections. Ed.]

10

The 1975 Result: How did it Happen and Why?

There are three questions which the dramatic reversals of the 1975 election pose for New Zealanders: Who or what did it? Just how did it happen? Could it happen again in reverse? The answers could hardly matter more for public or private life, for the overturn at the polls has been followed by equally lurching turns in economic, social and foreign policies.[1]

The committed zealot for a 'no growth society now' will argue that turns of much less than 180 degrees are insufficient, just as the economic socialist will maintain that these are mere zig-zags within the old, familiar, private enterprise-state capitalist mixed economy.

But such voices are few in New Zealand. All the independent Left and Marxist candidates in the 1975 election, for instance, secured between them only six ten-thousandths of the qualified vote.

Published polls on party standings throughout 1975 indicated that a reversal had already occurred over the 1974-75 summer and that it was becoming worse. Given the persistently gloomy state of our trading partners' economies during 1974, and the length of their unemployment lines for twelve months past, it appeared likely that New Zealanders were turning from one political side to the other in their growing anxiety about what would happen when the economic storm reached this country. By late January 1975 my own opinion was that only a sudden hard budget in March, followed by an election late in April or early May, could have saved the Government—albeit with the loss of seven or eight seats.

As the months and the polls wore on, it grew even more clear that the Leader of the Opposition had understood exactly how central anxiety about the economy would prove to be. In his campaigning around the country he employed his every skill to enlarge that central worry and supplement it with anxieties about law and order, immigration, union militancy, the welfare system, and the Government's role.

[This chapter includes five of the articles Robert Chapman wrote for the *National Business Review* and published during 1976. Chapman proposed the idea of a post-election survey to the Heylen Research Centre, designed the questionnaire and analysed the data which provided the basis for the articles. The titles of the omitted articles are indicated in footnotes to the text. Ed.]

He could not have made bricks without straw; the worries and resentments were there. Moreover the turnabout in party standing had already taken place, and it was Muldoon's aim to get every last seat possible out of that turnabout.

The surveys I jointly designed for TV1, with the help of the Heylen Research Centre, deliberately concentrated on public attitudes to major issues in the long campaign, not on the outcome. Two nationwide surveys were conducted—one in September and one in November—and they provide background to these articles. But the foreground is supplied by a third survey, planned well before the election for administering immediately afterwards. It was conducted in the week following the election before the public's memory of what it had just done—and its reasons—had been given time to fade or to be rearranged in the light of the consequences.

The electors were asked about the issues they considered had influenced them, and the roles of various factors—from party leader to local candidate—were enquired into. A second line of questioning concerned which party the electors had expected to win, both nationally and locally, and whether, if they had anticipated the real outcome, they would have acted any differently.

A third major element to be explored was the stability of the elector's party preference. How had she or he voted—not just in 1975, but in 1972 and 1969? In 1969 it was Holyoake vs Kirk; in 1972 Marshall vs Kirk; in 1975 Rowling vs Muldoon. With such a kaleidoscope of leaders how had party loyalty fared? Were New Zealanders still generally committed to their parties, regardless of coming and going issues and leaders? There were now two minor parties: could minor parties likewise count mainly on loyalty? After two landslides in seats was volatility increasing? Just which portion changed their minds, and was change alone the characteristic of what political pidgin English has labelled 'the floating vote'?

To answer such questions one must sort out the possibilities. A voter could be three times a National, Labour, or Social Credit voter, or a non-voter. They would all constitute stable preferences. To give Values an even chance, an elector voting for it in the last two elections would need to count as stable, remembering that Values' stable element would be rather reduced by the absence of candidates outside the cities in 1972.

New voters in 1975 had no opportunity to be constant or inconstant, so they made up a separate class of voter.

Then there were several ways in which those eligible might change. They might have changed between '69 and '72 and then stuck to their new-found guns in '75. This analysis calls them 'new stables'.

Another group could have left their party in 1972 but returned to it in 1975. They are here known as 'returners'.

Those who kept to one choice in 1969 and 1972 but then changed in 1975 were christened 'new changers'.

Finally those who lived out the metaphor of 'floating' constantly from one choice to another, made up the fourth group who are pinned down as 'entirely unstable'.

Altogether there are 28 categories, but the first thing to discover is how the New Zealand voter splits between the major types of stable, new, and changing voters. This survey gives these key figures as 53.6 per cent of stables, 13.1 per cent of new voters and 33.3 per cent of changers. The figure for new voters was much enlarged in 1975 by the extension of the franchise from twenty- to eighteen-year olds. In any event it is a matter for the future whether or not they will settle into a steady preference. So, setting them all aside, we get the final balance of 61.6 per cent stables and 38.4 per cent changers of one or another type.

This is a high figure for changers in the light of New Zealand research by Brookes, Mitchell, Robinson and others working normally at single or twin-electorate level.[2] Likewise overseas studies suggested that until quite recently about 70 per cent of voters could be relied on to remain loyal to one party from the time of first regularly voting until they or their party disappeared from the scene. From late in the sixties, however, reports of increasing instability or 'volatility' in voting have been coming in from many countries.

It is a phenomenon which has accompanied increased secondary and tertiary education, new and surprising levels of inflation, great but often disappointed economic expectations, rapid change in family patterns, and demands that new men and fresh solutions should emerge with extravagant speed from the aged party structure.

There may be a special element of coincidence in that New Zealand in the fifties was markedly unstable compared with the forties. Then came Keith Holyoake, the consensus maker, whose whole triumph was to dampen down issues and differences into a monotonous series of tight but very real victories. Then came Kirk and the politics of change, to be followed by polarisation practised as high art. Perhaps it is little wonder that, for local reasons, we have now caught up with our larger brethren overseas after the Holyoake lull.

But where does this leave our parties large and small in respect to their loyal core? If volatility is the sign of the times, are National and Labour equally well placed in basic support for the next round? Or was the third Labour Government, like the second, merely an interruption in the rule of a party with a natural majority, one with a constant edge in loyalists over its rival?

The answer lies in the graph which shows the percentages by parties, of all stable voters over three elections or, in Values' case alone, over two. The majors are within 0.4 per cent of one another.

With all those changers to be wooed and won, not to mention the next crop of new voters, 1978 is plainly no foregone conclusion. The tiny proportions of those constant to the minor parties—of which the most important is certainly non-voting—confirm that Social Credit is indeed a revolving door, filled and emptied afresh at each election, and that Values, as yet, has much the same character. So the survey has already answered one of the key questions posed at the start—yes, it could happen again in reverse.

Figure 10.1: Party Percentages of All Stable Voters, 1969-1975

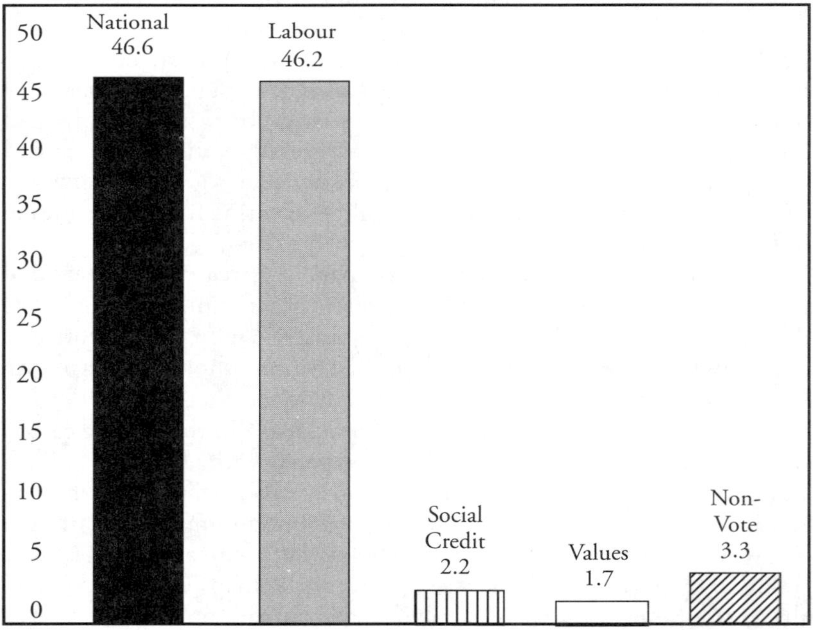

Party	Percentage
National	46.6
Labour	46.2
Social Credit	2.2
Values	1.7
Non-Vote	3.3

The Stable Voter: Predictability and Surprises

Given that National and Labour were within 0.4 per cent of one another in Heylen's post-election survey among the largest segment of the electorate—the stable voters—just who can the parties count on? What kinds of people vote consistently for the two parties of government? How do the usual social descriptions like education, occupation and income sort them out?

Is New Zealand unusual in the social shape of its National versus Labour contest when compared with Conservative versus Labour in the United Kingdom or even Republican versus Democrat in the United States?

A clear and straightforward contrast between the categories which regularly support each major party in New Zealand is provided by taking each category, say all women stable voters, finding the percentage of them for National and for Labour respectively, and then noting the majority of one party over the other—in this case 6.3 percent to Labour. By contrast the men show a majority for National over Labour of 7.7 percent.

It is not what one would have expected. Western European experience associates a small edge for conservatism with women voters, and all four New Zealand university studies of one or two electorates found women slightly more National orientated than men.

But the Heylen survey's New Zealand-wide finding could well be associated with a second finding that men are slightly more and women slightly less inclined to become changers, especially in 1975. That point connected in turn with a third finding that men favoured Rob Muldoon more than did women. Moreover, the issues which have flowed right through the three elections of 1969, 1972 and 1975—inflation, price control and subsidies; the state of the economy in general; or the best party to care for welfare problems—may well have impinged differently on the sexes.

The findings in this survey may reflect that men set more store by the general economy and on balance favour National, while women bother more about prices and welfare and maintain a lean towards Labour.

Age is another dimension on which parties divide, although again not sharply except at the start. The age group 18-21 contains very few who have been voting long enough to be stable, but their majority for Labour over National is 36.9 per cent.

The advantage reverses among the much larger category from 25-39, in which National leads by 8.1 per cent.

There is another switch in the next group of 40-54-year-olds where Labour is ahead by 3.5 percent while in the final group of 55-and-over, National just wins by 0.7 per cent.

The figures fit the concept that we carry forward in our voting habits of a lifetime an inclination towards the party which dominated politics when we were being politicised by parental, home and lesser influences.

David Butler, an Englishman, and Donald Stokes, an American, showed it operating in the UK, and it appears to characterise our stable voters too.[3] The 25-39-year-olds with a National lead would have been from 0-13 years old when National began its first period of office in 1949.

Likewise the 40-54-year-olds showing a Labour edge would have been 0-14 years old when Labour began its 14-year run in 1935. Only the 55- and-over group, whose early years saw Reform, United and Labour in three-way competition until Coalition and the Great Depression ended their lessons, have contrived to end up appropriately in the middle.

Sex and age are not great party dividers. The factors of education, occupation and income are—even in a country like ours with a pronouncedly homogeneous past.

Taking education first, the stable voters here with only a primary education give a 43.6 per cent lead to Labour over National. That large segment, with some secondary education but no certificate, put Labour ahead by 24.6 per cent. National draws in front by 14.2 per cent with those who ended their education at School Certificate. Among those who have obtained technical or trade certificates, National's majority drops a little to 10.3 per cent; but then climbs to a commanding 50.0 per cent with those who completed at matriculation or UE level.[4] Among the rather larger group who lay claim to professional or university training, National's margin is less, at 36.6 per cent, but still great.

Obviously education interacts with occupation and income so that these indices are also likely to show similar contrasts. Less obviously, however, age and the generation-of-politicisation effect have reinforcing links with education. Those in the 55-and-over bracket and some towards the top of the 40-54 age group are far more likely to have had only a primary education.

The surge of sixth-form and tertiary education in the 1960s interlocks with the experience of National preponderance among those stable voters in their twenties and early thirties.

Turning to occupation, there is a sharp but meaningful gradient from 'other', including students (Labour majority 61.6 per cent), through 'Manual worker' and 'semi-skilled' (Labour 35.3 per cent), to 'craftsman/ skilled tradesman' (Labour 31.2 per cent), 'housewife' (Labour 12.5 per cent), and 'clerical, sales and service' (Labour 6.0 per cent). It is only within the category of 'retired or pensioner' that we pass over to a National majority (6.2 per cent).

Then comes a cliff-like climb to National's majority of 56.4 per cent within the surprisingly populous category of 'administration, managerial, directorial and professional'. It is worth stressing that this group is so big

(22 per cent of all stables) and so enthusiastically National that, in alliance with the retired, it just outbalances the political effect of all the rest of the occupations put together.

Lastly we consider income. All goes simply from under $2000 per annum (Labour majority 21.8 per cent) up to $2-3000 (Labour 10.0 per cent) and $3-4000 (Labour 6.2 per cent) and so over the dividing line to $4-5000 (National majority 10.0 per cent). But then the gradient reverses abruptly and we go back to the Labour camp for $5-6000 (Labour 21.7 per cent) and $6-8000 (Labour 8.7 per cent). Again the line climbs and crosses the divide for $8-10,000 (National 10.1 per cent) and so up to $10-12,000 (National 20.7 per cent). Finally it shoots up to $12,000 and over (National 57.1 per cent) and ends with 'refuse to say' at a National majority of 76.2 per cent.

So the whole political response to personal income is double-peaked.

The first peak records the political response of the great majority of women, young and old. First come those working at home, or studying, or on benefits. Then there are those with part-time or low-paying jobs in services or manufacturing. Towards the upper reaches of office work women move into incomes which are just average for the semi-skilled and skilled male.

The second peak describes principally the political responses at various levels of male income earning. Both peaks are far from exclusive to one or the other sex but it is a matter of more or fewer women or men. The levels of the second peak between $5-8000 are Labour levels.

Beyond that, the National majorities increase as one climbs the income slopes towards the icy crags of 'refuse to say'.

In all this New Zealand is not in the least unusual. Labour parties in Australia or Britain are parties of the 'have-less' (to quote Austin Mitchell's modification of 'have-nots') while the Conservative, Liberal, Country and National parties are *per contra*, parties of the 'have-more'.

Seymour Lipset demonstrates in *Political Man*[5] that, despite all the rugged independence of party consistency and principle displayed by US Senators and Representatives, American voters nevertheless approach British or New Zealand levels of correlation between socio-economic factors and party preferences. Everywhere those correlations are far from perfect. At under $2000 or over $12,000 these percentages given are only majorities.

There is a minority of National voters at the base of the income heap as there is a Labour-voting proportion at the top. It is one of the arts of politics to enlarge those minorities and to lever more than your fair share from categories mainly committed to the other side.

The Changers: Who Won and Who Lost in November '75

Last week we saw that it is possible to get an excellent picture of where the returners came from and went back to. But with what party did the new changers spend 1969 and 1972, and where did they end up in 1975?[6]

Table 10.1 shows us the pattern. The column on the left demonstrates that Labour was the great loser in supplying well over half of the new changers followed by non-vote with just over a fifth, and National with just under a fifth. Social Credit, starting low, lost less and only to National.

Table 10.1: Movement of New Changers, 1974

	Total %	to Nat	to Lab	to SC	to Val	to N-V
from Nat	19	n.a.	4	3	9	3
from Lab	56	28	n.a.	13	11	4
from SC	3	3	0	n.a.	0	0
from N-V	22	9	5	2	6	n.a.
Total %	100	40	9	18	26	7

Nat — National Party
Lab — Labour Party
SC — Social Credit
NV — Non-Voting
Val — Values Party

Exactly half of all the ex-Labour voters went to National and it is interesting that ex-Labour changers marginally preferred Social Credit to Values given that they had decided to leave Labour. The ex-Nationals, by contrast, put Values well ahead and even placed Labour ahead of Social Credit.

Those who had not voted in 1969 and 1972 were not so decisively for National as the ex-Labour people. Indeed, amongst those past non-voters two-thirds as many saw virtue in Values as saw it in Muldoon's campaign, while over half as many saw Rowling and his Government as worth emerging to support. Only Beetham's Social Credit showed little power of attraction for them.[7]

Simply looking along the line at the bottom of the table to compare final party gains can produce an illusion, however, as to which party was the net victor. It leaves out of account, for example, that Values did not exist in 1969 and therefore had no-one to contribute to other parties who was stable with Values in 1969 and 1972 but then left in 1975.

Table 10.2 looks at the new changers to see which parties profited and which lost how much by the whole process.

Table 10.2: Final Party Gain/Loss Among New Changers, 1975

	% Lost	% Gained		Nett Result %
National	-19	+40	=	+21
Labour	-56	+9	=	-47
Social Credit	-3	+18	=	+15
Values	n.a.	+26	=	+26
Non-Voting	-22	+7	=	-15

Remembering that the table represents only one of three types of changer engaged in bringing down the Third Labour Government, it remains very clear that Labour's losses are the main feature—not National's gains. Indeed Values did better out of the goings and comings of the new changers than did the party which acquired the Treasury benches. This will later be shown to have wider application than simply amongst the new changers.

The verdict which I passed on the dismissal of the Second Labour Government in 1960 would appear still to apply—this time with redoubled strength—that National did not win the election, Labour lost it.

We have now sorted out that hazy, criss-crossing, amorphous mass, known at worst as 'the floating vote' and at best as 'the changers', into four component types. Each has proved to possess its own character in age, make-up, income, occupation, education and even in having areas of greater concentration.

The changers, all four kinds, were not all the same kinds of people, nor were they all moving at the same rate, nor necessarily in the same direction. It is no wonder that when they are lumped together the significant differences are lost by cancelling one another into insignificance and the precise informative silhouettes blur and blend into the simple lines of the general average.

Now that they are separate and we have their descriptive features, how did they vote in 1975? The graph [Figure 10.2] supplies the dramatically varying answer.

National's great coup with its 1975 campaign was scored among the returners. National's overriding aim to achieve a 'Great Restoration' of men of past power to present power, and of past policy emphasis to present implementation, was in considerable part accomplished by the restoration of past voting habits among those who had interrupted them to surge towards Labour and change in 1972.

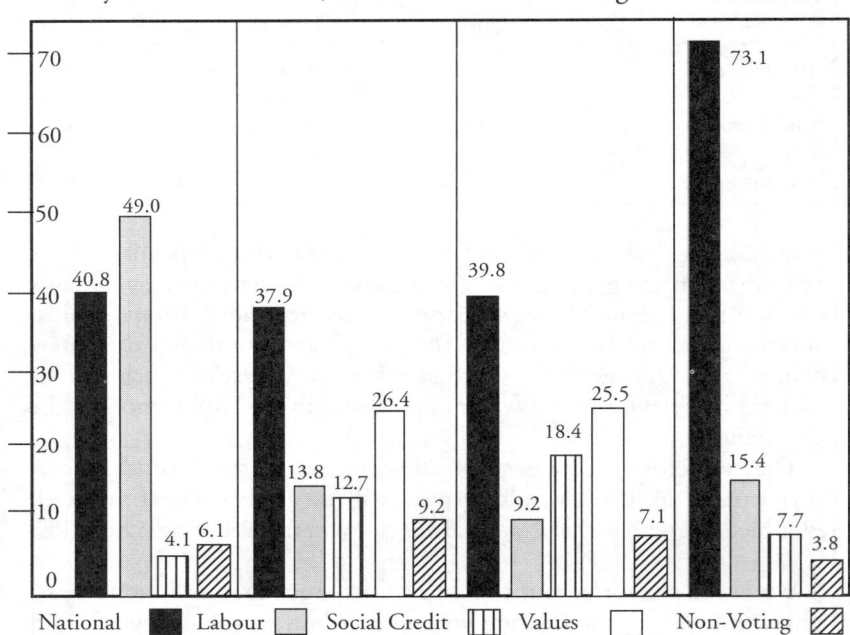

Figure 10.2: The Parties and the Vote Changers, 1975

Coming back to National was not hard for this group, so well above average in income, so frequently managers, administrators or prosperous skilled tradesmen of middling age and education.

Some 15.4 per cent of the whole were actually returners to Labour. Having skipped 1972 and victory, they returned in time for defeat, although, along with most New Zealanders, they did not expect it. Social Credit, too, recovered 7.7 per cent of past adherents. Though no doubt disappointing to Social Creditors in the absence of Values competition, this was still nearly three times as good a performance as Social Credit's showing among all stable and new voters which, it will be recalled, was a bare 2.8 per cent. As for Values, of course, one could not return to what had not been there in 1969, so Values gains had to be made elsewhere.

The entirely unstable gave more of those gains to Values than any other segment of the electorate. But by their nature, of course, the entirely unstable voters remain perfectly capable of retrieving gains subsequently.

Values took a little more than a quarter of the whole vote, Social Credit, an eighth, National two-fifths—which was worse than it achieved among the stable and new voters—and Labour a miserable seventh.

Here again with the entirely unstable we encounter what was earlier noted among the new changers, namely, that National's unimpressive harvest coupled with Labour's horrendous losses suggest a group of electors fleeing from something rather than marching resolutely towards an agreed and happy choice.

Because the entirely unstable were predominantly young and better educated than anyone except their juniors, many of them found a suitable temporary resting place in Values or, half as often, in Social Credit. More than any other type of voter they admitted to not voting in 1975.

When one recalls the high proportion of sales, service and clerical workers among entirely unstable voters and their concentration in the $8-10,000 income band, it is easy to see why any lodgement with the Labour movement they may have made in 1972 was quickly and easily discarded. They left Labour in droves but not necessarily, as it proved, in favour of the blunt clarity and simplicity of the Muldoon campaign.

Those newly changing voters who had to be lured away from more firmly-fixed opinions produced very similar results. They gave a shade more to National than did the entirely unstable, but still noticeably less than the stable and new voters. They were a little less enthusiastic about Values and definitely more favourable to Social Credit, indeed more so than any other segment of the electorate. Occupationally and economically the new changers were more evenly spread than the other changers of 1975. There was, however, a definite emphasis on skilled trades, trade and technical training, the $8-10,000 level and the 25-39 year olds. Mostly it was Labour that lost these votes and, if we look only at the graph, [Figure 10.2] National got the largest benefit—although understanding the beginning as well as the end of the process reveals the real victor as Values.

But among all the changers of 1975 the loser was undoubtedly Labour. National genuinely won the battle of the returners and Labour's column there looks as though half the Labour column in 'new stable' had been snapped off and added to National. It was snapped off shorter in 'entirely unstable' and 'new changer' but not added to National. Instead it was broken again and handed to Values, Social Credit, and non-voting in that order.

Delving into the Non-Vote Phenomenon

Last week I posed two questions.[8] Could the 1975 non-voting record be in some way a sectional quirk, the product of savage shifts in some, but not most, kinds of electorate? Is the suggested linkage between soaring failure to vote and Labour loss a phenomenon which appears consistently all over New Zealand and in all types of seat?

To answer these questions, the New Zealand electorate has been divided along the main lines of social difference: urban, town and rural; richer, mixed and poorer; Maori and Pakeha. This yields eight types of electorate and the results for each type have been analysed.

The 1975 non-voting record certainly proved to be no sectional quirk for a surge into non-voting appeared in every one of the eight types of New Zealand electorate and all over the country. It was somewhat less here, rather more there, on an individual electorate basis. But non-voting was also the biggest gainer out of the election in each one of those eight kinds of seat.

The next biggest gainer was the Values Party in the Special Country, Farmer, Mixed City, Town, Richer City and Maori electorates. Only in the Poorer City and Rural seats did National come second. Elsewhere National was either third or actually showed a drop as it did in the Richer City and Special Country categories.

The Social Credit movement—an overall loser in 1975—declined in its share of votes in five out of eight types of electorate. It managed a tiny rise in Special Country and showed the fourth biggest improvement in the Town and Farmer classes of seat.

So an analysis, designed to pick up the effects of social variation amongst kinds of electorate, returns the same description of the gainers of 1975 as do the graphs of the New Zealand qualified vote as a whole [omitted].

Does the association of Labour losses with more non-vote also hold across the different types of electorate? Here again the answer is 'Yes'. Labour losses were the biggest feature of the election in every kind of seat. Overwhelmingly the net losses came from Labour and, as has already been stressed, the leading gainer was everywhere the non-vote.

If one applies even harder tests, the results are still positive. The most consistently and most heavily Labour seats in New Zealand are the Maori seats and Labour loss and non-vote gain were stronger there than anywhere else. Poorer City seats rank next in loyalty to Labour and Labour losses there in 1975 were likewise second only to the Maori defections.

The Special Country class is a small one composed of rural seats with timber workers, miners, fruit-growing and tourism to render them unlike other country seats. The then Labour Prime Minister stood in one of them. There was a combination of Independent and National candidacies in another. As a result Labour's loss was not so heavy nor non-vote's gain so great as the third-most-Labour class of electorate should have displayed to make a perfect gradient.

But the fourth ranking class, the Mixed City seats, picked up the role and produced the third-largest Labour decline. The Town category should have come next and it did; then Rural, Farmer and Richer City. Farmer went 0.9 per cent higher than it should have done and the other two were very even with 0.02 per cent as the difference.

Revealing and tidy from the point of view of social science analysis, but disastrous for Labour in the consistency with which Labour's own, in the proportion they were Labour, turned away from their own government.

They turned very regularly to non-voting, not with such proportional exactitude as they demonstrated in leaving Labour, but in a sufficiently orderly way to isolate only two exceptional types. One of these, the Special Country electorates, has already been examined. The other type was the Richer City category where what was out of line was not the under-average Labour decrease (-7.56 per cent) but the big jump (+7.08 per cent) in non-voting. Social Credit and National were not attracting Labour's departing flocks, indeed both National and Social Credit declined themselves. Values rose by +1.81 per cent and the Independent Right collected a few (+0.40 per cent), but non-vote was the disproportionately attractive recipient in this, the most traditionally National kind of seat.

So the larger New Zealand pattern is repeated and even underscored in the different sections of the New Zealand electorate and the twin features of the design are picked out clearly and plainly: out of Labour; into non-vote.

So heavy and so doubly negative a movement raises with redoubled force the question 'Why?' The other two general retreats into non-voting over the past sixty years accompanied the stresses, the personal tragedies, and the social dislocation of the First World War and the Great Depression. In each case there was a confused and confusing multi-party situation and we do have that again now. But the three attackers and one defender situation can scarcely account for so great a retreat. Where this time were the equivalents of the miseries of the Great War or of the unemployed camps and the years of real want during the Great Depression?

New Zealand in 1975 had by international standards no unemployment to speak of when all the Western world had endured eighteen months of it. New Zealand's international credit was excellent. There was an abundance—too much so—in the shops; the voters were in jobs and earning rising wages, even if inflation was beginning to bite harder and chew fragments off the real standard of living. There were more houses built and building; pensions and benefits had been raised and more added; the economy was busily occupied and ready, said the Government, to profit from the big lift which overseas recovery would surely produce soon. Then we could do as we had done before and pay off over the good years the overseas debt contracted when the terms of trade turned savagely, suddenly bad.

Ironically in all of this, the only element which was at all a parallel of anything in the Depression years was the harshness of the terms of trade and they were an equation for bankers, not a commonly-understood daily experience.

So what we are left with, as an equivalent of the desperate realities of war and depression in causing a major negative movement in political opinion, are the doubts, anxiety and distrust engendered by a masterly campaign of political accusation concerted and led from the front by the Leader of the Opposition. He was assisted by attacks from dozens of directions, coming frequently from enthusiasts for some one issue who demanded entire satisfaction at once for their cause.

The 'fifties were a decade of great expectations and the 'sixties a time of causes. The Third Labour Government was expected to realise on an insatiable jostle of deferred hopes and fresh issues at the same time as Labour implemented its own crowded programme aimed, it said, to correct the errors and omissions of twenty immobile years. Those who had grown up to or were profitably adjusted to things as they had been for so long were now shaken by all this clangorous activity and added their complaints from the right to the demands from the left. It was all grist to the Opposition's denunciation. And not only the press but now also radio and two channels of television all separately and energetically reported every deputation, demonstration, complainant or spokesman.

So much we can all recall, but the effects still look larger than the causes. We have discovered from analysing the official results what we do *not* have to explain, namely, a great attractive force in the National programme and its leader. It was not to them the tens of thousands moved. Mr Muldoon appeared to anticipate this, and to grasp that he was a master of negative rather than positive politics, for he confined his positive appeal and his financial commitments to the promise of his superannuation scheme.

In other respects—apart from foreshadowing a transformed industrial law—he pacified the aroused and anxious voters with a generalised intention to return them to where they had been before Labour. This general licence to construct a private, happy fantasy was evocatively summed up in the slogan 'New Zealand the way you want it'. The direction of the response was similarly ambiguous as the voters massed themselves in that limbo of suspended judgment, the non-vote.

To look at personal motives and preferences and to explore how individuals interpreted what was happening we must go back to individuals through the survey method. Like the other methods, it is not final. It, too, has limits.

But in concert, the three kinds of data and analysis can eliminate, suggest and confirm so that we at last arrive in the vicinity of understanding.

We have thus much reduced and defined the further questions which other methods must answer by locating what has still to be accounted for after the official results have been properly and fully analysed. We must supplement the analysis of the official results because no analysis depending on the characteristics of electorates as wholes can go beyond definitively eliminating some possibilities and strongly suggesting others. Nor can the history of the times pass beyond confirming the events and factors present and their proportions, order and linkages.

The Principal Reasons We Voted the Way We Did on 29 November 1975

What did the voters themselves think moved them to the turnabout of 1975? Was it the policies or the leaders, Labour's performance or National's promise, the local candidates or the nationwide issues?

If you, like many voters, feel you already know the answer and have known it all along, even before acquiring the advantage of hindsight, pause now and note down which factor caused it all before reading further. If you feel there was a mixture of factors at work, then give their approximate proportions. Go on to pick which were the issues of the election and jot down their relative importance.

It would be a worthwhile check, because commonsense suggests not one but many plausible answers. Indeed the role of social measurement is to establish as correct the real answer, which anyone might have guessed and possibly did, along with a dozen other possibilities, some half right and a lot of them quite wrong.

In the week immediately following the election a nationwide sample of voters were interviewed and asked to give their version of why they had acted as they had. Time was of the essence because, with every extra week after the event, more subsequent developments were bound cumulatively to colour and skew the voters' memories of their motives as the consequences of their decisions, good and bad, piled up.

It was therefore vital to conduct the enquiry as near as possible to the decision and this was done. It was also important to carry the survey out by professional interviewing rather than trust it to postal questionnaires with their unpredictably distorting third or more of non-responses.

As a basic sorting out of the factors involved, the voters were asked what had most influenced them to support the political party they had just voted for. Rather more than a third (34.6 per cent) gave some or all aspects of their party's policy as the most influential factor. Since the diverse issues of any election are either met, fudged or missed by each party's policy, party policy should involve a standpoint on at least a selection of the issues.

The personality and capacity of the party's leader or his opponent's qualities, however, may well constitute the crucial issue for a substantial number of electors. In 1975 several factors ensured that this was the case.

The Leader of the Opposition had made it a major item of his Parliamentary tactics to disparage the Prime Minister almost from Rowling's assumption of office following the death of Kirk. A constant drip can wear away stone, and repeated slurs a reputation. But what was directed at Rowling was more like a jet of jibes and assertions of incompetence for which it is difficult to find any parallel in modern New Zealand politics.

While the deliberate association of Nordmeyer with just a single act—the 'black' Budget of 1958—among his many political deeds was undoubtedly damaging to him, it was not in the same class with the year-long campaign of denigration from platforms all over the country which descended like a gritty smog on the Prime Minister.

When, very late in the day, a political outsider organised a campaign of support for Rowling, and when his advocates then questioned Muldoon's Parliamentary conduct and what they considered would be the authoritarian consequences of his well-established style, this was greeted with an instant of outraged silence and then furious counter-charges of 'character assassination'.[9]

Looking back at this remarkable record it would have seemed an appropriate preparation even for an election decided mainly on a contest of personalities as the principal factor. The television news cameras clustered around the faces and doings of the prime contestants. The doctrine of balance prevailing in those days pitted the Labour team against the National leader almost shot for shot. Journalists played follow the leaders so much that voters might have been excused the error of thinking that theirs was a Presidential instead of a Parliamentary system.

With all this weight of personalities pressing down upon them, the voters nevertheless gave the factor of party leadership first importance in only one quarter (25.3 per cent) of their replies. In a way that quarter share pays a tribute to the lingering powers in every man to resist manipulation by the pressures of publicity even though probably they were yielded to more than in any normal election year.

The record of the Government is always at issue in any election. Moreover an active Government will have done much that provoked policy alternatives from its Opposition. Such policy causes and effects, of course, appear in the survey responses already examined as part of the 'policy' basis for electoral decisions. But in 1975, Labour's performance as a whole was also certainly bound to be on trial because Muldoon had not only attacked Labour's leadership, he had continually accused the Government as an entity of mismanagement of the country's affairs.

So what proportion of voters say they cast their vote on the basis of Labour's performance? The answer is 17.2 per cent and this is a good deal nearer to a sixth than to a fifth of the electorate. But, naturally, such responses cut both ways in that they could be National voters condemning the Government's performance or Labourites giving it as the reason for their support. Actually 20.7 per cent of Labour and 19.7 per cent of National gave this basis for their vote.

Thus, proportionately, Labour was very slightly more satisfied than National was condemnatory, while minor party and non-voters were much less moved by it at 15.7 per cent for Social Credit, 6.9 per cent for Values, and nil for non-voters. Plainly those whose votes were going past the major parties had other things more in view than Labour's record.

Was this perhaps an election where the local candidate for one's party made up many minds? MPs and aspirants, after weeks of struggling round their electorates, certainly hope they have won a useful personal vote. And those incumbents, who have carefully attended to their constituents' requests for years, trust that some of it has been bread upon the waters which will come back to them as ballots.

In the outcome, a touch over one-eighth of the electorate (13.0 per cent) gave their party's candidate in their own electorate as the precipitating factor in casting their vote.

This is, indeed, not a smaller but a higher proportion 'voting the local man not the party' than I would have expected, especially in a year noisy with the battle of the leaders overhead and on screen. But in a way that battle did impinge on, and even enlarge, the proportion looking to local candidates as their best reason for voting. For when we look at the choices of the partisans we find that whereas 10.5 per cent of all Nationalists pointed to their constituency candidate, 20.4 per cent of Labour voters found the merits of their local representative to be the best reason for voting as they did.

On the face of it, it would appear perfectly possible that proportionately far more intending Labour voters who thought first of men not measures were looking for virtues in their local contender because they were not markedly attracted by their leader.

To check this, the parties' data were broken down into those who in 1975 were stable in their voting and those who changed last November. Among National voters who stayed stable in 1975, 29.9 per cent gave the Muldoon leadership as the biggest influence on their vote, while 8.9 per cent picked the party standard-bearer in their seat. Looking at the Labour loyalists, the proportions were much more even. Rowling's leadership was cited by 30.5 per cent—a shade ahead of Muldoon's drawing power on his side—but more than twice the parallel National percentage, 18.6 per cent, looked to the local Labour man.

When we come to those who changed in 1975, a really startling statistic pops up. Nationalist changers still look first to their leader with 29.4 per cent compared with 14.5 per cent for the constituency aspirant. But with changes to Labour, the proportions actually reversed and 37.9 per cent of those moving to Labour indicated the electorate candidate as their major reason, while just 10.4 per cent attributed their vote to Rowling's appeal.

It would appear that, as with Sir John Marshall in 1972, Rowling was still being overshadowed by contrasting memories of his predecessor. To this was added, in the case of Bill Rowling, a sustained campaign to belittle him which apparently succeeded with many changers who nevertheless voted Labour in the name of their MP or who, frequently, did not vote at all.

As for Social Creditors, one-third fewer than among the supporters of the major parties gave credit for determining their vote to their leader's qualities. The figures by party were National 29.4 per cent, Labour 28.6 per cent, Social Credit 19.6 per cent, and Values—which makes less of its youthful and articulate leaders by rotating them—picked up just 6.9 per cent on that basis.

Neither Values nor Social Credit, however, turned as a strong alternative to their self-sacrificing spear-carriers in the constituencies. Finding a motive force in the local representative was first and foremost a Labour phenomenon: then National, fairly closely followed by Social Credit at 9.8 per cent, and Values at 5.6 per cent.

Which leaves one remaining general heading among the motives for voting for a party or not voting, namely, those who 'did not know' what their prime cause was and those who 'did not support any' party. A little less than a tenth of all voters (9.5 per cent) came into this last, least, double category.

Appropriately, 91.8 per cent of non-voters said they did not support any or knew of no basis for their inaction, although six per cent pointed to the leadership of all existing parties, and two per cent indicated the party programmes they had to choose amongst as reasons for giving the whole process a miss. Among voters, this 'do not know' category drew 7.8 per cent of Social Credit, 6.6 per cent of Labour and 4.2 per cent of Values. Only 2.4 per cent of National were unable to specify what had principally led them to give their vote to the party which received it.

It would be wrong, however, to assume that these figures indicate careless or perhaps irrational voting. Sensible electors need not necessarily find it possible to pick one rather than another basis as constituting the most influential factor in making their choice. But it is helpful and significant that more than nine-tenths of electors could do so or, if one excludes non-voters, then as many as 19 out of every 20 could.

A last question on this line of inquiry will already have occurred to many readers: what can be learnt from comparing the balance of motives among one party's supporters with the proportions in the other parties?

We have already discovered that Labour and National are close overall in looking to their respective party leaders, but that Labourites are almost twice as likely to find the key appeal in their constituency candidate. Both major parties see Labour's governmental performance as important to nearly the same degree, but in opposite senses of being pro and con.

What, then, is the complementary contrast to the difference over local candidates? The answer lies in party policy which moved only 23.7 per cent of all Labourites, but propelled 38.0 per cent of those choosing National.

This time there is no vital difference between those stable with and those changing to Labour concealed by the overall figure. Party policy was specified by 23.6 per cent of Labour's stable followers and by 24.1 per cent of those changing to it. Every other party's followers put policy first as an attraction.

For Labour supporters, policy came second to leadership among stable Labourites and second to the local candidate among Labour changers. Patently, Labour's voters were on the defensive. They found much to approve of in past performance and in either their leader or their MPs, but aimed mainly to conserve their achievements rather than hopefully look forward with fresh policy expectations.

Just as plainly, National supporters were principally rivetted or captured by what their programme promised in general terms to do, albeit most of those changes were intended to restore the *status quo ante* the Third Labour Government—or further back still.

Social Credit voters also put policy first (47.1 per cent) as a motive and, correspondingly, leadership and the Government's performance fell in comparative importance for them. But it was among Values voters that the attractions of the *Manifesto* as against all other factors reached its height of 76.4 per cent. The Values supporters' concentration on the pre-eminent desirability of their policies only underlines the implicit contradiction in voting for candidates who would certainly not—in contrast to major party candidates—become MPs able to implement those policies. And this paradox looks likely to persist at least for the easily foreseeable future.

Thus the priority assigned by Values to policy also identifies voting for Values as demonstrative politics rather than functional politics.

How Voters Responded to Muldoon and Rowling in November 1975

The post-election survey we conducted asked an entirely open question: 'Of all politicians in New Zealand that you know of, which one would you personally prefer to be our Prime Minister right now?' The response, as shown in Table 10.1, was clear.[10]

Not only was Rob Muldoon preferred to Bill Rowling by 9.3 points, but the other leading National figures were picked more than three times as frequently as their Labour equivalents. Sir John Marshall (3.0 per cent), Duncan MacIntyre (2.7 per cent) and Brian Talboys (1.1 per cent) each

Table 10.3: The Choice for Prime Minister in 1975

Party Leaders	Percentages
Muldoon (National)	41.4
Rowling (Labour)	32.1
Other National	6.8
Other Labour	2.2
Beetham (Social Credit)	3.1
Clough (Values)	1.9
Others	3.0
None	4.1
Don't Know	5.4

outweighed any among Dr Finlay (0.6 per cent), Colin Moyle (0.6 per cent), Mike Moore (0.6 per cent) or Bob Tizard (0.4 per cent). The leaders of the minor parties—who had received for that very reason much personal publicity on television, radio and in the press—ran well behind their own primarily ideological parties despite an articulate, innovative campaign on Reg Clough's part and despite Bruce Beetham's attraction and intensity.

The fine print of preferences for Prime Minister registered by various social groupings initially appeared to present nothing unusual. Muldoon's lead over Rowling was greater among males than females. Looked at by age groups, Rowling beat the National leader among the 18-24s, while

Muldoon's appeal peaked among the 25-39s and, though he still won, his lead was less by two-thirds in the older categories. So far then, the same general shape in the results as we have seen in the judgment on Labour's performance or the final party preference. The rungs of the educational ladder likewise continued to display the appropriate party leaders ahead on the same levels as before. But the proportions were distorted so that Rowling's predictable lead at the 'Primary' level was 8.9 per cent, not his party's generous voting margin of 27.9 per cent. Indeed, his expected lead on the 'Some Secondary' rung had disappeared. Conversely, Muldoon at School Certificate, UE and Professional/University levels was leading right enough, but not by nearly as much as his party.

The picture by occupations turned out to be even more awry, like a familiar face seen in a fun-fair mirror. The Muldoon victories, judged by the National Party's own lead, were not nearly large enough among the Managerial, Administrative and Professional group, among the Retired and Pensioners, or in the Clerical, Sales and Service group. The Rowling leads, by comparison with his own party, were overly large among students and others, whereas he actually lost the party's lead among manual workers and semi-skilled and among housewives.

A breakdown by incomes picked up similar wavering outlines, as though half-recognisable and half-transformed beneath water. Results of the leadership battle broken down by 1975 Stables and Changers and by parties likewise showed marked departures from what the National against Labour Party contest would have led one to expect.

Table 10.4 sets out Muldoon's lead over or lag behind the National Party's performance in various categories, and sets that alongside Rowling's leads and lags with Labour. The last column measures the jointly-produced divergence resulting either from a triumph beyond his party achieved by either man, and the other's corresponding failure, or as the product of the marginal difference between two poor personal showings.

The left and middle columns of the table show whether each leader ran behind or ahead of his own party. In the left-hand column the percentage wanting Muldoon as Prime Minister is measured for each category against the percentage picking National as its party choice. Where Muldoon lags behind his party, that shows as a minus; and where he went ahead, that appears as a plus. In the middle column Rowling is measured in the same way. It is a notable feature of the table how frequently both men ran behind their parties and, if not both behind together, then at least one of them. Only among young people from 18-24 and among the miscellaneous occupational category, 'Other', was the appeal of both leaders greater than the pull of their respective parties.

Table 10.4: The Pull of the Leaders Compared with their Parties

	Muldoon's Lead or Lag of Nat Pty	Rowling's Lead or Lag of Lab Pty	Divergence to Muldoon or Rowling	
SEX				
Male	− 4.1	− 0.9	R	3.2
Female	− 1.8	− 5.9	M	4.1
AGE				
18–24 yrs	+ 1.4	+ 5.7	R	4.3
25–39	− 0.6	− 4.1	M	3.5
40–54	− 7.9	− 7.0	R	0.9
55+	− 4.9	− 4.9		0.0
AREA				
Northern N.I.	− 1.9	− 4.2	M	2.3
Southern N.I.	− 3.4	− 5.2	M	1.8
South Island	− 4.6	− 0.4	R	4.2
EDUCATION				
Primary	+ 2.5	− 16.5	M	19.0
Some secondary	0.0	− 9.3	M	9.3
School Certificate	− 6.2	+ 1.3	R	7.5
Tech/Trade Certificate	− 5.6	+ 1.0	R	6.6
University Entrance	− 7.7	+ 1.3	R	9.0
Professional/University	− 3.4	+ 2.3	R	5.7
OCCUPATION				
Other	+ 5.0	+ 10.0	R	5.0
Mnl Worker/Semi Skilled	+ 12.8	− 12.8	M	25.6
Student	− 7.4	+ 3.7	R	11.1
Housewife	+ 2.6	− 7.7	M	10.3
Skilled Trades	− 1.8	− 3.7	M	1.9
Clerk/Sales/Service	− 10.1	− 7.7	R	2.4
Retired/Pensioner	− 8.4	0.0	R	8.4
Mngt/Admin/Professional	− 9.8	+ 4.0	R	13.8
INCOME				
Under $2,000	− 3.0	− 8.0	M	5.0
2 – 3	+ 0.4	− 5.3	M	5.7
3 – 4	− 1.8	− 7.2	M	5.4
4 – 5	+ 6.0	− 10.0	M	16.0
5 – 6	− 2.6	− 10.2	M	7.6
6 – 8	− 11.6	+ 3.1	R	14.7
8 – 10	− 1.5	− 0.8	R	0.7
10 – 12	− 10.4	+ 6.2	R	16.6
12+	− 5.6	− 2.8	R	2.8
Refuse to say	− 11.4	+ 11.4	R	22.8

The right-hand column shows which of the two leaders had the comparative advantage in personal pull as against his party for each category. In the grand categories like sex, age, and area, it is principally a comparison of who lagged further behind. As before, Muldoon gets stronger going northwards, and again he peaks in the 25-39 age group. But this time his extra personal pull is shown to be relatively stronger among women than men.

It is when we turn to education, occupation and income that the divergences become really enlightening. Among those with 'primary education only' Muldoon on balance was way ahead. Rowling's poor appeal at the level of 'some secondary education' confirmed the Muldoon lead up to this group—populated as it was with a great many voters. Then, at the 'School Certificate' stage, Rowling started to show positive appeal while the National Party commenced to outdraw Muldoon. Thereafter the divergences favoured Rowling all the way to the top of the educational lift.

The occupational categories show a closely related result in the basic and numerous categories of 'Manual Worker Semi-skilled' and 'Housewife'. Muldoon showed extra strength beyond his party in both groups and remarkably so among working people.

By contrast, Rowling lagged markedly so the divergences went heavily towards Muldoon. He preserved an edge among the 'Skilled Trades' but the edge transferred to Rowling in the 'Clerical, Sales and Service' category. 'Other', a small mixed bag, went to Rowling and so did the 'Retired and Pensioners' and the 'Students'—very definitely so. It can be seen that the educational factor was shining through from behind the structure of occupations.

Lastly the 'Managerial Administration Professional' group displayed a strong divergence towards Rowling both because he ran ahead of his party and because Muldoon was running well behind his.

The analysis by income repeats and confirms what education and occupation have indicated. Muldoon's relatively greater personal appeal ran right up to the $5999 per annum level. At $6000 the change was sudden and heavy and thereafter all the divergences were towards Rowling.

Simple irony would suggest that both parties had the wrong leaders and that they should swap. Reflection, however, shows that we have, in charting the particular appeals of the two leaders, come upon something fundamental to the way the whole 1975 election worked and how a reaction against it might yet work in the future.

Muldoon's forte was being able to reach beyond his party and convince the lower income groups, the lower educational levels, the semi- and unskilled workers and the housewives. His simple, declaratory, assertive style; the unflagging energy with which he repeated his charges and drove them in with anything that came to hand; the intellectual force with which he seized on one aspect only of a complex situation and hung on to that grimly whatever qualifications or other aspects of the question his opponents raised—these all contributed to his power on television to reach precisely into the ranks of Labour supporters and throw them into confusion, anxiety and inaction.

Two fairly elementary psychological responses were at work here. People subject to strong and conflicting forces, which call for the taking of entirely opposed courses of action, frequently respond by freezing and taking no action at all. The Muldoon message of total mismanagement and of an economically ominous future called for one kind of action and their Labour loyalties another. Tens of thousands responded to the situation by staying home and not voting, thus determining the basic trend making up the 1975 result.

The second point concerning the response to Muldoon has to do with the role he assumed so naturally as an aggressive, assured, tough, figure of authority. Here was the upholder of law, order and economy against what was pictured as a great variety of threatening groups from union militants, street bashers and protesters to immigrants and islanders and social security spongers.

A recent article in *Psychology Today* by Gerbner and Gross points out that the high tide of violence which washes over us from television raises the anxiety level and the expectation of encountering crime and brutality. Viewers identify not with the criminal aggressors but with the victims. The heroes are the Kojaks, the Barlows and the Cannons who fight ruthlessly to guarantee the anxious victims against the menacing world which surrounds them. Heavy TV viewing 'breeds suspicion' and 'breeds fear' say Gerbner and Gross. Correspondingly, it creates the role of protector, the authority figure who will stand between the public and what threatens it. The man and the role fitted like hand and glove.

Now that those other roles, the roles of Prime Minister and Leader of the Opposition, have been exchanged, Rowling can take encouragement from that very same set of indicators about where his particular appeal lies. Now that he is the Leader of the Opposition, it is Rowling who will increasingly have the opportunities to reach across into the ranks of National supporters in the appropriate occupational, educational, and income brackets. The qualities and style of the present Leader of the Opposition will provide an alternative kind of leadership which time will only place in deeper contrast to that of the Prime Minister.

Those tens of thousands of ex-Labour supporters now in the limbo of non-voting will be able at the next election to decide on the facts of how the threat to our economy was tackled rather than on fearful anticipation. Rowling will not require extra personal appeal to move those groups most likely to be pushed by unfolding reality.

Nevertheless, the present Leader of the Opposition is at risk from what might be called the Nordmeyer syndrome. Pressure from the very groups which deserted Labour in droves in November 1975 could build up against Rowling and make him the scapegoat for their own confusion and non-voting. That would be the crowning irony of the election of 1975.

Notes

1 [In November 1975, after one term of office, the Labour Government was overwhelmingly defeated by the National Party, led by Robert Muldoon. Norman Kirk, who had led Labour to victory in 1972, had died in 1974, to be succeeded by Wallace (Bill) Rowling. Ed.]
2 [Ralph Brookes, Austin Mitchell and Alan Robinson. For specific references, see Clive Bean, 'An inventory of New Zealand Voting Surveys 1949-84', *Political Science*, Vol. 38, No. 2, 1986, pp. 172-84. Ed.]
3 [See especially D. E. Butler and D. Stokes, *Political Change in Britain*, 2nd edn. (London, 1974). Ed.]
4 [UE = University Entrance. Ed.]
5 [S. M. Lipset, *Political Man* (London, 1960). Ed.]
6 [The previous two articles, entitled 'The New Voters: Perfect Equality Between the Major Parties' and 'The Changers: Four Groups with Distinctive Characteristics', have been omitted. See the Introduction to this chapter for the definitions of the four types of changers. Ed.]
7 [Bruce Beetham was Leader of Social Credit between 1972 and 1976. Ed.]
8 [The omitted article was entitled 'What Really Did Happen at the 1975 General Election?' It analysed the official results published by the Electoral Office and emphasised the importance of the non-vote in electoral analysis. Chapman also stressed that, 'The disturbing fact is that at no New Zealand election during the Great Depression or since has non-voting risen so fast nor so high as in 1975.' The non-vote in 1975 was 17.46%. Ed.]
9 [A former television interviewer, David Exel, organised the 'Citizens for Rowling' campaign. Ed.]
10 [The two articles that preceded this one have been omitted: 'The Issues in 1975: Most of the Anxieties were Economic Ones' and 'Was it Really Three Years Hard Labour?' In the latter piece, Chapman showed that the general verdict of the electors on the Labour Government was a 'favourable judgment'. Ed.]

11

The Case of the Pulled Punch: The 1978 Election

General elections in a democracy are first and foremost about choosing between alternative governments. So the prime significance of 25 November 1978 for New Zealand was that by their actions the voters showed that they had found both their alternative governments wanting. The popular vote condemned National to second place by dealing out a savage drop of 7.8 percentage points of the valid vote. Yet at the same time the voters neglected to replace the Muldoon Government decisively when they raised Labour only a mere 0.8 from the nadir of 1975. In short, the central decision of the election was burked.

Instead of picking between governments one way or the other, a horde of voters hared off after strange gods both Social Credit and Alternative National. Not really strange, of course, for the Social Credit League had been around for a quarter of a century now. But the League and the public were both deeply aware that there had only been two Social Credit M.P.s in all that time.[1] (At eight general elections there had been just one success in supplying 658 vacancies.) So, with a single M.P. in the House as the result of a by-election and having come second in only two other seats in 1975, the League could present no credible way in which it might become the Government in one bound.

Indeed, Social Credit and its Leader did not pretend in interviews that they hoped for more than four or five seats at the most. Had history or Mr Beetham been believed it followed that in 87 or 88 electorates those who voted for Social Credit candidates stood no chance of seeing their candidate elected. More importantly, there was no chance that those candidates would appear in Parliament and affect its balance and thus the policies put into action over the next three years. Thus in voting Social Credit in 1978 the great bulk of its electors were neither voting for an alternative government nor even for possible Parliamentarians. They were doing something else or avoiding something else.

Let us turn for a moment from the mass to the happy fraction who could perhaps believe that their man—there was no woman candidate so placed—would reach Wellington and, if not sit upon the Treasury benches, at least affect something. What could he or they do? That in

---

[This chapter was first published in *Comment*, New Series, No. 6 (February 1979). Ed.]

turn depends on what the other five-sixths (1978) or nine-tenths (1975) of validly voting New Zealanders have done. If they have produced a normal majority of nine or ten or more, then a lone Social Crediter or even a bevy of four or five can do nothing of consequence except attempt to make propaganda for their party. As Mr Cracknell's efforts between 1966 and 1969 illustrated, that could prove counter-productive.

But suppose that all the aces have turned up at once. Suppose that, say, four Social Crediters have got in and that, coincidentally, major party New Zealand has presented Parliament with the close margin for one party of government or the other which it just once did produce in Social Credit's time, namely, a margin of two between Labour and National in 1957. To suppose as much is to put two very long shots together, but its extreme improbability has been somewhat disguised by a dense cloud of speechifying and advertisement urging voters to give a third party 'the balance of power'. What would that do for the essential function performed by our electoral and Parliamentary system which is to give voters the choice between alternative governments with well-known records and announced programmes?

The answer must be that our hypothetical third party foursome could only frustrate the choice of the vast majority of major party voters by preventing, slowing down or distorting the implementation of the winning party's programme. When Parliament met the four could plan in the light of the Government's legislative proposals for the year to do either of two things. They could strike at once with a no confidence motion in the hope of throwing out the winners and substituting the major losers at the election with the extra support of the foursome. That would put the losing major party in the power of Social Credit and neither Mr Holyoake and his supporters in 1957 nor Mr Muldoon and his supporters now could be expected to accept such a position, particularly as agreeing to any instalment of Douglas Social Credit or its principles would represent a direct contradiction of National's basic economic policies.[2]

So preliminary soundings would soon show the balance of power holders that their power was remarkably negative and limited and they would probably opt for the second possibility of deferring their attack until some major measure like the Budget was being debated. At that point, however, they would discover that they were in the same fix as before in being able to block government but not to govern themselves, nor to persuade others to govern on their minority's conditions. Either way they could only frustrate the great majority of the electorate's intentions.

What is more, we have so far been leaving out of account the intentions of the winning major party. If, as in 1957, the party had been Labour in 1978 — and it was so in votes—then we have a guide as to how Mr Rowling and his team would have acted.[3] Because Labour's leader stated before the election that, in the event of a Labour win being confronted by a potential Social Credit veto, then his Government would at once move to secure a fresh election. No doubt like any sensible general he would first have occupied the high ground for the next battle by surveying the situation in the government departments and then have set out his intended economic and social measures in specific detail. But with the real electoral question thus posed for a second time and in a matter of months and with the essentially frustrating and negative effect of conferring the balance of power on a third party having just been displayed to the country in vivid terms, then one can be reasonably certain that this time a decision would be taken and the third party blockage politically removed to the great and lasting benefit of both major parties.

If Mr Muldoon and National had won more narrowly in seats—and they won in vexed but increasing comfort —and been faced with Mr Beetham and party brandishing a veto, then one could count on the Prime Minister to dispose of the obstacle just as soon as he had remodelled his image and his Cabinet even more drastically than he did do and after renewing the easement of the economy for two or three months longer. He might even have chosen to go into reverse and to tackle the basic problems of economic restructuring which he pointed to and pictured so dramatically in 1975 but which unfortunately still lie before us all. Whichever route he chose, a forewarned and chastened Prime Minister could have broken through a Beetham roadblock and so could Mr Rowling if he had won the major party battle in seats.

But until a critical minority of New Zealand electors have been taken through this scenario in actuality and have seen for themselves the nugatory and diversionary effects on clear choice should they hand the balance to a minority party, then they seem incapable of thinking through or imagining the possible outcome of their own political actions. As things stand such electors have never been faced with the consequences if both long shots—a small band of minority Parliamentarians and a closely-won major party battle—came home together. And so they can go on being quite vague about the possibility and yet attracted to it as though the imposition of a minority obstruction would somehow prove to be or to reveal a third and hopeful way forward.

As a result of this recurring and dreamlike temptation to dodge out of the choice between alternative governments, our political system seems fated every dozen years to produce elections like those of 1954, 1966 and 1978. These are occasions when voters by the tens of thousands stream away from one alternative but not towards the other, with the result that the government of the time—in each case a National government—stands deserted and rebuked yet able to go on essentially unscathed.

The departing voters both strike out against the government yet deliberately miss their ultimate target of replacing it with its opponents. Instead they pitch temporary camp with Social Credit off to the side of the battleground, while some may even wander right off the scene for a time into non-voting as they did in 1966. After three years the camp breaks up either partly or entirely. In 1957 many returned to National but the main body proved decisive in electing the Second Labour Government. In 1969 the process was slower. More moved on to Labour than returned to National in 1969, but the emptying of the camp was not completed until 1972.

Those who recall the three-and-a-half party politics of the 1920s and especially the 1928 general election will recognise how old in our politics the process is and how deep are its roots in our perennial conservatism and reluctance to choose change. But the pulled punch syndrome in its modern form appeared along with the arrival of the Social Credit Political League on the hustings for the 1954 election. That election and its results certainly provide the best parallels to those of 1978 and they are worth pondering.

The first concerns the broad economic background. After National triumphed in 1949 on Mr S. G. Holland's promise to 'Make the Pound Go Further', that unlucky currency did take off but in the wrong direction and into a faster inflation than any which had preceded it.[4] Fortunately for Holland's Government and for his Party, the industrial troubles of 1951 and the smashing of the waterfront union took the electors' minds well away from the contradictions between economic promises and performance. Better still for Sidney Holland, the snap election of 1951 was won on the defeat of industrial militancy. Nevertheless the haunting economic issue returned with the newly-introduced 'credit squeeze' and the sharp import curbs in his next term of office. By 1954 the electors stood ready to strike at the Holland Government for disappointing the economic expectations their promises had raised.

The second parallel concerns Labour's leadership. Walter Nash was at least as sophisticated an economic guide as Sidney Holland and a good deal more prone to take firm and even puritanical decisions on his own initiative.[5] Yet by exploiting the quandary into which the rhetoric and actions of the union militants pushed the Labour Party and by adroit and partial quotation out of context the National Prime Minister and his men had successfully decked out Walter Nash with the label 'Neither For Nor Against' and bound him with a reputation for weakness on unionism and indecisiveness on policy.

The third parallel concerns the attractiveness and even novelty of the way out of decision, the third way, the Social Credit way. By 1954 Major Douglas's overseas prescription for the intense deflationary—not inflationary note, but *de*flationary—woes of the 1920s had been widely canvassed in New Zealand for over twenty years. But Douglas's adherents were organised as a propagandist body and pressure group for the adoption of certain economic devices and not as a political party. It was only in the early fifties that Douglas Crediters abandoned hope that either Labour or National, faced first with wartime scarcities and now by an age of inflation, would ever adopt their devices born of so different an era.

So the form of presentation was metamorphosed into that of a political party and the core of financial devices reappeared but freshly togged out in all the finery of a full political programme with a leader, policy speeches and a complete stage company of candidates. It looked like a new party; it operated like a party; it was treated like a party.[6] The new party was unconnected with the unions, believed strongly in private enterprise, and it was enthusiastically for capitalism—except of course that the financial heart of the capitalist system would have to be replaced with another to the Douglas design. But above all, though the ideas were old, the approach was new and the party glittered with the possibilities of cheaper credit.

When surveying the League's fortunes in the early seventies—with Owen long gone, Cracknell replaced and the party split for 1972 by the O'Brien New Democrats—any observer might be pardoned for making a gloomy comparison. But that would be to underestimate a truly remarkable loyalty displayed by the hard core of the League and consequently the League's remarkable recuperative powers. The New Democrats faded away and the League edged up a trifle in 1975 while New Zealand's attentions were otherwise occupied. But it was Bruce Beetham's comparative youth, Bruce Beetham's constant activity and Bruce Beetham's good fortune that combined to be ready with a fresh face when New Zealanders' tired eyes turned from the ever-present image of their Prime Minister on the television screen.

Mr Beetham was drafted into the leadership while young because the Cracknell-O'Brien struggles fortuitously cleared the spot for him and he was ready, knowledgeable and energetic. He learned to campaign as a leader on the job. He caught the ear of the press by getting elected as Hamilton's Mayor, but got out in time for his great opportunity. This was the Rangitikei by-election which could not have come at a better place for Bruce Beetham nor at a better time.

The 1978 Election

He had already contested the seat twice and, as Social Credit's Leader, had gone into second place in 1975. There was no problem of edging out the League's regular candidate when Sir Roy Jack's death vacated this particular Government-held seat. And the time was ideal because it was at the start of the third year for an Administration on which farmers and townsmen had pinned enormous hopes. Those hopes were most decidedly not being fulfilled as costs soared, inflation and debt rolled on, disputes multiplied and unemployment rose. It was a far, far better time for electors to switch allegiances than at a general election. For discontented and wavering electors knew that the Government was safe behind a huge majority in Parliament and a firm lead over Labour in the opinion polls. So they could afford to strike at the Government without causing it major hurt or giving Labour encouragement and they did. It was all the perfect rehearsal for the year's end drama and it revealed a fresh new lead and unsuspected possibilities for the script. Bruce Beetham's standing in the polls and that of Social Credit were on their way up.

Television treated it as an unpredictable, inexplicable, personal triumph. Parliament was not in session and this was the lull before the storms of election year. So it was Bruce Beetham's smiling success which drew the camera lenses. Television with its ache for new faces and heroes and its incapacity to look behind events at their meaning or significance was the perfect medium for conveying into the home and for generalising what was, after all, a wildly special case of a by-election on the doorstep of an attractive young party leader facing, in Mr Bull, the inexperienced representative of a Government in disarray. The fortunate Social Credit League found itself renewed behind the amiable grin of its television matador.

The fourth and final parallel between 1954 and 1978 concerns the size of the flight from the National Government, the direction the departed then took, and the way in which the Muldoon Government's majority was reduced but preserved against its alternative.

I shall present the trends in net movement calculated in the popular way as percentages of the valid vote cast (see Table 11.1).

It is plain that in these terms both elections involved major movements of opinion (the 1972/75 nett was +14.9 for comparison); that in both cases basic trends were from the Government to Social Credit and that, in the case of 1978, they ran also from a fourth party, Values, and towards *ad hoc* alternatives—so great was the rush.[7] In both cases a strong margin collapsed leaving National 0.2 or 1,548 votes ahead in 1954 and Labour 0.6 or 10,737 ahead in 1978.

Table 11.1: Net Movements of the Percentages of Valid Votes Cast, 1975-1978 and 1951-1954

	1975	Change'75/8	1978	1951	Change	1954
Labour	39.6	+ 0.8	40.4	45.8	- 1.7	44.1
National	47.6	- 7.8	39.8	54.0	- 9.7	44.3
Social Credit	7.4	+ 8.7	16.1		+ 11.1	11.1
Values	5.2	- 2.8	2.4			
Independent Labour	0.0	+ 0.2	0.2	0.0	+ 0.1	0.1
Independent National	0.0	+ 0.9	0.9			
Ind. Social Credit	0.0	± 0.0	0.0			
C.P., S.U. etc.	0.1	- 0.1	0.0	0.1	± 0.0	0.1
Micro parties	0.0	+ 0.1	0.1			
Ind. & Right	0.1	± 0.0	0.1	0.1	+ 0.2	0.3
	100.0	± 10.7	100.0	100.0	± 11.4	100.0
Majority N:L	N 8.0	L +8.6	L 0.6	N 8.2	N -8.0	N 0.2

Ind. = Independent
C.P. = Communist Party
S.U. = Socialist Unity

But such was the way in which the constituencies were drawn in both instances that National's margin in seats over the alternative Labour government in 1954 was 10 and in 1978 it is now 9. So it was not only the restraint of departing voters in avoiding Labour and camping out with Social Credit that saved first Mr Holland and now Mr Muldoon. The operations of the Representation Commissions of 1952 and 1977 contributed their mites and so did the way party strengths were heavily concentrated here and there throughout the country.

There is much more to be shown both by a seat-type analysis and a regional analysis and by estimation of the real results in terms of the qualified vote. These I have now completed, but they deserve another article. Nor do they change the essential message of this article which is that a major section of the electorate threw a pulled punch at the Government in 1978 as it did in 1954. Thanks to Social Credit, to Representation Commissions and to divided intentions, all things New Zealand have once again happily conspired to save the country from having chosen change.

Notes

1 [They were Vernon Cracknell, MP for Hobson 1966-69; and Bruce Beetham, Leader between 1972 and 1986, who had won the Rangitikei by-election in February 1978, remaining in that seat until his defeat in 1984. Ed.]
2 [Keith Holyoake led the National Party between 1957 and 1972; Robert Muldoon was Leader between 1974 and 1984 and, of course, had won the 1975 general election. Social Credit had based its policies on the ideas concerning monetary reform of Major C. H. Douglas. Ed.]
3 [Wallace Rowling became Leader of the Labour Party in September 1974 after the Prime Minister, Norman Kirk, had died. Ed.]
4 [Sidney Holland led the National Party between 1940 and 1957, and was Prime Minister between 1949 and 1957. Ed.]
5 [Walter Nash led the Labour Party between 1951 and 1963, and was Prime Minister between 1957 and 1960. See Keith Sinclair, *Walter Nash* (Dunedin, 1976). On Labour and the 1951 dispute, see Sinclair, pp. 280-9; and Michael Bassett, *Confrontation '51: The 1951 Waterfront Dispute* (Wellington, 1972). Ed.]
6 [The Social Credit Political League became the New Zealand Social Credit Party in 1953. See Raymond Miller, 'The Democratic Party' in Hyam Gold (ed.), *New Zealand Politics in Perspective*, 2nd edn. (Auckland, 1989), pp. 244-59. The Party was led by W. B. Owen until 1960. Ed.]
7 [The Values Party was formed in 1975. Ed.]

12

New Zealand Defers Decision: The 1981 Election

On election night television the Prime Minister seized with apparent delight on what was for him the essential outcome of the 1981 election—that he could continue to govern.[1] But even that was uncertain, for 1981 was the kind of election a country has when it is not ready to make a decision. Even the vote counting and discounting dragged on for five months through electoral office revisions, district court recount and electoral petition hearing. It had indeed proved 'too close to call', as I predicted it would be, and the 4,122 votes which finally separated the major parties put Labour ahead of National while the seat result reversed that advantage into 47 National against 43 Labour MPs. And as an appendix there was Social Credit's twosome, confusingly pledged on a no confidence motion not to turn out whichever government had appeared.

Social Credit and the 'Balance of Responsibility'

All high hopes were disappointed in all parties. Social Credit saw the thirty and more per cent which the polls had registered twelve months before shrink to 20.65% of the valid vote on the day. Instead of the anticipated half-dozen or more Socred members vaulting to power then seizing the balance in the House and making the final choices between items in the Government programmes and Opposition proposals, the surge of support for the third party (+4.59%) accomplished no more than returning its two previous incumbents with reduced majorities.

Bruce Beetham's margin over National fell 2.60 percentage points while Garry Knapp's lead in September 1980 decreased by 2.17 points to an insecure 758 votes in November 1981. Indeed Social Credit's best chance for a third seat had undoubtedly lain with Nevern McConachy in Kaipara who was only 520 votes behind National's Peter Wilkinson in 1978. Yet the close prospect of defeat acted to galvanise National's organisation and voters, and their representative drew ahead by nearly doubling his majority to 1,029. So the seats where it mattered most to Social Credit to do well were precisely those where their performance faltered or drooped.

[This chapter was published in *Comment*, New Series, No. 16 (August 1982). Ed.]

How much more so was this the case with Labour. They captured four socially-mixed city seats: Hunua in Auckland and Kapiti in Wellington, both prizes which they thought to have been theirs in 1978, and then startled the Prime Minister by adding not only Wellington Central but Miramar as well. In addition they reclaimed Nelson from Mel Courtney who had deserted Labour's standard, and successfully defended the four Maori seats against Mat Rata who had not only departed but had hoisted a standard of his own. In the twenty-one city seats south of Auckland, National retained just the two well-to-do electorates of Ohariu in Wellington and Fendalton in Christchurch. But there Labour's successes ceased. Despite its loss of Hunua the National organisation in Auckland proved capable of holding target seats like Eden and Helensville and of actually making relative gains against Labour in Albany.

Even that much Labour progress would have been enough to have deadlocked the House eventually. What is more it would have forced Social Credit to do one of two revealing things. On the one hand it could have identified itself to both its ex-National and ex-Labour supporters— at the risk of offending one group or the other—by making a principled choice between the two overall programmes of the parties of government. If it had gone on burking and dodging such a coherent choice, on the other hand, it would thereby have exposed its own indecision, its powerlessness to advance its own prescriptions, and would thus have demonstrated the bankruptcy of its basic strategy of seeking the power to choose without choosing. 'The Balance of Responsibility', would then have looked neither responsible nor a balance but simply muddled and muddling.

In turn that would have cleared many electors' minds. If they had supported the third party as a way of seeking political change then they would have learned from the temporary survival of the Muldoon Government and the accompanying constitutional confusion and standstill that they had achieved just what they had not intended. On the other side, if they had voted Social Credit in order to safely register an alternative conservative protest then they would have been faced with the prospect that one outcome of their actions could be to let Labour in—as well as putting the Prime Minister out.

The very spectre of such a 46:44:2 situation when Parliament met was enough to provoke an erroneous assertion from Social Credit's Leader that the Speaker had both a deliberative and a casting vote so that the Speaker could and would relieve Mr Beetham of the cup of decision. But the ultimate effect of 46:44:2 would have been either to bring on an identifying alliance, coalition or arrangement or to have precipitated a fresh election in a much clarified atmosphere with the mass of voters impatient to make genuine decisions with understandable and predictable consequences this time round.

Taupo's tottering fall to National avoided or deferred all that. Little wonder that Mr Muldoon is reported to have added sotto voce to the Speaker's opening prayer of thanks: 'And for Taupo'.[2] Judicial decision, however, had appended only the final, formal seal to the results of the Prime Minister's own remarkable foresight in matters of political and social engineering. For Labour had been set the compulsory task of parties wishing to govern New Zealand with an assured Parliamentary majority which necessitates winning decisively in both kinds of marginal seat, in the provincial town electorates like Taupo, Gisborne and New Plymouth as well as in the socially-mixed city constituencies like Hunua or Miramar.

Labour's Failure in the Provincial Town Electorates

In the event Labour passed this test in the cities but failed it in the towns. In the town electorates Labour came up against the regional economic hopes stirred by the provincial location of so many of National's 'growth strategy' projects. In vain Labour urged that the gigantic capital sums for 'Think Big' infrastructures and construction would be better left unborrowed or else invested in agriculture, horticulture, primary processing and smaller, manageable ventures. The technicoloured hopes of the townspeople pointed them instead towards National.

Likewise there was spin-off from farmers to townsmen when the supplementary minimum prices [SMP] scheme was suddenly transformed by the Government deciding to fix support levels far above international market prices. Federated Farmers' leaders worried at the public nature of the subsidies and would greatly have preferred lowered costs of production. Labour candidates fulminated that it was all no more than a 'marginal seat retention plan'. If so, it worked because, as centres for servicing their regions, every provincial town had businesses by the dozens or hundreds which felt the benefit and knew whom to thank. Credit, too, was eased in election year and, if New Zealand's international borrowing had to be just about doubled, that was next year's bad news whereas the precarious and sectional prosperity was here and now.

Above all, there was the divisive distraction of the Springbok Tour looming ever closer during months of ineffectual exchanges with an adamant Rugby Union who would be moved by nothing less than specific directions. Then the Tour was on us in an obsessive cascade of newsprint, television and indignant, impassioned, dangerous social conflicts. It went on through July, August and September, travelled with the Prime Minister to London and the royal wedding, and in October it confronted the Commonwealth heads of government in Melbourne. There seemed to be no end to it until finally its animosities and revenges were merged into the election season with scarcely a break.

The elements of those struggles ran back for decades. They stretched back to 'No Maoris, No Tour' in 1960, to Norman Kirk's suspension of the 1973 Tour, to the Muldoon town meetings of 1974-75 at which he denounced Kirk's reversal, to the African boycott of the Montreal Olympics in 1976, to the carefully-placed ambiguities in the Gleneagles Agreement of 1977, to the Prime Minister's sports pledge in National's 1978 Manifesto, and to the test timetable of international rugby which had been planned and known for years in advance.[3] Assuredly the Tour could have been seen coming, the passions it aroused were anticipated, and its political consequences could broadly have been calculated.

Past polls had shown huge pro-tour majorities back in 1971 and 1972. The Kirk decision seems to have been followed by a turn-around of sympathies to a sizeable 56% to 35% lead in 1976 for the 'No' forces. By 1980, however, the country had reverted to earlier views with 'Yes' leading 'No' by 50% to 34%. All the issues and costs had again been canvassed by the time the May 1981 poll was taken, while the horrifying risks of Hamilton were present and visible to all by the time of the next July poll.[4] In these professional surveys there appeared a slim but growing anti-Tour margin, first of two, then of seven per cent. Moreover, underneath such nationwide totals there lay a further and critical division of opinion.

As the Herald-NRB reported on 13 August, 'In general the main metropolitan centres continue to oppose the tour. Most provincial centres support it—[nine did] although five do not and one, the Napier-Hastings area, is evenly divided.' These July figures for the pro-Tour sympathies of individual towns by no means correlate exactly with what specific towns did in November. For there were a cluster of factors in play: 'Think Big', the SMP spin-off, the election year splurge, candidate-induced variations, the entire context of the nationwide campaigns.

But the general way in which the Tour factor worked in the towns is plain enough and it combined with the other elements to ensure that Labour was blocked from securing any of its town objectives and even found a key town was prised loose from its grip. With Taupo gone, the beckoning vision of 46:44:2 and the clarification such an impasse would have compelled thereupon faded away and changed back into 47:43:2. As Labour's chance for power dimmed, so too did the electors' opportunity to have the drama of deadlock played out before them so that they could really have seen what a two-and-a-half party decision produces by way of good and coherent government.

At this point the trends in the election results for the towns are well worth pondering (see Table 12.1).

Table 12.1: Change in Majorities in Town Seats, 1978 to 1981
(In percentage points of the valid vote)

1.	Nelson	LAB -8.33 t°	(NAT 2nd '78; INDLAB 2nd '81)
2.	Manawatu	NAT +8.13	
3.	Wanganui	LAB -7.10	(NAT 2nd '78; SC 2nd '81)
4.	New Plymouth	NAT +6.99 t	
5.	Invercargill	NAT +6.49 t	
6.	Marlborough	NAT +6.27 t	
7.	Kaimai	NAT +5.25 t	(SC 2nd at both elections)
8.	Taupo	LAB/NAT + 3.81	
9.	Wairarapa	NAT +3.70	
10.	Palmerston North	LAB -2.81	
11.	Rotorua	NAT +2.75	
12.	Hamilton West	NAT +2.39	
13.	Whangarei	NAT +2.30 t °	
14.	Timaru	LAB - 1.74	
15.	Hawkes Bay	NAT +1.47	
16.	Horowhenua	NAT +0.46	

(Party direction of GAIN/LOSS)
(henceforth reverses.)

17.	Napier	LAB +0.05	
18.	Gisborne	NAT -0.39	
19.	Hamilton East	NAT -1.02	
20.	Tauranga	NAT -6.82 t°	(SC 2nd at both elections)
21.	Hastings	LAB +7.22 °	

1978 NAT 14: LAB 7.
1981 NAT 15: LAB 6.

---

t = Towns expected to benefit most from 'Think Big' or the surge into horticulture.
° = Affected by personal factors such as the unexpected withdrawal of a major opponent, an impending court case, competition from an ex-MP of the same party, replacement of the sitting MP by a fresh candidate, etc.

The Leadership Issue

For Labour 1981 was therefore a fourth heavy blow. The sequence of Norman Kirk's death, the disaster of 1975, followed by two near-misses has proved a disheartening succession of setbacks with a destabilising effect on the Parliamentary team. This has in some ways been reinforced and in other ways offset by the sharp rise in Labour's turnover of caucus numbers. First there were the losses of 1975, then eight captures in 1978, four more— with one loss—in 1981, and in addition the replacement of six former members from 1975 to 1978 and of eleven between 1978 and 1981. In the present caucus of forty-three there are twenty-seven or just on two-thirds who have entered or re-entered Parliament in 1975 or since. Instead of these newcomers starting at once upon the disciplined work of making their way into the Ministry while the experienced proved themselves in Cabinet, the result of Labour remaining out of office has been that the vigour and competitiveness of old hands and new has too often been turned inwards rather than against the Government.

The result has been public perception of disunion, dispute and doubt about Labour's Prime Minister-in-waiting and his future Cabinet. Given the continuing drumfire of popularity ratings put out by the various polls and the preoccupation of television with people rather than proposals, it is only to be expected that 'leadership' would assume the prominence it has as a factor in election decisions. (11.8% of eligible voters gave liking the leader as their main reason for supporting their party with a further 5% choosing out of a dislike of Mr Muldoon, according to the extensive Heylen-*Listener* post-election poll). The Prime Minister's personalisation and polarisation of politics have certainly exacerbated these tendencies with effects not only in his own party but also among the opposition. Indeed for both major parties 1981 was a post-coup election.

Those two attempts to change leaders in October and December 1980 were major eruptions, but the three inter-election years were spattered with minor explosions. In December 1978 Mat Rata, former Minister and long the Chairman of the Maori Policy Committee, was omitted by Mr Rowling from the temporary list of official Labour spokesmen and from then on relations began to worsen.[5] It took sixteen months for Mr Rata to arrive at the point of resignation from Parliament. By that time an organisational skeleton plus the groups of activists and the rough outlines of policy for a new party, Mana Motuhake, were in being. Mat Rata carried with him many concepts from his Labour days and drew also on recent thinking at the Maori Affairs Department. Especially, though, he emphasised the demand for as much cultural and economic autonomy as could be secured.

No-one could be sure whether the Maori electors' forty-year tradition of loyalty to Labour would withstand Mana Motuhake's appeal. For by-elections are notoriously times for experiment and Mat Rata possessed mana of his own. Labour's anxiety was relieved and the threat was contained when the June 1980 by-election result showed that Mat Rata had garnered only the kind of percentage (37.90%) that his National opponent had taken (35.96%) at the by-election seventeen years previously when Mat Rata himself had entered Parliament for Labour. The share gathered by Mana Motuhake in all four Maori seats at the general election showed a considerable reduction from its proportion at the by-election. Nevertheless the new movement emerged as the largest of the non-Labour parties: Mana Motuhake 15.08%, Social Credit 10.12%, National 9.26%, Independent 0.74%, Labour 64.80%, all as percentages of the valid vote.

This result raises the intriguing question of whence that Mana Motuhake vote came. The valid vote figures alone cannot supply the answer, but the leap of 8,499 in the total numbers voting validly points to an explanation. Using an estimation procedure to put the percentages on the basis of all those qualified to vote both in 1978 and 1981 yields the following net exchange as between the two elections.

Table 12.2: Net Movements in the Maori Seats Between 1978 and 1981

Mana Motuhake	+11.01%	Non-Voting	- 6.94%
Social Credit	+ 0.68%	Labour	- 2.77%
Independent	+ 0.53%	Informal votes	- 2.06%
National	+ 0.33%	Values	- 0.78%
	+12.55%		- 12.55%

In short, over seven-tenths of the gains registered by all three minor parties and the independents as well came either from decreased non-voting or from returning officers deciding that far fewer votes were informal. The principal effect of Mana Motuhake's appearance was not therefore to draw support from Labour's ranks but, on the contrary, it was to revive interest in or recruit fresh groups into electoral participation. As it happens this was an objective that Mr Rata as an MP had worked towards for many years.

There were other flare-ups of lesser significance. Mel Courtney's differences with his electorate committee and clashes with majority opinion in caucus led him first into independence and then to opposing his duly-selected Labour successor.[6] The effect was to siphon votes quite as much from his National rival as from his Labour opponent and to skew the totals somewhat for the town section and the Upper South Island region. Doubtless time will smooth out the disturbance as it did for Island Bay after the O'Brien candidature as Island Bay Labour in 1978.

In the end Richard Prebble was given a job he was interested to do in the shadow Cabinet. Roger Douglas eventually came back to the front bench having published his views at length and been repeatedly interviewed. Mr Lange, having been elevated to the Deputy Leadership in record time, did not lose that position after the run for the top but his popularity ratings descended instead.[7] And on the other side, Mr Quigley stopped rising in Cabinet, Mr Birch passed Mr Bolger and Mr Gair stayed as usual at the same level with a different difficult job, while Mr Cooper rose like a rocket and Mr McLay was definitely forgiven.[8]

There is little sign that any specific rebellion on either side continued on independently in the public mind and made a great and separate difference. Instead, the strife and the frictions were absorbed and subsumed by the electors into their overall pictures of the parties and the quality of their leadership. It was through the voters' cumulative gestalt or impression of each party and its head that these internecine struggles had their effect. Mr Rowling's sporadic embarrassments and his patient adjustments probably fed his image as a quiet, decent man, sorely tried. The Prime Minister's rapid recovery against 'the colonels' and a majority of his caucus were attributed at the time by supporters to his capacity for ruthless command and not to the colonels' blunder in failing to ensure beforehand that they had a candidate who would stand against the Leader.

The Heylen survey showed that among 280 party switchers National lost 30 for leadership reasons and gained 2, Labour lost 2 and gained 22, while Social Credit lost 9 and gained 17. Overwhelmingly these movements proceeded from negative judgments which caused voters to switch away from a given leader rather than being positively attracted to another. Looking at the whole body of electors surveyed including party loyalists and first-time voters, however, reveals a very different picture. Those giving liking for their leader as their main reason for supporting their party constituted 29.4% of National, 2.5% of Labour and 2.7% of Social Credit supporters. Conversely 10.7% of Labour and 6.8% of Social Credit specified dislike of Mr Muldoon as their main reason for voting as they did—which still leaves a worthwhile margin for Mr Muldoon.

We may well conclude that the benefits derivable by National from the Muldoon style and 'Rob's Mob' had mainly been capitalised upon in 1975 and 1978 and that by 1981, the returns in fresh party switching could well have ceased. The Muldoon campaign was toned right down as though just such a reaction to a full throttle performance had been anticipated and provided against. Since a third of the switchers at the election reserved their final choice for the last month, including 27.1% who kept their counsel until the last week or day, they were certainly watching—and it did prove right enough on the day.

The Mixed City Electorates
But not, be it noted, in the mixed city electorates nor the poorer city seats. Here it would seem the cumulative impression of the Government's economic performance over six years told against it. There were not the countervailing forces like SMPs and growth projects which saved the situation in the towns and, less so, the countryside. Even Dunedin, where the Prime Minister predicted he would win a seat, moved strongly against National. For after embittered and prolonged debate in the city, just at a late and damaging moment, the string on the growth package came loose and their smelter's prospects fell away.[9]

Among all eligible voters the Heylen Research Centre found that the main reason for supporting one's party was given as 3.8% unemployment; 4.8% 'Think Big'/growth strategy; 6.4% inflation/tax/economic issues and policy; 5.2% better deal for workers/people's party. Altogether economic reasons moved a fifth of the voters. Among switchers to Labour the same headings covered 8.6%; 7.2%; 15.9%; and 5.8% respectively, a total of 37.5%. Likewise despondency about the economy was widespread among voters in general but markedly more so among switchers to Labour and less so among switchers to National. 49.5% of all voters thought the economy would be in a worse state in twelve months, 68.3% of switchers to Labour held that view, but only 33.8% of switchers to National. Of recruits to National, on the other hand, 42.3% said the economic situation would remain 'the same' whereas only 22.3% of Labour's switchers said so.

The opinion survey figures above were nationwide. So to find what the marginal mixed city seats made of these and the other issues in their voting a table on their changes in majority between 1978 and 1981 should be useful (Table 12.3).

The contrast this table presents to that for the towns is remarkable. Their prevailing trends are opposite and this continues a divergence between the mixed city and town sections which had already appeared in 1978 but is now widening further, a growing difference which has little precedent in the last fifty years. Not only is the way the economy is working a differentiator, so is the way it is fostered by Government policies.

Table 12.3: Changes in Majorities in Mixed City Seats, 1978 to 1981 (In percentage points of the valid vote)

1. Lyttelton   *LAB + 11.39
2. Wellington Central NAT/LAB + 9.98
3. Western Hutt   *LAB + 6.40
4. St. Albans   LAB +6.33
5. Hunua   NAT/LAB + 5.77
6. Helensville   NAT - 5.29
7. Papanui   *LAB + 4.97
8. Miramar   NAT/LAB + 4.55
9. Papakura   NAT - 3.77 (1978 LAB 2nd; 1981 SC 2nd)
10. Onehunga   LAB +3.12
11. Birkenhead   NAT -3.05
12. Eden   NAT -2.67
13. Kapiti   NAT/LAB +2.45
14. Yaldhurst   LAB +0.96
15. Papatoetoe   LAB +0.78
16. Manurewa   *LAB +0.24

(Party GAIN/LOSS now reverses)

17. Albany   NAT +2.47

1978 NAT 9, LAB 8
1981 LAB 12, NAT 5

* =Already recaptured by Labour in 1978.

The different verdicts passed might have been pulled closer together if the cities had approved of the Tour which they did not, or if, for example, there had been serious industrial disputes in election year, or the unions had pushed harder on the wages or redundancy fronts. This was not so and such union restraint was very marked by contrast, say, with 1969 or 1975 and represented a measure of their desire for a change of government.

In view of the post-election dispute about the system of union affiliation to the Labour Party and the political effect in 1981 of the image it conveyed, one further Heylen finding is particularly germane. As a main reason for voting as they did, 0.8% of all eligible voters gave answers such as 'Labour leaning towards communism/socialist trade union involvement/Communists in other parties.' That 0.8% were concentrated exclusively under the heading of voters for National and, amongst National, they constituted 2.2%.

The Rise of Social Credit

There remains the continued but slowing phenomenon of the rise of Social Credit. Why did it happen, where and how did it happen, and whose party ox is being gored?

First the causes. At base the answer is obvious for it was and is economic failure, first felt here in 1967/68 but growing more and more serious from mid-1974 onwards and intensified as the impacts of the successive oil shocks arrived, primary produce prices fell and recovered unevenly, international inflation worsened and flowed in, protectionism spread and interest rates exploded. After thirty-five years of full employment and fluctuating but bankable prosperity, our governments had got used to distributing growing resources and our voters had developed great and demanding expectations which were hard to reduce and impossible to satisfy. Nor were leaders or the led proving adept managers of less. Though these difficulties were international and western-style governments everywhere were encountering degrees of resistance or rejection, yet the quality of economic management displayed overseas had varied greatly and New Zealand too had plainly created or compounded many of its own problems.

Bad times struck towards the end of the third Labour Government, and they were elaborated on and fixed in the popular memory by Robert Muldoon's tremendously skilful and destructive campaigning. The majority of the electorate including tens of thousands of Labour supporters were convinced that New Zealand's overseas borrowing in a time of spiralling oil costs and collapsing export receipts was conclusive proof of Labour's lasting economic incapacity. Then when Mr Muldoon's record by 1978 had proven no better on borrowing and worse on growth and unemployment, the doubly-disappointed who wanted to switch turned to Social Credit instead of turning out the National Government and turning to the alternative Labour government. It is the case that the high numbers not voting in 1975 were beginning to come back to the polls in 1978 and that Labour's vote rose in real terms, but the big wave of discontent washed towards Social Credit.

This doubled Social Credit vote of 16.1% fascinated the news media and provided publicity for the predominantly young and hard-working men at the top of Social Credit's organisation. From December 1978 to May 1979, however, they were just treading water as was Labour. The first four polls on party standings showed a minor shift towards the Government. Then in May 1979 after Labour's Conference and the election of a new and energetic President from the branches, there was a lurch to Labour which fell away slowly until December 1979 but averaged a Labour lead over National of 4.0% which would have translated, thanks to the boundaries, as a Labour majority of six seats over National and two to the League.

Up to this point Mr Muldoon had done little that was striking with his victory and the weight of the previous six years seemed to promise small chance of a third success in 1981. Somehow the attention of the electors had to be refocussed on the future and its prospects and taken resolutely away from both immediate past and present. At this point the Liquid Fuels proposals on energy were coming together and the revolution in Iran had lit the fuse to ignite oil prices once again. Labour's economic policy was as yet being ground fine in its Policy Committee and was to remain so until election year. So the early and middle months of 1980 became the time when Mr Muldoon and his key ministers added end uses for more hydro power to methanol and gas-to-petrol and refinery expansion and five times more New Zealand steel and pulp and the whole parcel which Mr Muldoon dubbed 'Think Big'. New Zealand would solve its export earning imbalances in the long run by a massive investment leap forward in the 'eighties.

The signs and portents of this vast and innovatory programme were accompanied by a fluctuating progression in the polls back towards the centre-line then over onto National's side. The average from February to September 1980 was a National over Labour lead of 0.5% which represented a National seat majority over Labour of about thirteen with only one seat for Social Credit. There was unease in agricultural and horticultural circles at plans for all this investment to pass them by, as they read it then. Both the Opposition parties began to criticise aspects of 'Think Big' but it was hard to get a grip on all of it or to be convincing with counter-proposals when the figures for planning alternatives were with Government and the departments and not available.

What Social Credit needed was an outsize piece of luck, something dramatic and on the human scale like the good fortune which had placed the Leader of the League in a seat like Rangitikei where a not-very-charismatic National member died thus bringing on a by-election and where the intended replacement was already an MP and Minister and so was not available to fight the seat. Add in an awkward National temporary stand-in and scatter hypnotised television coverage and, presto, Social Credit's first new series victory in February 1978 and the breakthrough to doubling Socred's vote at the 1978 general election.

Now again, with Social Credit becalmed, a hugely favourable wind blew in from the most unexpected quarter. The Prime Minister unwittingly obliged by choosing his close friend, Air Commodore Gill, as the new Ambassador to Washington after first getting a check-up on his seriously threatened health. East Coast Bays in 1978 had combined the highest urban Social Credit vote with the second highest National Alternative vote anywhere and, though Socred had come third in 1978, another alternative conservative protest at taxes, mortgage interest, executive cutbacks and disappearing second incomes would travel easier through Garry Knapp than the Labour candidate. After all, the Government's majority was in no danger from one by-election escapade. News media interest was intense and the Prime Minister said something adverse about academic economists when the occasionally critical investment banker, Dr Brash, was selected as National's candidate against Mrs Sue Wood. There was a muddle over admission and attendance at the Prime Minister's one meeting and, to cap it off, the bridge tolls raise was announced. Mr Muldoon then proceeded to go abroad on a long-planned tour.

Despite having heard and seen all the details of a National disaster in the making on the box, when Social Credit's second victory came it was still a thunderclap.[10] At the very next opinion poll Socred's standing shot up and suddenly anything seemed electorally possible to those many electors whose grasp of the workings of Parliament and the relation of opinion polls to elections was tenuous at best. Television was besotted by these fresh faces and instant authorities who appeared to promise change in a new way, a non-Labour, untired, intriguing third way. As Socred soared, National's lead over Labour lengthened. From October 1980 to March 1981 the average of nine surveys showed Labour 8.3% behind National and gave Social Credit 29.1%—which probably meant six seats.

There followed the two successive attempts to change leadership, National's failed coup growing directly out of alarm at the significance of East Coast Bays while Labour's parallel manoeuvring arose from prolonged destabilisation and every aspect of the polls. It was time for the major parties to take a grip on a sliding situation. Bill Rowling and half the Labour caucus held the pass coolly until Jim Anderton and the branches rode to the rescue.[11] By February 1981 that same caucus was unanimously endorsing the Rowling-Lange combination in that order. At National Mr Muldoon with his ever-ready mailbag and Mr Talboys routed the colonels and again by February the Prime Minister had reshuffled the guilty, promoted the innocent and forgiven the penitent.[12]

By then it was election year and the occasion to consider easing credit, pondering the right height for SMPs, and awaiting the gathering storm of the Tour. What could be done would be done—like renaming 'Think Big' as the 'Strategy for Growth'. And it was only the last kick of the departing high Social Credit polling that caused the BCNZ to decide quite unjustifiably to equate opinion polls with official election results and give equal time to all three parties.[13] Undoubtedly that was of real assistance to Social Credit, and its leaders had been shrewd to fight for it for years past. Like Rangitikei and East Coast Bays themselves, equal time was just one more of good fortune's gifts.

Social Credit's most promising prospects in 1981 lay in the countryside and provincial towns of the North Island away from its cities. Nevertheless, in view of the astounding upset in East Coast Bays it might have proved possible to exploit the parallel social and political factors present in Pakuranga, another richer city seat in Auckland which in 1978 had registered an even higher Independent National vote than East Coast Bays. This fact was nearly but not quite managed as may be seen below (see Table 12.4).

Table 12.4: Changes in Percentage Shares of Valid Votes between 1978 and 1981 in East Coast Bays and Pakuranga

	East Coast Bays			Pakuranga		
	1978 %	Change	1981 %	1978 %	Change	1981 %
Social Credit	19.99	+24.91	44.90	14.05	+23.64	37.69
National Alternative	16.55	-16.55	—	21.46	-21.46	—
Labour	27.45	-14.50	12.95	26.51	- 5.58	20.93
National	34.49	+ 7.47	41.96	36.68	+ 4.25	40.93
Values	1.52	- 1.52	—	1.30	- 1.30	—
Independent	—	+ 0.19	0.19	—	+ 0.45	0.45
1978 NAT:LAB majority		7.04		1978 NAT:LAB majority		10.17
1981 SC:NAT majority		2.94		1981 NAT:SC majority		3.24

Apart from these exceptions it behoved Social Credit to concentrate its effort on what had always rewarded them most, the countryside, and in particular the north, centre and west of the North Island. As I put it in a broadcast the night after the election of 1960: 'Within the countryside it would seem that it is the dairying districts that especially look to Social Credit. It is in the old stamping grounds of the conservative independent, like Taranaki and Northland, or in the heartland of Douglas Credit in depression times, the Waikato, that the modern League does well.' Since then much has altered such as Hamilton which has drawn itself and its surroundings somewhat apart from the rest of the Waikato. With that modification, however, the rest of the observation holds true. For the motivation behind these lasting political tendencies lies in the century-old search by onerously-mortgaged farmers and small businessmen alike for that colonial elixir, state or publicly provided cheap and easy credit.

For National a Tremendous Last-Ditch Save

National had good reason to fear for the 1981 result in these northern, central and western North Island seats. Social Credit had already made itself the principal rival in the region by climbing from 14.74% in 1975 to 28.85% in 1978. Instead of coming second in only three seats out of the region's fourteen, Social Credit had moved up past Labour in 1978 to being first in one and second in nine. The problem for National was whether SMPs, eased credit, the growth strategy and rural identification with rugby, law and order would suffice to hold the region against Social Credit the way the same factors assisted National to more than hold the towns against Labour.

Table 12.5: Change in Majorities in the Northern, Central and Western North Island Region, 1978 to 1981
(In percentage points of the valid vote)

1.	Rural Waipa	NAT	-13.35
2.	Rural Waitotara	NAT	- 7.27
3.	Town Wanganui	LAB	- 7.10
	(NAT 2nd 1978; SC 2nd 1981)		
4.	Town Tauranga	NAT	- 6.82
5.	Rural Matamata	NAT	- 6.79
6.	Farmer Bay of Islands	NAT	- 5.44
7.	Rural King Country	NAT	- 4.83
	(LAB 2nd 1978; SC 2nd 1981)		
8.	Rural Hauraki	NAT	- 2.15
9.	Rural Taranaki	NAT	- 0.89

(Party direction of GAIN/LOSS reversed)

10.	Town Whangarei	NAT	+ 2.30
	(LAB 2nd in both elections)		
11.	Farmer Kaipara	NAT	+ 2.33
12.	Rural Rangitikei	SC	- 2.60
	(NAT 2nd in both elections)		
13.	Town Kaimai	NAT	+ 5.25
14.	Town New Plymouth	NAT	+ 6.99
	(LAB 2nd in both elections)		

1978: National 12: *Labour* 1: *Social Credit* 1
1981: National 12: *Labour* 1: *Social Credit* 1

What made National's task in the regions more difficult was that Social Credit opposed 'Think Big' root and branch. So rural doubters who wanted Government investment to flow towards them directly instead of indirectly through multinational projects could make their protest without supporting Labour. As to credit, Mr Beetham was himself the amiable if unspecific personification of new horizons in eased credit. Mr Beetham was careful to moderate his questioning of SMPs by confining criticism to the conditions that had made them necessary. And on the Tour Social Credit's Leader wondered aloud whether the Prime Minister had done enough to meet with and put pressure on the Rugby Union, but then took care to identify with the continuance of the Tour itself and against the kind of protest which developed.

The upshot can be read in Table 12.5 which displays the changes in the region's majorities electorate by electorate.

The essence of the answer is that National held off Social Credit's assault, as witness the fact that the tenure of the region's seats by the three parties remained unchanged over the two elections. Certainly National was shaken and shaken severely in spots. Marilyn Waring's role in the Tour and her months away at Harvard were ill-received by the voters.[14] The Hon. Venn Young in Waitotara and Keith Allen in Tauranga would remember this rebuke though both were safe for the time being. They could console themselves with the thought that Labour's Russell Marshall had been hit just as hard in Wanganui.

But that would be to miss the point of the containment of Social Credit in its heartland so that it gained not one further seat nor any additional leverage in Parliament wherewith to throw the major parties and the governing process into confusion and eventually extract some arrangement with National or, more probably, precipitate another election. At such an election the presently divided majority against National might well decide to resolve effectively the issue of securing a change in government. Social Credit's recent windfalls of protesting rather than ideological supporters might make up their minds to abandon Social Credit as a blind alley towards change. Instead they could put Labour in firmly enough to deliver that change.

Of course there was always hope for National even with an early election that the electors, driven back to the ballot too soon, would blame both Labour and Social Credit and swing forcefully to the Prime Minister and 'Think Big'—however shaky various projects began to look. No; whichever aspect a National supporter examined, the Party and its Leader had already secured the best result possible given the difficult circumstances. It had been a tremendous last-ditch save. They had kept the power to govern, blocked Labour once again, contained Social Credit at a harmless two-seat total, and staved off an early election with all its unpredictable consequences and threatening odds.

The National supporters in the northern, central and western North Island seats might well have added that their region had demonstrated at the critical point that this was National's and Reform's core before it was Social Credit's heartland, and when put to the test the region preferred its conservatism to be of the established variety and not the alternative hybrid.

Other regions and sections like the Eastern and Southern North Island and, far more so, the poorer and socially mixed city seats had taken a different view. Urban New Zealand in 1981 made clear its choice of Labour to govern. Only the seven richer city seats and a handful of five Auckland marginals offset this thrust of Labour towards the Treasury benches. The cities returned thirty-one Labour to eleven National MPs and one Social Crediter. Furthermore the four Maori MPs stood with the party of the urban majority so it was 35:11:1 in all.

For their part the country electorates had it the other way round. They divided twenty-one National to two Labour and one Social Credit. With the provincial towns added that made 36:8:1. Such a contrast with the city marked a deeper and simpler sectional-cum-political alignment than New Zealand had seen since the last war which in turn reflected sharper divergences of social attitude, economic interest and political belief than the country had witnessed since the Great Depression.

They were deep and inflamed divisions which had produced a tiny and insecure margin on which to govern and no mandate one way or another. The Prime Minister's strategies had preserved that political margin while those strategies also had the effect of widening an abnormal rift between marginal mixed city and marginal town. Between them those classes of seat usually pick our government unitedly by moving in the same party direction at the same time. In 1981 they were opposed and did the opposite. Only increasingly common economic and social experiences in the next few years will bring the two back together again and produce the increasingly common verdicts and positive choices which New Zealand society and government require. For the 1981 election, anyway, the balance of choices made amounted to deferring these decisions.

Notes

1   [The Prime Minister was Robert Muldoon who had held this post since 1975. Muldoon remained Prime Minister until National was defeated by Labour in July 1984. Ed.]

The 1981 Election

2   [Labour held Taupo between 1972 and 1975, National between 1975 and 1978, and Labour between 1978 and 1981, when Jack Ridley very narrowly lost his seat for the second time after a roll recount. Ed.]
3   [The Gleneagles Agreement, concerning sporting contacts with South Africa, was negotiated amongst Commonwealth leaders. Ed.]
4   [On 25 July 1981, due to anti-tour protesters, the rugby match between the Springboks (the South African team) and the Waikato was cancelled. Ed.]
5   [Wallace Rowling was Leader of the Labour Party from 1974 until he resigned from that position in 1983. Ed.]
6   [Melvyn Courtney entered Parliament in 1976 in the Nelson by-election of that year and resigned from Labour in 1981. Ed.]
7   [Roger Douglas was removed from the informal shadow Cabinet after he published his Alternative Budget, unauthorised by Labour. David Lange became Deputy Leader of Labour in November 1979, having entered Parliament at a by-election in March 1977. Ed.]
8   [At the time of the 1981 election, Derek Quigley held Housing and Tourism, Bill Birch held Energy and National Development, Jim Bolger held Labour, George Gair held Health and Social Welfare, and Warren Cooper held the Broadcasting portfolio. Jim McLay was Attorney-General and Minister of Justice. Quigley, Bolger, Gair and McLay were involved in a plan to remove Muldoon from the leadership during 1980. This was known as the 'Colonels' coup'. Ed.]
9   [This refers to the planned aluminium smelter at Aramoana, near Dunedin. Ed.]
10 [Garry Knapp, Social Credit, won the East Coast Bays by-election of 6 September 1980 against National's Don Brash. Ed.]
11 [Jim Anderton, later to leave Labour and lead the Alliance, was President of the Labour Party between 1979 and 1984 (when he became MP for Sydenham). Ed.]
12 [Brian Talboys was Deputy Prime Minister until February 1981. He did not seek re-election to Parliament in 1981. Ed.]
13 [BCNZ = Broadcasting Corporation of New Zealand. Ed.]
14 [Marilyn Waring, MP for Waipa, argued against the Springbok tour being permitted to go ahead. She also took part in the anti-Tour demonstrations. Ed.]

13

Voting in the Maori Political Sub-System, 1935-1984

This Annex is offered with the twin purposes of adding recent voting details to Professor Sorrenson's historical account, and of helping to clarify the operations and outcomes of the parallel Maori electoral system over the last 50 years. The essence of the evolution to be examined can be read from the graphs included, but perhaps a commentary on the indicative trends they display, some of the factors behind the trends, and the methodology and limitations of the graphs may be of assistance.[1]

Figure 13.1 shows the party outcomes of the last 17 general elections in the 4 Maori seats taken as a whole and percentaged on the conventional basis of 100.0% equalling all valid votes cast. Insofar as MPs, the press and the public have moved on from attending to the relative size of majorities in numbers of votes from one election to the next, it is to valid vote percentages and comparisons they have gone. The advantage of basing percentaging on valid votes is that the figures are carefully scrutinised and compiled and widely published. They cover all the votes which 'count' in deciding seats and therefore appear to cover all the trends which affect the final result.

The main features of the last 50 years of Maori voting shown by Figure 13.1 are first, the rise of the Ratana-then-Labour vote from a shade above one-third of the combined electorate to the current level of nearly three-quarters of the vote over the last 6 elections.[2] The rise was rapid, very much so between 1935 and 1938, then strongly so until 1946 and was still lifting until 1951. Between 1951 and 1957 Labour support formed a plateau somewhat above two-thirds of all valid votes. Then, at the end of the second Labour Government, there was a minor to middling reverse (down 4.9 points). The climb was thereupon resumed both in 1963 and 1966 and more strongly again in 1969 and 1972 until it reached an absolute peak of 80.4 per cent or four-fifths of all Maori valid votes.

Once more a 3-year Labour period in office was followed by a minor to middling reverse (again down 4.9 points). In 1978 the regaining of

---

[This chapter was published in the *Report of the Royal Commission on the Electoral System: Towards a Better Democracy* (Wellington, 1986). The *Report* included appendices on New Zealand's electoral law and Maori representation. Chapman's analysis was included in Appendix B, 'A History of Maori Representation in Parliament' by M. P. K. Sorrenson. Ed.]

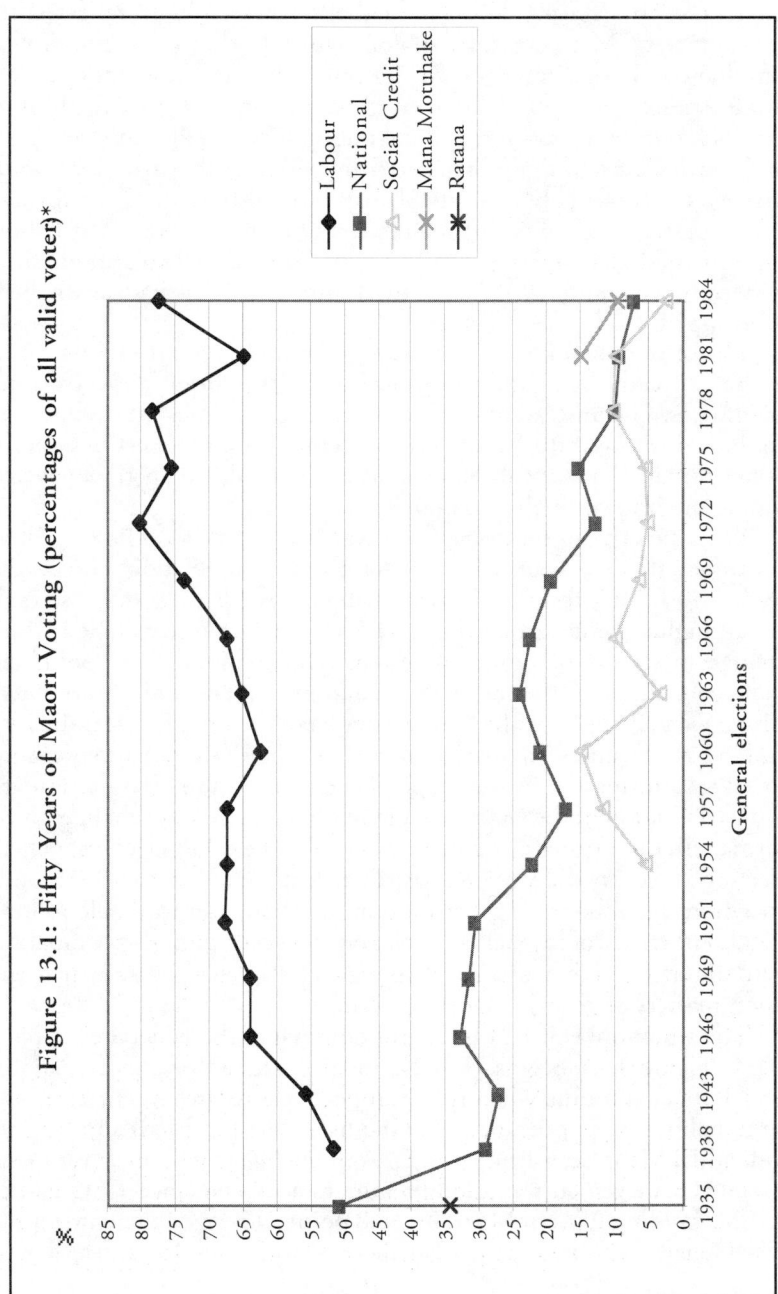

Figure 13.1: Fifty Years of Maori Voting (percentages of all valid voter)*

* [Other minor parties and Independents omitted. See the original Graph 1. Ed.]

ground began as it had in 1963. Only this time the process was suddenly interrupted by a heavy fall. This Labour fall seemingly reflected the appearance of Mana Motuhake alone, for all other competitors were simultaneously declining (down 2.3 points in sum) save Independent (up 0.7 points). In 1981 Labour continued to draw nearly two-thirds of the vote, but such a result raised the question of whether this new party of the articulate and those alienated from parties as they had been would manage to reduce Labour to its plateau of the fifties and keep it there. That question was answered for the time being in 1984 when Labour support made its largest single leap since the Ratana-to-Labour surge between 1935 and 1938. The three-quarters level had again been overtopped.

The second major feature of the developments set out in Figure 13.1 is the unsteady but continuing decline in support for the National candidates. The unsteadiness of the decline and at times the decline itself are linked to the third feature on the graph, the proneness of Labour's opposition to divide and even, as in the earliest and latest periods covered, to fracture into competing fragments.

Why the opposition to National was so divided in 1935 and why it continued divided against Labour for a time, why National descended so decisively and, reciprocally, why Labour rose, paused and rose again are all highly complex questions. The answers are intermingled with a change in the Maori political system which sprang from politically induced changes in the social and economic situation of Maori voters. There were changes in the way parties were organised, in candidature and in basic loyalties. In turn the altered system was tested by a profound social transformation in the shape of the accelerating urbanisation and industrialisation of the Maori people. It is true there were changes in the formal electoral system: the secret ballot for the 1938 election; general elections held on the same day as the pakeha voted from 1951; a new and more equal boundary distribution for 1954; and workable rolls for 1957. The effects of these alterations were, however, minor by comparison with the effects of refocused loyalties which followed a government acting upon matters of general Maori concern.

The situation as it had been still dominated the general election of 1935. Figure 13.1 begins with National possessed of a clear majority over Ratana at a time when the 'European' electorates were returning a large Labour preponderance. As Graphs 2 to 5 [omitted] showing the individual Maori seats bring out, Sir Apirana Ngata with his great mana, personal achievements and long tenure as a Liberal since 1905 had no trouble holding Eastern Maori by 37.8 points. Likewise the Reform MP, Tau Henare, who had sat for Northern Maori since 1914, was able to gather an ample majority of 14.7 points. In Western Maori, by contrast, Sir Maui Pomare, the Reform stalwart, had died some years before in 1930. His successor, Taite Te Tomo, had proved unable to equal Sir Maui's attractive powers and in 1935 a full fifth of the vote was split away by Democrat and Independent Labour candidates. Even so, Te Tomo barely lost the seat by half a point to Haami Tokouru Ratana. He was the Prophet's eldest son who had contested the electorate 4 times before and was widely known and respected.

Only in Southern Maori was the prestige of occupancy working for rather than against the Ratana candidate. Eruera Tirikatene had fought the pocket borough electorate—it had just 966 valid voters in 1935—twice before finally becoming the first of Wiremu Ratana's 'Four Quarters' to become an MP. Tirikatene had lost by 1 vote in 1928 and 19 in 1931. Then death removed the Coalition United MP in June 1932 and at the ensuing by-election on 3 August the way was further opened by a 6-candidate struggle which Tirikatene won easily. The general election narrowed his lead to one-fifth of what it had been but the main challenger proved to be an Independent while the National aspirant worsted only the Democrat.

In 1935 the name 'National' was new and did not yet represent a fresh organisation or a different reality. Beneath the label the faces were the same and the tradition was still of candidates lining up loosely tagged as one or other of the 2 old former parties, Liberal and Reform, or parading their hopes and independence usually in vain. There was still little or no organisation and few benefits for Maori from the old parties to point to. Belonging to the party of Government was of value and, because Maori since 1919 had to vote the day before Europeans, they had less chance to pick up the tremors and excitement of impending change in Government from the rest of the voters on the day. So the mana of notable men, their efforts to ventilate land and fishing grievances, the cumulative prestige of occupancy and links with tribes, federations and churches all mattered the more when there was no history of effective political change to the status quo.

The 'party of the morehu', Ratana, was different in manner, basis and objectives. Prophetic in leadership and inspiration, supra-tribal in aim, it was congregational and sectarian in fundamental organisation and this made it unusually strong in experienced speakers, ministry and committee work. Moreover Ratana was an entirely Maori party with easily-grasped objectives flowing out of Maori concerns and ideals for the land, health, education, their economic needs and opportunities and, above all, the proper place of the people under the Treaty of Waitangi. Yet the party stood checked at general and by-elections between 1922 and 1935. Its church adherents, supporters and political sympathisers could muster between one-quarter and two-fifths of the voters. Such limits on support, apart from the quirks of one by-election, had proved too narrow to win seats until 1935.

Had there been a system of strict proportional representation in a 4 MP Maori electorate there might well have been a Ratana MP in 1931 and perhaps 2 in 1935. As it was, there was 1 by 1932 and 2 in 1935. Given that proportional representation would also have yielded a new and Labour-led Government in 1935, albeit probably dependent for a slim margin on Country and Independent allies, then the adherence of the 2 Ratana members to that governing coalition or alliance would also have resulted then as it did in fact. PR would have made the conjunction far, far more of a critical matter even while PR at the same time rendered the new Government so shaky that it would not have risked the active programme which in reality it could and did safely undertake. As it was, Eruera Tirikatene had voted with Labour through the depths of the Great Depression so, after the Prophet and the new Prime Minister had formalised the Ratana-Labour alliance early in 1936, both Tirikatene and H. T. Ratana voted with Labour and joined the Labour caucus.

The major changes after 1935 to the shape and outcome of the Maori political system were neither the result of having 2 Ratana members in Parliament nor simply the consequence of their joining Labour in alliance and caucus. It was not until 1946, long after Labour's principal innovative legislation was passed and after the 'post-war' initiatives like the Maori Social and Economic Advancement Act of 1945 were in place, that Labour found its majority down to 4 and every last MP in caucus needed for defence.

What profoundly altered the Maori relationship to Government was the presence of a party in power which was prepared to make successive changes in the legal and administrative status of Maori, to include them as citizens in the structure of welfare and social security it was building, and ready to spend disproportionately on the health, education and housing of individual Maori in the name of more equal opportunity for all. This was not done on an ideological basis nor done in the name of 'affirmative action', 'positive discrimination' or 'cultural identity' for those concepts and terms were two decades off in the future. Nor was it done in a coherent, consistently executed fashion. On the basis of a philosophy of the value of the common man, the new Government felt its way forward and found its way, for example, to the structure of tribal executives and committees which was later crowned by National with the New Zealand Maori Council. Before 1935 there had been leading politicians such as Sir Apirana Ngata and Gordon Coates who individually achieved much for Maori causes. After 1935, however, a party in Government began to achieve what only Governments can carry into effect.

Certainly the major change came after and not at the 1935 election which was in most respects, as has been indicated, in the style of the first 3 decades of the century as modified but not transformed by the advent of the Ratana candidates and the deprivations of the Depression. Figure 13.1 shows the change came in 1938 following the torrent of legislative and administrative activity which characterised the intervening years. In 1938, Sir Apirana Ngata and Tau Henare stood again, still with their mana, still sitting members but, as Graphs 4 and 5 [omitted] demonstrate, with very different results from those of 1935. Tau Henare lost Northern Maori after 24 years to Paraire K. Paikea who had tried 3 times before and not once reached two-fifths of the valid vote. Sir Apirana's reputation, deeds and connections had not altered but his margin shrank from 37.8 to 10.7 points in the face of a divided candidacy which set an endorsed Labour candidate—Reweti Kohere, 30.6%—against the regular Ratana standard-bearer, Tiaki Omana, who took 21.3%. As for the 2 sitting Ratana and Labour MPs, Tirikatene's lead of 4.5 became 47.0 points while Tokouru Ratana's climbed from 0.5 to 20.6 points.

One is always wary of the fallacy in *post hoc, ergo propter hoc* ('after this, therefore on account of this'). Nevertheless only a sweeping and powerful set of factors could have moved so many voters so far and simultaneously in the same party direction. Voters changed to Labour despite opposition candidates' occupancy, mana or connections, more easily in their absence, but whether the opposition possessed them or not. Plainly, the motivation was Maori approval of Labour's political upheaval of the status quo. That had the strength and comprehensiveness in its emotional and practical effects to produce such a widespread result especially when action contrasted so positively with the dull endurance demanded by the Depression. The consequence was a climb in Labour support which outlasted the Labour Government and only paused in 1954 and 1957.

There was no sign of the new Maori loyalties being shaken at or after the first Labour loss of office in the way Liberal and then Reform had seen their vote eroded and some of their MPs displaced. By the time the Labour setbacks of 1960 and 1975 arrived it would be more reasonable to ascribe Labour's sags in Maori support to great expectations disappointed by the party's performance in office than to reverse the sequence and view the diminished vote as the product of losing the prestige engendered by governing. Moreover the reversion of some Maori seats to National as the new party of Government did not occur as it had when Reform succeeded Liberal. Instead the process had yet to begin although National had been the party in office for more than three-quarters of the time since 1949.

What this long succession of Labour members in Maori seats suggests, like the exceptionally high percentages of the valid votes cast in their favour, is that the separate Maori seats permitted their voters to choose and maintain a different course of political action from their fellow New Zealanders, one to which they have shown remarkable fidelity for over 4 decades. The Maori political system is part of and contributes to the general party system in that Labour continues to be one of New Zealand's two major parties from which governments come. But the Maori course is removed from pakeha practice in that a very small portion indeed of Maori voters shift back and forth from one to the other major party. Furthermore the origins of earlier Labour candidacy in the Ratana movement gave an independent and Maori style as well as a Maori organisation to this distinct and only partially parallel Maori political system.

At first the Labour leadership did not fully grasp the advantages the Ratana alliance had conferred on them. A small group of Maori Labour activists believed, in the face of failures in 1925 and 1928, that the general pattern of Labour organisation and selection could be applied within the Maori context. Kohere's endorsed Labour candidacy for Eastern Maori in 1938 was a challenge to Ratana selection and to the 4 men chosen by the Prophet and, in particular, to Tiaki Omana, the Eastern Maori 'koata'. Both candidates and both movements lost by this test of whether either could do without the other. Looking at earlier and later results on Graph 4 [omitted], it is debatable but unlikely that Sir Apirana Ngata would have lost in 1938 even if the test had not been permitted and if the alliance had been upheld in all 4 seats instead of in 3. Just the same the sudden, sharp dip in the trend line for Ngata—followed by a subsequent rise in 1943—shows that the combined extra pull exercised by running a pure Labour candidate plus a pure Ratana candidate could drag National's result down by 8 to 10 points. Both the Labour and Ratana men did well but neither, thanks to the other, did well enough to win or come close to winning the seat. Having learned the consequences of unfaithfulness to the alliance and rediscovered the penalties of disunity, Labour endorsed Omana in 1943 and Sir Apirana's long and distinguished tenure ceased.

By the point at which National's last MP in a Maori seat was defeated, National as a whole had descended from 50.7% in 1935 to 27.2% in 1943 partly as the converse of the secular shift towards Labour which has been examined. There was a recovery (+4.8 points) for National in 1946 when the men of the Maori Battalion were home from the War. But it did not represent a National success in relation to Labour for at the same election Labour had grown nearly twice as fast (+8.2 points). In search of an explanation for both major parties rising simultaneously, one has only to look down at the base of Figure 13.1 to see that the succession of Democrat, Independent and Independent Labour candidacies had at last subsided in 1946, pulled down eventually by their persistent and complete lack of success for individuals. Adding all the Independent and mini-party candidates together, they had in 3 elections successively preoccupied 14.8%, 19.0% and 17.1% of the voters. Released at the coming of peace, and with 5,660 additional valid votes in the 1946 total, the result was a rise for both major parties in the ratio of roughly 2 Labour to 1 National.

The years from 1946 to 1951 saw National climb to its zenith in General voting, followed by the Korean War boom, soaring prices, industrial battle on the waterfront and Sidney Holland's successful snap election of 1951. Despite all these stirring developments on the general political stage, those same years were, by contrast, stable years in Maori politics. This would have been paradoxical if Maori politics had been simply a subdivision of pakeha politics. As a Maori political sub-system taking its own course, however, its independent results were clear enough. Labour moved up very faintly (+0.1) as it sank from power among other voters, then went up definitely (+3.8) during the 'Strike Election'. Independency rose slightly and fell again. National sank in the Maori seats (-1.2) as it came to power elsewhere and sank again (-1.1) as it acquired a massive majority of 24 in the other 76 seats.

This was the era of the Hon. E. B. Corbett as Minister of Lands and Maori Affairs in both the first and second Holland Ministries and the first Holyoake Ministry of 1957. The new Government might have been able to strike out with fresh policies and to a degree overlay with National's activity the deep impression Labour's changes had made. For the need to go on adapting to and providing for the consequences of the spreading urbanisation and industrialisation of the Maori people was increasing with the acceleration of the transformation itself. The first Labour Government's thinking in relation to Maori apprenticeships, job training and professional opportunities had moved on from the once universal conception of rural solutions, but not so fast towards an evolving mixture of urban and rural answers as the facts now required. It was an opportunity which the conventional Corbett administration chose not to seize even though the Minister's regular and friendly presence on marae was welcomed.

Without initiatives to counteract Maori loyalty to Labour, National's descent became steeper in 1954 and reached a nadir of 17.1% at the 1957 election which returned Labour to power in the country at large.

Among Maori voters there was no build-up to this event nor any visible addition from National's exodus. Labour's vote stayed above two-thirds of the valid vote for 3 elections while declining gently in 1954 (-0.3) and more gently (-0.2) in 1957. Little was happening in Labour's Maori ranks with the party out of power and a stable set of MPs. Eruera Tirikatene had been there since 1932, Tiaki Omana and T. P. Paikea since the general election of 1943, while Mrs Iriaka Ratana had succeeded her deceased husband, Matiu, at the general election of 1949.

If they were not going to Labour, where then were National's departed supporters going to and why? Here again we encounter the phenomenon of splits in the anti-Labour opposition such as could be found in 1935, 1938 and 1943. Among Maori voters in 1954 the 3 Social Credit candidates took 5.8% while Independency went from 1.5% to 4.5%. In net terms National's outflow contributed 8.5 points and Labour's trickle 0.3 points. The 1954 rejection of National and the consequent filling up of the ranks voting for an alternative conservative or at least non-Labour party was by no means a peculiarly Maori phenomenon. Among General voters the economic strains and discontents of the early fifties drove National down even further (-9.8 points) and that pushed the newcomers in the Social Credit Political League up far further to 11.3%.

Maori and General voters alike felt the pressure of credit squeezes, import cuts and exchange allocations as participants in a common economy. Resentment at this pressure had conjured forth within the General system a hastily-assembled party to express this indignation without having to vote Labour and, in that, it was successful. The enthusiasts for Douglas Credit and the League leadership no doubt hoped for power or, at a minimum, a change to National's economic policy. In those aims the League's activists failed and, instead, prolonged the Holland Government's life for 3 years in a way that a traditional transfer of support between alternative governing parties would not have done.

The Maori sub-system's variations displayed in 1954 were, however, to prove indicative. Independency in General seats went from an insignificant 0.1% in 1951 to an insignificant 0.3% in 1954 while Independency showed a clear secondary response in Maori electorates by lifting 3.0 points. Social Credit found 76 candidates for 76 seats in the General system but could fill only 3 out of 4 Maori slots. Most important for the long term was the disparity between the 11.3% accorded by General voters and the 5.8% from Maori electors. After 2 further elections which embodied a noteworthy Maori departure to which we shall return, the generally lesser but parallel Maori share for Social Credit was to reassert itself and continue through to 1984. The following table illustrates this. The bracketed figures indicate fewer than the optimum number of candidacies.

Table 13.1: General Seat and Maori Seat Electors' Support for Social Credit, 1954-1984

Election	1954	1963	1966	1969	1972	1975	1978	1981	1984
'European' SC%	11.3	8.1(73)	14.6	9.2	6.7	7.5	16.2	21.0	7.8
Maori SC%		5.8(3)	3.4(3)	10.0	6.5	5.3	5.8	10.5	10.1	2.4

Seemingly, the conclusions are obvious. The Social Credit Political League was utilised as a fluctuating opposition within the opposition to Labour both by General and by Maori electors, although to a diminished extent by the latter. Social Credit's best years were those elections reflecting a degree of rejection for both major parties, in 1954, 1966, 1978 and 1981. The appropriate rises and falls show up in Table 13.1 along both the 'European' and Maori lines, so that conclusion stands and represents a common response to political and socio-economic circumstances among both General and sub-system voters. But is the other conclusion that there was a 'lesser' or 'diminished' Maori tendency to split the opposition to Labour correct?

To doubt it one has only to recall the major difference between the Maori sub-system with its decisively declining line of support for National and contrast it with the situation obtaining in the General system where the battle lines of National and Labour intertwine around the 50% down to 40% parallels. In the General system, opposition to Labour—in the sense of voters for all other parties or Independents—will normally constitute over 50% and even 60% of the entire valid vote. A look at the height of Labour in Maori voting emphasises the contrasting fact that the anti-Labour opposition there may run from a third to a quarter and as low on occasion as one-fifth. For Social Credit to have picked up, say, 10% of an opposition amounting in all to one-third of the Maori voters could be to display a greater propensity for third party splitting than for Social Credit to capture, say, 15% of an anti-Labour sector of 60% of the whole General vote.

Table 13.2 tests the proposition by expressing the points scored by Social Credit as a percentage of all points won by non-Labour candidates at each election among, first, Maori voters and, second, General voters.

Table 13.2: Maori Seat and General Seat Support for Social Credit Expressed as Shares of the non-Labour Voting Sector, 1954-1984

	1954	1957	1960	1963	1966	1969	1972	1975	1978	1981	1984
Maori Election											
A. Total non-Labour	32.5	32.7	37.6	34.9	32.5	26.2	19.6	24.5	21.7	35.2	22.4
B. Social Credit share	5.8	11.8	15.0	3.4	10.0	6.5	5.3	5.8	10.5	10.1	2.4
B/A as %	17.8	36.1	39.9	9.7	30.8	24.8	27.0	23.7	48.4	28.7	10.7
'European'/'General' Election											
A. Total non-Labour	56.7	52.3	57.2	52.3	59.4	56.8	52.6	61.4	60.6	61.8	58.1
B. Social Credit share	11.3	7.1	8.4	7.1	14.6	9.2	6.7	7.5	16.2	21.0	7.8
B/A as %	19.9	13.6	14.7	13.6	24.6	16.2	12.7	12.2	26.7	34.0	13.4

By comparing the last lines for Maori and for 'European' it can be seen that Social Credit's share in each non-Labour sector was close in 1954. It then shot up in the Maori case in 1957 and 1960 when Social Credit's share among Maori was greater than among General voters regardless of the size of the non-Labour sector. In 1963 the Maori figure fell sharply back but rose again to be greater than Social Credit's share in the General sector for the next 5 elections, far greater indeed. The last 2 comparisons reverse, though not very markedly when it is remembered that the appearance of Mana Motuhake in 1981 and 1984 threw the Maori non-Labour sector into an unprecedented realignment when the new party at once became the principal non-Labour party at both elections. Furthermore, the irruption of the New Zealand Party in 1984 upset the General side of the comparison when Mr Jones's creation notably out-polled Social Credit.[3]

Seven cases of larger Social Credit proportions in the Maori sector, 5 of them much larger, weigh heavily against 4 reverse instances, 2 of them confused by extraneous developments, 1 clear case and 1 reasonably close to even. It is to reiterate this same point about the greater Maori propensity for splitting its opposition to Labour to emphasise that Mana Motuhake's share of the Maori non-Labour sector was as high as 42.9% both in 1981 and 1984 whereas the New Zealand Party's proportion of the General non-Labour sector in 1984 was 21.7%.

It would seem safe enough to say that, if cumulative National weakness was one peculiar feature of the Maori sub-system, so was the linked phenomenon of a greater Maori tendency to divide its opposition to Labour. It was not a new feature which arrived with Social Credit for it can be seen in 1935, 1938 and 1943 when Independency was far better supported among Maori than among General voters. It reaches back to the twenties and earlier when there were other dominant parties. It was a particular feature of Maori by-elections when, in the absence of a sitting member and his mana, candidates positively flocked in to try their fortunes. And now this fractionalisation of the opposition to the dominant party can be seen stronger than ever in the eighties.

How, then, did Maori Social Credit's contrary performance in continuing to rise both in 1957 and 1960 fit in with National plumbing a new low point in 1957, then shooting up again by 1963 to its best result in a dozen years? Partly it was a matter of overall political developments but the prestige of the candidates played an increasing role, especially in 1963. National's inactivity in Maori affairs and its tightening of the economy continued to drive its results down whether its team of candidates were widely-known or not. In 1954 such distinguished names as Carroll, Bennett and Waetford all lost points and when they retired from the fray in 1957, their replacements—with the exception of Pei Te Hurunui Jones in Western Maori—fared worse again.

On the other hand, in 1957 the now familiar Social Credit League was reinforced by 2 outstanding candidates. Instead of finding no candidate in Western Maori, this time Colonel Awatere appeared and captured 11.5%. At the same time in Eastern Maori, H. T. Reedy's manifold connections on the East Coast raised Social Credit's level from 5.3% to 18.4% (Graphs 3 and 4 [omitted]). Elsewhere results were mixed with -5.2 points in the North and +2.1 points in the South. Nevertheless, overall Social Credit rose 6 points in Maori voting while it was falling (-4.2) in General electorates.

Now the record of a one-term Labour Government came into play. Great expectations were disappointed particularly by the Prime Minister being both Minister of Maori Affairs and a supporter of the Rugby Tour of South Africa despite the 'No Maoris, No Tour' movement. There were other factors which I examined in *New Zealand Politics in Action*,[4] but suffice it to say that they all produced a strong reaction which appears as the loss of 4.9 points. That and a minor decline of 2.3 in Independency made possible the simultaneous rise of both opposition parties, National gaining 4.0 points and Social Credit 3.2.

For Social Credit H. T. Reedy continued to gain (+6.3) in the East, W. Clarke succeeded T. Maihi in the North and rose (+7.3), while Southern crept up (+1.2) and Western descended (-2.7) when H. Tuwhangai replaced Colonel Awatere (Figures 13.4, 13.5, 13.2, 13.3

respectively). Only Pei Jones was a notable candidate for National and all the others were new since the last election, yet just the same they went up in percentage terms in 1960. The lesson of 1960 was that a strong tide carries candidates up or down almost regardless of quality or mana. The same lesson appeared to have been taught in 1954 but then was partially contradicted in 1957. Now 1963 was to reinforce the 1957 demonstration of the importance on occasion of the Maori candidate's heritage, reputation, achievements and tribal and confederal connections.

Meantime National was back in power and the Rt. Hon. Keith Holyoake calmly disposed of a similar but smaller foreign exchange crisis than the one Nordmeyer had dealt with by taking the opposite tack. The Prime Minister had his Minister of Finance borrow and wait for export prices to rise—as they did. His Government was rewarded by the General electorate with a fall in support of only 0.8 points in the 'No Change Election'. The Hon. E. B. Corbett had retired in 1957 and this time Keith Holyoake chose the third-ranking man in his Cabinet, Josiah Ralph Hanan, to be Minister of Maori Affairs as well as Attorney-General, Minister of Justice and Minister of Island Territories. A lawyer from Invercargill, Hanan claimed no experience or expertise on Maori Affairs but he had strong opinions about equality before the law in all matters and a growing suspicion of institutions like the Maori seats which might recognise and actively express cultural differences.

Above all Ralph Hanan was a contrast to Ernest Corbett in being a widely influential and indefatigable legislator. By 1961 the Maori Education Foundation was established because education was the key to integration as set forth in the Hunn Report which, ironically, was a deferred and interpretative summation of much data-gathering under Walter Nash's regime.[5] From 1961 separate registration of Maori births and deaths was abolished and Maori became eligible for jury service. The following year came the New Zealand Maori Council which federated the district and tribal committees, thus producing an alternative leadership system at the centre with which the Government could have more sympathy than with the 4 Labour Maori MPs. From this period also there was an acceleration in the phasing-out of the traditional and valued system of Maori schools with their dedicated corps of teachers and emphasis on Maori 'language, history, arts and crafts'. By 1963 they accounted for only 20% of Maori pupils at primary and 6% at secondary schools. Such changes and innovations received a mixed reception because they at first appeared to point in different directions and their full effects were hard to anticipate. The Education Foundation seemed to many, however, to promise particularly well.

It was plainly time for a special effort on the National Party's part to break Labour's hold on all 4 Maori seats. Before this could be attempted at a general election, there was occasion for a trial run at the Northern Maori by-election which followed on the death of Tapihana Paikea in January 1963. Nine candidates contested the by-election on 16 March including 2 unofficial Labour and 1 Independent Labour candidates, 2 Independents and 1 Kauhanganui. National secured J.C.T. Henare, a former Colonel of the Maori Battalion, son of the Reform member for the seat, and himself National's contestant in 1946, 1949 and 1951. Social Credit continued with J. Clarke, their representative in 1960.

Labour with Ratana advice selected a surprise candidate in Matiu Rata, a registered minister of the Ratana Church, a youth worker and unionist aged 28, who was well-known in Auckland but less so in country districts despite coming from Te Hapua in the far North. The result startled Labour when the majority dropped from 3,372 to 447 votes and their percentage from 60.8 to 42.0. Social Credit was disappointed to see Clarke go from 16.0% to 4.6% while National was much encouraged by James Henare lifting their results from 23.2% to 36.0%, the kind of level he had maintained in the late forties. Incidentally, the 6 unofficial and Independent candidates collectively drew 17.4% with E. M. Pou, a former National candidate now running as 'unofficial Labour', taking 7.7%.

When the general election arrived, National had gathered its strongest team in many years. James Henare stood for the fifth time in Northern Maori and Pei Te Hurunui Jones represented National for the third successive time in Western Maori. There was a fresh candidate in Southern Maori, an ex-All Black and future MP for Wairarapa, M. B. R. Couch. National's unexpected acquisition in Eastern Maori, however, was the Social Credit League's leading vote-gatherer, H. T. Reedy, who changed party banners presumably in the hope of combining his own following with National's steady 22%.

The results only partially justified the hopes that were held for them. Reedy raised National from 22.1% to 34.2% which was still 12.6 points short of a total combination of the 2 parties' forces in 1960. James Henare improved his by-election result by adding 1.6 points but had to watch Matiu Rata rise from 42.0% to 58.4% which was within 3 points of the last Paikea victory. Pei Jones added another 5.4 points to reach 25.7% but that was less than the 33.6% he had garnered as Independent in the February 1945 by-election or his 28.5% as Independent Labour in 1943, although rather better than his 21.5% as Independent in 1938 or his 11.5% as Young Maori Party in the October 1930 by-election. Only Couch's vote was less than his predecessor's, by 3.5 points. As for the

Social Credit team, it was symptomatically back to 3 people again with nobody once more in Western Maori. As the by-election had foretold, all those who stood lost heavily; Smith in Eastern down to 6.0% from Reedy's 24.7%, Clarke in Northern down from his own 16.0% to 3.6%, and Nia Nia in Southern reduced from 7.0% to 3.8%.

Can one conclude that this was a limited victory for National personalities and personal connections? In part no doubt it was. But what contribution was made by Ralph Hanan's active role, probably perceived on balance at the time as beneficial? And what share in it all should be attributed to the disappointment and disenchantment of Social Credit's ex-supporters who for 3 elections past had been investing votes, each time in increasing numbers, in the hope ultimately of dislodging a Labour MP or 2 or at least surpassing National, but had succeeded in doing neither? Moreover what part was played by the fortuitous occurrence of the by-election? It came at such a point that its results could well have roused more National voters, who duly turned out; discouraged Social Creditors, who in fact did not; and stirred Labour voters to take corrective action at the following general election, which they did do with enthusiasm.

No precise allocation of weights or percentages to these 4 considerable factors can be made. We cannot take the results of the 1963 general election as demonstrating the predominance in Maori voting of personal attributes like achievements, mana, and tribal and confederal connection because the 3 other factors were not personal but impersonal political sequences which, taken apart or together, may well have been far more important to the outcome within the sub-system. The 1957 result may assist an argument for the importance of the personal factor in 1963, but then 1954 and 1960 show that personal factors can be quite swept aside.

What can be said is that, by comparison with General New Zealand politics, the factors we have reviewed take on rather different proportions in Maori politics. Whakapapa, mana, achievements and connections can combine to work individual variations in results that are on occasion noticeably greater than those seen in General voting. However, they remain within limits set by the characteristics of the sub-system itself. Moreover, because in 1963 there were no parallel pakeha factors nor in the outcome any National rise or sudden fall for Social Credit such as Maori voting produced, we have been confined in explaining these Maori results to examining factors working on or arising from the sub-system alone. This powerfully underlines the fact that Maori politics do define and constitute a sub-system.

At this point we can also sum up or point to the continuation of other characteristics of the sub-system that have appeared before or confirmed themselves by their works or have begun to do so. First, in 1963 Maori Labour sailed up 2.7 points in the Maori seats as a whole, apparently little affected (Figure 13.1, Graphs 2-5 [omitted]) by the hubbub within the opposition below. Maori Labour was on its way up to a higher peak than ever from which only discontent among its own supporters with the performance in Government of the Party itself could dislodge it—as it had done in 1960 and would do again in 1975.

Second, the battle within the opposition between National, Social Credit and Independency was once again confined there in 1954, 1957 and 1963. National's 'ups' again corresponded with third party and Independent 'downs' and, as in many earlier and later elections, vice versa. Third, the amplitude of the waves of opposition within the opposition in 1957 and 1960 had again proved far greater proportionately among Maori voters, given the size of their opposition sector compared to Maori Labour, than did the General surge to Social Credit in 1954 or in 1966 given the size of the General non-Labour sector. Indeed, that was shown over the whole range of elections to have been normally the case.

Fourth, despite hope springing up with National's two rises in Maori voting in 1960 and 1963, analysis showed the underpinnings to be transitory, unrepeatable and as fragile as baulked political ambitions. Moreover the high point of this second National recovery in 1963 was distinctly lower than the first in 1946. The third 'rise' rather than 'recovery' in 1975 was to prove no more than a slight elevation lasting for one election only. In truth, notwithstanding the second recovery, the National Party had been and remained in decline.

If one sets aside the 1935 election result as the last of the previous era of Maori politics, and disregards National's disastrous fall of 21.6 points in 1938 as the equivalent of what happened to National in the General seats in 1935, then the whole span of 46 years from 1938 to 1984 may be seen as the single, latest era in Maori politics that it is, an era with common characteristics. If one of those characteristics is a prolonged National decline, then a straight trend line should economically describe the general run of results and evenly divide all the variations. Just such a trend line starts at 34% in 1938 and runs down to 7% in 1984. There are 8 elections above the trend line and 7 below it while the last result is, naturally, almost on trend.

The actual results begin below the trend line in 1938 and 1943 for these are the years—like 1935—of lingering Independency. The results are above trend in 1946, 1949 and 1951, the years of 2-party contests which followed the subsidence of Independency and preceded the appearance of Social Credit. Actuality for National then drops sharply beneath trend for 1954, 1957 and even 1960, the elections of Social Credit's cumulative growth. At last in 1963 National's result climbs out to an inspiriting peak for reasons already pondered and in the election year which marked Social Credit's first Maori disaster. So far, then, all the variations above and below the trend line have to do with the presence or absence of Independent or third-party competition.

Results for 1966 and 1969 are in quickly descending order but do not fall below National's overall trend until 1972. Social Credit did rise much faster than Labour in 1966 and can take most of the credit for pulling National back in that year. But in the next 2 elections in 1969 and 1972 the Social Credit League's results themselves declined. Therefore it was the net effect of National's own policies and of Labour's pull in those boom years for the Party which brought National back under trend by 1972.

In the most recent Muldoon phase National was almost 3 points above trend in 1975, the year when Maori confidence in Labour was deeply shaken and a reduced Maori National contingent could still overcome the appearance of a little Values vote (+2.2) and a faint upturn (+0.5) by Social Credit. In 1978, however, Social Credit doubled its share and for the first time surpassed National in Maori politics. The National trend line was now so far down that the actual National result was only driven a half point below that line. Mana Motuhake's advent in 1981 was so successful that it soared (+15.1) into the opposition lead. Social Credit fell slightly (-0.4) but still managed to come second, which left National in third place in an opposition sector which had grown by 13.5 points thanks to Labour's apparent collapse. Paradoxically that put National, which had fallen further (-0.7) and lay third, nevertheless a half point above trend. At the terminal election in 1984 National sat one-tenth of one percent above its trend line.

It was a trend which had carried National from dominating the opposition to Labour down to the position of having to concede that opposition leadership to others for the final 3 elections. Overall National's actual results had come closer and closer to the trend, particularly as they reached the bottom of the line. It was a case of increasing congruence between projection and reality. The party was losing support at an average rate of six-tenths of 1 percent every year for 46 years so that prolonged National decline did indeed characterise this era and lay at the heart of the overall decline of the opposition which was the converse of Labour's rise.

In a way National seems to have concluded that its recapture of Maori seats was out of the question after the 1966 result and recognised that the trend was what it was so long as the sub-system was permitted to continue. For 1966 did come as a blow. Matiu Te Hau, who became Maori Vice-President of the National Party, told me before the 1966 election that he believed they would take a seat, probably the Northern electorate because of James Henare's fine showing there in the 1963 by- and General elections. Alas for such hopes, F. R. Wilcox contested Northern and his result halved National's percentage (-19.0). In Western, M. Te Heu Heu succeeded Pei Jones and the new man dropped 8.4 points. H. T. Reedy fought again but saw his score diminish by 3.4 points. Only in Southern Maori where Baden Pere replaced Ben Couch was there a gain of 7.8 points. What had happened was that both in General and Maori seats Social Credit bounced back at remarkably similar rates (+6.5 and +6.6 respectively). National's second term was seen as lacklustre with farm protests, Vietnam debates and economic difficulties. National fell (-3.4) in General seats and faster (-6.5) in Maori electorates, the difference being that Labour rose (+2.4) among Maori but among pakeha it just as definitely descended (-2.4), new leader, Norman Kirk, notwithstanding.

Ralph Hanan's conclusions as Minister of Maori Affairs can be judged from his words and his acts. He spoke with approval of the eventual removal of separate Maori representation and thought the right time would come in about 10 years. In Parliament he introduced the Maori Affairs Amendment Bill in 1967 and, despite widespread and bitter opposition to major and minor aspects of the Bill from all over Maoridom, even including objections on several points from the New Zealand Maori Council, the Bill with minor alterations became an Act. At the next 2 general elections National lost 3.2 points then 6.5 points to reach the hitherto unprecedented level of 12.8%. Not that some notable names did not appear to struggle for National in 1969. H. K. Ngata in the East, G. S. Latimer in the North and N. W. Pomare in the South tried for the last time, but the die was cast. The gains Labour made in these elections were made primarily at the expense of National and secondarily from Social Credit which was also sinking modestly.

Labour also successfully negotiated the risks of changing the guard among its MPs during these years. The first challenge was met and overcome when Matiu Rata won his by-election entry and proceeded to gain back most of the support formerly accorded the Paikeas at the general election of 1963. At that same point Tiaki Omana retired after 20 years as MP for Eastern Maori. His selected successor was P. T. ('Steve') Watene, a Mormon of 53 who had made his name as a chairman and initiator of Maori and social policy within the Labour Party organisation. The relationship between the Ratana Church and the Labour Party was altering publicly when a non-Ratana candidate could be accepted, albeit in the least Ratana of the 4 seats. The Ratana Church remained a very significant force, but it tended increasingly henceforth to concentrate on religious and welfare concerns.

Two deaths and a retirement then widened the break in generation. Sir Eruera Tirikatene died in January 1967 after 34 1/2 years of service in the House as Member for Southern Maori. The first and last of the original 4 of the Prophet's 'koatas' to be an MP, he died aged 71 and his daughter, Mrs T. W. M. (Whetu) Tirikatene-Sullivan, at the by-election triumphantly improved on her father's high standing by lifting Labour from 72.3% to 74.3%. Unexpectedly Steve Watene died in June of the same year. Labour made a more conventional selection in choosing P. B. Reweti who was a well-liked trade unionist and watersider and a most effective speaker on the marae. Brown Reweti was 51 when he won Eastern Maori against H. T. Reedy for National, C. M. Paul for Social Credit and two Independents including D. M. Bennett. Labour's vote dropped from 58.8% in 1966 to 49.5% but it rose above Watene's 1966 level to reach 62.0% by the next general election in 1969. That election also marked the retirement of Mrs Iriaka Ratana at the age of 64 after 20 years as MP for Western Maori. Koro T. Wetere who was selected to succeed Mrs Ratana was 30 years her junior, a farmer, and worker for church and party who formed close links with the King movement and the Maori Queen. In his first election Wetere managed the feat of improving on Mrs Ratana's 1966 vote of 73.4% by contriving to capture 77.5%.

Thus between 1963 and 1969 all the electorates had acquired new members, 3 of them born within 3 years of one another: Mrs Tirikatene-Sullivan, Matiu Rata and Koro Wetere. The first 2 were to become Ministers of the Crown in 1972 at the ages of 40 and 38 respectively. The third had to wait for the fourth Labour Government to become a Minister in 1984 at 49. Their thinking was of an utterly different era from that, say, of Paraire Paikea who was a Member of the Executive Council from January 1941 until his death in April 1943. Eruera Tirikatene was in a way an important bridging figure. He was in the Executive Council from May 1943 to the end of the Fraser Cabinet in 1949 and Minister of Forests in the Nash Cabinet between 1957 and 1960. Tirikatene urged Fraser to go further and faster towards Maori institutions and self administration by extending the advances in the Maori Social and Economic Advancement Act of 1945. In the second Labour Government he broke away from Nash and his Cabinet colleagues to publicly oppose the Rugby tour—both of them issues that lasted and grew in importance.

Nevertheless the way that Matiu Rata's views on the land issue developed, for example, was keyed not to the past but to his own leading role in the parliamentary struggle against the Maori Affairs Amendment Act of 1967 and his determination to undo the policies and attitudes it represented. Likewise, as Maori Studies developed in the universities and teachers' training colleges, new or revived views on the value of Maori culture and language were aired by Maori lecturers, students and graduates. In parallel the spread of television documentaries, debates and news film of protest marches and occasions provided popular extraparliamentary arenas for political activity. So much visible exhortation doubtless promoted some broader changes in attitude but it conjured up resistance to them at the same time.

The scene was being set for a new Labour Government to produce the most active legislative programme on Maori affairs that Cabinet support and 3 crowded years would permit. Such were the expectations, however, and such the interested public's swirling, altering conceptions of what was possible, which directions the Government had pursued and which in the critics' view it should, that the result was bound to be confusion and disappointment. Years of effort concluded with a Maori Minister of Maori Affairs looking out on a Land March which, for example, loosely united the protests of a National stalwart in her seventies with those of hundreds of all ages, most of them young people from all 3 parties and from none except the activism of the streets.

However busily these events filled the television screens they were marginal to the life and work of most pakeha New Zealanders and most Maori. They provided emotional colour and stereotypes for political argument but the structures of politics generally and of Maori politics did not alter. The 1975 election brought big swings in General voting to the National Party and a sharp drop to Labour in Maori voting. These were traditional forms of rejection with normality in control and in demand. Yet the taste of change mixed with the fear of too much change left the electorate uneasy and half expectant.

The verdict in 1978, bringing the sudden rise of the Social Credit alternative to both the major parties, suggested that the third National Government had not been able to deliver a reality which matched the vague and multiple promise of 'New Zealand the way you want it' any more than the third Labour Government had been able to answer 'Time for a Change' with the correct amount of it. We earlier noted that pakeha and Maori ran roughly parallel in the rise of Social Credit with the Maori line lower and slower to rise. National lost 7.8 points among General voters and 5.3 points among Maori voters while Labour rose 0.8 points and 2.8 points respectively.

This was in fact the commencement of a minor change in the structure of Maori politics. Social Credit had briefly become the first party of opposition and fragmentation was on its way—but within the opposition, not the system as a whole. The precondition of this alteration was the already-examined cumulative decline of National going back in its latter phases to the sixties rather than to the swings and arrows of the early seventies. The emotional force behind the searching expressed in fragmented opposition arose from the dragging economic pressures of 'stagflation' and rising unemployment, a dreary cramping of opportunity and continued strain and stress which, from 1974 onwards, fluctuated but did not cease whatever the policies of the Government of the day. Proportionately far more of the Maori than of the General population suffered it and sought relief. Yet most Maori voters continued to rest their hopes with Labour.

A minority did not. For them the personal wrangling between the leader of the Labour Party and his front-bench Maori spokesman which led to temporary demotion, indignant independence and resignation for Matiu Rata were the occasion for action.[6] The process of creating Mana Motuhake brought the ex-Minister and his personal assistant from that period of legislative effort together with critics of party and pakeha institutions, theorists of autonomy and self-direction, believers in Maori resources for independent economic and social ventures. The Treaty of Waitangi was to be given its full meaning in Maori culture and applied to redress the past and the present. Above all, the language was to be saved by recognition as an official language and every educational measure available.

No-one could be sure of how far the appeal of such ideas might stretch. Matiu Rata chose the by-election in an electorate he had represented for 17 years as the most favourable testing ground and medium for advertising the ideas and policies of the new party. Labour responded by selecting a 43-year-old, Anglican, medical practitioner. He was well-known in the North, a former chairman of the Tai Tokerau District Maori Council, on the Kaitaia College Board of Governors and with an active interest in social services. Incumbency, mana, achievements and the fact of the ministry in the Ratana Church were all with Rata. The Labour Party's standing was Dr Gregory's principal asset. Instead of the 71.5% Rata had secured in 1978, at the by-election on 7 June 1980 Dr Gregory took 52.4%. Dr Gregory dropped 19.1 points. Matiu Rata 17 years before had dropped 18.8% from the 1960 results. J. C. T. Henare had achieved 36.0% against Rata. Rata managed 37.9% against Gregory. It was a tribute to continuity in Maori politics, while the fact that Social Credit took 8.2% and that National did not run a candidate was a sign that the opposition to Labour was in flux.

In the months before the oncoming 1981 general election, health problems and his 65 years brought the particularly popular member for Eastern Maori, Brown Reweti, to announce his forthcoming retirement. The Labour selection was a critical one in that the party organisation was vividly aware that a challenge of unknown size and from a new direction awaited them at the general election. Their choice fell on a second medical practitioner, Peter Tapsell, 51 years old at selection as Brown Reweti had been when selected, a University Rugby Blue and former Maori All Black, and a prominent orthopaedic surgeon in Rotorua. He had served on a Tribal Lands Incorporation Board, been on the Maori Health Advisory Committee, and was chairperson of the Maori Arts and Crafts Institute in Rotorua. His most unusual recommendation was that he had already twice stood for a General electorate, Rotorua, in 1975 and 1978. It recalled the figures of Carroll and Buck who had stood for both Maori and 'European' electorates. At the election of 1981 Peter Tapsell easily withstood the challenge of A. Tahana for Mana Motuhake who drew 15.0%. But Tapsell's result at 64.1% was 10.7 points down on Reweti in 1978, a fall Tapsell recovered amply when Labour went up by 20.1 points in 1984.

These 2 changes of MP in the early eighties were little affected by questions of denomination. One was a committed Anglican, the other a churchgoer but eclectic. The important alteration to the Maori Labour team was the fact that in 2 further steps it had become heavily professional in background: a graduate social worker, a general practitioner and a surgeon in Mrs Tirikatene-Sullivan, Dr Gregory and Dr Tapsell. The changes in the sixties had been generational, with consequences for ideas as the seedbed of policy. The replacements of the early eighties, because they had entered politics later than the two who came on from the sixties, brought all 4 Labour MPs into a cluster aged between 44 and 51 at the 1981 election—a cluster into which Matiu Rata would have fitted neatly at 47.

The ideological and attitudinal fit would naturally have been less happy. Matiu Rata was out of the party and Parliament which formed him politically and into a vigorous exchange with other groups. Labour's 4 MPs were by now less crusading, more interested in the detailed workings of institutions and measures, more moderate and pragmatic than their predecessor appeared, and certainly more suited to the Government that was to come. Given that the conceptual challenge of Mana Motuhake had proceeded primarily from tertiary institutions and those professionally concerned with teaching about Maori language and society, this re-balancing of the Labour team towards professionalism could be seen as a parallel but different outcome of the same process of change in Maori political and social leadership, or as a riposte to the graduate middle-class element in Mana Motuhake, or as both.

One question the nature of the new party and the balance of the new Labour team both raised was which would attract the urbanised, unionised, lower to middle income workers—and unemployed—of the cities and provincial towns? And what of the people still on the land, the older more traditional folk? The Northern Maori by-election had given a strong hint. Indeed the same thoughts could well have moved the 1984 Labour caucus when it chose Koro Wetere, the experienced politician with a country base, and Peter Tapsell, the oldest of the quartet and from a provincial town, to be the fourth Labour Government's two Maori Cabinet Ministers.

That was in the future, however. After the Northern Maori by-election and the Tapsell selection, the question in November 1981 was how well would a Maori party, running on a platform of Maori issues as conceived by the policy-makers of Mana Motuhake and running in all 4 seats, compete against the party which had been chosen by an increasing majority of Maori voters for more than four decades? Those seeking guidance on how Mana Motuhake would fare in the 4-electorate total now had the warrant of the by-election result to look to the past for precedents. They could have taken the height reached by all the Independent Labour and Democratic Labour candidates in 1943 which was 14.8% [shown in the original Graph 1]: or picked Social Credit's zenith in 1960 which was 15.0%. Of course National had been much stronger in those days, so in 1981 one might expect there to be less National opposition within the opposition sector. Or would it mean that there would just be fewer opposition voters to persuade into the new party? It might have cut either way.

The actual result was that Mana Motuhake took 15.1% of the whole Maori valid vote, which was remarkably close to the 2 likeliest precedents of well-prepared and widely-known opposition within the opposition. Had this support indeed come over from other opposition parties? On the face of the net trends in the results, apparently very little. Values was down (-1.2 points), National down slightly (-0.7), Social Credit faintly (-0.4), and Independency was actually up a touch (+0.7). By contrast it was Labour which had shed 13.5 points. The conclusion seemed plain that in the main it was Labour loss which had fuelled Mana Motuhake's rise and that in turn might possibly indicate that Labour's long-term increases, only dented sharply in 1975, were at last to be eaten into seriously, if not this time, then next.

There was another and firmer conclusion to be drawn. Looking at Graph 6 [omitted], which aggregates all non-National, non-Labour support into one category of 'Other' valid votes, makes the matter very visible. This opposition to both major parties comes at the beginning, the middle and the end of the latest era. Comparing the 3 with each other shows that they have not greatly altered in magnitude over the whole era which otherwise was characterised by a long-running Labour climb and a long running National decline. Periodically, then, there have been waves of opposition amongst Maori voters against the 2 parties of Government in the overall party and electoral system. These have risen to successive crests of 19.0% in 1938, 16.5% in 1960 and 25.9% in 1981, or between one-sixth and one-quarter of the whole, then subside over a total cycle of 3 or 4 elections.

The breaking of the 2 previous waves could have brought reassurance to Labour's 4 Maori MPs after 1981, even though Mana Motuhake came second in all 4 seats. What did reassure Labour's MPs was that the new party was not a credible threat to them anywhere, not even in Northern Maori where Matiu Rata had lost 16.6 points of his by-election percentage and was now down to 21.3%. Mana Motuhake persisted to fight again in 1984 only to find it was facing a Labour Party invigorated by a change of leadership, major improvements in organisation and the circumstances of the snap election.

In 1984 Labour picked up once more by 12.8 points which was only 0.7 points less than all it had lost in 1981. With so much of substance removed by Labour, Mana Motuhake sank by more than one-third of its previous strength (-5.5) and lodged at 9.6%. That the fall stopped there must be attributed principally to the net effect of Social Credit's major collapse of 7.7 points, National's descent of 2.2 points and to the New Zealand Party in Maori seats being held down to a gain of only 2.7 points. There were therefore enough voters departing from Social Credit and National to compensate in net terms for between one-half and two thirds of Labour's retrievals.

In earlier describing the 1981 election the words claimed only that the 'conclusion seemed plain that in the main it was Labour loss which had fuelled Mana Motuhake's rise'. The caution indicated that we had arrived at a classic instance of the limitations of analysis based on valid vote percentages. There was in fact a force in the vicinity of that 1981 struggle other than Labour's regiments and the battalions of National and Independency. This was the leaderless and fluctuating force it has been my habit since 1960 to refer to as the 'non-vote', the thousands of non-participants, abstainers or protesters who are entitled and qualified to vote and registered yet who, with reason or without, choose not or neglect to do so.

When the non-vote shrinks then one party, some parties or all parties may gain. When discontent or disillusion grows and the non-vote swells then its expansion may take from one, some or all but there are no party gains, simply losses. A change of party adds to the new and takes from the old, a double effect. When the non-vote enlarges, a particular party may lose much more than the others or be more prone to desertion yet, equally, it may be more likely to receive back its losses when the mood of protest fades. This is not only associated with other characteristics of the party, it is also normally the case that parties are differentially open to losses into non-vote and to recoveries from non-voting. This is especially significant in the Maori sub-system where the non-vote is normally at least double the non-vote percentage in the 'European' or 'General' electorate.

Much research overseas has established that in Western countries there is an association between poor voting participation and lesser or low levels of information on and interest in the political scene, weak identification with parties, reduced feelings of personal efficacy, and lesser educational attainments and economic resources. There are a multitude of further factors at work such as societal change breaking up the formation of voting habits or, on the grand scale, the size, party history and federal constitution of a country which can complicate and obscure from the voter the lines of political responsibility so that a fringe or even a major sector of voters may retreat into apathy interspersed with sallies out to support colourful personalities. Suffice it to say that, in the huge, federal entity that is the United States, the general rate of voter participation is low and, within it, the participation rate of black voters is lower again. The University of Michigan vote validation study reported white voter participation in the 1984 Presidential election as 70.2% and the parallel figure for black voters as 52.0%.[7] In New Zealand in 1984 the General rate was 92.3% and the Maori rate 77.0%. Neither in General nor Maori seats do New Zealanders approach either of the American levels. Yet the choice of not voting is always an exercised and often significant option in New Zealand elections by both General and Maori in differing proportions.

Graph 8 [omitted] on its left half makes 100.0% equal the whole valid vote and on its right half makes 100.0% equal all those qualified to vote. Looking at Graph 8 one can compare the pictures of the Maori voting record in 2 different mirrors, one reflecting all the qualified potential participants including those who do not vote or vote informally, and in the other, only those who do vote and formally so. In the qualified vote half, the inclusion of more potential voters has lowered National's silhouette while making no major change to its shape. Something the same can be said for 'All Other Valid' down to 1960 although thenceforth there are certainly changes especially in the period since 1972. Labour's climb is reduced then flattens out sooner and after 1957 the shape is quite different and altered in significant ways.

Lastly we come to the other force on the outskirts of electoral battles, those temporarily or normally withdrawn, together with the platoon of informal voters. First they decline somewhat in proportion and are then recruited so fast that they surpass National in 1954 and then rise from 1957 onwards in 3 successive surges to reach a peak only 6.6 points below Labour in 1975, only thereafter to fall away to the 23.8 level by 1984. Undoubtedly one's understanding of the record of Labour, Independency and National in that order is increased to greater or lesser degree by using an analysis which comprehends all the factors available.

In order to see what the comprehensive analysis tells us which the partial valid vote analysis did not, let us take the latest phase from 1972 to the present when the greatest differences appear by comparing Graphs 6 and 9 [both omitted]. According to the valid vote Graph 6 [omitted], Labour fell by 4.9 points between 1972 and 1975, a middling response to the Muldoon onslaught. Graph 9 [omitted] reveals a devastating desertion of 14.9 points from the Labour regiments. Who benefitted in net terms? According to the valid vote trends the middling loss from Labour was picked up almost evenly by National (+2.5) and 'All Other' (+2.4). On the qualified vote trends National lost a shade (-0.4), 'All Other' picked up very little (+0.3), while Non-Vote and Informal made a huge leap of 15.0 points upwards. The comprehensive record shows the net movement. The essence of the result was an alarming desertion from Labour and a formidable fresh contingent of non-voters off the battlefield. The switch had left the other battalions much where they were.

The exchanges between 1975 and 1978 are altered only mildly by comparison. Labour now recovers faster on qualified vote figures (+4.2 not +2.8), National loses less (-2.9 not-5.3) because the largest net source is now some former non-voters (-3.3) returning to the struggle. 'All Others' are +2.0 points instead of +2.5. The lesson from this is that where non-voting does not alter greatly, the valid vote picture of what was happening corresponds much better to its reflection in the qualified vote. Of course it can be and has been objected that this picture of net movement itself does not represent all the cross-cancelling exchanges between the various forces which also take place. That is obviously so. But as I found in designing and analysing a large questionnaire survey of the 1975 election which did pick up these cross-cancelling exchanges, it is still the net movement which carries the message and measures the operative trends of the election.[8]

Now we come to the altered picture of the 1981 election and what really happened when Mana Motuhake appeared on the field. In order to pick out Mana Motuhake and other battalions and companies from 'All Other', it would be clearest if the comparison were now made between Figure 13.1 and Graph 7[omitted]. The valid vote version on Figure 13.1 shows Mana Motuhake shooting up (+ 15.1 points) and Labour tumbling (-13.5), the one seeming to draw upon the other. Graph 7[omitted] reduces Mana Motuhake's leap to 11.0 points but at the same time dramatically arrests Labour's tumble and turns it into a modest descent of 2.8.

The cause of the contrast is easily detected. The qualified vote record attends to non-voting and reveals that its huge increase and the corresponding desertion from Labour occurred back in 1975. Non-vote's battalions shrank in 1978—while Informal rose, equally unnoticed—and this shrinkage helped to recruit not only Informal but Labour and Social Credit as well, but not National or Values. Then in 1981 a much larger detachment came back out of non-voting (-6.9). The Labour loss in 1981 was as mentioned 2.8 points. Informal dropped 2.1 while Values disappeared with a loss of 0.8. Adding the 3 together, they do not equal the detachment from non-voting. Add the 4 together and they indicate the net sources for Mana Motuhake's leap, with enough left over for slight gains of 0.7 points for Social Credit and 0.4 for National.

Finally between 1981 and 1984 both kinds of calculation—on a valid vote and a qualified vote basis—agree that it was, within the Maori sub-system, a case of Labour up drastically and the New Zealand Party a little, with every other party or group down. Table 13.3 sets out the 2 versions of the changes.

Table 13.3: Maori Seat Voting Changes between 1981 and 1984 Expressed as Percentages of Valid and Qualified Votes

In % of Valid Vote				In % of Qualified Vote			
Labour	+12.8	Social Credit	-7.7	Labour	+11.8	Social Credit	-5.6
NZ Party	+2.7	Mana Motuhake	-5.5	NZ Party	+2.1	Mana Motuhake	-3.6
		National	-2.2			Non-Vote	-3.2
		Independent	-0.1			National	-1.4
						Independent	-0.1
						Informal	—
Total	+15.5	Total	-15.5	Total	+13.9	Total	-13.9

It can be seen that the qualified vote measurement reduces every component because of the larger numbers in its base of 100.0%. Nevertheless it keeps the same order and roughly the same proportions although its additional elements—the non-vote, and Informal which in this instance did not change—can alter those proportions radically if movement into or out of non-vote is a major trend. This was so in 1960 (+8.5 points), 1966 (+10.6), 1969 (-5.6), 1975 (+14.8) and in 1981 (-6.9). By following through changes in the non-vote and interconnected changes in other parties and especially in the Labour vote, one can see why on Graph 7 [omitted] the 'W' formation appears in Labour's silhouette between 1957 and 1972 and again between 1972 and 1984. On valid vote's Figure 13.1 the shape is a steepening climb from 1960 to 1972 followed by a small 'v' from 1972 to 1978 and a much deeper 'v' between 1978 and 1984.

The characteristics of the Maori sub-system of electoral voting which remain much as before in this deeper qualified vote analysis are:

1. The continuing decline of National with limited recoveries in 1946 and 1963 and the reduction of this party of Government to second or third place even within the opposition to Labour in the last 3 elections.
2. The greater tendency of the opposition to Labour within the Maori sub-system to sustain an opposition within itself; and the larger proportion that internal opposition constitutes relative to the size of the opposition sector as a whole when compared with similar elements in the General system.

The characteristics of the sub-system which are shown by the qualified vote analysis to have altered, or to be additional, are:

3. Labour's climb to dominance flattens out one election sooner while the plateau now stretches from 1946 to 1957. Labour thereafter plunges in 1960 twice, and in 1975 three times as far as the valid vote calculations revealed. Consequently, after 1957 instead of 6 buoyant elections on or above the plateau line, there are only 3. Nevertheless the Labour Party continues to dominate this latest era of the sub-system with an average support of 50.3% of all those qualified to vote as compared to 65.8% of all valid voters.
4. A fourth force in non-voting and Informal is thereby added to Labour, National and Independency with third-party voting included. This fourth force shows up on the figure in third place, its 2 elements together pass National in 1954 while the non-vote alone does so in 1960. With a one-election exception this continues to be so. The real contest for dominance after 1963 is between a surging non-vote and the Labour Party, an unequal contest in which non-vote falls away after 1975.

The 2 analyses employed have, to change the metaphor, introduced different sets of actors in the amphitheatre of Maori politics. First the adolescent Labour giant soon grown to full stature, the mature National figure bending with increasing years and ever less with time, and a tribe of changing, cartwheeling patch-coated Independents thrust aside by the privates and sergeants of Social Credit until, as a finale, a second adolescent warrior climbs to the top of the giant's boots. Next the qualified vote analysis introduced a chorus of non-voters—and the Informal dwarf—who commented on the economic fates and the success of the play and often took off their masks and walked on as bit players as it pleased them.

Now there is a last and numerous group who remain in the shadowy audience, the unregistered potential voters who therefore are not even qualified to vote. Their thousands among the rapidly growing Maori population impressed me a quarter century ago when doing research for an article.[9] It was the increasing disparity between the estimated population and the first 'hard' reliable roll numbers in 1957 which alerted me, while the trends backwards and forwards showed the problem to be growing as rapidly as the urbanisation which helped cause it by interrupting or suspending the teaching by family example and small community interaction of those political attitudes and habits like voting which have to be learned.

Anthony McCracken explored the problem and expanded on and reached beyond my answers in a fine MA thesis.[10] The problem grew and the necessary research on the underlying figures which could only have been done officially was never undertaken. Instead there were *ex cathedra* pronouncements by Ministers that ever larger numbers of Maori were 'going over to' or, from journalists and fearful candidates, 'being put onto' the 'European' or later the General rolls. So one can only introduce the subject and hope that, before any conclusions are drawn, resources and officially-conducted research will clarify the numbers and the motives involved, and discover also whether the neglect of the recent past may not have left tens of thousands quite outside the patterns of participation as well as the records of our electoral system.

For if there is, particularly after the reforms of 1975,[11] a permeable boundary between the Maori political sub-system and the General electoral system, then is not that a further creditable adaptation by Maori of a special representation system they have made their own and use for their own purposes? If National declines in the sub-system, it usually governs in the General system. Indeed, as Maori candidates have come onto the General roll and been selected for National, and subsequently won, they have reflected a transition by individual Maori before them in time and who shared their values. Nor is the choice of voting on the General roll confined to National voters. Labour and Social Credit organisers have sought and enrolled those available in marginal General electorates. For it is now an entirely free choice and, despite the accusation in the 1960s that it smacked of apartheid, it has been largely choice for decades.

Those who chose to stay on the rolls of the Maori seats are participating in a unique and valuable sub-system. Here electors can choose representatives of their own culture who can express their constituents' attitudes, views and responses, articulate their needs, and attend to their contacts with Departments and officialdom and mediate one to the other. No MP in a General electorate could consistently perform such a task, for he or she is tied in terms of time and is responsible for expressing the interests and considering the views of constituents predominantly or overwhelmingly of another culture. Reading Hansard or the newspapers with an attentive eye will reveal the force of this fact.

This Annex has been devoted to showing how the sub-system differs from the General system with which it interacts in many vital ways. The sub-system is distinct and different because it is supposed to do the different job of representing the other culture in our country in its Parliament. Maori electors and MPs see to it that it does.

Maori voters have invented their own parties, adapted other people's parties, and coalesced where it suited them. Maori voters display different policy priorities, values and party choices from those of the system in general. Ironically, by their consistent choice of 4 Labour MPs, the voters have made the sub-system work to balance the tilt in favour of National as against Labour displayed by the 'European' or General system over more than 3 decades. The great merits of the present sub-system, however, lie in the uses to which it has been put. Maori have thus made it their creation. They have endowed it with functions they need to have performed and which only MPs representing voters of their own culture could perform. They are supported by a political sub-system which has its own characteristics and uniqueness.

LIST OF GRAPHS

GRAPH 1 [i.e. Figure 13.1]: 50 Years of Maori Voting: 4 Maori Seats Combined (percentages of all valid voters)
GRAPH 2: 50 Years of Maori Voting: Southern Maori (% of valid vote)
GRAPH 3: 50 Years of Maori Voting: Western Maori (% of valid vote)
GRAPH 4: 50 Years of Maori Voting: Eastern Maori (% of valid vote)

GRAPH 5: 50 Years of Maori Voting: Northern Maori (% of valid vote)
GRAPH 6: Phases of 50 Years of Evolution: Percentage Changes in Valid Vote, 4 Maori Seats Combined
GRAPH 7: 50 Years of Maori Voting: Percentages of All Qualified Voters
GRAPH 8: Graphs 6 and 9 compared
GRAPH 9: A More Penetrating Analysis: % Changes in Qualified Vote, 4 Maori Seats Combined
GRAPH 10: Percentage Change in Qualified Vote: Southern
GRAPH 11: Percentage Change in Qualified Vote: Western
GRAPH 12: Percentage Change in Qualified Vote: Eastern
GRAPH 13: Percentage Change in Qualified Vote: Northern
GRAPH 14: The 4 Maori Seats Compared: Ratana/Labour Vote 1935-84 (% of all qualified to vote)
GRAPH 15: Decline and Convergence: National's Vote in the 4 Maori Seats (% of all qualified voters)
GRAPH 16: The Search for an Alternative in the 4 Maori Seats:
(i) 30 Years of Social Credit
(ii) 50 Years of Independents and Mini Parties
GRAPH 17: 1935 to 1984—Phases in the 4 Maori Seats (% of qualified vote): Southern
GRAPH 18: 1935 to 1984—Phases in the 4 Maori Seats (% of qualified vote): Western
GRAPH 19: 1935 to 1984—Phases in the 4 Maori Seats (% of qualified vote): Eastern
GRAPH 20: 1935 to 1984—Phases in the 4 Maori Seats (% of qualified vote): Northern

Notes

1 [Although the original List of Graphs is included in this chapter, only the first graph (now called a figure) has been reproduced. The text is otherwise unchanged, except that where omitted graphs are mentioned [omitted] has been inserted into the text. Ed.]
2 [Tahupotiki Wiremu Ratana founded the Ratana Church. The Ratana movement stood candidates for election from 1922 onwards. During the early years of the first Labour Government, Ratana allied itself with the Labour Party. Ed.]
3 [Bob Jones, a prominent business entrepreneur, founded the New Zealand Party. Ed.]
4 R. M. Chapman, W. K. Jackson, A. V. Mitchell, *New Zealand Politics in Action. The 1960 General Election* (London, 1962), pp. 71-2 and 283-4. [The Prime Minister referred to was Walter Nash. Ed.]

5   [J. K. Hunn, *Report on Department of Maori Affairs* (Wellingtcn, 1960). Ed.]
6   [Wallace Rowling was the leader; Matiu Rata resigned in 1980. Ed.]
7   P. R. Abramson, and W. Claggett, 'Race Related Differences in Self-Reported and Validated Turnout in 1984', *The Journal of Politics,* Vol. 48 (1986), pp 416-8.
8   [See Chapter 10 in this volume. Ed.]
9   R. M. Chapman, 'The Response to Labour and the Question of Parallelism of Opinion 1928-1960', in Robert Chapman and Keith Sinclair (eds.), *Studies of a Small Democracy* (Auckland, 1963), pp. 247-52 and 279-80. [Reprinted here as Chapter 7. Ed.]
10 A. J. McCracken, *Maori Voting and Non-Voting 1928-1969. A Study of Change in Voting Patterns Preceding and Accompanying Urban Migration,* unpublished MA thesis (University of Auckland), 1971.
11 [Electoral Amendment Act 1975. Ed.]

14
Deaths and Entrances

In seeking to define the subject of this paper by outlining it with a title, I called it 'Death and Re-election'—but that has too sepulchral a resonance, so I borrowed instead the title of Dylan Thomas's first book of poems, 'Deaths and Entrances', in this case out of and into the role of politician. I shall borrow from Dylan Thomas in addition something equally useful, his brevity. For this is intended as a working paper; not an end but a beginning on by-elections as one among the many processes by which the composition of Parliament constantly changes in its parts, but only slowly in its major party outlines and structures.

For it is the truest of commonplaces that ours is a government by party and, in order to govern as much of the time as possible and as effectively as ample majorities permit, parties must structure entrances and exits from the arena of Parliament to gain or at least not to lose through them. By-elections are one such door. But how large a door is it?

The first problem here is posed by the state of the records themselves. Only since 1957 has the Electoral Office seen fit to print by-election booth figures and roll numbers and all the other data we have about general elections. In earlier times the gross totals for each candidate, with or without informals and roll numbers, might or might not appear in the *New Zealand Year-book* or the *Appendices*.[1] Sometimes by-elections were acknowledged to have occurred by listing that fact together with the names of the departed and the newcomers. But no details were given of how these members found their way into Parliament. Perhaps public voting was and is one of New Zealand's many state secrets. Certainly when I enquired of the Chief Electoral Officer some years ago whether I might see the Returning Officers' returns for by-elections in the 'forties and 'fifties, he confided darkly that, so far as he knew, they had disappeared. Even now, repeated requests by an M.P. have failed for the last two months to produce one copy of the returns on the basis of which Messrs Lange and Falloon confidently take part in our government.[2]

So one is reduced to working with whatever the newspapers of the day passed on to their readers—sometimes only the overnight figures, or happily the final count or even, *mirabile dictu*, the corrected roll figure. But it does pay to know where to look, which in turn necessitates an

[This chapter is the text of a paper presented to the Annual Conference of the New Zealand Political Studies Association, University of Auckland, August 1977. Ed.]

accurate list of the by-elections. Thus far I have established and cross-checked such a list back to 1908, which gives us nearly seventy years of data with which to measure the proportions of the by-election door into Parliament. In those sixty-nine years since the general election of 1908, when the Liberals triumphed and the Reformers were as yet simply His Majesty's Opposition, there have been ninety by-elections proper and ten of what I call 'quasi by-elections', in all, a neat hundred.[3]

Let me explain the concept of a quasi by-election. It shares with most by-elections the consequences of the removal by death of the sitting member together with whatever personal pull he or she might have exerted. Individual connections have been broken but, in the case of quasi by-elections, the member's death has occurred too near to an expected general election to justify issuing warrant and writs. So the seat stays vacant until that general contest and is decided then between candidates none of whom has the familiarity and possibly the special appeals of the late sitting member. In looking into what death in office does to entry into Parliament, the effect of all M.P.s' deaths—however carelessly timed with respect to the electoral calendar—seemed worth including.

But there are other causes of by-elections proper than simply death. Two out of three since the last general election have been occasioned by resignation; one by-election so that a former Prime Minister might pass on to even higher things and one as a response to the most extraordinary allegations so far made in a New Zealand Parliament.[4] Both the making of the allegations and the elevation of Sir Keith were within the control of the present Prime Minister who would have considered how any consequential by-elections might serve to register an ebbing electoral tide since November 1975. Nevertheless Mr Muldoon proceeded as he did. So some resignations are evidently risked for other gains. Since 1908 M.P.s have caused by-elections in order to become respectively a mere Legislative Councillor and, more significantly, a Supreme Court Judge. Six of the sitting M.P.s, no less, have gone off to grace that formerly most prestigious of posts, New Zealand's High Commissioner in the United Kingdom. And now Parliament itself has been drawn on in mid-term to supply Her Majesty's representative who must be her impartial arbiter of constitutionally grave and party-tangled causes.

There are more simple, plainer reasons for resigning, of course. One and possibly two have departed because of ill-health; one went out to test public opinion on his opposition to conscription; another because he had pledged himself to go when his friend had served out his one-year disqualification from Parliament for election-time bribery. The Bay of Islands voters put the convicted Reform member, Mr V. H. Reed, back into Parliament at the ensuing by-election while Mr Reed's trustworthy friend found himself installed in the Legislative Council not long afterwards, no doubt much to his surprise. And then there was the United Party M.P. for Parnell electorate, as Remuera was known, who became so disenchanted with the then 'Wizard of Finance', Sir Joseph Ward, that he acted upon and admitted publicly that he, Mr Jenkins, had 'suffered a change of political heart' and departed Parliament accordingly. Disillusion may still be as common nowadays, but such readiness for action has diminished. Whereas in the 27 years before 1935, 11 resigned for all reasons, in the 42 years since, only six have so decided.

As between the earlier and the later periods, another cause of by-elections, the voiding of the general election result because of procedural and other irregularities, has not just diminished, it has disappeared.[5] Before 1935 five results were overturned for such causes while Labour's Paddy Webb had his seat adjudged vacant for absence without leave of the House because he was being detained in prison at the time for his anti-conscription views and activities. Before 1935 six such by-elections; since 1935 none. Voided results caused just over an eighth of all by-elections then, just as resignations were responsible for almost a quarter. In the age of Labour and National governments, however, electoral irregularities have apparently vanished while resignations are down from a quarter to a tenth of by-election producers. Either the comparative comfort and status of Parliamentary seats has increased or party vetting and discipline have hardened and clarified. Most probably both factors have contributed to these contrasts which emerge so clearly from the data. Only reliable death remains fairly constant. The 30 deaths over the 27 years from 1908 to 1935 represent a rate of 1.11 per annum whereas the 47 deaths over 42 years since 1935 represent a rate of 1.12. At least something has proved safe from inflation.

But let us return to that central problem of measuring the size and significance of by-elections and quasi by-elections as a door into Parliament. The size of this door, in the first place, is to be compared to what, to which other doors? For when one thinks about it, Parliament is in a way an arena without walls in that every general election could, in the abstract, empty out the whole of the last Parliament and replace it entirely with new members. There are as many chances of replacement as there are seats to be contested and that figure must then be multiplied by the number of general elections to be considered. Since 1908 there have been eighteen elections each with 80 seats at risk, one with 84, and two with 87. Subtract the 10 quasi by-elections and you have a total of 1,688 unimpaired general election choices for continuity or change of member and party. Adding in the chances provided by by-elections pure and impure brings the grand total to 1,788. Against this massive array of choice, our hundred exceptional elections constitute just 5.59% of the total or a touch over one-twentieth of all elections.

So much for the comparative size of the by-election door measured across nearly seven decades of use. But what of the linked question—its significance as a door? Who passes through it and to what party effect? And again one must ask further questions, significant compared to what number of new entrants of which party stripes coming in by what regular channels? For we know that the walls of the Parliamentary arena are in practice not flat on the ground of that mound on Molesworth Street or, at least, not up to now. Allegiance to parties and loyalties to men build walls of custom and habit around the cockpit of power sufficiently strong to repulse every third November the great majority of those who try to enter for the first time. But what proportion do manage to enter when and how?

To find the significance of by-elections, in short, one must first chart the regular channels. To do so I have compiled a record of the electoral and Parliamentary lives of all those who have served up to now in the ten Parliaments of the conservative era of National predominance since the 1949 election. This record therefore begins by covering the 844 chances for change at the 1949 general election and at all elections since. That by itself represents 47.2% of all electoral choices after 1908.

In addition, however, the last ten Parliaments have contained 72 M.P.s, 38 of them National and 34 Labour, whose Parliamentary careers were begun before 1949. The Rt. Hon. Peter Fraser, for example, reached right back to a by-election victory in October 1918. From their first successful elections and onwards, the 34 Labour representatives who had been in before 1949 had fought in 125 contests while the equivalent 38 National M.P.s had contested 101. Between them the records of these pre-'49ers who went on into the last ten Parliaments brought with them a further record of 226 prior contests or another 12.64% of the total since 1908. What had begun as a test of the total transition process in Parliament by looking only at the Parliaments of these last 28 years turned out, thanks to the longevity of stalwart M.P.s, to encompass 59.84% or a fraction under three-fifths of all the transition points not just over 28 but over 69 years. Any researcher who has endeavoured to restrict and trim his field will recognise the inevitable dismay as one vainly hacks at the inherent longitudinality of institutions and processes.

Perhaps then we could commence our analysis of normal and abnormal entrances to Parliament by looking first at these 72 early inhabitants, 70 of whom were there when the first National Parliament met and two of whom, the Hon. Arnold Nordmeyer and Dr Martyn Finlay, re-entered the Chamber later after absences of one-and-a-quarter and 14 long years respectively.

How did these 72, then, make their initial entry into Parliament? How many, for example, came in at a by-election or quasi by-election bearing in mind, of course, that such events afforded only one-twentieth of the opportunities to enter Parliament. The facts, however, do not seem to have borne that proportion properly in mind. For they answer that just under a third (32%) of the 72 came in at a quasi or full by-election. This result is roughly six times what the ratio of opportunities would have suggested. Intending Parliamentarians should take note that a by-election appears to be a most promising time at which to begin a long tenure, at least if one is a member of a major party of the near future or the present, like our National 38 or our Labour 34 were when they began.

Consider Peter Fraser, still Leader of the Opposition in 1950 and most recently Prime Minister. He struggled in for Wellington Central at a by-election and so did the next Labour Leader of the Opposition and Prime Minister, Walter Nash, member for Hutt from 1929. Arnold Nordmeyer re-entered Parliament at the by-election for Brooklyn which followed Peter Fraser's death and, while Nordmeyer missed the Prime Ministry, he did lead the Opposition. Both Michael Savage and Norman Kirk fought their way in at general elections. But it is more characteristic that both the competitors to succeed Kirk as Prime Minister, Bill Rowling and Hugh Watt, should have come in at by-elections—Watt in 1953 for Onehunga and Rowling in 1962 for Buller.[6]

On the other side of the House, the right channel for entry is by no means so clear. Yet the young Keith Holyoake found his way in via the Motueka by-election of 1932 even though, after his defeat in 1938, he had to wait five slow years for the death of Sir Alfred Ransom to produce a quasi by-election at which he could succeed for Pahiatua. Robert Muldoon, naturally, battled his way into a marginal in 1957, like Norman Kirk, but Sidney Holland sank gratefully into his father's comfortable and secure old seat when Henry Holland retired in 1935 from Christchurch North. John Marshall, too, made a gentleman's entry into the new and moderately plush Mount Victoria when that electorate was drawn into short-lived existence in 1946. However, at its abolition in 1954, John Marshall's unbroken career depended on the happy conjunction that Charles Bowden chose to retire from neighbouring Karori at just the considerate and well-mannered time. As for Gordon Coates, he neither fought nor sauntered his way into the House in the shifting uneasy election of 1911. Rather, he sidled his way in under the *nom de guerre* of Independent Liberal. But the father figure of all Conservative Prime Ministers, William Ferguson Massey, understood the other New Zealand tradition and chose to appear in Parliament fresh from a by-election for Waitemata in 1894.

I have tested the connection between forms of entry and long tenure by means of these party leaders' careers partly because Holland, Holyoake and Marshall, Fraser, Nash and Nordmeyer, were all numbered among our 72 bridging M.P.s, but also because they illustrate party variations as between the forms of entry, party variations which appear also among the 72 as a whole. Consider initial entry by all forms of by-election. Fifteen of the 34 Labour M.P.s (or 44%) came in by this route, whereas only 8 of the 38 National members (21%) followed suit. It was the other way around in respect to convenient retirement on the part of one's own party predecessor. Ten Nationalists followed a departing colleague compared with only five Labour newcomers who greeted a voluntarily disappearing back as their best omen for a long occupancy in a safe seat. Insofar as senior Labour colleagues paved the way for younger men, it was much more likely to happen involuntarily when death in office and a by-election opened the way—which was the case with 9 Labour and five National entrants.

The last two styles of entry again reveal party difference. Labour was more likely than National (3 as against 1) to arrive via the creation of a new seat. In those more stable days the creation of fresh seats was rare except when the burgeoning cities were recognised and especially in 1946 at the time the Country Quota was removed.[7] But it is in the entries by straight victory that the difference between the National party in the ascendant and the Labour party of survivors really shows. Of the National 38, 19, or exactly half, came in by displacing an incumbent of the opposed party. Among Labour's 34, 11, or fractionally less than a third, arrived in the same fashion.

Reflecting upon these bridging 72 M.P.s has thus uncovered a much more significant role for by-elections among the mechanisms for replacement of members, especially in the Labour Party, than measuring the size of the by-election door at first suggested. But these same 72 members—less Messrs. Nordmeyer and Finlay—only constitute most of the membership of one Parliament, seven-eighths of the 1949 Parliament to be precise. Are we being led astray by the accidents which are attendant upon taking any one cross-section through ongoing phenomena? To find out, only an examination of many Parliaments together will suffice. So now I turn to analyze the pattern of entry for all members of the last ten Parliaments, the results, you will remember, of 1,070 opportunities for choice.

The first intriguing answer is to the question 'How many members has all that picking and choosing produced? Besides our original 72 from the past, only a further 165 turn out to have arrived in Parliament over the next twenty-eight years containing ten general, two quasi, and twenty-six pure by-elections. Somehow it all rather smacks of conservative stability, despite the wholesale eviction notices served in 1972 and 1975. As for the party complexion of the newcomers, well, 92 Nationalists were added to the 38 who came through the 1949 curtain into the era of National predominance, while Labour gained 72 to mix with its 34 survivors. And, of course, there was briefly one Social Crediter. The 55:45 party balance of these later entrants rather exaggerates the difference in votes between the parties. But that exaggeration hardly begins to parallel the heavy distortion in the ratio of party years in power which stands at 22:6.

Given the conservative weight of this post-war age and in view of the changed proportions of the party intakes, has this more than doubled sample greatly altered the previous findings about the function of by-elections among the forms of entry into Parliament? The answer, briefly, is 'No'. At 21% of all initial entries, by-elections retain their disproportionate importance, but that importance is sharply reduced by one-third from the 32% share it held among the 72 representatives of previous political eras.

What has happened within this overall reduction in by-elections as a source of initial entry is a down-grading of by-elections as victorious occasions for one's party, and a relative increase in their significance as favourable points of admission into safe seats. Different relative rates of shrinkage as between the two types of by-elections has done the trick. Taking the larger type first, we find that by-elections caused by events within one's own party, such as the resignation of the Rt. Hon. Sir Keith or the death of the Rt. Hon. Sir Walter, events which led to the replacement of elderly and aged men by juniors of a like party stripe if hardly of the same capacity, such replacement by-elections shrank by a quarter from 22.2% of all entries to 16.4%. On the other hand, the victorious by-election, the second and smaller type, was reduced to less than half its former proportion. The kind of occasion represented by E. R. Neale's capture of Nelson in 1946 after the death of Labour's grand old Independent, Harry Atmore, or Joe Walding's victory in Palmerston North when National's W. H. Brown died in 1967, such lively turnabouts have got very much fewer. Indeed, they have declined from 9.7% of the whole entry to 4.2%. So that is one style of victory that has much diminished, leaving the genuine fight in pure and quasi by-elections to those party rooms to which the electorate properly belongs where the future M.P. is really selected ready to be endorsed with enhanced predictability at the subsequent poll.

Is it the case, then, that the scenes of dubious battle and victorious outcomes have shifted from by- to general elections? Has entry with battle honours merely moved its timing and surroundings? Looking at those thirteen ill-fated in-and-outers who arrived with laurels in 1972 only to lose them in 1975 (12.3% of all Labour entries) and then gazing speculatively at the twenty-three first victories by party overturn from 1975 (17.7% of all National participants in these ten Parliaments) one is led automatically to form the hypothesis that these successive and massive tidal waves of victory would sweep victory as a form of entry to new heights which would mark off this age of individualist aggression from those less unstable times represented by our 72 pre-'49ers. But not so. The proportion entering by victory at general elections increased by only 0.9 points, from 41.7% to 42.6%. The explanation of what other kind of entry took up the slack from by-elections cannot lie here.

Yet before we move away from successful entry by combat let us ponder the slaughters of 1972 and 1975 a little further. They will not go away from the political record or the statistics, even though they seem to have drowned in them without a trace. Since they constituted in reality 15.2% of all entries of any kind by all parties, Norman Kirk's one-term warriors and the counter-victors who fought under the banner of Mr Muldoon are a large collective fact to be swallowed up. Indeed, they represent over one-third of all entrants by victory in the ten Parliaments. Therefore, it follows that the rest contributed only two-thirds as high a figure as we have been considering. So the even level maintained in the gross comparison must actually conceal a drastic ebbing away of victories at general elections—which we remember as the peculiarly static Holyoake years—to be followed by the astonishing onset of two crashing waves, the second even larger than the first. The tsunami or tidal wave can take, I understand, precisely that form—an unprecedented ebb followed by two great walls of water, which afterwards rapidly subside and disperse, leaving little except wreckage behind them.

Withdrawing from these scenes of public, private and party confusion, let us return to our problem about which form of entry engorged itself as by-elections shrank and especially those victorious by-elections—reduced perhaps, as part of the general ebb of victory but not, so far, explosively restored. Certainly entry by seizing on suitable new seats does not answer our question. Despite two enlargements of Parliament[8] and seven fresh seats extra to those which the redistribution process has always conferred, entry by means of sizing up and claiming fresh and accommodating electorates nevertheless advanced only from 5.6% to 5.9% of the whole initial entry. So naturally we turn with expectation to entry by successful replacement of retiring or shifting party grandees, the mode, you will recall, far more favoured by National's than by Labour's leaders. Sure enough, among the pre-'49ers this mode represented 20.8% of all entries whereas, in the Parliaments of the National age, it has shot up by a half to 30.9%. As being ready in the wings for death and by-election was to Labour's heyday, so nowadays is spotting the succession to a weary National Minister wanting to exchange his bench for an armchair.

And, of course, the Parliamentary superannuation scheme, a late benefaction of Labour's welfare state, arrived in 1947 just before these ten Parliaments. Undoubtedly that has encouraged thoughts of retirement even among Labour's sempiternal back-benchers for, after all, Ritchie Macdonald did retire, not die, in the end.[9] Since so many more of National's representatives were men of property or professional substance—accountants, pump manufacturers, farmers and such—they could always afford to retire once they had achieved what they came for, that term as a Minister. Labour's stalwarts, comparatively, had come in from less or little, had only their Parliamentary salaries and allowances to rely on and, moreover, wished to hang on to what conferred status upon them, the fact of the Parliamentary seat itself. No wonder it took the experience of the failing Sir Walter in his eighties, the apparently ageless Rex Mason setting New Zealand records for Parliamentary longevity and the hard young eye of Norman Kirk to produce a Labour age limit for its candidates. But set the limit was and will already have contributed to some retirements to our statistics.[10]

This suggestion that Labour, too, will find that replacement of the retiring has become and is becoming an ever more important form of entry to their Caucus is borne out by the figures when we look at them by party colours. R and R, retirement and replacement, has gone up by nine points among the Nationalists (from 26.3% to 35.4%) and by eleven points among Labour (from 14.7% to 25.5%).

Other forms of entry have changed less. Obtaining selection for a newly-designed electorate, with the correct party persuasion from the start, is rather more likely nowadays with National (up from 2.6% to 3.8%) and fractionally less so for Labour (8.8% shading down to 8.5%). New seat entries are the least significant of ways into Parliament, although the recent Redistribution Commission has done its level, well, its energetic best to enlarge this form of entry for 1978 and, if their precedent is followed, in future. Perhaps it will have the side-effect of bringing National's share of new seat entries (3.8% over the ten Parliaments) much closer to Labour's equivalent (8.5%). Looking back at it, Labour used to get most of the fruits of the drift to the cities in the creation of their Te Atatus, Mangeres, Poriruas and Wigrams. Now a two-and-a-half class society of upper, lower and brown basement is bringing forth for National its upper Pakurangas, East Coast Bays and Hunuas as a top to match Labour's bottom.

Just as the smallest mode of entry has not changed dramatically, but holds some surprises, so does the largest mode, entry by victory at a general election. National in its age of triumph, and despite that 17.7% contingent of Muldoon shock-troops, has witnessed victory as a form of entry drop from 50.0% to 47.7%. Even at a shade under half of all entries, however, it is far more the right way in for Nationalists than general election victory is for Labour men. Their proportion hovers around a third although it has improved from the pre-'49er's percentage of 32.3% to the overall figure for ten Parliaments of 35.8%. Here too, of course, that 12.3% of Kirk and Rowling in-and-outers more than account by themselves for the entire improvement.

But it is in our final form of entry, by pure and quasi by-elections, that party differences are still most clearly revealed. By-elections are not what they were in either party, thanks to the rise of R and R. By-elections used to introduce, among the pre-'49ers, a solid fifth (21.1%) of all National entries and a startling 44.2% of the Labour newcomers. Nevertheless, this door into Parliament, whose size, remember, represents only one-twentieth of all possible points of entry, continues to be so busily used that through it have flowed 13.1% of all Nationalists and 30.2% of all Labourites coming into the last ten Parliaments. It is not the front-door of general election victory nor the back-door of retirement and replacement, but it is a side-door as busy with traffic at all seasons as death and resignation can provide.

To analyse further what is, in effect, a flow-chart of Parliament and to check precisely the place of by-elections, I have made a series of subsidiary studies of modes of entry by type of seat. But I will not abandon brevity entirely by including them. Suffice it to say that, among Maori representatives, entry at a by-election is overwhelmingly popular. It is a major way into poorer city seats and is heavily used by farmers but not when compared with retirement and replacement either among intending farmer or rural members. Victory at general elections, on the other hand, finds its natural arena in the towns, the mixed city electorates and the special country constituencies. It should all make sound sense to the aspiring candidate and to the new M.P. estimating his tenure and the worth of what he has beneath him. The rules are now plain. Entry by victory and the front-door for an uneasy electoral life; and do not count on many Parliamentary terms. If you favour longevity, try to find a hole in the wall cut by the Representation Commission, or try the back-door of replacing an obliging party colleague entering retirement, or try that Labour favourite, the swinging side-door of by-election—the doorway of leaders.

Notes

1 [*The Appendices to the Journals of the House of Representatives*. Ed.]
2 [David Lange won the Mangere by-election for Labour on 26 March 1977; and John Falloon won the Pahiatua by-election for National on 30 April 1977. Ed.]
3 For a list of by-elections from 1911 until 1994—when the last by-election for a Parliament elected under the First-Past-the-Post electoral system occurred—see G. A. Wood (ed.) *Ministers and Members in the New Zealand Parliament* (Dunedin, 1996), pp. 107-13. Ed.]
4 [Sir Keith Holyoake, former Prime Minister and MP for Pahiatua, became the Governor-General on 26 October 1977. Colin Moyle, a Minister in the 1972-1975 Labour Government and MP for Manukau between 1963 and 1969 and Mangere between 1969 and 1977, resigned from Parliament after allegations were made about his personal life. Moyle returned to Parliament in 1981. Ed.]
5 [In two cases between 1977 and 1998, however, post-election court decisions overturned the election night results. Winston Peters, National, successfully filed an election petition after the 1978 general election and won the Hunua seat, defeating his Labour opponent, Malcolm Douglas, the initial winner. After the 1987 general election, Wyatt Creech, National, successfully petitioned against the victory of Reg Boorman, Labour. The first case concerned the electoral roll, the validity of votes cast and voter qualification irregularities; the second concerned voter qualifications and candidate over-expenditure. In neither case was a by-election held. Ed.]
6 [Note that two further Labour leaders continued in the tradition of by-election entry. David Lange won the Mangere by-election on 26 March 1977 and later held the posts of Deputy Leader and Leader, and was Prime Minister (1984-1989). Geoffrey Palmer won the Christchurch Central by-election on 18 August 1979 and later held the post of Deputy Leader, succeeding David Lange as Leader and Prime Minister on Lange's resignation in August 1989, a position which he held until September 1990. Ed.]
7 ['Throughout the twenties a special provision of the electoral laws—the country quota (1881-1945)—added a greater weight to the votes of those living outside the cities and towns.' R. M. Chapman, 'Appendix: The Effect of the Country Quota', *The Political Scene, 1919-1931* (Auckland, 1969), p. 66. Ed.]
8 [As a consequence of the Electoral Amendment Act 1965, the House of Representatives went from 80 to 84 seats in 1969 and to 87 seats in 1972. Ed.]
9 [Ritchie Macdonald held Ponsonby (1946-1963) and Grey Lynn (1963-1969). Ed.]
10 [Rex Mason held Eden (1926-1928), Auckland Suburbs (1928-1946), Waitakere (1946-1963), and then New Lynn until his retirement in 1966. The Labour Party's age limit made candidates ineligible for nomination if they were either 70 years of age or would become 70 during a parliamentary term. Ed.]

Part Three

Governing Democratically

15

The Mechanics of Representation

Democratic representation in countries with which New Zealand might be fairly compared—the United Kingdom, Australia, the United States—is less equitable than in New Zealand and less sensitive to growth and change in the centres of population. Fundamentally the system is fairer in New Zealand because the House of Representatives has made redrawing the boundaries of electorates an automatic occurrence which must follow each census. This is a frequent occurrence since censuses are taken every five years, a relatively impartial process since it is carried out by a commission of seven, only two of whom represent party viewpoints. If one looks at the recent squabble in Britain—when a threatened government picked which revisions it would accept to cries of 'Foul' by the opposition—or contemplates the history of gerrymandering in such states as South Australia and Queensland, we have much to be thankful for in New Zealand.

Our system, however, is far from perfect and some of its biases have been intentionally incorporated. Overall the system displays a mild favouritism for National against Labour. This is most visible when the nationwide votes for the two parties are nearly equal. In 1957 Labour was 2 per cent *ahead* of National on the European voting, yet National obtained 39 seats to Labour's 37—thus reversing the results on the votes. Only the addition to Labour of the four Maori seats caused the seat totals to correspond with the winner on votes, still leaving Labour with only a working majority of one after providing a Speaker.

In the opposite situation in 1954, when National was under 2 per cent ahead of Labour in the European voting, National took 14 more European seats than Labour. Even if 1954 is dismissed as 'the bad old days', it is worth noting that in 1966, when National was just 3 per cent ahead of Labour in European voting, National received 13 more seats. If the Maori electorates had not been overwhelmingly Labour, lessening the disparity, more notice might have been taken of this characteristic outcome before now.[1]

The Tilt
How does this tilt in the system come about? First, because the law orders the Representation Commission to draw electorates on the basis of the

[This chapter was published in the *New Zealand Listener*, 24 October 1969. Ed.]

total population, man, woman and child, instead of on the basis of those over 21 years old (now 20).[2] Since country electorates, which almost all elect Nationalists, contain proportionately more children than the less fecund urban electorates, these electorates contain fewer actual voters. To put it another way, there are more country National electorates than the number of voting adults would justify.

Secondly, the tilt proceeds from how the Representation Commission uses or does not use the latitude given it by Parliament to draw electorates a little larger or a little smaller than the average (the law says plus or minus 5 per cent), and whether that use is analogous to the movement of people within the nation. Everyone knows that the outer suburbs of the big cities like Auckland, Christchurch and Wellington, and some towns like Hamilton, are growing most rapidly. These are predominantly, though not entirely, Labour voting areas. If the Representation Commission drew these suburban electorates at the minimum size allowed for, they would grow to at least the average size by the time of the next election and, if experience is any guide, be overpopulated by the first and certainly by the second election under a given set of boundaries. Instead, successive Commissions have drawn the outer suburban growth electorates to include average or above average numbers, while tending to draw the emptying inner city and country electorates with smaller numbers. By the time the 1969 election takes place, of the 14 electorates which were drawn with below average numbers, 12 are either country or inner city electorates which could have fallen further behind. On the other hand, of the 15 electorates drawn to be decidedly fuller than normal, 11 are in fast-growing suburbs or towns which are all too likely to pull further ahead. The result of the Commission's blindness to growth when it employs its latitude is slightly fewer Labour members and one or two more for National.

The third factor behind the tilt has nothing to do with the electoral law or the Commission's habits. Labour voters have packed themselves into fortresses like Birkenhead, Grey Lynn, Mangere, Porirua and Avon and their surplus votes beyond a winning margin show up only in the size of majorities and nationwide totals. In the countryside, National's growing margin over Labour is similarly 'wasteful' so the two wastes may increasingly balance out.

The final factor in the tilt is a political one. During the last 20 years, in which New Zealand has six times out of seven preferred the more conservative party, National has consistently augmented its lead in seats by winning more of the genuinely close contests in towns and marginal city seats. A slightly longer reach in each case has allowed National to pick a whole row of plum electorates. This phenomenon, of the winning party gaining disproportionately more close seats, is a widely-recognised characteristic of any first-past-the-post system of counting votes. It should work evenly and add to Labour's haul when they win, yet in 1957 it did not. So the first three factors I have outlined must bear some of the blame, and perhaps the precise way those marginal city and town electorates are shaped makes more of a difference than is recognised.

Boundaries
Here again population change is sharpening a problem for Representation Commissions. More and more towns like Napier, Hastings and New Plymouth have not only filled up their own electorates but have grown so big that some townsmen must be decanted into surrounding electorates. Which townsmen are poured off can make all the difference to an electorate evenly balanced between the parties. If New Plymouth's southern National booths go, that will yield one result; if certain eastern booths are transferred, perhaps the opposite can be expected. When one examines the Hastings seat, and sees that it runs from west to east to include all of the conservative Havelock North booths—when it might run from south to north to pick up Tomoana, Whakatu and Clive—one sees how delicate a task faces the Commission's presiding retired magistrate, the Surveyor-General, the Government Statistician, the Chief Electoral Officer, the Director-General of the Post Office and the two party representatives.

Quite often the real force which determines boundaries is tradition. For generations the people of Woolston in Christchurch, the well-to-do of the Port Hills and the port workers of Lyttelton have been yoked to rural Akaroa in defiance of the Law's instructions to preserve 'community of interest'. Whatever that loose phrase may mean, it certainly cannot be an invitation to cut across one of the two most notable social differentiators in New Zealand—the distinction between country and city. Yet this has happened with Lyttelton, Rangiora and the old Selwyn seat. Three rural-urban mixtures were maintained around the fringe of Christchurch instead of two city seats and one farming electorate. At times all three mixtures were National and always two. One rural electorate and two city seats might have voted the other way round

Some mixtures are unavoidable, as in the mingling in two electorates to the north and south of Auckland. But only the odd statement that a truly rural Waikato constituency would be 'large' and 'unwieldy' was proffered by the Commission as a reason for trisecting Hamilton and joining each piece to an arbitrary wedge of countryside. Yet the majority of country electorates are both larger and more 'unwieldy' than any seat which could be made from the populous countryside round Hamilton.

One is driven to wonder, in the absence of tradition, necessity or instruction, whether the Commission might not have overlooked an opportunity to even the odds a little, at the same time giving some content to that vague formula, 'community of interest'.

Plainly, a prime object in drawing boundaries for a system of popular choice between alternative parties is to ensure that enough of the resulting electorates swing easily back and forth between the two so that gains in popular favour by either major party are evenly rewarded by more seats. As we have seen, this is not quite the case. Nor in recent decades has the balance between rural and city seats sensitively reflected the explosive growth of the latter. When the country quota was removed at the end of the Second World War, city seats numbered 34. As recently as 1966 they numbered only 33. Thanks to the recent enlargement of the House, four city additions have been made for the 1969 election. Undoubtedly future Commissions will need to show more awareness of urban/rural delimitations if they are to do full justice to all citizens.

For this is what our system operates towards: an accurate reflection of a decision between two parties made by all citizens equally on the basis of their experience of the Government and Opposition. We do not choose candidates for their debating qualities, or to argue for the locality, or even to be ex-farmers, ex-unionists or ex-accountants. We choose them to support a party which equals a leader, a team, a reputation and a programme. It will be part of the representatives' functions to see that the views of occupations and regions do not go unheard, but always they will be co-ordinated into meaningful choices by the fact of party competition. Either or both parties can be relied on to discover that whole sections of the community can be neglected only at their peril. It is a misconception of the representative system to over-represent one kind of region in order to give extra defence to some 'separate' interest it may be thought to have; for that strikes at the basic principle of the system which is the equal value of one man's experience of government with another's.

Those who still hanker for over-representation, in the fashion of the long-gone country quota, must now be few. There are more, however, who complain that electorates are getting too large, whether in numbers of constituents or in geographic size. There is some justice in the complaint that there are too few MPs to perform all the functions that New Zealanders expect of them. It is seeking for government on the cheap in trying to man Cabinet, committees, caucuses, and debating chamber (as well as to provide part-time ombudsmen for all) by employing just 84 individuals. Our Parliament and our party system would run better with a larger pool of talent available. The companion complaint that rural electorates are unworkably large is less serious. Air services alone have greatly increased time in the electorate available to MPs, while cars, better roads and more telephones have shrunk distances faster than new boundaries have stretched them. Campaigning from settlement to settlement was and is strenuous, yet door-knocking in a suburb can be just as frustrating and wearing, particularly when unsympathetic local bodies are allowed to restrict times and techniques for reaching gatherings of people.

Correction by gradual enlargement of the House has commenced, largely because the South Island objected to the inconvenience arising from the steady loss of seats because population growth was faster in the North, while the overall size of the House remained fixed. Now the South Island is guaranteed at least 25 European seats in an expanding House and their average size, divided into the population of the North Island, determines the number of North Island European seats—which is at present 55.[3] The North will have to keep growing faster than the South if the House is to enlarge further. On present trends New Zealand will be well into the 21st century before Parliament approaches the size political scientists have long recommended as efficient.

Maori Seats

One kind of electorate is not governed by the same rules as the rest: the four Maori seats are not increased in number by the Commission to six or seven according to total relevant population, because they come under a separate clause of the 1956 Act which provides that the four Maori electoral districts may have their boundaries changed only by proclamation. Instead it has been suggested that they should be done away with either inside 10 years or when four or more Maoris have been elected to European seats. Another proposal, not necessarily directed at ending separate Maori representation, is that those who are more than half Maori by descent should have the same choice of which roll to vote on as possessed now by those who are precisely half Maori and half European. It has also been suggested that, since this is a cultural matter, those who choose to be Maori regardless of inheritance should be free to vote Maori, with the same or stiffer guarantees against frequent roll-hopping that now exist.[4]

The agitation to abolish the Maori seats is an interesting case of New Zealanders being tempted in pursuit of an abstraction to abandon their customary pragmatism—trying it for size and seeing if it works. Separate Maori representation is certainly a contradiction of our general principle of representation, though it is a case of under-representation not over-representation. Moreover, its existence has worked to correct the tilt in the system against Labour. But that is not its purpose or function. The job of the Maori MP is to represent and interpret one of two distinct cultures in a bi-cultural nation and to act as mediators and interpreters between an overwhelmingly Pakeha people and Parliament on the one hand and, on the other, a minority culture in the crisis of transference from country to city and from one way of life to another. This is no mere regional difference or occupational interest that is being interpreted, but a culture as much entitled to preserve itself as the European. The encouragement of that cultural identity is as much a true New Zealander's objective as the right working of the representative system itself. And, if Maori MPs are increasingly significant leaders in that culture, then at least four of them should be retained, free from the necessity to represent also a majority of Pakeha constituents with their quite different outlook and demands.

This does not mean that every Maori values his right to vote or even obeys the law and registers. Because young Maoris are passing from one community to another, they are failing to learn the habits of registering and voting which the rural family and community used to teach. As the needs which ought to be represented increase, the means are let slip. It is hardly a cure to do away with Maori representation and leave young Maoris to become non-registrants and non-voters in Pakeha city seats.

Rather, New Zealand should finally enforce the existing law by giving the Electoral Office a properly-sized staff which could personally check registration by household visitation as is done overseas, and by following up information such as that derived from new connections for electricity and telephones.[5] If registration for Parliamentary and local body rolls was made the full-time, year-round concern of one adequately staffed office, we could do as much to improve the electoral vote as we have already done for television licensing. This would go far towards reducing the number of those unknown thousands of New Zealanders, Pakeha as well as Maori, who remain outside the representative system because, quite illegally, they are allowed to go without enrolment.

Notes

1 [Note that in both 1978 and 1981 Labour received more votes than did National but the latter party won the most seats. This was a factor in the Labour Government's decision to set up in 1985 the Royal Commission on the Electoral System. Ed.]
2 [In 1974 the qualifying age for voters became 18 years. Ed.]
3 [The Electoral Amendment Act 1965. Ed.]

4   [The Electoral Amendment Act 1975 gave all adult Maori the right to choose whether to enrol on the Maori or the General electoral roll. Ed.]
5   [Robert Chapman personally campaigned for improvements to be made as outlined here. Since 1975 there has been a series of changes in voter registration and administration. In 1998 the structure was as follows: the Electoral Office, headed by the Chief Electoral Officer (in the Ministry of Justice), was responsible for the overall conduct of elections; and the Electoral Enrolment Centre (New Zealand Post), was responsible for voter enrolment and maintaining up-to-date registers. The Electoral Commission registered political parties and educated voters about the electoral system; and the Representation Commission continued to draw the constituency boundaries. Ed.]

16

On Democracy as Having and Exercising a Clear Choice of Government

Arguing for any particular political system at the end of the nineteen-seventies can be a disheartening task whether one argues for systems which include PR or use first-past-the-post vote counting.[1] For voters expect governments to show a recognisable degree of success in tackling basic problems like inflation and unemployment and that success has not been forthcoming for the voter in Denmark or New Zealand, the Republic of Ireland or the United Kingdom. To pick up that *Economist* quotation about countries—not governments incidentally—being stable or unstable despite their voting systems, one could rephrase it as: 'Governments seem to be unsuccessful in the late seventies despite the political and voting systems which produced them'.

Therefore, the initial linked points to make are, first, not to attach great expectations of socio-economic solutions, nor, indeed, positive transformations to schemes for a different way of electing Parliament and, second, that the way votes are counted is only one part of a whole political system in which all parts interact to provide the final outcome. The final outcomes since 1973 have been poor enough to raise doubts about the contemporary effectiveness of political systems with single *or* with multi-member constituencies. By the same token, the relative failure of both does not suggest a basis for preferring one kind of system as against the other nor for picking out one part, such as the way votes are counted, as being the key to success.

Who Chooses the Government, When and How

The two kinds of system do work in quite different ways despite both of them arriving at their disappointing confrontations with the problems, inadequacies and contradictions of the mixed economy. Perhaps the most striking and vital difference between the British and Continental systems is who does the choosing of the government and its policies. Under the British and New Zealand system the norm is for the vast majority of voters—from nine-tenths to four-fifths of them—to be divided into adherents of two major parties each presenting a possible alternative

---

[This chapter was published in J. Stephen Hoadley, (ed.), *Improving New Zealand's Democracy* (Auckland, 1979). Ed.]

government and policies. That vast majority of voters then decides by majority between those alternative governments. Just once in New Zealand's post-depression years has the alternative government with fewer supporters secured office thanks mainly to the 1977 redrawing of boundaries.[2] But that has been the one exception to the norm which remains that the vast majority picks between alternative governments and the party with the greater support provides the kind of government and policies its supporters and opponents expect, if not the prosperity they hoped for.

Under PR counting, by contrast, choice of government and policies is not normally completed by the voters at the election. It may be so if a clear majority of all votes appears for one party. That is not normally the case however. Either a coalition government or a minority government must be negotiated subsequently and the viability of the government will depend upon support from others secured upon negotiated terms and conditions. Choice of government is thus not made directly by the voters but instead choice migrates and is made indirectly and later by representatives of the parties in Parliament. The negotiations of terms and conditions concern not only what policies are to be pursued, when and how hard, but also turn on which party personalities are to receive what posts and exercise influence over what departments. As Sweden has recently illustrated, even an expected combination, in this case of the 'bourgeois' parties in government, may well not survive in the form originally negotiated. So a fresh balance of policies and set of ministers may have to be arrived at with or without a fresh election. Meantime the record of performance and the policies pursued—which the voters will some day have to judge by—are the results of negotiations and combinations which the voters cannot control, which they are not fully informed about, and for which they cannot clearly fix responsibility.

On Giving Disproportionate Weight to Minor Parties

West German policies illustrate another recurring feature of PR systems, the disproportionate bargaining power which can be lent by the system to very minor parties. The Free Democrats, despite drawing a tenth or less of the available support, have partnered first the Christian Democrats and subsequently the Social Democrats in coalitions which guaranteed to Free Democrats ministerial posts including critical ones like agriculture. The only way round them was found to be the formation of a grand alliance between the two major parties, the Christian Democrats and the Social Democrats. As it proved there was also a heavy cost to that stultifying misalliance in terms of the sharply reduced credibility of both major parties and of government generally. It was in that period of obviously compromised principles and immobilism that urban political terrorism got a hold.

Governments in New Zealand whether National or Labour have been free to act on their own in a concerted way and in public where it is plain which set of ministers and which party has been responsible for the government's programme and record. Since 1954, however, there has been a minor party in the field (the Social Credit Political League), and, since 1972, Values as a fourth mini party. If New Zealand had elected Parliament by a proportional system Social Credit would have landed in the position of the German Free Democrats at its first jump. So, incidentally, would Labour at its first 1919 election after the Labour Party's formation in 1916. We can only conjecture about what would have happened in the long run after 1919 or 1954 had Labour and later Social Credit been able from their beginnings to force policies, appointments and priorities out of either one of the major parties of their time.

But in the short run such forced concessions to the incompatible programmes, principles and personalities of the minor party would have represented the great majority being steered by the small minority. Worse still for future electoral judgments, it would not have been at all clear from month to month just who had been responsible for which veer, surge or lurch. All that would have been clear in 1919 was that three-quarters of the voters had not voted for legislation shaped or influenced by Harry Holland, McCombs and Savage.

Likewise in 1954, eight-ninths of the New Zealand electorate had not voted for the implementation of the ideas of Major Douglas. It is difficult indeed to see how either National or Labour could have assumed responsibility for directing New Zealand's mixed economy in an inflationary age and then, to obtain a majority, have conceded any part of that direction to the devotees of 'costless credit'. Just because so much of Social Credit's thinking revolved round changing the very heart of the economic system it would not have been possible for National or Labour to fudge or compromise about conceding Social Credit's central demand. It concerned too vital an area. Fortunately as things were under the simple majority, single constituency system neither of the major parties had to attempt to square the circle of basically contradictory economic policies and allow one-ninth of the voters to sway the other eight-ninths. Nor would the 1954 type of dilemma for a PR New Zealand have gone away by November 1978 just because the proportions for the time being had become slightly less than one-sixth proposing to sway the other five-sixths.

On Arrangements Privately Arrived at between Leaderships

It is of course possible to flatter the whole process and praise it as tolerant government. It is certainly to be predicted that the major party's ministers and MPs would spend a great deal of time talking and listening in antechambers. But they would be attending out of public earshot, not to all the parties in Parliament nor their MPs, but to the leaders of those parties supporting, negotiating and then administering the compromise programme. For it must be remembered that under PR also there would continue to be adversary politics in the House—to which objection has been made in New Zealand as it is—because likewise under PR some party or parties would be excluded from or antipathetic to the deal on which the government of the day rested. In Italy with PR it has proved possible for the Christian Democrats by continual factional recombinations and arrangements with minor and mini parties to exclude for decades the second largest party, the Italian Communist Party, from a share or a voice in power. Those arrangements in a very different way from the German alliances have also produced 'immobilismo' but of a more lasting, damaging sort with worse guerilla violence from both the right and the left.

The Necessity of Judging Parts in the Context of the Whole

One should not argue that PR in New Zealand would reproduce the Italian or German situations here, any more than one should argue that changing to multi-member constituencies would reproduce the Danish, Swedish, Dutch or Belgian situations, all of them different. The entire politico-economic systems of those countries, not just their methods of translating votes into seats, have been involved in their variety of outcomes. One must add that the culture and history of the peoples, their resources, their defence problems, and the geography of their markets have all contributed materially to the way the political economy of each works. Each is a complexity of interacting systems not a static blueprint from which it is possible to snip a part, transfer it and anticipate its working in an alien context.

Has Our System Proved Responsive? The Labour Example

Consider the two different cases already mentioned of parties trying to break through to power in the context of New Zealand. Labour in 1919 at the first opportunity took 24.5 percent of the votes and there, throughout the twenties, it more or less stuck with 23.4 percent in 1922, 27.2 percent in 1925 and 26.9 percent in 1928. It had persuaded the majority of voters in two sections of the New Zealand electorate, the poorer city seats and the mining and forestry constituencies, that Labour policies were relevant and beneficial for them so that, by 1922, Labour held fourteen such seats. But it failed in its efforts to reach outside those sections and convince a substantial proportion of electors in the rural, the town, or even the mixed city constituencies. Labour remained a minor party in the twenties because it had not persuaded the great majority. The single-member system meant that Labour politicians were not granted the leverage which PR would have given them to bargain for or force changes while the mass of New Zealanders remained unconvinced. That can be seen as a great virtue in the existing system.

Meanwhile Labour's attitudes and policies were being fought over and modified, their MPs and candidates were learning their trade, and together they were familiarising the voters with Labour's sharply different answers to the contest of alternative conservatisms being conducted between the Reform and Liberal parties. Then the onset of the Great Depression, the widening exposure of the old parties' helplessness and further alterations to Labour's programmes all combined to convince the other sections of New Zealand society—most reluctantly as always in New Zealand—of the need for and the possibility of major socio-economic change.

Once the Labour minority broke out of its sectional confinement and began to become a majority the first-past-the-post electoral system proved most responsive. It took two further elections for Labour to reach power. In 1931 Labour secured 33.5 percent of the vote and 32.9 percent of the seats and in 1935 those figures had become 47.1 percent and 71.1 percent respectively. The re-named National opposition, by contrast, stood at 33.6 percent of the vote and 25.0 percent of the seats. Labour's Parliamentary majority was much strengthened by its candidates winning many three- and four-way contests against Nationalists, third party Democrats and independents. The result was that it had the assurance and the numbers to undertake and carry through a whole series of radical reformations in economic and social institutions. The upshot at the next election was endorsement by 57.0 percent of the voters.

The System Responded as the Tasks of Persuasion were Met
In sum then, the New Zealand political system initially allowed Labour quickly to capture the bulk of the seats in the two types of constituency where its policies persuaded and matched the needs and attitudes of the majority of the voters. Where those conditions were not met, Labour penetrated with difficulty and only sporadically. As the minority party representing a little over one-quarter of the voters, Labour in the 1920s was not able to influence or shape New Zealand's legislation to fit its basically different approach. Nor is it obvious, as advocates of PR assume,

that Labour as a minor party ought to have been able to do so. When Labour's approach had been fully articulated and modified, when the existing politico-economic structure could be seen to be crumbling under strain, and as voters in every kind of electorate were persuaded by Labour and even more so by events, then Labour rose rapidly to major party status and to sufficient power to accomplish major change It had taken nineteen years from party formation in 1916 to power in 1935.

The Social Credit Example

Social Credit's fate has been very different. It is twenty-five years since it first fought a general election and it has not yet captured a sectional majority even in the rural seats. It has had three encouraging elections, 1954, 1966 and 1978, with respectively 11.1, 14.5 and 16.1 percent of the valid vote. But it has also had to endure six disappointments at 7.2, 8.6, 7.9, 9.1, 6.6 and 7.4 percent. Social Credit's sequence of high points each twelve years have been registered at low points in the record of one or both major parties. In 1954 National was heavily rejected without Labour having recovered its drawing power after the 1951 strike election. In 1966 Labour's new leader, Mr Kirk, and National's familiar Mr Holyoake had so little that was convincing to offer that their parties declined together in the 'protest election'. Again in 1978 National was hit very heavily but Labour gained little because of the demolition of its reputation for economic management by Mr Muldoon in 1975. In each case Social Credit was the recipient of, rather than the force attracting, its windfall of votes. The electoral evidence points to the conclusion that Social Credit's fundamental task of persuading majorities that its financial programme is relevant, necessary and practicable has yet to be accomplished at the sectional level, let alone nationwide.

If Social Credit could focus and intensify its efforts in rural electorates and if it were able to exploit the present pervasive economic malaise by presenting a convincing alternative, then the existing electoral system could deliver noteworthy gains to Social Credit in 1981. Victories could come in at least one region—the northern and central North Island— and in at least one category of seat—the eleven seats with a high proportion of farmers. Social Credit finally overtook Labour to secure second place in those seats in 1978. With an equal step in 1981, Social Credit could reach the position which Labour arrived at in 1922 of being the predominant representatives of a specific kind of constituency. They would then have their band of MPs because they would have surmounted the higher hurdle of persuasion set by this system. By the same token Social Credit would still have much to do successively to achieve major party status and then power. Once achieved, however, the prize proves worth the seeking. The New Zealand political system has provided and will provide to the winners of the major party battle the means to effect genuine structural change undeflected by any system-induced need to negotiate coalitions or pay in compromises for additional support from minor parties.

The Real Contrast between the Systems
For the contrast between the British and Continental systems is not a contrast between more and less democracy, more and less fairness, more and less choice. Instead it is a contrast of systems with different proportions to be persuaded before the threshold of regional or sectional representation is crossed, with different bonuses in increased numbers and effectiveness for parties being distributed at different points along the path of growth, and with quite different rewards in terms of power to effect change being granted for a party win, place or show under the two kinds of system.

As a voter one is looking at two kinds of choice. Under PR one can choose one's party list and/or representative, depending on the type of PR, hoping that in the inter-party bargaining at the capital some undeterminable but preferably worthwhile proportion of your party's programme will find its way in some form into legislation and into the hands of a friendly minister. What you are going to get, however, will normally be in the lap of other people's gods. Under the British system the norm is a choice between alternative governments, programmes, and prime ministers expressed through support for a local party candidate. One can ignore that choice and vote out of belief in a minor party programme or candidate or in protest at the deficiencies of both major alternatives. But British rules on the practical returns for supporting minor parties make such action much less rewarding, though not overwhelmingly so, than it is under PR. Correspondingly the British connection between a voter making his choice of alternative governments and then getting generally what he expected in leadership and action whether his choice wins or loses is satisfyingly close, predictable and public.

Is Government Without Coalition or Combination Normal under PR?
It may be objected that there are considerable periods in the politics of some PR countries such as Sweden, Israel and Eire where a major party has attained an absolute majority and not had to manage by negotiating support in return for concessions. The brief answer is that, while these exceptions have existed, such British freedoms for the largest party under

PR to govern undeflected have indeed been exceptional. Remembering the examples cited above but also then adding in West Germany, Italy, Norway, Finland, Austria, the Netherlands, Belgium and Denmark, the statistics for PR numbers involved and the length of time spent under coalitions and combinations when compared to years and PR numbers under absolute majority government must be as many to one.

How Would New Zealand Fare? Division on the Left

To believe that New Zealand under PR would join the exceptions and become a kind of sunnier Sweden in its Social Democratic heyday of absolute majorities is to ignore the burden of New Zealand's political record. Ours are inherently fissiparous parties. Craft unionists and industrial unionists, Social Democrats, ULP men[3] and Socialists spent more time in the late nineties and the early part of this century learning by bitter experience about the need to come together than they spent thereafter on reaching power once they had founded a viable common organisation and had forged an initial programme from their disparate attitudes. When Labour had reached power, success and an absolute majority, the Lee-ite split speedily developed and the traumas of 1940 and the 1943 election ensued.

It requires little expertise about current tensions among unionists, between some unionists and the Parliamentary Labour Party, and within the ranks of Labour activists, not to mention among Labour voters, to realise that under PR a Social Democratic versus Socialist division could easily appear and perpetuate itself in a PR New Zealand. After all, the hope of promoting just such a split in the UK and thus isolating powerless Bennians on the left is one of the benefits *The Economist* foreshadows in its undeviating promotion of PR as the way to a permanently centre-right, 'Liberal' Britain.

Division on the Right

Compared to division on the left, however, New Zealand's record displays even more division on the right which is the predominant end of the New Zealand political spectrum. The Reform and Liberal struggle was not ended until 1935. Having two alternative conservative parties up till then did not prevent a third or Country Party endeavouring to establish itself in the twenties and thirties. When in 1935 the National colours at last covered the remaining Reformers and Liberals at once another conservative party, the Democrat Party, sprang up in 1935 but faded away after drawing only 8.1 percent of the vote. That left the scene clear for a two-party contest in 1938, a split on the left in 1943, and more two-party elections in 1946, 1949 and 1951.

But then in 1954 Social Credit appeared on the right as a party of private enterprise, but private enterprise with a difference when it came to paying the market price for money as opposed to all other commodities. Social Credit has persisted with admirable tenacity for a quarter-century despite attracting an average of only 9.8 percent of the vote and despite having itself suffered a split in 1972 when Mr O'Brien's New Democrats hived off. In 1972 Values also appeared with little by way of economic policy at first but initially with particular attraction for ex-Nationalists disinclined to vote Labour.

National itself represents an amalgam of sections and interests containing as it does farmers selling on the world market and city manufacturers desirous of measures of encouragement and protection. There are plenty of other potential lines of fracture as past struggles and present stresses both indicate. PR would open the prospect of at least a separate Country Party for farming and rural interests untrammelled by the need to compromise with city interests—at least until its MPs arrived in Wellington and tried to negotiate a role in the governing combination of the day.

Is PR a Persuasive New Zealand Option for the Eighties?

Thus the proposal to alter our electoral system and install some form of PR, when judged by New Zealand's political past or its present contained tensions, amounts to this. The proposal invites our two major parties to risk or undergo an unpredictable future of potential or actual splits and comparative ineffectuality except insofar as inter-party negotiations after the elections might reconstruct what one or the other major party has now under the existing system, namely, the power to govern undiverted. The proposal is made in the name of granting much increased representation and immediate possession of the power to make and unmake governments to Social Credit, a minor party which has not yet persuaded a majority in even one section of the electorate, far less having persuaded the great majority to consider it as an alternative government or the legitimate source of a new course in economic and social affairs.

The wide-ranging consequences of making any such change, once understood, are most unlikely to recommend PR to either of our major parties or to their supporters who remain the great majority of voters. To put forward PR as a likely New Zealand option for the eighties is therefore to run the danger of creating a massive diversion from more practicable options.

The Options We Could Attend to
Preferable options would include:
- implementing and improving compulsory voter registration to obtain regularly-issued, accurate rolls;
- revising the criteria and procedures for redistributions so that the 1977 fiasco cannot be repeated;
- strengthening the Parliamentary select committee system and matching it to a more sensible grouping of departments and portfolios;
- enlarging Parliament's numbers;
- establishing a decidedly longer Parliamentary year with regular intervals;
- making provision for more publicity and access in legislative and administrative procedures;
- bringing in public funding of political parties.

These options would adapt instead of fracturing and replacing the present political system, which represents a well-understood and interlocking process of choice and the balancing of social and economic interests arrived at by New Zealanders over nearly a century.

Notes

1 [PR = proportional representation. Ed.]
2 [Chapman is referring to the 1978 election. National won the most seats, having won fewer votes than Labour, again in 1981. Ed.]
3 [ULP = United Labour Party. Ed.]

17

The Politics of Division?

My given title is 'The Politics of Division?' and, if that is a question, let me settle it at once by saying 'Of course New Zealand's politics are a politics of division'. All politics rest on, and get much of their impetus from the recognition of natural divisions in society together with their accompanying differences of interest. Societies produce differences of interest according to age, sex, wealth or the lack of it, race, region, religion, morality, lifestyle, even sport and its claims and consequences. Politicians organise their parties and us as voters by recognising those inevitable divisions of interest, relating as many as possible into a coherent programme and pulling us in behind them to jointly forward our, as against some other, set of interests.

All this seems obvious enough, except that it is becoming quite fashionable to deplore 'adversary' politics and to suggest that a middle way, an embracing way, a third way is available if only party interests could be put aside and Parliament as a whole left to decide solitary MP by solitary MP. The abortion debates showed just what that accomplished, even if the pre-party history of the English and New Zealand Parliaments had not already proven the wisdom of our ancestors in evolving out of that chancy and structureless phase of policy incoherence. Others call for proportional representation (PR) to encourage third, fourth and fifth parties as though more hung Parliaments and ad hoc alliances would be a gain in democratic choice instead of the begetter of confusion, collusion and cobbled-together agreements to do what nobody had expected and most had voted against.

Such appeals to change the rules of government or the electoral system have been heard before. They usually accompany any prolonged failure of the national and/or international economies to support us in the style to which we have accustomed ourselves. Since the first oil shock finally hit New Zealand in 1974, the 'seventies and early 'eighties have witnessed an unsteady but deepening economic decline with possibly worse to follow. Neither major party has matched their results to our high expectations.

One consequence has been that a fifth of all New Zealand voters has turned towards Social Credit as a possible, if ill-defined, escape route

---

[This chapter was published in Graham Bush (ed.), *New Zealand—A Nation Divided* (Auckland, 1983), Ed.]

from the local version of difficulties which beset the whole western world. Like the anti-party cries for Parliamentary predominance or the pro-multi-party cries for PR, so the uncharacteristic retreat of so many New Zealanders into third party voting is a protest against disappointment in the fruits of the existing system. It does not represent the discovery of a comprehensible alternative. Nor will a Parliament of 92 independents or executives drawn from multi-party coalitions cause the underlying divisions of society and its interests to go away. All three nostrums would complicate or already have complicated the problem of aligning a body of interests behind a coherent programme to reduce, though hardly eliminate, our spreading morass of problems.

For politics is also about harmonisation and linking of interests as well as about division. Politics must concern itself with the competition to promote individual and group interests, but there are also common interests in plenty which affect every member of a given society and economy. Ironically one can recognise this truth behind the summons to other people to tighten their belts and contribute to fighting the common threat of inflation by taking a tuck in their own particular standard of living. The restoration of prosperity must be of general benefit, although the distribution of that prosperity is another matter. Our common interests in social peace, in international order and security, in retaining the trading opportunities which are the preconditions of internal prosperity, all these are objectives which once achieved must reward each and every citizen.

Party dispute in this sphere therefore begins, not with differences of interest, but with conflict on how such objectives can best be pursued. We all, for instance, want peace and protection in our corner of the world. But would that be maintained most securely under the full nuclear panoply of the U.S. Navy and ANZUS as now interpreted or via a more delimited version of that alliance along with a diplomacy of disengagement from the nuclear contest? Politicians do not normally create such contests of method or of interest. Instead they recognise and define them, then marshall the groups involved, and according to their skills, help in large part or small towards arriving at a decision.

Respect for Majorities
In doing so, politicians are required to legitimate their decisions democratically by 'carrying the people with them'—in the words of our Prime Minister.[1] At the least they should respect majorities whenever discovered and even if the majority is discovered amongst their opponents. Such a majority eventually appeared against the continuation of the tour by the South African rugby team. Nevertheless the tour continued to its

bitter end. Opinion polling found that a majority had assembled for a liberalisation of the laws on abortion and an overwhelming majority of the general practitioners certainly concurred.

Yet Parliament gave New Zealand what pleased no-one wholeheartedly while satisfying the largest body of opinion to the very least degree possible. The Johnson Report and years of intensive public discussion likewise provided the best warrant ever prepared to do something civilised and optional about sexual and marital education for youth. The alternative was to do nothing much and that was an alternative which presented no warrant whatever to the public. Just the same it was no warrant which triumphed.

It may be objected that, while in each case it was not the majority view which was attended to, nevertheless these are not vital matters of economic policy, property rights, foreign affairs or trade. They simply affected aspects of our daily individual or family lives which Parliament or government had chosen to control or to decide upon. Testing the nature of what was being decided brings out that, insofar as such matters are peripheral to the normal politico-economic concerns of government, it is precisely there on the margins where majority opinion should be closely followed and the entire consensual basis of government in general reinforced.

Significantly, it was the opposite which occurred. Neglect of majorities tore at the consensual process which is essential to the ongoing legitimation of government. The passionate feelings thus aroused, the rallies and lobbying and, on the tour issue, the massive and peaceful demonstrations and the unprecedented disturbance and sporadic violence which followed from pros, antis and police, all go to prove that such issues are rarely peripheral and, with mishandling can escalate into critical tests of the democratic nature of our governmental process. What is more, the tour issue had from the start quite predictable and major adverse consequences on our standing overseas and on our Commonwealth and foreign relations, not to mention its continuing effects on other sports. The entire process struck unevenly at the relationship between the two principal cultures within the New Zealand community, a relationship already strained by economic adversity. Even more fundamentally, it upset the habits of social peace which every government should nurture as a primary concern. So the struggle over the tour involved core issues in the political process from the beginning while the depth of feeling evoked was proportionate to the centrality of those issues.

Respect for the Law

An almost equally important part of ensuring the legitimacy of all governments in the minds of their citizens is that governments should respect the laws they themselves produce and support the judicial process which helps implement and interpret what they and previous governments have done. Mr Muldoon was reminded of this at the outset of his Prime Ministerial career over the way he disposed of Labour's superannuation scheme. That incident and his critical remarks on the judgment then rendered do not compare, however, with the prolonged drama of seeking the water right to build the Clutha high dam under the Water and Soil Conservation Act 1967.

If the Act's procedures were complicated and lengthy that was because the previous National Government had so designed it to test and protect the interests of all. Once Cabinet had chosen to proceed under the Act they had to live with the consequences of that Act if they were simultaneously to show respect for due process of law. If matters dragged and faltered while the political stakes on success grew higher, that was a measure of the importance of keeping to the rule of law. Only an overwhelmingly urgent and demonstrable case of public need for that power would justify Parliament in cutting across the rights and procedures which it had itself set up.

Parliament could do so. There was no question of Parliament lacking the constitutional power to pass special legislation The real constitutional question was: should it do so? The need was urged as justification, yet if it could be clearly proven and shown that the electricity was essential, then the Tribunal would recognise the force of those facts, award the water right, and away would go the necessity for a special Act while the rewards of having respected due process, despite difficulties, would also have flowed to the Government. There might be short-term delays which would involve finding interim work for the men. But the costs would be as nothing compared to the costs and benefits of an essential dam while the Government had been used to coping with many long deferments in the course of negotiating for oil exploration and the huge commercial investments connected with the growth strategy.

So why the drastic decision to cut loose and legislate instead of proving the need for the power and gaining double kudos as both upholders of law and beneficiaries of it? Could it have been consciousness that the need for so much electricity so soon was highly debatable and the Tribunal case was, accordingly, unpredictable in its outcome? Was there dismay because so many international investors were climbing out of the 'Think Big' package that it had become urgent to take compensatory action where matters were controllable within the country and especially within

Parliament? Perhaps it was a desire to demonstrate the impotence of the Labour and Social Credit opposition because of its division by party and despite its numbers. Possibly, too, the instinct was to distract Labour from the case on power by facing it with the prospect of unemployed Clyde workers and the demands of the local P.S.A.[2] and of Cromwell generally.

Underlying the hasty resort to legislation do we not discover, firstly, a tactical miscalculation about the probable resoluteness of Mr Minogue in his despairing defence of the rule of law?[3] Secondly, can we not detect also a somewhat cavalier indifference to, or underestimation of, that principle itself? There is scant evidence that Cabinet was conscious of how much the precise observance of the implications of the rule of law could accomplish towards reassuring opponents and supporters alike. For New Zealanders have need of the assurance, in face of the untrammelled powers of our unicameral Parliament and notwithstanding the dominance within Parliament of one Leader with his Cabinet and his Caucus, that Government will recognise its limits and limitations and keep responsibly and constitutionally within them. The quest for full legitimacy of government in the minds of its citizens lies not only in respect for majority opinion but also in respect for limits and the balance of our constitution, simple and straightforward as it is.

As it proved, it was not Mr Minogue who crumbled. The heat was turned up when the Government announced that, without their legislation, work on the dam must cease and the workforce be paid off. Television played its all too frequent role of ministerial echo chamber by amplifying and illustrating just what that might mean. There were treks by all parties to the Clyde and the Leader of the Opposition, stung by the Prime Minister's assertion that he had only one option available, replied that there were five, including to proceed by Order-in-Council, though that was a bad option.[4] As frequently happens, the qualification got drowned in the hubbub and the public was left wondering whether this cure was not worse than the disease.

Meantime, back in Social Credit's core region, National's deregulation of the freezing industry had claimed another works at Patea. Something should be done about small town unemployment and something made of Mr Minogue thrusting the balance of power into the hands of the Beetham-Knapp combination.[5] Moreover, the Social Credit MPs had discovered that farmer opinion round Cromwell now favoured the high dam for its irrigation potential to grow late, rather than early, stone-fruit harvests. Adding it up the Social Credit commanders decided to admit to a total change of heart about their longtime pledged policy and offered support for the Government's legislation if it met a list of conditions.

There were also references to Parliament as 'the highest court in the land' and to a special meeting of Parliament constituted as a court. But the Clerk of Parliament made short work of that muddle just as the Speaker, after the election, had swiftly disposed of the hypothetical two votes he was supposed by Mr Beetham to possess.

The negotiations between the Government and the Social Crediters provided a scale-model test of how 'holding the balance of responsibility' would work out in practice. The Prime Minister beamed on Mr Beetham's 'constructive' suggestions and, after their first encounter, made clear to the public what the terms of trade were by fairly chortling that he 'still had all his horses', having had to concede nothing that was not already intended. It was all as tragi-comic as Labour's earlier efforts to round up their maverick MP for Dunedin Central who was backing and filling around their otherwise unanimous adherence to principle and policy.[6] For his part, Mr Beetham was offended but, after a long second meeting, the arrangement was confirmed without any perceptible improvement in its terms.

What the rule of law had been presented with was a worse arrangement than any which had gone before. Notice had been served that a joint Parliamentary majority would be forthcoming to nullify the effect of any wrong answer the Tribunal might come up with. Nevertheless the hearing would proceed—with some gain in information no doubt—but to a predetermined end for the appellants' interests. There was rich visual symbolism in the picture of the Tribunal meeting gathered together in a hospital around their injured member, the chance victim of an unfortunate accident.

'Streamlined' Modes and Procedures

So what have we here for the politics of division, apart from some loose forward play with the rule of law and an exposure of the present futility of third-partyism and the confused compromises it engenders? First, the seeming unconcern of the Prime Minister with the objections of professional and specialist opinion to the trends in our constitutional development and to the strained relation of its parts. Second, that the Prime Minister's seeming unconcern was catching. Mr Birch, the Minister of Energy, of National Development and of Regional Development, had announced the Government's intention and his personal conviction that all the planning checks, hearings and consideration of the various interests involved should and will be condensed by new legislation into one decisive process. This will save time, reduce appeals and provide an altogether more streamlined basis for carrying on the Government's programme. Plainly, the executive does not intend to expose itself again to the embarrassments of the Clyde saga. If a deficiency in its case is suspected, and much more so if it should be found by the process, then it is the process and not the case which should be remodelled. Even should the Government case win clearly, it is intended to find another, faster way.

Third, there is the Prime Minister's mastery of the news media. His dramatic skills at press conference or in interview permit him with just a few sentences ground out or with a penetrating and apparently unstoppable exposition or simply by employing a throwaway phrase or grin, to dictate the terms in which political dispute in New Zealand is conducted. The cameras and the microphones follow his agenda. They bring up his topics, his arguments, his judgments in interviews with his opponents.

If the Prime Minister wants to take the focus off the recalcitrance of Mr Minogue, or away from Social Credit's part in opposing him, a Muldoon phrase about Brian MacDonnell will suffice to dispatch the press to Mr Rowling to find out whether Labour's rebel has been quelled. Or when the Prime Minister wants the media diverted or distracted from some awkward development, he understands how to ensure that other spokesmen vary the pace and the subject. This happened when Mr Birch's ultimatum on high dam employment transferred New Zealand's attention from the potential end-use of Clyde electricity to the immediate family consequences of Cromwell joblessness. President Theodore Roosevelt once said that the White House was 'a bully pulpit'—meaning a fine rostrum from which to speak to the nation. But the Prime Minister of a small country with just two TV channels leading into everybody's living-room is in a much more 'bully pulpit' yet again.

Fourth, we must grasp how many objectives the Prime Minister can keep in mind and pursue almost simultaneously. In this situation he was primarily shoring up his electoral theme, the growth strategy, but also searching out any weaknesses in Social Credit's tactics or Labour discipline to judge if he could indeed go the full three-year Parliamentary term. As a by-product he was appealing past the environmentalists to the farmers and their neighbours in the small towns, besides reinforcing his friend Warren Cooper's Otago constituency[7] and rousing the loyalties of the Awarua and Invercargill smelter seats.

His incidental jibes about Mr Rowling's Order-in-Council and Mr Beetham's horse-trading were not intended to enhance their standing with either their parties or the public. So shrewd a man as the Prime Minister would be conscious that as between party leaders, like begets the demand for like. In a way, Norman Kirk's dominance in Parliament and on the platform had called Robert Muldoon out from behind Sir John Marshall and into the leadership of the National Party.[8] If the Prime

Minister could tough this Parliamentary situation out and manoeuvre one of his rivals into helping him against the other to override this vexing legal sequence, that would certainly inject fizz into Labour's leadership struggle and raise the question of who among Labour's crop of contenders could stand up against Mr Muldoon. As for Social Credit, the same manoeuvre would reduce Mr Beetham to the 'also helped me' category. Turning to his own party, with the successive Quigley challenges in mind,[9] there was no harm in having the party ruminate on who else could have pulled off such a double victory over both a third party and Michael Minogue, the rebel MP, alike.

The Formation of a Prime Minister
Is there more, then, to the Prime Minister than a clear, incisive mind and style; the power to plan flexibly and surely, at least in the short-to-medium term; a natural performer's gift for timing and communication; and the ruthlessness to win at the cost of reducing rivals and troubling the governmental process itself? There is: the clues are to be found in the basic political attitudes and preferences he has revealed through time and in his habit of working by increments, sometimes with surprisingly distant perspectives.

Robert Muldoon is a New Zealand conservative and, therefore, as he said himself, a pragmatist. He comes out of the New Zealand which Labour built, welfare and all. He can still reach out to many Labour supporters and throw them off balance with his insight into their feelings. His 1975 campaign showed just how devastating that capacity could prove by pouring Labour supporters in their thousands into non-voting. His superannuation scheme likewise had and has retained strong cross-party appeal and he has held on to it without alteration. Whether the issue is police, patriotism or sport; overstayers, union stirrers or protesters; he can still touch a great number or cause them to doubt. The effect, however, is fading with age and social change in the cities. Outside the cities, in the provincial centres, the effect lingers and there voters can move with fewer cross-pressuring social constraints from Labour to National, or Socred, and stay there.

As with others of his generation, Robert Muldoon's wartime experiences of service and combat were vital and formative. At war's end he used his energy, talents and the basic security of the 'forties to vault into professional life, the world of private enterprise and preferment in the National Party. It was this next era of the First National Government from 1949 to 1957 which gave him his final moulding. He worked and prospered both professionally and politically. There was plenty of growth and solid international prosperity underneath. New Zealand's whole system, taken over from Labour and revamped and remodelled for different social purposes and beneficiaries, must have seemed to fairly hum along. In his basic responses the Muldoon of today still embodies this era and represents the values of that background and those formative experiences.

As a result, Robert Muldoon is certainly no classical economic ideologue nor prone to the tempting simplicities of a new-found Friedmanism nor to supply-side mysticism. Instead he is an economic eclectic. His conservatism is defined by what he is conserving. He is no adherent of some new-fangled radical right but rather a proponent of attitudes which have been around if decreasingly so since the nineteen fifties and the days of Sidney Holland.[10] They are attitudes he believes to have been tested against reality and found to work and be adaptable.

So, within the range of National Party opinion, he is certainly for private enterprise, but within the mixed economy or mixed enough to allow of government intervention, government investment in massive infrastructure and some superstructures, and the continuation of Treasury's shaping control. He has a compulsion to conduct and is a fine tuner by temperament. Therefore he is very loath to leap from the direct taxation basis he has lived and burgeoned with to the nirvana of indirect taxation his more theory-prone juniors put their faith in.

In his lingering and cautious incrementalism the Prime Minister is a bridging figure. For he stands against rapid changes to the economic mix which most New Zealanders still believe in and which their governmental and business institutions were designed to suit. By standing pat or shifting only slowly he prevents the clear party and social divisions which a more rigorous, classical attack on the New Zealand way would precipitate. A Quigley, McLean or Cox among the MPs, a Bayliss, Sir Frank Holmes or even a Dr Brash among the economists, might well set us by the ears in short order, and there are in the National caucus and party plenty of younger supporters to back them.[11] In basic policy attitudes there is a half-concealed element of 'conservator' about the Muldoon role as he binds the generations uneasily together in caucus, party and electoral programme.

Volatility and Continuity
It is, however, as a wily politician, a Parliamentary tactician and campaigner in winning elections that the Prime Minister has scored his triumph. Here, too, he is traditional but also realistic in counting first on the enduring divisions and loyalties of the New Zealand political scene. By carrying back the 1977 boundaries and adjusting the figures to cover four successive elections from 1972 to 1981, we can analyse what

continuities the Prime Minister—or Mr Rowling for that matter—can rely on. These totals and percentages have all been based on the qualified voters by making a close estimate to correct the Election Office's huge roll errors of 1978 for which 92 separate median interpolations have been substituted. These are not valid vote percentages only but rather more informative because they let us also watch portions of the electorate making the politically significant choices of whether to move out of voting, enter voting, or decide to re-enter.

The dozen years of politics on which these four elections were the people's verdict were tempestuous compared with politics in the age of the Holyoake consensus. As elsewhere in the western world, this period in New Zealand witnessed the product of increased and lengthened education; the personalisation and immediacy of politics on the box and in the sitting room; the accelerating speed of transformation in social habits with its concurrent rise in privatism, social atomisation and its emphasis on judgment by and for the individual. All three factors conspired to heat up and set the atoms dancing and the atmosphere was suddenly full of volatile votes. In addition there was the first onset of recession and unemployment in 1967-68, then a saw-toothed recovery, a boom, the oil and import price explosion and from 1974 the lurching, disappointing then depressing decline. Little wonder that we saw Labour triumph in 1972, National arrive at its peak within only three more years, then the Social Credit rocket coming out of insignificance in 1978 and getting a second-stage but weaker boost in 1981 so that it may be well over the top of its arc and descending by 1984.

It could have been expected that so many rapidly raised and lowered hopes, so many demands made and so few met, would have convulsed the electoral landscape over the last ten years. Yet this has not happened. The 92 constituencies so defined by the 1977 boundaries divide into three remarkably even classes. One-third or thirty seats were never anything but Labour come Muldoon hell or Kirk high-water. One-third or thirty seats remained inviolately faithful to National come Kirk hell or Muldoon high-water. The remaining one-third or thirty-two seats are those which have swung between the parties, thirty of them between National and Labour and just two between National and Social Credit.

Like the three parts of Caesar's Gaul, the make-up and social composition of each third is worth a closer look. Nineteen of Labour's thirty were poorer City seats where the average majority over four elections did not come below 10% of the whole enrolled and qualified vote. In Labour's disaster year of 1975 when non-voting in this group of seats shot up by over eight points and Labour's vote plunged by over thirteen, the majority in many of these poorer city electorates fell below the margin of safety and a companion seat, Dunedin North, was actually lost to National for three years. The overall majority picked up sharply by 9.71% in 1978 and rose again by 3.01% in 1981 so, despite everything, these urban workers have shown little sign of permanently deserting Labour or its current leader, Bill Rowling. The same is true of the four Maori electorates notwithstanding Matiu Rata's setting up a rival party in Mana Motuhake, for its main effect was the beneficial reduction of non-voting. The remaining seven constituencies had long histories of Labour predominance: a mixed city seat in Onehunga, the four towns of Napier, Timaru, Wanganui and Nelson, and the two traditionally Labour mining, timber and orcharding seats of West Coast and Tasman.

Where, by comparison, has the Prime Minister been able to rest his case with relative assurance? The thirty always National seats include six out of the seven richer city seats—the other being East Coast Bays, an alarming capture by Social Credit. Instead of Labour's four, National held five town seats throughout: Kaimai, Tauranga, Rotorua, Hawkes Bay and Manawatu and, in the first two, Social Credit led the opposition. Like Labour, National always retained a clear margin in the area of one mixed city seat, in this case Mr Wellington's Papakura with its sizeable fringe of well-to-do farming country.[12] In all there were 12 urban electorates of one sort or another.

But the heart of the matter for National beat in the 18 farmer and rural seats. If the heart skipped a beat in 1981 it was because Social Credit passed Labour to come second in ten out of the eighteen. A second front was entrenching itself within National's constant possessions and, while it harmlessly divided the opposition in most instances, it constituted a genuine threat in Hauraki, Kaipara and the Bay of Islands besides foreshadowing a second East Coast Bays in Pakuranga. This menace from within received due attention from the Prime Minister but as part of his general strategy to hold all he could along the normal front lines. His high SMPs, and relaxed business and credit conditions, to specify only two kinds of precaution, proved helpful in beating off the internal challenge where it was most dangerous, but it still left four of National's faithful thirty with majorities of less than five per cent in 1981.[13]

The Arena of Battle

That brings us to the conventional arena of battle—the thirty-two constituencies across which the front lines have shifted back and forth for the last decade and, in most areas have crossed and recrossed since 1938. Overwhelmingly they are of two types: fourteen mixed city seats to which can be added the errant poorer city Dunedin North and richer city East Coast Bays; and a dozen provincial town seats together with four rural seats which, like the towns, gather those who are farm-bred or have country clients and attitudes in a mixture with those of more urban interests and assumptions. It was sixteen a side, and in 1975 National had held all thirty-two, both city and town-country marginals.

What seems to have dictated the strategy for the election of 1981 was the outcome of the 1978 election, an election of disillusion and third party protest following a shapeless three years which neither yielded electors the promised New Zealand the way they wanted it nor dispelled the structural difficulties of the economy which the Prime Minister had so stridently denounced. Labour's organisation had been reinvigorated and grown in numbers several times over so that, not to its own but to National's surprise, it reoccupied seven of the city marginals and two towns, Palmerston North and Hastings. At the same time Social Credit was confirmed in its by-election capture of rural Rangitikei.

The lesson was clear enough to the Prime Minister now thrust on the defensive but disinclined to repeating the passive, smoothing-over tactics of Sir Keith Holyoake.[14] A plan of counter-attack was required with the main thrust at a major area of weakness in the economy, a diversion or two, and a device for underpinning rural production until inflation and markets could be tackled or righted themselves. If the planning had to risk one kind of marginal to save another, so be it. National was first of all a party of the countryside and its towns and measures to shore up marginals of that sort would check Social Credit's second front among the previously faithful behind the lines. Moreover, an energetic counter-attack on a series of salient issues was bound to appeal to and preserve some city marginals while Labour's caucus was baulked and strained by a second defeat despite this time beating National in terms of votes. The Labour caucus could crack and any disunity be played upon with press conference references to leadership polls and Mr Rowling's qualities. The news media would clutch at every word, every incident, every gesture.

Planning Ahead and Picking the Targets

The main thrust took nearly a year to develop and arose from the harsh consequences for New Zealand's balance of payments of the second, 1979 oil shock; the investigations of the Liquid Fuels Trust; and the Electricity Department's custom of generously estimating further power needs and building accordingly. At last New Zealand would utilise its natural gas to supply alternative fuels, manufacture ammonia-urea fertilisers for export, sell methanol and, as the Prime Minister later explained, sell the rain behind the dams in the form of aluminium ingots. Oil refining capacity would expand, New Zealand's steel production would quintuple. We must, declared Mr Muldoon, 'Think Big'. In several features it was a belated successor to Labour's 'manufacture in depth' of the late 'fifties. The scale of the risks involved was uncharacteristic of the Prime Minister's normal caution. But the incremental way it had evolved and went on being added to—and subtracted from—was vintage Robert Muldoon.

'Think Big' was part import substitution, part export earning and altogether expandable so that somehow pulp, paper and kiwi fruit were also wrapped up in what was discreetly relabelled 'the growth strategy'. Foreign capital was to flow in to pay for some of this great leap forward and we would have to pay high interest now to gain export capacity and import savings eventually. At the same time it would stimulate the economy and especially the project towns. If inflation continued to soar in the short term, a rough ministerial estimate indicated that 410,000 new jobs could finally result. The plan was no mean thrust as a counter-attack. Accordingly in early 1980 the lead in party standings veered towards the Government.

Farm leaders responded initially with strong concern at the likely effect on farm costs of intensified inflation and borrowing and with indignation at the sheer volume of capital which would be passing by what they saw as New Zealand's most fruitful fields for investment in exports. Manufacturers had export incentives already. Now multinationals would receive aid and comfort while the economic prescription preferred by farm leaders—a major devaluation—was rendered highly unlikely because overseas interest repayments would therefore become more onerous. Labour's criticism, too, was somewhat shakily focussed on the virtues of supporting the small man whether primary producer or innovative manufacturer. Labour would prefer to funnel investment into intensifying the doing by New Zealanders of what they already did best. As for fuel, the manufacture and fitting of kits to convert vehicles to CNG or LPG was considered by Labour an admirable use of New Zealanders' talent for light engineering. It would provide much more employment than massive foreign-designed plants with imported skilled staff. Social Credit was even fiercer about borrowing for transnational projects instead of increased primary production.

For a time it appeared as though 'Think Big' might back-fire politically at least in the countryside. That chance would increase if opposition groups and parties could complete their case by discovering the underlying costs and demonstrating poor markets and profitability for all this extra steel, added refining capacity, potentially expensive synthetic petrol, urea, methanol and aluminium by the boatload. The crucial planning figures, however, were in government departments, under negotiation, or were commercial and economic secrets. A lone internationally-recognised expert did question in detail the economics of the Aramoana smelter project and encountered a heavy ministerial rejoinder dismissing his conclusions. If New Zealand was indeed repeating the Polish syndrome of the seventies by investing borrowed foreign money too heavily in the wrong industries too late then the opposition found it could not prove its case conclusively.

Public attention was fixed instead on a series of televised political dramas which featured personal struggles rather than complex issues. First came Social Credit's startling by-election triumph at East Coast Bays in September 1980.[15] In consequence there followed the October revolt of National's 'colonels' against Mr Muldoon and there were gyrations in the opinion polls. These led in turn to Mr Lange's caucus group attempting in December to overturn Mr Rowling's leadership, an attack repelled both by Labour's MPs and organisation.[16] Far from 'Think Big' having settled things down decisively in National's favour, public uncertainty, disillusion and division had invaded the House and infected both major parties. Meanwhile the surge to Social Credit in the opinion polls had strengthened their second front inside National's thirty basic electorates besides posing a threat to several National marginals in the countryside. Something more was required from Mr Muldoon.

The Prime Minister was prepared. As far back as 1978 he had introduced the supplementary minimum prices scheme as a further weapon in his armoury of assistance to farm production. The significance of SMPs went largely unremarked until, for the 1981/2 season, he suddenly shifted the levels at which this scheme would pay out. They had been set as normally inactive reserve prices. Now the levels for wool and meat were lifted far above what the current international markets were returning and the taxpayer would make up the difference. Fortunately market prices for dairy products were high enough not to need such energetic resuscitation and, in any event, dairy farmers retained most of their fertiliser subsidies, cheap credit for their Dairy Account, development loans and other help. They might not feel so directly beholden to the Government, yet in parlous times the value of this sectional guarantee could be readily understood. When some farm organisations said they would prefer lowered costs, Mr Muldoon insisted that SMPs were essential to retain New Zealand's export production and overseas income thus playing a key role in the grand strategy of growth.

The chosen targets were being ticked off. The project towns and far more had been attended to with 'Think Big'. Then seats in the countryside had been shored up with SMPs. There was danger for some town and city electorates, however, in the menacing rise of unemployment here and now, whereas those 410,000 jobs 'Think Big' could bring were mostly off in the future when the projects were built, prospering, and returning proceeds to New Zealand which in turn would finance new businesses and thus furnish fresh employment. What deferred the problem for election year was the heavily increased foreign borrowing and project capital which flowed in and, along with a relaxation of constraints on credit, stimulated business generally. In consequence the last two-thirds of 1981 was a time of growing optimism and consumption for that great majority who remained in employment. City firms did surprisingly well and customers for the goods and services of provincial centres were still there in plenty. The city workforce was less impressed for it was a force-fed, brief prosperity and unevenly spread. Yet it could well prove politically sufficient in more comfortable electorates.

In doing so it had strong help from the Tour, a deeply divisive issue with a twenty-one year history of development counting from the 1960 'No Maoris, No Tour' campaign. After Mr Holyoake had damped the issue down and Mr Marshall had built his bridges there were high pro-tour poll majorities in 1971 and 1972. Despite them Mr Kirk suspended the 1973 Tour on grounds of public safety and order, a decision which was followed by a public change towards the Kirk position so that in 1976 'No' led 'Yes' by 56% to 35%. Nevertheless Mr Muldoon has always claimed that resentment at the Kirk decision helped National win in 1975. The new Prime Minister's convictions were apparent when the Africans boycotted the Olympics in 1976. The intent of the Gleneagles Agreement of 1977 and its carefully added ambiguities were followed up by the committing clarity of the Prime Minister's sports pledge in his 1978 Manifesto. Given this lead, public opinion again swung by 1980 to a 16% pro-tour advantage. Everything was set for the issue to reach a head in 1981 if the test time-table of international rugby proceeded.

It did. The early months of 1981 were packed with ineffectual interviews and exchanges which made it obvious that only specific direction from Government would move the Rugby Union. None came.

> Then the Tour was on us in obsessive cascade of newsprint, television and indignant, impassioned, dangerous social conflicts. It went on through July, August and September, travelled with the Prime Minister to London and the royal wedding, and in October it confronted the Commonwealth heads of government in Melbourne. There seemed to be no end to it until finally its animosities and revenges were merged into the election season with scarcely a break.[17]

The Tour, in slowly bearing down on the country, then moving inexorably all round New Zealand, changed opinion in several ways. The pro-tour 16% lead of 1980 became a 2% anti tour margin in May 1981, then a 7% anti-tour lead measured in July. Not only did the majority shift while divisions hardened and grew bitter, but the cities on the one hand and the provincial centres and the countryside on the other tended to move in opposed directions. The *Herald*-N.R.B. poll on 13 August 1981 made this major point succinctly: 'In general the main metropolitan centres continue to oppose the tour. Most provincial centres support it—[nine did] although five do not and one, the Napier-Hastings area, is evenly divided.'

The combined effect of all this forethought, preparation and experience of division can be readily tested. The Table [omitted] above displays the percentage change from 1978 to 1981 in the majority of the final winner in each of the crucial 32 constituencies which at any election in the seventies or eighties ever switched from one party to another.[18] In view of the Prime Minister's prime targets, the list is divided into the 16 town and country switchers as most likely to be influenced in National's favour, and the 16 city switchers which could well react otherwise to the same set of factors.

As can be seen from the Table [omitted], the selective power and effectiveness of the Prime Minister's long-term planning and whole-time campaigning were very considerable in the electorates at which he was particularly aiming. In a time of international strain and depression he could not prevent victories going to his opponents in the city marginals; but he could retain and usually strengthen all the town and country marginals National held as well as weakening two out of three of such Opposition seats. Much more than that, by National's capture of the town seat of Taupo the Prime Minister preserved his power to govern with his Executive and that they hold by a working majority of one.

If his planning has utilised divisions of interest and values much more frequently than harmonisation and common objectives, that may be as much a commentary on how our society is now structured, and is therefore most easily shaped, as it is a matter of Prime Ministerial personality, preference and choice. Insofar as the rule of law and the balance of our constitution have been disturbed in the process, we have no other guardians than alert electors ready to apply the sanction of their votes. For that to happen effectively in New Zealand a more sophisticated awareness of political and economic realities is patently required.

Notes

1 [The Prime Minister referred to was Robert Muldoon who held that position between 1975 and 1984. Ed.]
2 [Public Service Association. Ed.]
3 [Mike Minogue was National MP for Hamilton West between 1975 and 1984. Ed.]

4   [The Leader of the Opposition was Wallace (Bill) Rowling who led the Labour Party between 1974 and 1983. Ed.]
5   [Bruce Beetham, MP for Rangitikei between 1978 and 1984, was Social Credit's Leader between 1972 and 1986. Garry Knapp, MP for East Coast Bays between 1980 and 1987, led Social Credit between 1988 and 1991. Ed.]
6   [Brian MacDonnell was MP for Dunedin Central between 1963 and 1984. In 1983 he resigned from the Labour Party and sat in Parliament as an Independent until his defeat. Ed.]
7   [Warren Cooper was MP for Otago Central between 1975 and 1978 and for Otago between 1978 and 1996. He was a National Party minister between 1978 and 1984 and again between 1990 and 1996. Ed.]
8   [Norman Kirk was Labour Party Leader between 1965 and 1974 and Prime Minister between 1972 and his death two years later. John Marshall was Prime Minister briefly in 1972 and led his party between 1972 and 1974 when Robert Muldoon took this position. Ed.]
9   [Derek Quigley was a National Party MP between 1975 and his retirement in 1984, representing Rangiora. Between 1972 and 1982 he was in Cabinet, a critic of the 'Think Big' policy. In 1982 Quigley was dismissed from Cabinet for his public criticisms of both the policy and his Leader. In 1996 Quigley re-entered Parliament as an Act list MP. Ed.]
10 [Sidney Holland was Leader of the National Party between 1940 and 1957 and Prime Minister between 1949 and 1957. Ed.]
11 [Ian McLean, National, was MP for Tarawera, 1978-1990; and Michael Cox, National, was MP for Manawatu, 1978-1987. The economists are Leonard (Len) Bayliss and Don Brash. Ed.]
12 [Mervyn Wellington was MP for Manurewa between 1975 and 1978, MP for Papakura between 1978 and 1990 and a minister between 1978 and 1984. Ed.]
13 [SMPs refers to the Supplementary Minimum Prices scheme. Ed.]
14 [Keith Holyoake was Leader of the National Party between 1957 and 1972 and Prime Minister during some of 1957 and between 1960 and 1972. Ed.]
15 [Garry Knapp, Social Credit, defeated the National candidate. The incumbent National MP and minister, Frank Gill, had resigned. Ed.]
16 [David Lange became Leader in 1983 after Bill Rowling resigned from that position. Ed.]
17 Robert Chapman, *Comment* No. 16, August 1982, p. 12. [See Chapter 12 of this volume. Ed.]
18 [The data presented in the omitted Table can be found in Table 12.1 (p. 212) and Table 12.3 (p. 217). See also Table 12.4 (p. 221). Ed.]

18

Restructuring Broadcasting

The Principle of Independence

The new structure flows from general principles, the primary principle being independence in the service of the public. Independence in this plan has several forms and purposes. The structure seeks first to give independence to the corporations so they can present a real choice to the public in programme style and content. The structure aims next to guarantee independence in resources to allow the two TV services and radio all to set their own priorities and pursue their own improvement and development. By its design the structure is planned to extend independence from ministerial control and from indirect pressure exercised through close capital works supervision. In the individual corporations the structures outlined are shaped to promote creative independence by focussing the organisation on those who produce the programmes in the studios and on the stations. Finally the structure pursues independence from the unitary, centralising tendency, which gathers as much as it can into one place and one pyramid of power and resources, thus over-riding or neglecting the country's spread of talent and its regional variety.

The Separateness of Radio

The first kind of independence, independence to present a real choice to the public, necessitates first the separation of radio from the very different medium of television. Radio has a different pace; its appeal is less gripping but can be more sustained. It is omnipresent and immediate—the perfect vehicle for the latest news—yet sufficiently inexpensive compared with television to make radio the adaptable medium of the locality. Radio calls for a different kind of broadcaster. As a service it has different ends to pursue. Both the radio and its guiding corporation require to be devoted to their medium undistracted by another responsibility and a different set of priorities.

[This chapter is from *The Broadcasting Future of New Zealand. Report of the Committee on Broadcasting* (Wellington, 1973). *The Broadcasting Future for New Zealand* began by setting out the Committee's 'aims and principles' for the future. Next it discussed 'The New Structure'. This chapter contains extracts from that section. The location and subtitles of the omitted passages are contained in the endnote. Ed.]

Therefore, the radio corporation, which we propose to call Radio New Zealand, is to have its own staff, its own financial resources, its own studios and equipment, and its own sphere of broadcasting 'to develop, extend and improve'. In a way it is a restitution. From the 1920s to the 1960s radio had its independence and in those days it had impetus. For a decade now radio's development as a medium has been slowed while television grew and took money, attention, and men. To get radio under weigh again it needs to have its independence restored. With that impetus will come a freedom to find its own style, develop its own strengths, make its own more regionally-based comments on life in New Zealand. And at that point radio will be offering the real choice that an entirely different medium of communication can and should present.

Television Independence
In respect to television the basis for independence is the fact that the public wants and expects choice between two channels, and that the Government was elected on a pledge to secure expeditious establishment of a second television channel with a colour capability. Furthermore, there was a general expectation of two channels in that the previous Government had been committed for some years past to seeing a second channel built. The new Government's manifesto promised corporation control as the form, stated that it favoured continuing 'the present policy of ownership of the facilities' and set out its main goal as 'the best, most independent, and enterprising television and radio that can be provided.' The structure therefore establishes a radio corporation and two publicly-owned television corporations. From their independent basis in policy, studios, staff, and revenues, the two television corporations which we propose to call Television Service One (TV-1) and Television Service Two (TV-2), will compete to produce two services of the best and most enterprising television they can put before the public. Thus the bases, goals, and methods have been publicly set for us by the continuing democratic process and the form of the structure adopted follows immediately from them.

It is also worthy of remark that as earlier policies have developed and come to fruition there has not proved to be a conflict here on the issue of one television corporation or two. The conception of warrants was introduced as early as 1961 into the Act setting up the NZBC. Then in 1968 the previous Government established the Broadcasting Authority which in turn held extensive warrant hearings on the future control of television in New Zealand. The Authority's conclusion was the same in respect to the independence of the two television corporations as the conclusion upon which we are now proceeding. Nor is there, in countries whose experience New Zealand has customarily drawn upon, much precedent for unitary control of all channels and the whole television medium. The United Kingdom, Canada, Australia, and the United States all have pluralistic systems.

The Mixed System of Support

As to the resources necessary to sustain independence, New Zealand has been familiar since the 1930s with a mixed system of support for public broadcasting from commercial and non-commercial revenues in the form of earnings from advertising and receipts from licence fees. When we consider that, as the representatives of large advertisers pointed out to the Committee, the costs of advertising are eventually passed on into the levels of commodity pricing adopted, then paying in part for broadcasting by selling advertising may be a circuitously expensive form of support. But it is one which New Zealand is used to and it arises naturally enough from the fact that New Zealand is in itself a mixed economy.

What does matter is that there was no proposition put before the public to eliminate the mixed system. Indeed, the new Government stands pledged to nationwide radio and television coverage of both a commercial and non-commercial character. Accordingly each of the corporations, whether radio or television, has been given this same mixed commercial and non-commercial character by providing that each have a share in licence revenue and that each corporation will broadcast in part with advertising and in part without it.

Equal and Independent Bases for Competition

The decision to give each corporation the same mixed character has some important consequences for the structure and for its viability. So far as the television corporations are concerned it gives them an inherently equal and independent basis from which to compete and develop once the phase of establishment is passed. Two national networks with the same number of advertising and non-advertising days a week have equal opportunities to vie with one another to enlarge their revenue by attracting and holding the viewer. TV-1 and TV-2 will have their 4 nights of advertising staggered through the week so that only on 2 nights will both be advertising, Sunday will remain free, and on 4 nights a commercial programme will be opposed to a non-commercial alternative. The corporations will be aware in designing their programmes that they must aim at carrying their viewers with them, not only from hour to hour, but across from non-commercial to commercial nights. So neither can afford to neglect the chance to keep or build a following with good features just because on that night the other corporation is advertising. To do otherwise would be to make a present of the audience to its commercial competitor.

Avoiding a Minority/Majority Split

New Zealand has over three decades of experience with popular preference as between two nationwide public radio services one of them commercial and associated with light entertainment, the other not. The audience has consistently divided with a large majority on the light side. This has obvious consequences in developing semi-permanent majority and minority audiences and cutting down the variety of communication which the audience will encounter by tuning to their favourite station. Mixing the character of both TV channels and alternating their commercial and non-commercial programmes must have the effect of reducing this self-segregation and minimising the division of communicated experiences within the community. Precisely because the channels will be fighting to develop 'brand loyalty' they will be struggling to maintain it on commercial and non-commercial nights alike. In so far as they succeed, 'their' loyalists will see the whole range. No doubt there will be a big section of viewers determined to steer consistently for the lightest option, but it will take rather more effort and have none of the cumulative impetus provided by segregating the channels themselves from the start. It is in the public interest, in the Committee's opinion, that a wide variety of programmes not only be presented but presented with the maximum chance of being encountered by all kinds of viewer.

By giving a mixed character to each corporation the new structure does more than just equate their resources to support independent service. At the same time each corporation is given a non-commercial role to plan for and fulfil in the general interest. The Committee notes later the preoccupying, almost dominating effect on the staff of a public corporation which comes from being committed to the day in day out operation of a wholly commercial station. The wider aspects of public service broadcasting can be lost sight of in the struggle for revenue. Yet the public corporation was chosen as the form of organisation for broadcasting precisely to keep those wider objects always in view. The assignment of a non-commercial role to both television services will therefore act as a constant reminder to them that they exist 'to inform, to educate, and to entertain' and that their commercial activities are solely a means to a public end.

The Form of the Three Corporations

The form of the three independent corporations is straight-forward and their membership has been kept low to make them the spare, working bodies required. Each has a chairman and two other members appointed by the Governor-General on the advice of the Minister. Each corporation once appointed will then select its deputy chairman, and there are the normal provisions for filling extraordinary vacancies. The Committee might have expected in view of the number of concerned pressure groups to receive more submissions than it did which advocated large, representative, or delegated bodies. There were a few such suggestions that seats be reserved for women, educators, Maoris, clergymen, staff delegates, 'consumers', and even representatives of the interested manufacturers. These occasional suggestions were set aside, however, since they mistook the point in the structure at which numerous representative views should be sought and sizable bodies consulted which is at the advisory committee level. Instead we preferred to leave unfettered choice to the Minister in seeking men and women of proven judgment and distinction of mind who would have an interest in the wider aims and the practice of public service broadcasting.

The Terms of Office
The terms for which chairmen and members are appointed, we suggest, should in all cases after the first appointments be for five years with freedom for the Minister to reappoint. In order to establish a staggered system the initial appointments of the chairmen will be for 5 years, for one member in each corporation 4 years and, for the other, 2 years. From then on the 5-year terms will apply to all. Every 1 or 2 years, mostly the latter, one member will come up for appointment or reappointment. This will secure continuity of experience in the corporations and ensure that, even when the chairmanship is being transferred, a member who has served as deputy chairman will remain to facilitate the transition.

As for the 5-year term itself, the Committee was conscious that it takes time to become thoroughly familiar with the workings of anything as complex as a broadcasting organisation and that the trio in each corporation will be expected to take a very active part in the guidance of the organisation. With the existing 3-year term, as one member put it, 'It takes you nearly half that time to get a grip on what's going on'. A 5-year term also contributes to a proper sense of independence in the corporation since members are not so frequently aware of the imminence of an end to their term. Nor will a close, hard-working corporation be so often disturbed by retirements given the longer term. There is one further reason for preferring a 5-year period of service and that is simply to interest the calibre of person who wants to see in membership of a corporation the chance to really devote himself to a considerable task.

The danger with more rapid turnover, as with large membership, is that the corporation has difficulty in becoming truly a corporate whole, with the consequence that the bulk of work and decision falls on the chairman and his director-general.

Out of the same intention to make available the widest range of suitable people for appointment we recommend that all, whether chairman or members, should be part-time. This way the man or woman who is still contributing in his or her field can bring that experience to bear on broadcasting. Although the Committee realises that the chairmanship of any of the corporations will be a particularly responsible, busy, and onerous position, it is still the case that the maximum of choice should be kept open and the requirement of full-time appointment would preclude that being so.

The Directors-General

The key staff appointment in each of the corporations will be that of the director-general. Making this appointment and fixing the appropriate terms for the contract of service of their chief executive officer are powers vital to the independence of the corporations and to the whole style of service they want to create. Directors-general must retire at 65, but otherwise no limitations are laid upon the corporations in their search for the kind of person they want in order to make their service the best they can achieve.

All the directors-general will have the right under legislation to attend meetings of their corporation and to speak, but not to vote, on matters before it unless specifically directed to retire temporarily from a meeting because of the nature of the business being transacted. Each director-general will be there to set out the situation as he sees it, examine policies and their implications with the chairman and members, and together chart the course which the corporation will determine. As the chief executives of their corporations, the directors general will accompany the chairmen of the operating corporations to take part in the joint consultations of the common servicing body, the Broadcasting Council. Again their entitlement to attend and speak but not to vote at Council meetings is established in the legislation. Thus decisions taken at every level of the new structure will be made in the light of all the relevant operating considerations and the advice of the chief executives who will be able to speak to and be present when decisions are taken.

Figure 18.1: Structure of the Broadcasting Council and the Corporations
Broadcasting Council of New Zealand

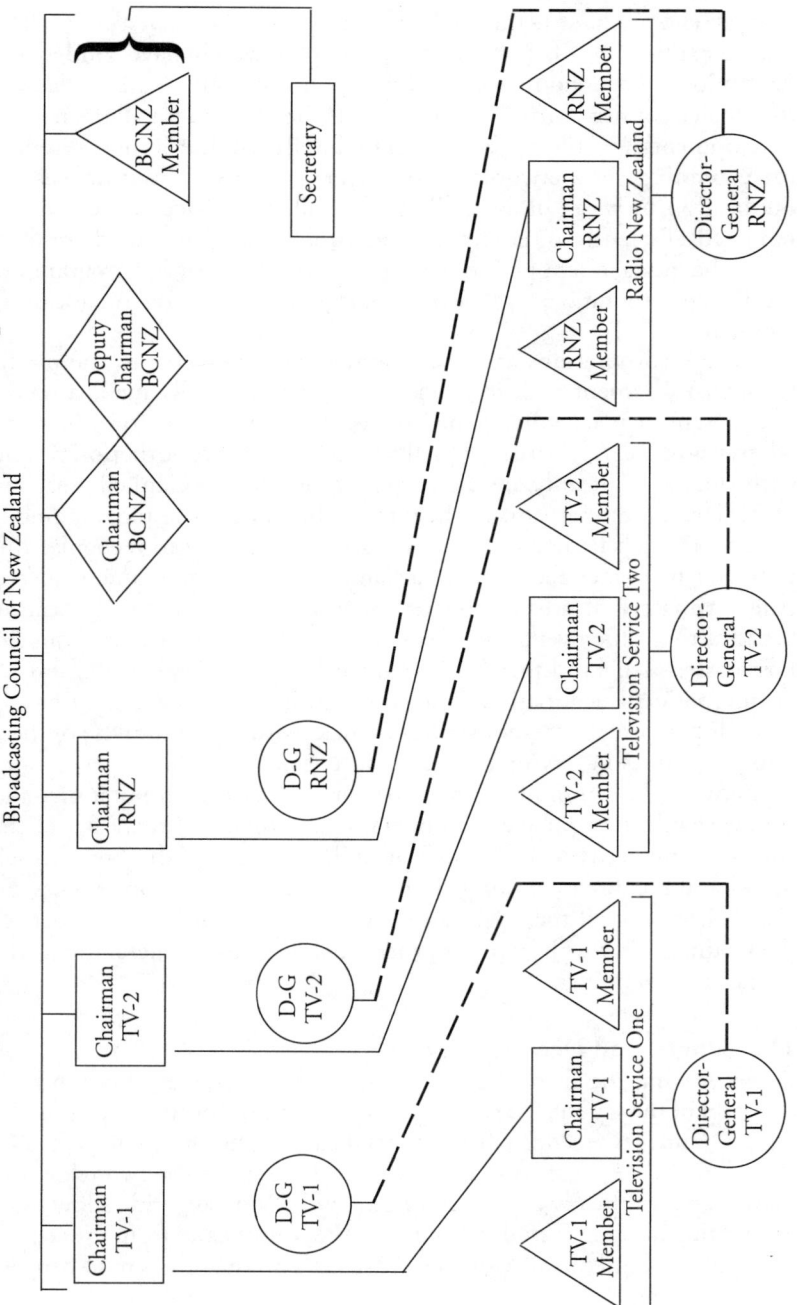

Responsibility and Economy

The presence in the structure of the Broadcasting Council of New Zealand makes explicit two other general principles which have guided the Committee throughout: responsibility and economy. New Zealand is too small a country, broadcasting revenues are too slim for all the needed developments, and the public interest in the efficient use of those revenues for extending the networks is too great, to permit any unnecessary duplication or waste of assets. Therefore all the services which can be rendered efficiently in common, and which would not in themselves affect the independent policy-setting and operations of the programme-producing corporations, will be rendered by a joint body, the Broadcasting Council.

All the corporations and the Council are responsible to the public through Parliament and, to effect this, all will annually make a report and present their accounts to the Minister for presentation to Parliament, whereupon an opportunity will occur to debate both policy and performance. Not only are the corporations and the Council creations of Parliament and servants of the public, they are also employing public resources which Parliament makes available. It is easy to recognise this character in licence fees which Parliament sets. But the same is just as true ultimately of advertising revenues which are earned by selling broadcasting time over scarce frequencies obtained by licence from the Postmaster-General. Indeed, the frequencies are themselves the subject of international negotiation. The corporations and the Council have a plain duty to exercise responsibility in making the optimum use of these public revenues in serving the public interest.

Because the common services are vital to all the corporations and connect with their policies and operations at many points, each of the corporations needs to be present at and be a part of the body which decides on the design, costing, and running of the common services. So the chairmen of all the corporations will be *ex-officio* full members of the Council. They will have with them their directors-general to put the operating viewpoints.[1]

The Council and Decentralisation

Before leaving the field of common services to consider the standards function of the Council, a related aspect of the Committee's stress on the regions and on freedom from centralisation should be noted. The counterposed regional bases of studio production for the two television networks have already been announced by the Minister and follow from the existing balance of studio facilities in the country and from the centres of population and broadcasting talent. TV-1's production is to be centred on Wellington and Dunedin, TV-2 on Auckland, Christchurch and Hamilton. Radio New Zealand's facilities are spread all round both Islands but are focused in the Wellington complex and that must remain so. But most of the BCNZ's common services either require no one specific territorial base or, like the *Listener* alongside its printer in Auckland or the news organisation headquartered in Avalon, they will be set up in the most suitable place for their activity independently of where the Council meets or its offices and other staff are situated.

In the new structure the headquarters of the Council will be established in Christchurch. The Council's chief executive officer, the Secretary, can be established there with his secretariat at the convenience of the Council. This does not call for a radical redistribution of staff. News, orchestra management, and the computer will be staying where they are. The few upper-level staff who will have to move can do so quickly enough without the necessity of having, for example, the design section of transmission engineering install themselves in Christchurch at precisely the same time. The NZBC is at present spread through a multitude of buildings in Wellington. The transition to the new structure and its decentralised locations will afford a good and economical opportunity for some sections to regroup. Last, but certainly not least, a location for the Council in Christchurch will end a desirable degree of detachment from the headquarters of all three corporations, and from the Wellington hub of the political world and the Auckland axis of the commercial scene.

Standards

That detachment will be particularly useful to the Council in the exercise of its 'power to prepare and make rules' on the standards which must obtain in the field of broadcasting. The NZBC under its Act had to satisfy itself that its programmes complied with certain requirements. The NZBA under its Act of 1968 had to ensure the same very general requirements under its authority to make rules. It was, in the opinion of the Committee, an advance in that it gave the NZBA the opportunity to lay out specific codes of practice and prohibition which would give some workaday content in the NZBA rules for such inherently imprecise concepts as offending 'against good taste or decency' or 'public feeling', maintaining 'a proper balance' in the subject-matter of programmes or presenting news 'with due regard to the public interest'. The problem with such phrases is that we all think we know what they ought to mean to others and then discover the wide variety of opinion that exists.

Operating broadcasters encounter just such problems themselves and have to act on behalf of the audience as well. So the real efforts made by the NZBA in its rules covering various fields to say what was permissible and what was not was a sensible beginning which is carried on, still in force, under the new legislation. The present legislation does not keep the imprecise phrases of the 1961 Act but it retains the power to get on with the task those phrases pointed towards which is the development of specific sets of standards. The existing NZBA rules apply until the Council can build on them.

The NZBA has begun to incorporate its rules into codes such as that on the portrayal of violence. The Council will require to extend the range into such diverse areas as children's programmes; fair representation of what was originally taped as an interview; or perhaps into finding some agreed broadcasting interpretation to that phrase of a thousand meanings, a 'proper balance in subject matter'. The same process of building on the rules of the NZBA will, of course, be applied by the Council to advertising where the rules in turn derive from those of the NZBC.

Conformity with the rules of the NZBA was part of the terms and conditions which governed the warrants it granted to private stations. Those terms and conditions carry on along with the NZBA's rules. When the Council amends the rules or extends the codes both Radio New Zealand and private stations will have to comply. In this way the common standards which have been worked out and applied up to now will be maintained throughout broadcasting.

The Council will monitor programmes and maintain a watch on breaches of the codes. Just as the Authority warned the NZBC and the private warrant holders of any infringements, so will the Council warn the corporations and the private stations. The sanctions against the highly unlikely eventuality of persistent infringement on the part of TV-1, TV-2, or Radio New Zealand will be the raising of the matter at the Council's next meeting, the right it has to report on its proceedings to the Minister at any time, and ultimately its annual report to Parliament. The Council's course if it finds private stations not obeying the terms and conditions of the warrant is equally clear. The Council will prepare a report stating the grounds for believing there has been a breach and dispatch it to the Minister and the Director-General of the Post Office. Beyond finding and establishing the pattern of performance and reporting it, the Council will not go.

The Renewal of Private Warrants

The Committee held that revoking, suspending, or renewing of warrants for private stations should be no affair of the Council which might be considered an interested party in any decision arrived at. The new legislation accordingly provides that applications for warrants must go to the Director-General of the Post Office who advises the Minister that the warrant should be renewed unless a breach of conditions has been reported. Without a breach, the Minister will renew on the same conditions or make new ones. If there is a breach reported, then the Postmaster-General with the Minister of Justice will appoint a practising lawyer of standing as a Private Broadcasting Tribunal who will hear evidence—normally in public—and who can revoke, suspend, or give a limited renewal to the warrant. If the tribunal revokes or suspends a warrant for any length of time then the holder can appeal to the Supreme Court and have his case heard by the Administrative Division. The holder cannot transfer or dispose of his warrant without the Minister's consent. But even a refusal of consent can be appealed to the Supreme Court. The minor fees for warrants paid to the NZBA disappear along with the Authority. The warrant holders are therefore very fully protected against arbitrary proceedings while the executive and judicial action in regard to them is entirely removed from the Broadcasting Council.

Freedom from Ministerial Control

Just as the new legislation draws a firm line between the Broadcasting Council and any judicial function, so the Committee has pursued in other ways necessary freedom of action for the corporations and Council in the pursuit of good broadcasting. Independence from ministerial control is exemplified by setting a limit on borrowing which allows minor accommodation to be sought without recourse to the Minister. Above $500,000 he must give consent and properly so. In a more major departure, the legislation does not include a section laying down that the Council or corporations 'shall comply with any general or special directions given by the Minister...by notice in writing pursuant to the policy of the Government ...' There is a provision for broadcasts as directed 'in the case of any national, regional, or local emergency', but the corporations, while following the direction, may at discretion announce this requirement as can the BBC.

To signalise the freedom of broadcasting from ministerial control, which the new Government itself has declared it seeks and which this new structure assumes as a basis, the Committee recommends that the position of Minister of Broadcasting should be abolished. The new legislation refers to the Postmaster-General when it refers to the Minister. The Postmaster-General or his equivalent, whatever the structure of broadcasting, must license the use of frequencies which have other users and are the subject of international agreements which he and his department negotiate for New Zealand. Accordingly, he is the appropriate Minister to handle the matter of private warrants and, as his department is the collecting agent for licence fees, he is the right Minister to consider first the recommendations on licence rates from the Council which are addressed to the Government. In making appointments to the Council and corporations it is the Postmaster-General who has most concern with the general field of communications and broadcasting. Moreover the disappearance of the portfolio of Minister of Broadcasting will not mean consequential departmental reconstruction, for in New Zealand there is a Minister of Broadcasting but no department.

The great advantage of the change is one of increased independence and clarified responsibilities. The Council and corporations will be responsible to Parliament and report annually to it. There will be no Minister of Broadcasting receiving advice both from a corporation and an authority and empowered to issue written general or special directions to them. The confusion in the public mind between the Minister of Broadcasting's responsibilities and the NZBC's day to-day responsibility for programming—so often attested in the pages of *Parliamentary Debates*—should diminish with the abolition of the name and fade in the light of the independence embodied in the new structure.

Creative Independence
The whole plan is designed throughout to encourage creative independence. At every point, therefore, the structure has been kept spare. The Council and the corporations taken together number 12 people. Common services are used wherever necessary, but considerable freedom of action is allowed to the divisions and units. Elsewhere the Committee discusses a lean design for the TV corporations which we recommend in outline to Radio New Zealand where its focus on the line from director-general through his programme controller to the producing teams could equally be followed. The same principles are applied to the problems of regional radio's management in the appropriate chapter. For we have been conscious as a Committee at every point that programmes are broadcasting. The more direct and short the lines of decision can be made in the operating corporations the sooner they will reach the producer and his team or the station manager and his staff. Concentration on the quality of programmes by organisations shaped to that end should release a fund of creative initiative, enthusiasm, and flair which broadcasting in New Zealand needs. It is the purpose of the new structure to promote and support that drive towards more vital broadcasting.

A System of Advisory Committees
The responsibility of the Council and operating corporations to Parliament and to the public interest has been built into the new structure. But responsibility to their audience demands a more continuous,

intensive, and rapid feed-back from their public to the corporations. The legislation provides powers to appoint committees to advise the corporations and these, we recommend, should be used to create a system of advisory committees.

At present the NZBC appoints and supports three regional programme advisory councils totalling 58 members. The Committee was able to draw on the experience of many of these members about the successes and problems of the existing bodies. The NZBC achieved a good representation on its committees of the distribution between cities, large provincial towns, and small towns and countryside with 31, 15, and 12 members respectively. This is near to the national balance and made them useful sounding boards on what had a national impact, namely, television and, to a far lesser extent, the networked 'national' radio programmes.

Several problems arose which affected their usefulness. One was the mixture of television and radio topics which meant a struggle to attend to either adequately. In practice the councils spent most of their quarterly meetings considering television and aspects of the national and YC programmes. Thus commercial radio with four-fifths of the radio audience got less attention and so did the variety in regional radio and its strengths and weaknesses in makeup and coverage. The NZBC was careful to confine its advisory councils to programme matters only with the consequence that this tended to exclude problems concerning anything which affected investment or the way in which the system produced what it did. The Director-General and several of his executive directors attended regularly and spent a great deal of time on the quarterly meetings putting the NZBC's position in detail to the members. But precisely because the three councils were each meeting in a major city and with the topmost executives of the corporation there was less linkage to the men and women at the programme and station level.

Future Advisory Committees for Television
It would seem reasonable in future to divorce the consideration of television network programming from the assessment of radio's performance. The present advisory council's sectional composition has proved well adjusted to this task. So each television network's programme could well be commented upon by its own New Zealand wide advisory committee selected in the present fashion and proportions and of up to 15 or even 20 members. A fair size is needed for variety of judgment, but experience suggests that active participation and debate decline when the committee numbers 20 or more.

A Design for Radio Advisory Committees

For adequately regionalised, indeed, localised, assessment of radio, on the other hand, a quite separate and different system is plainly needed. It should itself be regionalised and to a degree localised so that it can call on local knowledge and responses to the programming and coverage available in each specific region of New Zealand. Decisions of programme input and output have been decentralised to commercial radio station managers to a significant extent and differ according to the manager's understanding of his community and audience. Therefore the usefulness of the advisory committee will increase as it meets key staff responsible for the detailed decisions, emphasis and omissions on which the Committee is commenting. This interplay between the advisory committee and the makers of programmes in the region deserved every encouragement.

In visiting the stations round New Zealand the Committee has found that the regions recognised by most New Zealanders for other purposes tend also to be suitable for this purpose. Information about the reception areas for given stations has been drawn on in delineating the regions but each has a real unity of character as its base. All the regions save the West Coast have a town of at least 20,000 as a natural focus and meeting place and some, such as Hawke's Bay and Wellington Province, have more than one. Each region is sufficiently compact to allow all Committee members to drive to a centre, hold a usefully lengthy meeting, and return in a day without strain. Compact regions mean convenience and economy. Moreover, the natural meeting places in each region contain the radio stations and the key staff who will be the other participants in the regional dialogue.

These representative bodies must be small enough to be workmanlike and to attract members of real capacity who are genuinely interested in the problems of broadcasting. We have suggested 10 members each for all the more populous regions, 8 for those of around 100,000 inhabitants, and 6 for the East Coast and the West Coast which are smaller but still deserve separate consideration. These committees should cost far less than their worth in establishing contact with and responsiveness to the communities which radio should be serving.

Consideration for the Recommendations of Committees

Naturally the minutes of each committee will be passed on for consideration by the corporation members and senior staff who will also attend at times. Common problems can thus be isolated, defined, and answered and problems which are not common but particular to one region can be recognised and met. The Committee would recommend that regional committees be given more scope and more detailed general information than the former programme advisory councils. The radio committees' number and compactness will secure a far more intimate knowledge of what is and is not being done locally. They should receive increased consideration and imaginative action in response.

Linking the Committees
The chairmen of all the radio committees should certainly gather to exchange views and consider overall problems at the very least annually. And there would be advantages, too, in giving all advisory committee members for TV1, TV2, and Radio New Zealand the opportunity to meet in conference, if not every year, then every second year. These occasions would become full broadcasting conferences representative of the whole country's interest in public service broadcasting.

Notes

1   [The following sections have been omitted: 'Determining Major Financial Priorities and Means'; 'A Balancing and Moderating Element Completes the Council Membership'; 'The Mechanics of Division and Consensus'; 'Possession, Use and Ownership'; 'Salary Structure'; 'Common Services: Transmission, News, Sport'; 'The *Listener* and the Symphony Orchestra'; 'The Computer and Audience Research'; and 'Negotiation and Representation'. Ed.]

19

Political Culture: The Purposes of Party and the Current Challenge

Writing about New Zealand's political cuture and tradition at the end of the prosperous 1960s, Alan Robinson saw New Zealand as having a 'very homogeneous culture' and estimated that 'The degree of consensus in the New Zealand political culture possibly exceeds that in any other country'.[1] Writing at the end of the 1980s, one is struck instead by the confusion of party political beliefs and traditions; by public uncertainty about the role of government and the state in relation to the economy and about even the proper forms of government; and by the rising level of dislocation, conflict and, again, confusion in New Zealand society.

The contrasts between the two perceptions are so sharp that questions shape themselves about how such changes could come about. Just how solid or fluid or perhaps even precarious are our party political system and the assumptions of our political culture? And the answers to those questions are most likely to be found by examining what kinds of internal development or external influences could have given rise to the stability and consensus Robinson described and which now, a bare twenty years later, show so many signs of flux.

The reassuring view is to emphasise that, behind the confusion and flux, all the key elements of our accustomed political structure and tradition are still there. New Zealand continues to be a democracy with popular sovereignty. Virtually everybody of eighteen years of age or above, whether of New Zealand nationality or ordinarily resident here, is enfranchised. 'The people rule' by regularly choosing their representatives to make up a fresh Parliament at three-yearly intervals and, normally, nine-tenths or more of those qualified to vote freely take part in that choice.

Like most features of New Zealand's political structure and concepts, the occurrence here of representation, choice of governments and popular sovereignty, together with the idea of party as the means to organising coherent choices, are all consequences of a particularly pure transplantation of the British form of democratic institutions and ideas

---

[This chapter was published in H. Gold (ed.), *New Zealand Politics in Perspective*, 2nd edn. (Auckland, 1985). Ed.]

which made up an interactive set with a built-in direction for development. In turn that development was considerably reshaped in the course of adaptation to New Zealand's size and circumstances, while proving increasingly open, especially since the Second World War, to international tides of opinion and example.

Adoption and adaptation here were rapid. New Zealand as an entity was founded in 1840, was granted representative government in a dozen years, implemented it in 1854 after holding elections, and on most matters was given the essence of responsible government—responsibility of the executive to a parliamentary majority—sixteen years after the colony's founding. The expansion of the franchise was speedy indeed. The essential electoral elements of popular sovereignty were all established with one exception by the early 1890s. They were: Maori manhood suffrage although voting for only four specific seats (1867); secret ballots if polling called for (1870); general manhood suffrage (1879); triennial Parliaments (1879); all European elections by secret ballot (1890); and votes for women on the same basis as men (1893). The last element was added when women obtained the right to stand as candidates for Parliament in 1919.

Of the four interactive elements of British democracy, party was the last to be adopted and adapted in New Zealand. At first the raw jostle for government funds among little settlements scattered round the coasts meant swiftly shifting alliances among the representatives, all in pursuit of development and at different stages of it. Wretchedly slow communications threw voters back on locally known notables to represent local interests, while development of one's province became the highest common factor of politics. The preconditions for party were provided when Vogel demonstrated that central government borrowing could most effectively supply new settlers and the railway infrastructure of development. Proto-parties appeared in the late 1870s but collapsed or remained half-formed, while governments exchanged policies and proposals all through the depressed 1880s.

At the same time the dragging depression produced a ferment of ideas and proposals, drawing on thinkers from Aristotle to John Stuart Mill and Henry George. Recent scholarship has shown how many common attitudes were forming and were revealed in the resulting debates of the times, their concentration on the social and political virtue and the economic necessity of small farming settlement and the worth of positive state action to promote it. So when New Zealand's first viable party, the Liberals, won election in 1890, their doctrine was not the *laissez-faire*, negative state liberalism of a James Mill but the active state liberalism of a T.H. Green or a future Lloyd George chancellorship.

The Liberal legislation from 1891 to 1894 and sporadically thereafter set up a whole new political economy for New Zealand. The mounting voter support for the Liberals came from the backblocks settlers and leaseholding sections of the countryside, from little and large towns, and from the workingmen's areas in the four small cities. There was fluctuating opposition in the House of Representatives and, inevitably, from the Legislative Council. It came from representatives of the large landholders or simply from longer-established and financially more secure farmers and from the middling and well-to-do districts of the cities and towns. It proved difficult to draw this opposition together for it clung to its pre-party habits and the ethos of the individual notable standing on his own for his district or interests. Those interests differed, so opposition unity and leadership kept breaking down while the rudimentary attempts at extra-parliamentary organisation failed for want of an agreed and positive programme.

It was the consolidating sectional organisations like the Farmers Union which showed the way forward by generating programmes in their interest and pressing for them. Eventually a shrewd parliamentary leader emerged who first made his MPs into a fighting unit by articulating common attitudes, then solved the problem of extra-parliamentary organisation, and finally combined commercial and manufacturing interests with the established farmers and the emerging section of prospering ex-Liberal settlers. The Reform Party's espousal of freehold and free contract drew in both farmers and business. But its substantive promises of agricultural and rural development were borrowed from the Liberal's basic theme. Reform, too, was ready to use the positive state.

So in fact, if not in name, Reform's role was to furnish a more conservative administration of a hardening *status quo*. Thus a one-party situation had brought forth a two-party system by the process of organised persistence in the aggregation and representation of initially differing interests opposed to aspects of government policy but eventually readied for agreed common action of their own. This two-party formation quickly became an incipient three-party system as fractions of unionised labour sought their own representation. But the unions and proto-parties of the labour movement had to undergo conflict and defeats to learn the disciplines of party and common policy and it took until 1916 to acquire them and until 1919 before their core supporters gathered.

By then the functions of party were familiar to all at elections, in parliamentary practice and legislation, in the process of government and in the way individuals, organisations, and sections of society favoured given parties as participants or supporters. In a generation New Zealand's political culture had absorbed the concepts of parliamentary and electoral struggle between alternative governments resting on parties and their programmes. It was already expected that interests and issues, schemes for preserving what was valued, and projects for change would be sorted into coherent policies and manifestos which would accord with the broad principles and the past record of each party and the sectoral combination which sustained it.

These expectations of party did not change while consensus about New Zealand's political culture was intensifying. Even the replacement of the Liberals by Labour as the alternative party of government, and the consequential consolidation of Reform and the country remnants of the Liberals into the one National Party of 1936, scarcely disturbed the role which voters expected party to play. Instead it simplified the two-conservative-and-one-radical party system of the 1920s by turning it back into a two-party contest of centre left against centre right. Nor could Social Credit's subsequent thirty years of endeavour achieve a repetition of Labour's progress from a strong sectional base to a significant place in Parliament and then on to power, thanks to economic crisis and governmental failure. All Social Credit managed to mobilise were three bursts of voter discontent with both major parties simultaneously. In 1954, 1966, and 1978-81 Social Credit focused a variety of dissatisfactions into protest votes which skewed four electoral outcomes without ever transforming the overriding contest between the alternative parties of government, National and Labour.

What did change in the concept of party was the extension of party from Parliament to people or, rather, to that quite small section of the people who would commit themselves to participation and regular work for the principles of their chosen party. This development came in two stages. The Liberals led initially with an Association and then a Federation which were more effective at raising sizeable contributions from a few and for coordinating party leaders' tours and publicity than for gathering membership fees or regularly talking and listening to members out in the scattered electorates. Reform was likewise organised from the top down, while policy in both parties descended on MPs and supporters from the parliamentary leaders and close coteries around them.

The second stage was launched with the organisation of Labour from 1916 which spread in the 1920s as an expanding body of fee-paying members, on the union model, organised by branch and electorate, and expecting to discuss policy questions at meetings, select candidates, and be consulted at annual conferences. When this structure was basically reproduced—minus the affiliated unions—by National after 1936, the principle of the parliamentary party could be said to have been matched with a separately-led party organisation outside Parliament which would select the MPs and vigorously support them and their principles. Popular participation had thus gone beyond the triennial vote, occasional rallies, or putting forward resolutions or delegations from interest and pressure groups.

The domestication of party as the organising principle and practice within Parliament, among the politically active, and for voters in general, came rather later in New Zealand than in some Australian states and much later than in Britain and the United States. Its adoption into the political culture of New Zealand, however, has been so complete that no independents have been elected with that label since 1943, while all movements trying for a foothold in Parliament have been organised as parties for over half a century. Residual resistance to the idea of party direction of the MP by his or her party colleagues' resolution in caucus has been reflected in occasional party agreements to free votes—the 'conscience vote'. These deal with cross-polarising value issues like abortion, homosexual law reform, and the control of alcohol and gambling. The confused and patchwork state of most law achieved with free votes has up to now provided scant recommendation for the method. Individual MPs are also expected to, and do, set party aside to act as mediators for any vocal constituents encountering problems with government departments and agencies. Because busy MPs' 'clinics' are the norm, however, individual reward for them is largely subsumed in the party vote.

The deeper debates about the place of party concern responsibility, accountability, and control. The Executive Council or Cabinet as a whole is responsible to Parliament as a whole, and that remains true. But that is a latent consideration so long as Cabinet, which comes out of the party majority in Parliament, both retains the support of that majority and the majority is not eroded into a minority by by-elections or defections. Since the Parliament of 1928-31, there has been only one instance of a government being even in prospect of losing its majority, the debatable case of 1984. Caucus discipline is generally so compelling that the Labour government of 1957-60, for example, sailed through its three years with a working majority of one vote after providing the Speaker.

If governments are so dependent for a majority on their party caucus, does it follow that the executive is in the hands of its backbenchers? To ask such a question is to ignore the complex of relations which bind a caucus and especially a caucus in power. In the first place the Ministers are themselves part of caucus, and on the whole the most experienced part, the best informed through Cabinet discussion and their departments, and the most cohesive about policy thanks to their often prior participation in Cabinet committees and their part in the final determinations of the whole body. Moreover, New Zealand Cabinets work together daily in one building, not scattered in their departments as they are in London.

Besides these pressures and practices of the executive to ensure its cohesion and its superiority in information and experience, the executive inevitably borrows strength in caucus from the leading figure or figures of the government around whom and by whom it is largely built. Caucus may elect the leader and deputy leader but, once they are in government, National's leaders both choose their own Cabinets and allocate portfolios and Cabinet ranking. Labour's leaders since 1940 have had to accept caucus election of Cabinet's membership. Thereafter, however, the Labour Prime Minister decides portfolios and ranking as with National. What is more, the party difference between leader selection and caucus election of Cabinets would appear to affect the inclusion of no more than two or three in twenty because parallel considerations of party record and parliamentary experience, personal ability, capacity for teamwork and sectional representativeness guide both forms of choice. In the final analysis, in both parties and under either system each caucus aspirant to office knows that it is one's past and present record in caucus and the work of party in Parliament which the leader and perhaps one or two close advisors will review when deciding one's place in existing or future executives.

Another factor affecting the balance between the executive and backbenchers in caucus is also a matter of prime ministerial decision, namely the size and composition of his (or her) ministry and allied offices. Practice has varied through time and by party as to whether the Speaker attends caucus. But excluding the Speaker throughout, the numbers in office have grown with the years and particularly since Parliaments began enlarging after 1966. Cabinet members moved from eight for Ballance in 1892 to sixteen for Nash in 1957. By then Cabinet with the Chairman of Committees and the two Whips made up nineteen in a caucus of forty. In the Holyoake era of consensus his 1967 Cabinet and other office-holders numbered twenty-two in a caucus of forty-three, so at that point the balance had tipped numerically in the same direction as the weight of influence had always pointed. Twenty years later in David Lange's second term there was an elected Cabinet of twenty to which the Prime Minister had added a Minister not in Cabinet and three Associate-Ministers together with four Parliamentary Under-Secretaries, while the establishment was rounded out with a Chairman and Deputy-Chairman of Committees and two Whips, a grand total of thirty-two in a caucus of fifty-seven MPs.

Adding all these factors together, the conclusion that Cabinets have sharply increased their predominance within caucus appears inescapable.

It follows that government by party majority may be coming to mean government by Cabinet alone, and within Cabinet that the major figures grouped around the Prime Minister fix both the agenda and direction of change. Viewed superficially, there appears to be little alteration in all this. New Zealand has had Cabinets, Premiers, and a core group of more influential Ministers at the heart of governmental decision since responsible government began in 1856. The pre-party cabinets, however, could never be sure of their support in the House and had to steer, sometimes from bill to bill, with an eye to the crumbly margins of their majority in Parliament itself.

When viable parties arrived, their contribution was to take any existing or potential Cabinet and establish clear links between that party leadership and its candidates and future supporters in Parliament. At the same time the basis of party tied both groups to a programme of policies which either were being implemented or would be if a majority could be won from a general electorate aware of those programmes for action and aware increasingly of party records in office and party traditions and principles.

The gift of party to governments was stability of support by MPs reinforced in Labour's case by a pledge to abide by regular caucus decisions, a practice less formally cemented but almost always followed by the National caucus from the 1940s onwards. Apart from early situations temporarily vexed by further party formation and decay (1911-19) or by three-party equality in numbers (1928-31), governments could cease looking to the House as a whole and become primarily responsible and accountable to the electorate. Party's gift to the electorate was meaningful choice between alternative governments whose proposals were known.

In between those electoral judgements governments were secondarily responsible to their caucus. For example, the Savage-Fraser-Nash triumvirate were called to order and to their pre-election intentions by the Labour caucus during the genesis of the Social Security Act of 1938.[2] The caucus checks were rare—although one eventually led to caucus election of Cabinets—because they were rarely needed. And on the periphery as a third type of accountability stood the extra-parliamentary party organisation which acted as a reserve pressure towards consistency with party policies, principles, and tradition. It was this whole complex of responsibilities which came in with party and choice between predictable alternatives which had been absorbed by New Zealand's political culture. That three-way accountability also constituted a vital if familiar set of assumptions within the accumulated consensus of the 1960s.

Three factors now began to function together to challenge not just these operating assumptions of accountability, but the whole consensus about the political culture. By far the most significant factor was the pervasive influence of an adverse change in the international economic climate. This contracted New Zealand's returns from trade, distorted its access to markets, and drove New Zealand governments to seek radical internal answers to a hostile and worsening international environment. This country's politicians had generally been able for three decades to help to distribute rising standards of living within a full employment economy. There had been genuinely difficult fluctuations to negotiate at times, such as the sudden recessions of 1952-53, 1957-58, and 1967-69. Nevertheless, compared to the Great Depression or the 1920s, the long wartime and postwar prosperity underwrote governments and socioeconomic satisfaction until 'the end of the golden weather' came in 1974.

The second and ancillary factor was the combined result of rising educational standards and public attention to new forms of news media, the fruits of development in the 1960s. Successively radio news and current affairs, network television and regular opinion polling broke through the static conservatism of the old press and competitively moved it, too, to take a more analytical, domestically-interested stance. The result was an increasingly varied, sensitive, and powerful news media which could swing quickly from approval to forceful and personalised criticism either with or independently of changes in public opinion. Working together these two factors alone would have guaranteed that the drowsy acceptance of the 1960s consensus would be challenged and was bound to change.

But what opened the way to upsetting those assumptions about party and programme accountability was the third and directly political factor, the accelerating preponderance in governing caucuses of office-holders over backbenchers. That made possible the building of the fortress Cabinets of the 1970s and 1980s with their central keep of twenty Ministers and their outerworks of Associates, Under-Secretaries, Chairmen, and Whips. Later in times of threat, the accustomed career paths were dug into trenches for 'going along to get along', while the caucus pledge to vote with the majority and to keep silence on caucus debates became a guarded discipline for the few fractious exceptions remaining within the perimeter walls of caucus.

Like most fortifications, these began with a particularly large encampment, and it was only external threat and the possibility of internal division which gradually turned them to new purposes and fresh additions. The great Kirk majority of twenty-three in 1972 gave rise to a Cabinet of twenty with at first one, then three Under-Secretaries. This size simply facilitated the efforts of an especially active Cabinet busy fulfilling a party and electoral agenda overcrowded after twelve years out of power. Then in 1974 primary export prices collapsed, fuel and other import costs shot up, and the Prime Minister died. The caucus united round new leaders but it was an embattled unity because they were facing bitter terms of trade and economic shortfalls which precluded gains for the expectant voters.

Labour's plenitude of seats created seeming security in Parliament. The new opposition leader, Robert Muldoon, chose instead to campaign for a year mainly outside Parliament while press and television conveyed his meetings all over the country into the nation's living rooms. The multiplying eye of the network had peered critically at the end of the Holyoake-Marshall era. Now two channels focused their glare on the Rowling regime in difficulties. Polling picked up the dismay and disappointment among voters and the media spread the news. In the first of the contemporary and really volatile elections, Labour's very large majority melted into a triumphant Muldoon majority of the same size.

The Muldoon Cabinet was also as substantial as its predecessor but was apparently under no threat until the 1978 election revealed the extent of electoral dissatisfaction with meagre economic results by dropping National's majority to ten and putting their vote fractionally under that cast for Labour. Spurred to sudden activity, the Prime Minister's economic 'fine-tuning' was converted into a proliferating Cabinet programme of radical, large-scale state investment. The legislative, economic, and philosophical consequence of the 'Think Big' policies had benefited some but upset more National voters by 1981. Eventually they disappointed the expectations and the party traditions of so many National supporters that they produced an anti-Muldoon, pro-private enterprise party on what was now National's right which compounded the National disaster of 1984.[3] It can be concluded that the electoral check on radical departures from party principles was still operating, but it was slow to act decisively.

No earlier check from caucus had appeared despite cause for and signs of unease from the election of 1978 onwards. The fortress Cabinet could restrain the backbenchers providing the Ministers themselves kept together. Protest rose in the polls particularly in 1980 when the Prime Minister took the risk of causing a by election by appointing one of his Ministers as an ambassador, then departed overseas while the contest exploded into a Social Credit candidate's victory. This brought on 'the colonels' coup' of October 1980 in which Ministers divided the Cabinet, and consequently the backbenchers, on the proposal to replace the Prime Minister, a revolt which was only repulsed for want of a resolute leader.[4]

Once quelled, the Prime Minister still found it possible to reinstate discipline and scrape through one more general election in 1981 with farm subsidies, a divisive Springbok rugby tour and big state expenditures on investment projects. After that election, the National majority was so low that occasional shows of independence from a Minister and, separately, from two to three backbenchers became seriously threatening and drew drastic disciplinary action which the fortress Cabinet concurred in. Indeed, it was not so much the fortress Cabinet or its leader which brought a desperate kind of unity to the bulk of caucus at the last, but the looming threat of decisive electoral defeat.

Because the uses and implications of the fortress Cabinet were still under development in the Muldoon era, and since his personal role as Prime Minister and Minister of Finance was so extensive and powerful that it provoked revolt from within the Cabinet as well as from without, the effect of considering that period is partly to obscure what trends in the political system a fortress Cabinet represents and what can be achieved by it. Given a substantial or even sizeable majority to begin with, the decision to build a dominant official establishment makes possible the near-total escape of Cabinet from accountability to the remaining backbenchers in the party caucus as a whole. Tactical sense argues that those backbenchers in critical marginal seats should be heard on local and regional causes of complaint and on significant shifts in opinion, particularly as an election approaches. Listening, however, is by Cabinet calculation and choice. It does not constitute the internal check on the redesign or implementation of party policies furnished by caucuses in the past.

The second kind of accountability by government to party, that to the external party organisation, is the most contentious and insecurely accepted aspect of our political culture. It can be presented as disturbing the responsibility of governments to their electors or to an indefinitely-defined 'national interest'. The cry can be raised in correspondence columns and editorials that governments should govern and not yield to activists who in National will indeed customarily be to the right of National parliamentarians and voters, just as in Labour they are traditionally to the left of Labour parliamentarians and voters. The function of party organisations in keeping their MPs to their announced programmes can be overlooked because, like lenses, while they magnify departures from policy, they also polarise their light from the left or the right.

So however useful party organisations may be in person-to-person propagation of policies, however vital they are for party campaigning and fundraising, they start at a strategic disadvantage when trying to debate, correct or pull back Cabinet action to accord with manifestos or party principles. The party organisation finds itself standing committed by the Cabinet's record in office regardless of how far that may be from what the organisation thought was intended. In fact the situation imposes division upon them.

Some activists will want to go forward with Cabinet in the hope that future reward will compensate for any present pain and that, by keeping silence and office, a reconciliation will eventually be revealed between Cabinet's departures from policy and the principles and objectives of the party. Others will want to cry halt now and get guarantees for the future; and still others will demand reversion to the manifesto at the risk of public disunity. Providing the fortress Cabinet continues to argue for its programme before the split party and promises future reconciliation, it seems probable that freedom from organisational accountability will join freedom from caucus accountability, at least for an organisationally-confused and dispirited interim.

The controls which party caucus and organisation could deploy to bring a Prime Minister and Cabinet back to party principles therefore appear to have been temporarily disconnected with the building of fortress Cabinets. What then of the greatest control of all, the electoral commitment of potential governments to abide by their manifestos and campaign promises and to act in general accordance with past traditions and party principles because all of them are part of voters' electoral images and decisions? By 1984 it was plain that Cabinet's dominance over caucus and the strategic disparity between a united government in action and the organisation outside had presented Cabinet with the freedom to choose how to act—at least until the next election and possibly beyond it. They could act as announced and campaigned for, or once elected, strike out in fresh directions and legislate novel and interdependent structures which would be hard to unbolt and dismantle.

Such decisions are not taken in a vacuum and the Labour Cabinet's decisions were set against five and a half years of intra-party struggle and a tremendous momentum from events. First there was a long campaign to replace Wallace Rowling with David Lange as leader. It took a core group of experienced MPs to achieve it after two defeats and Rowling's retirement, and involved battles with the party organisation and a stand-off on economic policy. But it provided four of the five Ministers at the top of the Lange Cabinet. The elected deputy leader could be drawn in subsequently as were the other ex-Rowling half of the elected Cabinet by David Lange's campaigning skills as leader and by everyone's painful memories of adverse polls and media criticism during the years of disunion. No feature of the Lange Cabinet's first term was more valued and carefully nurtured than its unity.

The second factor bearing on Cabinet's choice of how to act was the influence of a generational set of attitudes favouring radical institutional change in many spheres and the spread of an international ideology about necessary economic objectives and the monetary, fiscal, and deregulatory path to reach them. The essential figure in gathering and projecting these views was Roger Douglas, an ex-Minister who took up a public position contrasting with accepted Labour approaches when he issued an alternative budget and a short book in 1980.[5] He became the centre of a group of MPs with academic and Treasury members which led on to the coalescence of the Lange core and Douglas conceptions. The final element was contributed by the loan costs and international consequences of the Muldoon programme of public investment, farm subsidies, economic controls, and a half-disengaged salary and wage freeze. As the 1984 election campaign progressed, a crisis mounted over New Zealand's international credit and exchange rate situation.

When Labour came to power in the snap election it was committed to an anti-nuclear stance, a manifesto array of social, employment, and welfare objectives, a consensus approach to industrial and other matters which smacked of the Australian accord, and an economic section so general as to allow Roger Douglas *carte blanche* if a prospective Cabinet agreed. The day after Labour's election triumph, officials of the Treasury and Reserve Bank informed Labour's key Ministers-elect of the critical state of overseas balances. Labour's leadership then decided on a major devaluation of New Zealand's dollar by 20 per cent. In a sense the future Cabinet's choice and the compelling economic role of Douglas in all that followed were also decided at that point. However, the outgoing Prime Minister disputed the necessity of devaluation and only acted as requested by the Leader of the Opposition under pressure from National's deputy leader and other Ministers.

Once the changeover was complete and the new Cabinet was in being, both Labour Ministers and backbenchers were convinced by what they learned of the parlous state of New Zealand's economy, which was initially seen as the outcome of and a verdict upon their predecessors' policies. 'The opening of the books' was intended to impress media and public with New Zealand's dire situation. Increasingly, however, the Minister of Finance, Roger Douglas, and his two Associate Finance Ministers,[6] also attributed the critical situation to twenty or even thirty years of systemic economic failure, over-borrowing, subsidies, protection, poor economic management by past governments, departments, and public bodies generally, and to welfare extravagance such as the National Superannuation scheme. The stage was set for drastic and indeed fundamental change.

It was in this preliminary, settling down period that Cabinet was given a second chance for choice. Taking New Zealand's immediate crisis as dealt with by devaluation, there was a second course of policy with which to tackle the underlying problems which was at least available, promised, and potentially more in accord with the manifesto's programme. This was to pursue the pledge of consensus and try for a corporatist solution. A quadripartite and indeed general economic and social conference was summoned. The conference could be seen on television to be a gathering of New Zealand's sectoral leaderships from business, farming, labour, and government—and its Maori leadership as well, which held a consequent conference.[7]

Despite the popular appeal of the consensus concept, the fanfare and size of the gathering did conceal organisational difficulties for a New Zealand corporatism. Indicative planning, sector by sector, had not gone far beyond conferences and pronouncements on planning by the National Development Council at the end of the Holyoake-Marshall era. A more basic consideration was that peak federations for employers, commerce, manufacturing, and unions had proven in the past to have only a weak hold over the actions of their constituent members. In any case, corporatism contradicted the thinking of the Douglas group and the exhaustive plans of Treasury which had greeted the new government with a volume on economic management as a whole[8] and for most Ministers' areas. Both envisaged parallel solutions quite different from sectoral negotiation and consensus. Step by step Cabinet chose to follow instead the Douglas lead, and all that was left of the alternative were doomed tripartite conferences before subsequent wage rounds which simply registered disagreement not consensus.

It is not the intention here to lay out the details of the end of farm subsidies, the free floating of the 'kiwi' dollar, the attack on protection, the end of foreign exchange control and the rest of financial deregulation which invited foreign capital and banks, unshackled private corporations and released the stock exchange boom. There was a rebalancing between the introduced, indirect and universal goods and services tax and lowered selective income taxation, more regressive and less progressive taxation for which there was some targeted compensation for the poorer in the form of the Family Support provisions. Then having restructured farming, finance, and taxation, notice was served on a list of government departments that they were post-haste to be 'corporatised' as 'state-owned enterprises'. They were to be organised and much slimmed on the model of big businesses and to be run by boards largely of business people, lawyers, and accountants and have chief executives attentive to dividends for the state.

Much of it fitted the standard Thatcher doctrine and so did Labour's second term sequel of privatisation for SOEs whenever the market was ready. Equally parallel were the advances towards lower taxes for business and the penultimate reduction of income taxation on the way to the grail of a flat tax rate. Yet parts of the Douglas programme were likewise to be found in social democratic Spain and Portugal as well as in Reagan's United States, Kohl's West Germany, coalition Italy, and cohabitational France. What distinguished 'Rogernomics' was the speed with which it was unrolled, its thoroughgoing doctrinal completeness, and the impression of inevitable momentum that it generated. And all of it challenged, confronted, and attacked the socioeconomic structure which the first Labour government had erected and within which all subsequent governments had lived and administered, with modifications to taste.

By the same token, Cabinet's deeds had challenged the traditions of loyal Labour voters and the principles of occasional waverers and the few absolutely unconverted in caucus. They had confronted the National opposition with a startling situation in which Labour had ended Sir Robert Muldoon's departures from National principles and cleared away past Labour institutions from the path of business as National activists had always intended some day to do. Cabinet had implemented much of the programme of Robert Jones' splinter New Zealand Party as Cabinet swept past the position on which Jones had stood and moved rigorously to the right of National. As for Social Crediters, now called Democrats, their anti-nuclear attitude was embodied in law, their leader was new and uncertain, and their results in the polls disheartening.

Altogether, Cabinet's new directions had confused the electoral basis on which they had received power since neither those who had voted for Labour's manifesto or record, nor those who had not, saw before them what they had expected. The electoral attachment of party to programme had been temporarily severed and the spectrum of parties shaken out of order.

If New Zealand's political ideology and the consensus of the 1960s had absorbed Labour as the party of the centre left and National as the party of the centre right, this assumption now required urgent reconsideration. Insofar as the voting public looked for records in office to fit the past of the alternative governing parties, that, too, was in flux and had been since 1979.

Most importantly, if New Zealand's political ideology incorporated conclusions about the uses and purposes of government, including presumptions about an active state and common upholding of high employment and the apparatus of welfare as established, then those conclusions were also in question. What faced the public was a major retreat from political action and the positive, active state. Under the guidance of Cabinet, the role of party and the scope of government responsibilities were contracting as they ceded large tracts of the state's accustomed territory and the form of state institutions to the direction and then the possession of private business. By those cessions and contractions Cabinet was removing great areas of vital decision from the judgements of popular sovereignty and substituting the impersonal and asocial judgements of local and international markets.

The meaning of these implications for the purposes of politics and government was not at all clear, nor made clear for most of Labour's first term. Attention was on more immediate matters when constant change at Cabinet's direction began and gained speed and variety. Labour's lead over National in the Heylen polls dropped from euphoric post-election figures of above ten per cent to safe-enough single figures in December 1984 when Sir Robert was replaced by Jim McLay as National's leader. Labour continued in front until April and May of 1985 when National edged the government behind and National then concluded the phase by winning the Timaru by-election.[9]

Thereafter Labour climbed back and National only barely recovered the lead at two polls in two years, those of March 1986 and February 1987. Otherwise a moderate Labour lead persisted or shot up for five halcyon months after GST arrived with its income tax changes, then more double figures at the end of 1986 and, just when they were most needed, five double figure polls prior to judgement in the 1987 election. If Labour Cabinet Ministers required any reinforcement about the acceptability of their programme, they had only to look at the polls as they did; and just to make sure, they ran advertising campaigns on new concepts. Moreover the media were full of encouraging comments from leading business and international figures, while by contrast National was having more disputes over leadership as Sir Robert and his followers persistently opposed both the leader and the president of their party. Disturbance continued over personalities until Jim Bolger displaced Jim McLay, but the underlying puzzle went on about what posture to adopt towards Labour's innovations almost to the eve of the election. Accordingly there was little threat to Labour to be found in the opposition until the campaign.

Labour's fortress Cabinet held every advantage from the start in embarking on its own programme. Even their action in taxing the better-off national superannuitants had at least the colour of financial emergency, although it was long resented. The financial changes appeared to be validated by the stockmarket and property booms. The stockmarket, despite sagging alarmingly for a while, recovered to greater heights in time to cast the rosy hue of partial success over election time and leave the tens of thousands of participants to learn and regret later.[10]

Labour's caucus was quiet. Jim Anderton MP, the former party president, appeared a lonely figure in his warning comments on Timaru's loss.[11] Party conferences produced sharp questions but not hard adverse resolutions. And as for future votes, Robert Jones endeavoured fairly conclusively to end the New Zealand Party in Labour's favour, while the Democrats ousted their leader, found an inexperienced successor and had their other MP promise retirement.[12] So there were plenty of votes seeking a new home. Overall success for the Douglas programme to lower inflation, however, could not be counted on before the election but would come 'in the medium term'. Since anti-inflationary success was in turn to bring down interest rates, moderate the surging kiwi dollar and revive farming and manufacturing, the prospects of economic victory remained in the future.

Most Labour voters held on instead to the hope of a more socially-oriented second period in office. They were determined after two one-term Labour governments, that at last there would be a Labour programme which had time to be fully implemented and to be fairly judged. Furthermore, the anti-nuclear legislation aroused genuine enthusiasm, just as American pronouncements and the French bombers stirred national sentiments and produced gusts of self-assertion.

When the acid test of electoral judgement was applied, Labour was returned with an increased proportion of the vote and three seats won from National. It had every appearance of a triumphant vindication for the Cabinet, for the Prime Minister who had led them and for the architect of their principal policies, Roger Douglas. Underneath, however, Labour's majorities over National were slipping, strongholds were showing losses to non-vote and only the wealthy and middling city seats shifted much towards Labour. Moreover on the night of victory David Lange spoke, as he had towards the end of the campaign, of the need to deliver in the fields of education, health, and welfare, while Douglas' televised comment was about the need to get on with the reforms they had yet to complete. Were these contrasting attitudes the seeds of division or did they present the opportunity to combine social with eventual economic success? Choices for Cabinet had reappeared and perhaps—if those choices were mishandled—the electorate would choose other than Labour at the third electoral judgement. For unfortunately the manifesto did not appear as a whole until after the election, just as the programme for the first term could never have been anticipated from the campaign of 1984.

Certain related questions crucial for the development of New Zealand's political ideology remain for the reasonably near future to answer. Will the next election shake the party spectrum again and economic failure— or success—prompt the assertion of changed party principles along with the restoration of caucus and organisational controls? Could the next election bring back electoral choice between alternative governments which will once again be tied to manifestos which are followed? Or will the wild card of a mixed (and conflicting?) first-past-the-post and proportional system be legislated into existence and popular sovereignty be mathematically completed with a range of several parties which will modify in coalitions instead of giving choice between alternatives? Will the 1990 outcome or some later electoral result produce Cabinet government strong enough to reclaim for popular sovereignty the responsibilities and social areas for decision now ceded to the markets? Alternatively, will the party traditionalists fall away into minor sectarian parties and a three-or-more party system appear in which the major parties dispute from 'new right' and 'old right' positions? And will New Zealand's political ideology see its party rules recast and adjust to a contracted state while popular sovereignty accommodates to a market-driven, international business-led future?

Notes

1 Alan Robinson, *Notes on New Zealand Politics* (Wellington, mimeo, 1970), p. 17; reprinted as 'The Political Culture', in H. Gold (ed.), *New Zealand Politics in Perspective* (Auckland, 1985), p. 13.
2 [Michael Joseph Savage was the Labour Prime Minister between 1935 and 1940; Peter Fraser was Minister of Health and Education during that time; and Walter Nash was Minister of Finance. Ed.]
3 [The reference is to the New Zealand Party led by Robert Jones. Ed.]
4 [For further details, see Chapter 12. Ed.]
5 [R. Douglas, 'Alternative Budget', June 1980; and *There's Got to be a Better Way!* (Wellington, 1980). Ed.]
6 [The two Associate Finance Ministers were Richard Prebble and David Caygill. Ed.]
7 [The Economic Summit Conference was held in September 1984; and the Maori Economic Summit (Hui Taumata) was held in October 1984. Ed.]
8 [The Treasury, *Economic Management* (Wellington, 1984). Ed.]
9 [Sir Basil Arthur, Labour MP from 1962 and a Minister between 1972 and 1985, died. Maurice McTigue held Timaru until 1993 when he was defeated. Ed.]
10 [The 1987 General Election was held on 15 August 1987. In October the sharemarket crashed. Ed.]
11 [Jim Anderton, MP for Sydenham, left Labour in 1989. He stood successfully for New Labour in 1990 and the Alliance in 1993 and 1996. Ed.]
12 [The Democrats, formerly Social Credit, were led by Bruce Beetham between 1972 and 1986 when he was replaced by Neil Morrison who held the leadership position until 1988 when he was replaced by Garry Knapp. Morrison and Knapp, MPs for Pakuranga and East Coast Bays respectively, were defeated in 1987. Ed.]

20

A Political Culture Under Pressure: The Struggle to Preserve a Progressive Tax Base for Welfare and the Positive State

An Endorsement, a Warning, or Both?

The result of the general election of 15 August 1987 was the return of the Labour Government with an increased proportion of the vote and three seats won from National. This simplified picture of what had happened could be and was widely interpreted in the media and among government members as a triumphant vindication for the Cabinet, for the Prime Minister who had led them, David Lange, and for the architect of their principal policies, Roger Douglas, the Minister of Finance. If the Government's return with almost as strong a majority of seats as before was to be the sole test, then triumph it was. It undoubtedly pleased the bulk of Labour voters who had held on in the hope of economic success in the ever-receding 'medium term' and in the further hope of a more socially-oriented second term in which an authentically Labour programme could be implemented while the nuclear-free policy was consolidating. At the same time Labour's re-election encouraged those new recruits who assumed that all Roger Douglas stood for would go forward in strength.

What first impressions overlooked, however, was that National's net gain since 1984, in terms of the qualified vote, was +5.31 per cent compared to Labour's +2.24 per cent and that the rise in non-vote plus informals of +4.82 per cent was also more than twice as great as Labour's improvement. National's gains exceeded those for Labour in six out of the seven sections of the electorate. Indeed, in the poorer city special country and Maori seats—all Labour's heartlands—the Labour percentage did not rise but fell instead. Only in the six wealthier city seats did Labour's vote really soar upwards, by +10.17 per cent compared to the +2.15 per cent lift for National.

As for the seventeen members of the first Lange Cabinet who stood again, instead of enjoying the endorsement of a rise in their majorities or simply paralleling the performance of other Labour candidates, those

[This chapter was published in *Political Science*, Vol. 44, No. 1 (July 1992). Ed.]

Cabinet members' majorities shrank by an average of -8.68 per cent against their National opponents and by -8.96 per cent against all nearest competitors. Even the tally of seats captured since 1984 tilted towards National. National candidates picked up the two new seats created in the redistribution; National took two from former Social Crediters; and it held its by-election capture of Timaru and eventually secured Wairarapa also from Labour. So National was up by six seats while losing three. Labour was up by those three, but had lost two. There was thus a sizable element of warning for the governing party when its Cabinet fared worst, its core support in its safest seats declined, and when its National alternative and then non-voting made the principal gains from the election. It at least constituted a signal that Labour's many marginals, which had been saved by a deluge of special attention guided by private polling, could well not survive a further National gain like that registered in August 1987.[1]

Moreover on the night of victory David Lange spoke, as he had towards the end of the campaign, of the need to deliver in the fields of education, health, and welfare, while Douglas' televised comment was about the need to get on with the reforms they had yet to complete. Were these contrasting attitudes the seeds of division or did they present the opportunity to combine social with eventual economic success? Choices for Cabinet had reappeared and perhaps—if those choices were mishandled—the electorate would choose other than Labour at the third electoral judgement. For unfortunately the manifesto did not appear as a whole until after the election, just as the programme for the first term could never have been anticipated from the campaign of 1984.

The Crash and the Thrust Towards Privatisation

Optimistic anticipation gave way to harsh and depressing facts all too quickly. The heaviest blow was dealt by the October collapse of prices on the world's stockmarkets which in New Zealand's case shrank further and recovered more slowly than anywhere else. Much of the banking and financial boom which had followed deregulation and engendered a superfluity of office buildings now proved to have been highly speculative and spectacularly ill-managed.

Consequently, when confidence fled, so did most of its promoters' pyramids of credit, much of their paper fortunes and with them went the savings and hopes of tens of thousands of shareholders. Three years later not all the consequences had yet been discovered nor unwound so that, for instance, the National Government on election was greeted by the Bank of New Zealand's compelling need for a further injection of $620 million.[2]

Altogether the crash and the subsequent catalogue of major failures hardly constituted an advertisement for the acumen of finance and big business in New Zealand nor an endorsement of its stock exchange as a reliable or even credible assessor of the value of companies. Yet Cabinet continued to put its trust in businessmen as board members of corporatised SOEs, as models or consultants, and ultimately as proprietors of former departments of the contracting New Zealand state. As Roger Douglas wrote, 'The real contributions to the formation of our policy came from those used to taking practical action—the business people.'[3]

Moreover, with the 1987 election behind them, Labour's Cabinet could be urged forward from corporatisation to privatisation. Well before the election there had been warning shots. There was the decision to sell out of New Zealand Steel and the 1987 Budget plan to sell shares in three corporations and issue equity bonds for a quarter of two SOEs.[4] But this plan was limited, for the future, and would require parliamentary action. Restive Labour conferences and the watching voters were reassured that some participation did not portend wholesale disposal while attention was focused on ongoing corporatisation as simply a better, more efficient, and profitable way to run public commercialised operations. Board control, defined objectives, and oversight by Treasury, ministers and parliamentary select committees would all render SOEs thoroughly accountable and their dividends would mean less debt and tax.

Before these checks for accountability and the form of the corporations could all become fully elaborated, familiar and tested, however, the opposite argument as advanced by Treasury[5] and such influential figures as the Chairman of the State Services Commission[6] appears to have triumphed. They held that only the 'discipline' of corporations being quoted and valued daily on the sharemarket and made subject to the possibility of takeover could provide true accountability, but it would be an accountability to private shareholders and not to government on behalf of the public.

The principal objective of privatisation as announced in the 17 December 1987 Statement[7] was, nevertheless, to reduce the public debt with the proceeds of sales and that intention may well have weighed more than considerations of corporate discipline with ministers conscious of the multiplying interest burden and alarmed for New Zealand's post-crash credit abroad. To explain ministerial consent to such a crucial, even fundamental change of course as privatisation, one which could also be taken as a breach of electoral trust, it must never be forgotten that this Labour Cabinet's career had begun with an inherited crisis when New Zealand's reserves overseas had dropped to a desperate level for which only radical devaluation had provided relief. It was a dramatic demonstration that, once deeply indebted, any New Zealand government would be surrounded by rigid limits on its freedom to choose in economic policy.

Certainly the foreign exchange crisis of 1984 was a formative experience, one imprinted on the minds not just of the three Treasury ministers but also of every member of Cabinet. Thus it was a paradox that subsequent Douglas policies by way of decontrolling foreign exchange, financial and general deregulation, tariff reduction and the free float together constituted a uniquely unguarded opening up to the world. In turn this openness served to amplify any signals from opinion in the great financial centres of New York, London and Tokyo and rendered waiting for the verdicts on New Zealand of the major credit rating agencies into occasions of foreboding and suspense. Now in December 1987 and only months into their second term, ministers again faced the effects of a crash, this time of the stock exchange. They were staring at savagely high interest rates, increasing bankruptcies and unemployment, a flat economy, and were well aware of the debt limits lying ahead. Selling the SOEs could ease the situation particularly if they sold to foreign investors when reducing external debt.

The Price of Privatisation
For attentive voters, however, and especially Labour's organisational activists and electoral supporters who had believed 'the family silver' to be safe, this announcement of future sales was a startling reversal. Curtailment of services, high user-pays fees, staff reductions, redundancies and unemployment could be regretted but explained as unavoidable and efficient slimming to meet hard times. Just so long as the state-owned enterprises remained in public possession their existing mandatory concentration on dividends and tax returns could always be revised to restore some social objectives in a brighter future. By contrast, sales would be so final and eventually so far-reaching.

It had been the century-long workings of the positive state, not bursts of ideology but pragmatism, not one party but four successive parties which had bequeathed these balancing public institutions to modify laissez-faire capitalism and produce the mixed economy and later the welfare state. Once the corporations were consigned to market ownership those multiple tasks of community assistance and social easement which the former departments had once fulfilled would go permanently unperformed. And who could say where the process of state contraction, user-pays and privatisation would halt? There was a pervasive sense of the importance of the changes proposed because the activities and assets to be disposed of were themselves expressions of New Zealand's political culture, the familiar products of basic attitudes evolved and maintained over long periods of time. They had been voted for, paid for and democratically sanctioned under both Labour and National whereas this new beginning most patently had not. What was being cut across, or at the least profoundly redirected, was the course which New Zealand's political consciousness and history had carved out almost since its inception.

The Flat Tax Proposal Unveiled

When David Lange gathered his core ministers for the television cameras on 17 December 1987 there was a second surprise announcement even more sweeping in the short term although of less long-run significance than privatisation. Roger Douglas foreshadowed doing away with what had survived in New Zealand of graduated income taxation—the mainstay of the modern state in the twentieth century. Instead from October 1988 there was to be a flat rate of tax of about 23 cents in the dollar and a precisely targeted system of income supports for those employed people most in need. With one bound Roger Douglas would have outrun Mrs Thatcher and outdone President Reagan while confirming his own position as a major innovator in financial circles.

Back in October 1986, when the regressive Goods and Services Tax came in at 10 per cent, there had also been a big cut in the top rate of progressive income taxation from the former 66 per cent down to 48 per cent.[8] Two years later, all, whether rich, middling or struggling, would pay income tax at the same rate—as they already paid GST—save those at the base of the pyramid where the families of the employed and the neediest individuals would find themselves granted rebates and supplements up to a guaranteed minimum income. Just as the 1986 changes had been kindest to the very top and bottom bands of earners, so once more with the flat tax proposal the base was shielded while for the upper fifth, and above all for the topmost fraction, the prospects for speedy accumulation and investment here or overseas were truly unprecedented.

In fiscal principle a flat tax was a great leap backwards in time to the age before the First World War and even before Lloyd George in Britain, but with a compensating gesture towards Walter Nash as Minister of Finance in the first Labour Government in the provision for the poorest employed sections of society. Coming from a Labour Minister of Finance supported by his key colleagues only three months after an election campaign in which not one word nor figure of such a flat tax proposal had appeared, it was undoubtedly disorienting for the concept of choice between known political programmes and parties each with recognisable principles and established traditions. It is true that Labour's headlong pace and free market formulas for change in its first term had already disturbed allegiances to the point where Labour recruited well-to-do and upwardly mobile voters in surprising numbers and places while losing more of its own to non-voting. But the December Economic Statement with flat tax and privatisation together promised a new scale of change in the social and economic framework of politics while posing a confusing challenge to New Zealand's political culture as a systematic whole.

What the Public Heard of the Split in the Leadership

From its onset the Statement bore an air of haste and erected a patchwork screen of lesser topics around its key messages. The country was then left with one busy week in which to ponder the necessity of privatisation and the consequences of flat tax before the Christmas-New Year vacation closed the subject for all but a few. Dramatically it flew open again on 28 January at a Prime Ministerial press conference[9] when David Lange revealed that 'advice tendered to us, as a result of the working party and the decision which was taken to await the findings of the Royal Commission' meant a perfected minimum family income and other protections for the 'less well off' could not be ready for 1 October 1988 and the 'other changes to personal tax will probably have to be deferred....' However, he held out the possibility of reductions in both personal and company tax rates by October. The quintessential question came back: 'are you saying that a flat tax rate might not necessarily come into effect from 1 October? [A] I am saying that, yes.'

At once Roger Douglas emplaned in London to return and defend his scheme. Before press and television[10] he concentrated on the benefits of the accompanying minimum family income, agreed that the figures were not final, quoted Lange reaffirming 'the direction of our economic policy', and concluded that he would only resign if the Prime Minister lost confidence in him as Minister of Finance.

The country added the two shocks together and realised that however impervious to caucus or party the fortress cabinet might be, it could still be riven by disunion from within. The Douglas dominance had been built on Prime Ministerial consent as well as general Cabinet agreement. It is worthwhile to recall that the previous Prime Minister had repulsed the leaderless colonels' coup in October 1980 and Muldoon policies had continued as before. Yet that could not happen this time when what the Prime Minister was checking was not yet rebellion but the onrush of the policies of another. When the figures were firm what would Lange's policies prove to be? How deep had division driven? Or was this, as Douglas implied when he offered a hurried television defence of his figures against those of the Working Group on Income Maintenance, just a minor dispute which could be smoothed away when Treasury's final and correct answer was understood?[11]

The conclusive proof of a restored Douglas-Lange unity, in that ideological order, would naturally have been the reinstatement of the flat tax. Again the Ad Hoc Committee of major ministers and the Cabinet met, reviewed the whole crucial situation, and a decision appeared. It took the form of an announcement by the Minister of Finance on 10 February that 'Cabinet had agreed to' a series of company, indirect and personal tax measures.[12] From 1 October 1988 24 per cent would be the standard rate and the marginal rate above $30,875 would descend from 48 per cent to 33 per cent. So the flat tax was out. As to the guaranteed minimum family income, that transmogrified into a rebate of 9 per cent up to $9,500, thereafter abating in steps although eligibility was yet to be determined.

Early Portents of Division and the Power to Allocate Portfolios

Thus the public phase of the crisis had lasted precisely a fortnight from Prime Ministerial doubt to Cabinet resolution. In truth, but in private, the early episodes of what was now a prime time struggle had run long before over the creation, membership and agenda of the Royal Commission on Social Policy[13] and again prior to the June 1987 Budget when measures on the labour market, health and education were set aside as electorally prejudicial.[14] Moreover, in his freshly elected second Ministry, sworn in on 24 August 1987, Lange's replacement of Prebble and Caygill as Associate Ministers of Finance by two newcomers to Cabinet, Cullen and Butcher, could be taken for a sign that the Prime Minister had found the former financial troika altogether too much of a winning combination. On the other hand, Prebble received the whole range of SOEs to guard or gut; Cullen as Minister of Social Welfare was under the Douglas gaze; while the pivotal welfare ministries of Health and Education were placed in the care of the transferred Caygill and of the Prime Minister himself.[15] So the new dispensation could just as easily be predicted to spread the Douglas discipline, and in many respects it did.

This ambiguity illustrates that the Prime Minister's power to allocate portfolios, though critical for individual ambitions, was not sufficient in itself to dam up the flooding in of doctrines which were well channelled and coordinated from other key positions and quite as likely as not to be shared already by those whom Caucus elevated to Cabinet membership. Considering also that the overwhelming element in the Caucus choice of a new Cabinet was the carefully negotiated preference of the outgoing

Cabinet and its confidants acting in concert, then the Cabinet mixture of the first term would be returned to power. That mixture would likewise be reproduced among the four additions—for which three retirements and the filling of the Speakership had opened the way. That is what occurred. Even had the Prime Minister then been of a mind to resist, the process of Cabinet renewal had left him as unable as ever to construct his own support and just as much Douglas-led and Cabinet-driven as before.

What of Checks from Labour's Conference, the Manifesto and the Mandate?

Nor could he turn to the Party organisation for he was bound by the first-term record of his own Government, increasingly remote in person and suspicious of 'outside' pressures, and far from sympathetic to what the organisation was seeking. Indeed at the Annual Conference early in November 1987, Lange lectured delegates on poor teachers and departmental waste in education then, having roused fears rather than hopes, added 'There will inevitably be some difference between the policy remits passed by this conference and the policy of the Government.'[16] Conference responded by passing a resolution to include in future election manifestos those policies which had been passed by a two-thirds vote in conference.[17]

The Deputy Prime Minister thereupon reiterated that the 'Government reserved the right to implement the policies it chose.'[18] He suggested that 'manifestos are merely statements of intent and cannot be seen as binding contracts' with which opinion a *Herald* editorial concurred, saying 'It is a sad and cynical position but it is clearly the case.'[19] As for the efficacy of the views expressed by delegates and by both the retiring and incoming presidents of the Labour Party, Margaret Wilson[20] and Rex Jones,[21] these pronouncements of Lange and Palmer were a comprehensive dismissal. Finally, lest the primacy of Rogernomics should be doubted by the newly-elected centre left majority on the Executive and the Policy Council, Roger Douglas stressed that his concern was not with them but with business confidence at home and abroad and promised 'It is not my intention to waver one iota.'[22]

Notice of termination had thus been served on two components of the nation's political culture. The more important of the two was that manifestos would inform the voters before they made an electoral choice about the major institutional changes and at times even quite minor measures which each party intended to put into law. An extension of this basic idea of parties seeking informed consent before being empowered to make changes of consequence was the concept of requiring a mandate whereby an elected government was not justified in taking legislative action in a field not marked out in its manifesto, and conversely that it should take action before the next election on all or nearly all its manifesto had promised.

Politicians of both sides for five decades before 1984 had made great play with the presence or absence of a mandate for this or that measure. Only the Great Depression was supposed by the 1931 Coalition to have called for an emergency 'doctor's mandate' or blank cheque which proved to be a licence for banker-approved cuts and economic contraction and made Labour all the keener to specify the design of its recovery programme in advance.[23] Thenceforth Labour became positively excessive in the length and particularity of its manifestos whereas National was more circumspectly vague in its phrasing of what exactly was to be done about the problems it nominated for attention—although National was equally emphatic on the necessity of having and fulfilling its mandate.

When the Deputy Prime Minister downgraded manifestos to non-binding statements of intent he back-lit the contrast between the Fourth and all previous Labour governments in respect to democratically seeking informed consent and then matching performance to promise. Indeed it was precisely this abandonment of Labour's traditional adherence to its programmes, its accustomed principles and its normal position in the political spectrum which the Conference was trying to control and reverse. It could not do so if a Labour Government had the unbridled power to choose what policies, and not necessarily Labour policies, it would implement. The right of conference as nominal governing body of the Party to contribute to binding electoral policy was thus the second, although far the less securely established, of the two components of the political culture to be set aside by the Party's parliamentary leaders.

It was perhaps both ironic and a predictable response to Rogernomics' inroads that in this period as Opposition the extra-parliamentary National Party put more energy and institutional innovation into electorate and divisional policy consideration than at any previous period. For Labour branch activists, however, the one power still remaining to them was to prepare for the next selection and reselection of candidates. They would do so as a declining force because the bulk of the disillusioned party workers had already preferred using the exit to giving voice. The rapidly dwindling third who remained also realised that party headquarters was deeply in debt and that large donations, not the portion of their fees sent to Wellington, had funded the sophisticated, computerised communications to the marginals and selected groups and the elaborate polling and advertising with which the 1987 campaign had been fought. The age of the hall meeting and party footsloggers on doorsteps was departing and their influence with it.

Restructuring the Public Service

What, then, was the Prime Minister's situation once the thrust from the Minister of Finance, his allies and the Treasury had been resumed as it had? Before the Annual Conference Roger Douglas had hinted at 'Faster Tax Cuts'[24] and it was 'no secret' to the press[25] that a package of cuts was coming. What was more, another struggle was joined when the public sector unions were confronted on 10 December 1987 with the State Sector Bill which applied private sector practices, executives and structures to what remained of the departments after the SOEs had been subtracted, transformed and shrunk.

The Public Service Association, following lengthy and anxious negotiation, had just confirmed on the evening of 9 December its members' acceptance of a whole new occupationally-based bargaining system yielding all the flexibility as between departments which had been sought.[26] So when next day and without warning the Minister of State Services put the Bill for a total restructuring of the whole state sector before Parliament, with the Prime Minister's and Cabinet's blessing, it was plain that it was not simply the pursuit of flexibility and efficiency which prompted this stroke of state, but rather the managerialist attitudes and neo-liberal arguments which lay behind corporatisation and the quest for the minimal state.

In the months of alarmed protest and demonstrations which followed, public servants were joined by teachers and health workers for they could all read in the recent past of corporatisation the early retirements, redundancies and uncertain futures actually or possibly in prospect. Another level and kind of criticism came from such authoritative sources as Dr Probine,[27] a former State Services Commission chairman, who said that the Bill 'would destabilise the public service and jeopardise the democratic system.' Eventually several improvements did appear in the final Act to do with appointments, training and coordination at the upper levels. But there was no reinstatement of traditional pay-fixing criteria, appeals and compulsory arbitration, the concerns of the great majority. The Prime Minister gave staunch support to Stan Rodger as Minister and, if the unionists involved had ever been considered as natural allies of the Labour Prime Minister and Government, there were few signs of it. Indeed, fashionable doctrine dismissed the protesters as congeries of vested interests. Once more a substantial change had been effected in the conventions of the political culture by substituting a set of chief executive led, shaped and disciplined departments on the model of profit-seeking, private businesses for a unified, articulated public service based on lifetime careers, training and experience.

Again in respect to state servants the usual image and reality of a united, untrammelled Prime Minister and Cabinet had been projected whereas the Prime Minister's contrasting and obscure account of policy change and implicit Cabinet controversy over the flat tax did not reach the voters until 28 February. But that was a montage of glimpses for the media and public which has been examined. We now know, thanks to the publication of the Lange and Douglas letters a year later,[28] that the dispute between Prime Minister and Minister of Finance was already well begun. The Douglas view of its commencement concludes his initial response to Lange on 3 December: 'After months of deliberation, we decided on a hold-the-line budget [in June 1987] before the election. It is now time to get back to work.'[29]

The Douglas and Lange Views when the Struggle was Joined

The Douglas version of that work was very clear, integrated and unyieldingly driven home by repetition throughout the correspondence. Because of the heavy fall on the New Zealand share market, high debt ratios, uncompetitive inflation and rising unemployment there was a need to show purposeful leadership by an early announcement of 'a package of mutually reinforcing changes.' The company tax reforms he was proposing would widen the tax base, close off tax avoidance particularly by companies with offshore operations, but at the same time he would lower the company rate from 48 per cent to 28 per cent, thus providing an incentive for investment for the large majority of companies. To have a single rate of personal tax and 'a revised and expanded GMFI [Guaranteed Minimum Family Income] is logically equivalent to having a progressive tax scale....' As for government expenditure, it was too high; it needed to be improved by efficient administration and by ending programmes serving 'the providers rather than the consumers' of services which ought to be targeted to new criteria. Then 'the rich' would find it 'not so easy for them to avoid paying health and education bills.'

For his part David Lange began the exchange about 1 December[30] with 'views on what is politically appropriate' which was certainly the function of a Prime Minister and elected Leader of the Parliamentary Party and Cabinet. He made clear that he had 'no problem with a programme of privatisation' and favoured 'selling control at a premium' in areas 'deemed socially neutral but revenue-efficient.' The reservation he did make concerned SOEs with monopolies where selling control 'not only should not be done but some protection will have to be invented to stop such control.' He also agreed that the tax base for companies 'is to be so broadly expanded that there would need to be a reduction in the nominal rate of taxation to keep them here and attract further investment.' He did, however, tentatively consider it 'a good time to implement a capital gains tax on shares' or some other way of addressing 'the apparent inequity of companies posting huge profits and making derisory provision for taxation.'

So far so amiable, or at least bearable, for Roger Douglas, although Douglas firmly rejected taxing capital gains on shares in his reply and offered only to review taxes on capital—which came to nothing—while no controls appeared to protect the mass of consumers from Electricorp and Telecom such as the Thatcher Government provided in Oftel and Ofgas. Instead the 'Kiwi share' eventually dealt with different concerns. But Lange[31] hit close to the heart when he wrote: 'I am certain that we would do ourselves a great deal of harm politically if we: (a) Increase the rate of GST. It is inflationary by its nature and regressive in effect. (b) Have a single rate of income tax. I do not think NZ is ready for an abandonment of progressive rates of taxation and as a high income earner I cannot justify them.'

Thinking back to the experience of October 1986 when 'the tax cuts cost about $600-700 million more than was to be initially recovered by GST', the Prime Minister added, 'I am really concerned that we do not end up in a situation where we have a reduced revenue post concessions and then say that we have to embark on a further round of cost cutting to achieve balance. The lesson of our economic history is that at a time of recession that has been tried and it plunged us into depression.'

Lange could see plainly the immediate targets of such a further round of cuts which bringing in a flat tax might necessitate. 'I am totally identified with the Royal Commission on Social Policy. I do not propose to commit political suicide by having radical changes to benefit policy during the currency of that review.' He wanted to preserve the family benefit at least until the Commission reported and believed vehemently that 'National Super is an entitlement. It is a right. It is paid irrespective of income. If other income exceeds certain amounts then taxation imposts are made on the other income.' As to broader welfare services, he could see them threatened in another way which involved Roger Douglas' own scheme to expand the Guaranteed Minimum Family Income. 'I have', wrote Lange, 'a fundamental philosophical problem with the provision of income support as a substitute for government social provision. If that becomes the basis of the social wage then our people are secure while we are in government but at the absolute mercy of an incoming government.' In conclusion Lange told Douglas he wanted him 'to know the parameters of my thinking before you wrap it up' for he believed 'my position is one which reflects the bulk of cabinet's view.'

Whether this was so or not was about to be tested, as was the unity of the fortress Cabinet, the powers of a Prime Minister and cultural assumptions about welfare and the state. David Lange had argued for 'temperate rather than radical means' and wanted government to remain 'a significant and efficient actor in the economy' and, implicitly, society. It was a narrower and more circumscribed role than modern New Zealand governments had exercised since the Great Depression of 1929-1935 and, in certain spheres, since the Long Depression of the 1880s and early 1890s. He had conceded the reduction of the state by corporatisation, privatisation and the restructuring of the public service on the model of corporate business. This was to accept in considerable part the primacy of economic and managerial allocation and decision over political balancing of social and economic considerations in pursuit of the public good. Yet now he stopped and, in the midst of the sands of the market, hopefully drew a line to preserve the welfare benefits and services of the state and the principle of progressiveness in taxation of the great majority of citizens.

The Intra-Cabinet Process of Persuasion, Amendment and Qualified Agreement

There were no further letters before the December Statement, but from subsequent letters and press conferences the outline of the struggle can be traced. The Treasury analysis of the Douglas package was presented to Lange on 3 December together with a briefing from the head of Treasury.[32] There was a Cabinet meeting on Monday 7 December which would have been preoccupied with the State Sector Bill announced that week. On Tuesday the Cabinet Policy Committee was to meet at 9 am.[33] The first item on its permanent brief was 'To define policy objectives and evaluate major social and economic proposals.' In view of the contents of the Douglas package and the Prime Minister's objections, this was the formally correct arena, but instead a committee of 'senior ministers'[34] met to consider the 'original package'. All were members of the Policy Committee, though three lesser members were absent.[35] Six were front benchers—Lange, Palmer, Moore, Douglas, Prebble and Caygill—while the last, Stan Rodger, was ranked 13 but was later to leap eight places and replace Prebble.[36] This was the core of the second Lange Cabinet and was a considerably more difficult body for the Prime Minister to sway than Cabinet as a whole or even the full Policy Committee.

Roger Douglas proposed three programmes to his confrères:[37] the package they decided to compromise on; an alternative which did 'substantially more ... on labour market policy, asset sales and regulatory reform, and was much harder on tariffs, motor vehicle industry changes and expenditure'; and a third option which took a more gradual approach and, if accepted, would cause Douglas to 'stand aside' for another Finance Minister. Not wanting to lose Douglas by taking the third option, nor to provoke Lange further by adopting the most radical alternative, the senior ministers rolled what was effectively the 'original package' towards the meeting of Cabinet on 14 December. Round one had undoubtedly gone to Douglas.

Under Lange's chairmanship, and with the full range of its membership present, Cabinet proved more cautious and less dry than its seven senior figures in conclave. Cabinet's Statement 'deliberately did not endorse ... specific proposals for housing and health',[38] existing benefits were preserved, Family Support was to be reviewed and a standard form of youth support provided, and the only expenditure reductions accepted were to come through rationalisation of departments and increasing cost recoveries from some services. Cabinet did not adopt the package as such but 'agreed to the statement of principles and major measures attached as Annex A'. This went on to become the 17 December Statement. Enough doubt had been raised about the underlying figures accompanying the original package, which had anyway been shorn of several of its features, for Cabinet to determine to present the Statement to Caucus without specifics as to the rate of flat tax or the rate of the expanded Family Income for the employed. On the other hand, Cabinet set up an Ad Hoc Committee under the chairmanship of Roger Douglas[39] to look into the detailed implementation of 'the principles Cabinet had already agreed'. This was to be supported by a Working Group on Income Maintenance made up of officials drawn from more than one department whom Treasury would assist.

Why this Uneasy Compromise became a Very Public Statement

Cabinet's partial and generalised approval of the package as amended was certainly no unalloyed victory for either combatant. It was too little for Douglas to rest content with and too much for Lange to believe sustainable. Both men thought time would be on their side. If Caucus accepted the Statement's release, the concepts of the flat tax and GMFI would be off and running in the public mind. Douglas was sure of their joint appeal both to the better-off who would be released from progressive taxes and the worse-off who would be supported either as employed or, at a distinctly lower level, as beneficiaries. He was also utterly convinced that, with a few more weeks of work by Treasury's number crunchers after the holidays, the basic concepts would be accepted by all as demonstrably workable. As for housing, health and education, there were more economically logical budgets yet to come and this Christmas budget, for that was its real nature, was as he wrote, 'not expressing a new view, but one I had been arguing for since the lead-up to the 1987 Budget.'[40] With further persistence from himself and a restoration of trust by others, Douglas believed that eventually the whole structure would be completed and vindicated.

For his part Lange needed time for information and analysis from independent economists, he needed the check on the Douglas figures which the Working Group could present, he needed the demographic data, the social facts and the policy considerations which the Royal Commission must have gathered by now. His political instincts told him he surely had a case against ending progressive taxation, more GST, and the vulnerable Family Income. But as he said, 'I was flying blind'[41] when it came to proving it. Above all he needed to put his whole argument and the detail in support of it before Cabinet and Caucus together to widen his appeal and perhaps go beyond them to the 'greatest exercise in consultation by the Government since the economic summit conference.'[42]

Lange hesitated and with Palmer met Douglas and Prebble at 'the eleventh hour'.[43] Roger Douglas was so confident that he could with fresh figures early in the new year get closer to his original package than the Statement had achieved, that he emphasised to the two leaders 'as I had to the Cabinet' that flat tax would end fiscal drag and impose 'fiscal discipline' and that 'we had very little room to move up from the 23 cent rate'. Then he made the proposal: 'that if we did not accept those things, we should pull out from the package right then.' But Lange was constrained by Cabinet's decision to make the Statement. Anyway, there was a great deal in the Statement he believed in such as the superannuation, imputation and international tax changes, the deregulation of occupations, and especially the pledges to achieve 'a sustainable fiscal position' and 'a revenue base which will provide sufficient resources to maintain effective social services'.[44] Even more, Lange had to bring Caucus into consultation, then gain that politically blank month in the holidays. So he decided to go forward and risk the release of the Statement. He briefed Caucus and got exactly what he had to have, an agreement to release the Statement later that day on the understanding that Caucus had the right to examine certain measures in detail before enactment.[45] When the time for consultation and legislation arrived he would not be drawing a line in the sand. He hoped to be armed and ready.

Preparing, Waiting and Refining Positions—By Letter

What followed indicated how inadequate were the resources of a New Zealand Prime Minister to counter an able and grimly determined Minister of Finance, the Treasury and a group of loyal fellow ministers all living in a climate of financial, corporate executive and news media opinion long convinced of the general correctness of the Minister of

Finance's approach and doctrines. Lange himself returned to his office from 4 January onwards.[46] He read intensively and wrote brief notes to Douglas on 6 and 11 January indicating that his doubts over fiscal sustainability were deepening, then had to wait for a reply. He had asked for a Treasury assessment of the impact of the 1986 changes, and subsequently wrote of 'commissioning an independent analysis'[47] of the economic package. Plainly his own staff could not provide the backing of economic data and analysis essential to debate major policy with a Minister reinforced by Treasury. He must wait for the Working Group report with Treasury officials participating. The irony of the fashionable use of the terms 'professional capture' and 'vested interests' could well have occurred to him.

Next he turned to Caucus opinion by writing a New Year letter[48] which reviewed the forthcoming year's challenges and problems including the risk to government which would come, not from the Opposition, but 'if we don't deliver on the election pledge on ... social policy.' He initially mentioned his major preoccupation when he forecast that the Royal Commission would be 'the first ... ever to have direct input into government budgetary policy' in regard to income maintenance. Then he posed the problem, 'How do we entrench the welfare state in the 80's?' Finally he referred to a two day caucus: 'By then the work of the officials' working parties ... will be to hand and Cabinet will have had its briefings. I'm not going into that top priority matter now.' However, the MPs were alerted that consulting them was in mind.

The following day the Prime Minister received two very long letters from Roger Douglas in reply to his notes. The first[49] was a firmly technical rebuttal of each and all Lange's arguments and doubts and a reassertion of all Douglas' major points. The second[50] was a more personal record and interpretation of the history of the package expressing genuine concern at the seeming lack of confidence 'in the objectivity, the competence or the integrity, not just of me personally as Minister of Finance, but also of the Treasury and its staff.' The letter ended with an appeal for face-to-face talks over these issues and the reflection that Douglas' fortnight's trip overseas from 23 January 'may be a good thing ... if it gives you a chance to clear your own mind about the package, without interference or further advocacy on my part.' The correspondence had two meanings which reflected the Douglas-Lange experience. First, that the unremitting advocate in Douglas was certain he should not yield anything to unjustified doubt, and second, that he recalled much past co-operation and still hoped to win Lange over. Lange was left in a quandary as to whether these memories of past co-operation might possibly permit the reverse to occur if he could show Douglas clearly the consultative Lange alternative.

The Royal Commission Interposes

An unexpected event then came to the Prime Minister's aid. The Chairman of the Royal Commission on Social Policy, Rt Hon Sir Ivor Richardson, called on the Prime Minister at the start of the day, on 18 January. He told Lange that a first report would now come in April, five months early. He and his Commission had been gazzumped and they knew it. As their press statement[51] put it: 'our experience since the inquiry began 12 months ago and particularly the Government Economic Statement of 17 December and the recently announced programme of the Social Equity Committee [of Cabinet] have brought home the need to make a report as quickly as possible.' Submissions from all over New Zealand had been received and would continue to be so until 31 January. They, along with the commissioned attitudinal survey, 'will provide guidelines as to the thinking of New Zealanders on a broad range of social policy questions.' There was much analytical work already done and together the material 'should be taken into account in charting social policy.'

The first report would 'present only an initial analysis', but with papers; and 'What, if any work,' would be done after April would be decided later. 'Finally, because of the Government's recent announcements, income maintenance and taxation matters become more urgent.' They were to be given priority and working papers would be ready 'in late February or early March.' When the *Report* did come out in May, this compendium on New Zealand's social values on the one hand, and the products of the rapid revision of New Zealand's political culture on the other, appeared to be in significant conflict. When a Government MP referred to the *Report* as useful only as 'a doorstop', he said much more about New Zealand politics and his own attitudes than he understood.

As a lawyer and a Leader who had himself been overridden, David Lange could sympathise with the distinguished Justice of the Court of Appeal, so he promptly issued a press release[52] putting the best public face on it he could. At the same time he recognised that the decision to report early would be of great aid to himself in supplying relevant data to counter the assumptions behind the Douglas package. 'I welcome the willingness ... to put in the extra effort required so that it can present its first report ... in April.' He also welcomed the help their working papers and analysis on income maintenance and taxation would give when considering the implementation of the Statement and emphasised that it was now practical to make 'No decisions' until the *Report* was received.

This unexpected strengthening of his position persuaded the Prime Minister to make an immediate effort to bring his Finance Minister, before his departure for overseas, round to at least concurring in how

Lange proposed to proceed. His letter to Douglas[53] began with thanks for Douglas' 'notes' on the proposals and urged working together for the best outcome and avoiding 'cabinet guerrilla warfare.' Then came his news: 'Rex Jones [NZLP President] has blown his stack. The Royal Commission packed it in this morning. Ivor Richardson ... tells me that he can't accept a flat tax regime.' The Government would be bound by a flat tax rate 'either to make large numbers of low and middle-income people (who do not qualify for GMFI relief) pay more tax or to avoid that by shrinking in arbitrary ways the size of government. That is intolerable.' In December ministers had not worked that out and it would carry 'heavy political costs in the management of cabinet, caucus and party.' A flat tax and the consequent need for expenditure cuts would not be 'sustainable if we have to take an axe to delicate issues of social policy, health and education' and if it would mean 'an end to the NZLP however deficient it may be.' He proposed to work with Cabinet and Caucus to examine the tax/benefit proposals in detail and in the light of the Commission's findings and, if necessary, vary the content of the proposals. Lange asked for Douglas' help and concurrence 'by tomorrow'.

The Douglas reply was back on the morrow:[54] 'I cannot do that.' To concur would involve 'throwing open the fundamental principles, decisions and directions of the December 17 economic statement for discussion and modification.... You do not have any mandate from cabinet, any more than I have, to depart from the decisions cabinet made'. Considering that Cabinet had omitted specific figures, set up both an Ad Hoc Committee and a Working Group to seek details for implementation and, as Douglas later argued in the same letter in respect to deadlines, 'Given that cabinet decided that no specific decisions would be made until late February,' the Douglas accusation of departing from Cabinet's decisions was overheated to say the least. But he could see his package being further interfered with, even though Cabinet had set the precedent by removing the wrapping and taking out some of the contents.

Douglas went on to defend the figures supplied to Lange and the Cabinet. He stressed that they 'show[ed] the package to be fiscally positive in 1990/91 to the tune of $1 billion,' but added, 'As I said ... "This package will not solve our fiscal problems. It will help. But we still face a financial deficit of around 2-3 per cent of GDP over the next few years."' As an argument for preferring a flattened rate of tax to retaining even a reduced element of progressivity it could hardly have been persuasive to the Prime Minister. To Douglas, however, it demonstrated that the original package was frank, correct and that the 'limited number of expenditure reductions' in the public sector it had contained 'should be carried out anyway.' Most of all he distrusted the effect of consultation: 'You know that open-slather public consultation ... would invite the worst sort of pressure group politics.' It would return the country to uncertainty, and, 'The sum of the wish lists of all the articulate interest groups who can find favour with the NZLP will not add up to a workable strategy, let alone an equitable one.' As for the Royal Commission, he questioned the adequacy of their advice, 'whether or not they will product fiscally sustainable recommendations', and their competence to assess sustainability.

A Public Contest on Fundamentals Appears Inescapable and Imminent

Despite Douglas' final sentence—'This is too important for us to allow a stand-off to develop between us'—matters had now gone beyond a stand-off with each faintly hopeful of persuading the other. It had become a contest between two concepts of equity and an effective state, two understandings of social welfare, two versions of New Zealand's society and economy. Each contestant prepared. On the day he received the Douglas letter, Lange wrote to all Caucus members[55] making doubly sure they could appreciate how 'unheard of' was the early wind-up of the Royal Commission and stressing the significance of its forthcoming Report which therefore must not be anticipated by Government action. It was for that reason that 'we would make no further decisions on income maintenance' until the Report was out. Lange thus reminded Caucus that his consultation timetable, which included them, now stretched past April.

Douglas was far more active and aggressively so. He had received a shock which turned out to be a fortunate warning and an opportunity. In his own words to the Deputy Prime Minister of 21 January,[56] 'A report still in draft form, and draft tables, have just reached me from the Working Group on Income Maintenance [also known later as the Preston Report].' He reminded Palmer that the Working Group reported to the Ad Hoc Committee. 'I am presuming, in writing this note you will be acting chairman on my behalf, of that Ad Hoc Committee in my absence [from 23 January to 3 February].' He had only the opportunity to look at the draft report and tables 'for only a couple of hours or so' but 'It is already evident to me' that the report was faulty in its static analysis and 'factually incorrect, incomplete and/or completely misleading' on redistributive effects. 'It does NOT, in its present form, provide a sound basis on which the Government could make decisions' and he added, 'I need to emphasise as strongly as possible that the Ad Hoc Committee should avoid coming to decisions on these matters until I return.' In the meantime he would give Treasury 'a programme of work on these problems' in direct consultation with him in the course of his trip and, in 'a matter of days after my return, we will be in a position to know what we are talking about'.

The same day Lange replied[57] to Douglas' refusal to concur by affirming, for the record as it were, Lange's consultative scheme to start again 'with a set of measures derived from the statement of December 17 which are agreeable to Cabinet and which have some chance of passing through caucus.' He asked Douglas to 'work with me towards its [the Statement's] implementation. You know the alternative which I would not welcome but which would become inevitable.' He ended positively about cooperation; but for the first time he had conjured up 'the alternative'. But which? Consultative debate and public disunity; a changed post in a reshuffle; a forced resignation from the Ministry like Quigley's departure from the Muldoon Cabinet? For a spurned Prime Minister there was a whole armoury constitutionally available because a Prime Minister is not, as the Douglas camp appeared to assume both before and afterwards, simply the first one among equals but, instead, *the one* who recommends to the Crown with effect whom to appoint and whom to dismiss within a ministry with a majority.

Despite or perhaps because of this Damoclean conundrum, Douglas met Lange before his departure. 'We in fact sat in your office and worked out the earliest date the ad hoc committee could meet to discuss the outcome of the working group's examination of ... income support and housing measures.'[58] That could have been in tune with the consultative scenario and encouragingly cooperative. But Douglas warned Lange in his turn that there was more than one weapon in play: "I did mention some problems with the analysis on which some of the points you raise is based". Notice had therefore been served that any negotiation about Lange's points and the basic analysis was going to become a battle of the figures.

As to when that was to be: 'I [Douglas] anticipated that we would work through the issues in it when I returned to New Zealand—you gave me your assurance that no decisions or action would be taken on the Economic Statement until then, so that we could have that discussion.' Whether Douglas' anticipation of mutual discussions on the problems in Lange's analysis was justified or not by what passed at the meeting, Douglas' statement that Lange had assured him 'that no decisions or action would be taken on the Economic Statement' was clear. It could not have been challenged then because the last letter from Lange exclusively released to the *Herald* in 'the Douglas Dossier' was dated 21 January 1988, while Douglas' letter recalling what happened between them at the meeting was not written until after his return to New Zealand

and is dated 1 February 1988. Nor was anything released in the Dossier challenged by the Prime Minister when suddenly published a year later. By then Lange treated the letters as mere despatches from the first big battle of an exhausting campaign which still raged.

By the time Douglas set off for London on Sunday, the Prime Minister would have been furnished with a draft copy of the eagerly awaited Working Group Report and tables and been informed first of all in 'broad'[59] terms by Douglas and then by the Prime Minister's Deputy, about the Finance Minister's denunciation of what Douglas considered were the draft's errors, omissions, misleading nature and worthlessness as the basis for decisions. Yet Lange had been relying on the Working Group to provide data and analysis which would support his position as they obviously had. Otherwise why would Douglas so strenuously and inclusively denounce them immediately after his very first sight of them? Furthermore, Treasury's 'number-crunchers' would be back by Monday 25th and, although Lange could not foresee how they would undermine the contents of the Report, the Prime Minister knew Douglas was counting on his supervised 'programme of work' to supply different and, from the Douglas point of view, conclusive answers on his return. Lange was also painfully conscious that in seven weeks of correspondence and confrontation Douglas had not moved an inch from his original position, while three and more years in government had taught the Prime Minister how often Treasury's advice had carried the day in economic and even social disputes within Cabinet. Both contestants believed their advisers; but the Prime Minister had reason to suspect that the playing field of decision would be tilted.

The Prime Minister Acts

So within the week David Lange acted. On Tuesday there was a Cabinet and on Thursday morning a Caucus which surveyed the state of the economy, the issues for 1988 and the lengthening timetable for implementation of the 17 December Statement,[60] but not the action. That came, carefully swathed in related matters, at Lange's post-Caucus news conference. The Prime Minister began gently with economic trends. He reaffirmed the directions of economic policy set out in the Statement, talked of securing enough revenue to look after the people without running dangerous deficits, and then hovered over the long period needed to consult widely and refine all the details correctly. At this point he introduced a principal deferment. Waiting for the 'pivotal' Royal Commission's findings on income meant 'that changes to GMFI almost certainly cannot be introduced by 1 October.' Then on to the heart of the matter. Perfecting the system for the less well off likewise meant that 'other changes to personal tax will probably have to be deferred because the introduction of a single nominal rate of income tax was dependent on the integrity of the fiscal arithmetic depending on each part of it.' That led, via the possibility of other and implicitly smaller reductions by 1 October, to the basic 'yes' answer to the journalist asking whether 'a flat tax rate might not necessarily come into effect from 1 October?' That was the essence of Lange's message, not a decision, which only Cabinet could take, but two major deferments, and those the news media rapidly condensed in their headlines into one Government U-turn over flat tax and a reverse for the Minister of Finance.

Lange knew deferments were not final decisions but, after the journalists had reported and editorialised, they might as well have been just that. Lange saw it this way in a much later interview.[61] 'I don't think there is any other occasion on which I have ever done anything by way of unilateral decision that [has] interfered in economic policy.' Certainly Douglas thought so. He was also offended and embarrassed to be asked in London about a development of which Lange's staff had given him almost no warning.[62] He cancelled his Swiss visit and was back to speak to a gathering of the press by Sunday.

The Minister of Finance Delivers Three Ripostes

It was characteristic that he defended his package by tying its measures to the need for growth, jobs and competitiveness. We would, he claimed, have 'the best guaranteed minimum family income so far proposed in the world.'[63] He emphasised his 'full confidence' in the advice from the Treasury 'on the equity and fiscal issues' and reaffirmed 'the package' as robust enough to 'accommodate any reasonable changes of detail'. Then he quoted Lange's words at his press conference: 'We can advance that Statement and its principles and it is our responsibility to do so.' Altogether Douglas presented a composed, politic speech which nevertheless fought fiercely for both the feasibility of flat tax and the merits of GMFI. After referring to the 'first-class working relationship' he and David Lange had always had, the Minister closed with a promise full of the possibilities of reversal: 'what we need to do is ... get on with the job of working through the detail, to reach final decisions just as fast as we possibly can.'

After Cabinet next day there was a joint press statement from both men.[64] It was pacificatory in tone and its appearance was a measure of the hubbub and questioning among the public and the business community to whom it was addressed. At great length it said all was well on track, then shifted the focus on to the Ad Hoc Committee of Ministers' meeting that day and the Deputy Prime Minister preparing the legislative

A Political Culture Under Pressure

timetable. On 3 February Douglas had the satisfaction of announcing the retention of New Zealand's AA rating for long term debt and interpreted it thus: [65] 'What Standard and Poors is saying is we've done well so far, but we have to see the process through if we're going to get the full benefits of change.' That day, however, there was also a noisy derailment which was heard and seen around the country after a Douglas press statement on 4 February and in a brief appearance by Douglas on television.

The statement[66] said 'that an officials' report likely to grossly mislead the public on key features of the economic package had been released to some media yesterday without Government authorisation.' This had 'forced him today, in fairness to Cabinet and the Government, to give the public accurate information on matters of vital economic and social importance.' Then Douglas went back to 20 January and the draft Report which 'had been written by a person in the Department of Social Welfare.' The Minister had consulted with Treasury officers in the Group and had been told the draft 'represented a majority view of the people in the working group.' Treasury officers had been doing their best 'to ensure the report was accurate and fair.' They had obtained 'some improvements ... but not enough.' It was a static analysis, done by Treasury well before 17 December and was a 'limited, inadequate view.' Douglas had told Treasury 'to go on trying to patch up' the Working Group Report but also to 'pursue their own dynamic analysis' and only present it when totally checked.

Then followed an exact copy of his 21 January letter to the Deputy Prime Minister, as again published a year later, and complete with Douglas' scathing indictment of the Working Group's 'ludicrously incorrect' statements. The press release ended in a cascade of figures comparing 'the Preston Committee's' maximum losses under the package at various income levels and in differing family circumstances with the results as calculated by Treasury. Losses all turned to gains and, in the roughly hand-written comparison, which went on and quickly off the small screen, the 'Average Error by Preston Committee' was 'Annual $233'.

A fully worked example was also appended which compared the results using the dynamic Treasury and static Working Group methods for an earner with a spouse and three children on an income of $29,000 'when they start receiving GMFI.' The difference came from Treasury—but not the Working Group—assuming two annual pay rises for the earner, one in October 1987 and one in October 1988 just before GMFI was to be received. Each was assumed to be a rise of 7.5 per cent, that is $1,882 and $2,023. They were then subtracted successively from the $29,000 to represent earlier pay levels and they, in turn, were averaged to yield the level over the 1987-1988 March year which became the base year for calculating the gains from GMFI. This lower base produced an increased weekly addition of $48.47, compared to the Working Group's $4.58. But could or should one make a general assumption of two such generous rises for those two years or for future years such as 1989, say, or 1991? And if large rises were not continuously forthcoming as the base years rolled forward, might not the Working Group's nil assumption prove as rational as Treasury's dynamic growth assumption, or even more so, when estimating the final results? The journalists who paused to read right through the press statement would certainly have cause to wonder whether the public denigration of the Working Group's methods and Report was wholly justified and why it was repeated from private correspondence within the press statement.

The Pressures on Contestants and Cabinet to Reach a Swift Resolution.

They would also note from this press statement that the Ad Hoc Committee did not meet on 1 February as then publicly announced by Lange and Douglas,[67] but was due to meet for the first time this day, Thursday 4 February.[68] That left a day perhaps for the Social Equity Committee, then Cabinet on Monday before the concluding announcement on Wednesday, a momentously busy period. The pressure was on all parties to come to a decision. The Minister of Finance had already expressed his deep concern about a degenerating situation for international and local business confidence in his more personal letter of 1 February[69] to the Prime Minister. Douglas anticipated increasing uncertainty offshore leading to exchange rate falls and interest rate rises and concluded: 'We are now in a position where the Government must crystallise its proposals into decisions and lay them before the public. We will gain nothing by allowing a lengthy period of uncertainty to develop.' Furthermore he had consistently opposed Lange's timetable for wide consultation and could now blame the Prime Minister for having 'seriously jeopardised' further development and decisions in April.

David Lange could see from the media that his January intervention had divided opinion and support for his Government and that each Douglas press conference set the two leading figures of the Government further apart in the public mind than his own press conference had initially placed them. From the days of Rowling: Lange combats, then the Muldoon: McLay and McLay: Bolger contests, he could vividly recall what disunion did to a party's standing in the polls and at the ballot box. It was also apparent that the Douglas blitz had put doubt where Lange might have hoped for reinforcement from the Working Group's Report.

Yet what he had heard from the Working Group and what he saw of the GMFI's costs in Treasury's dynamic analysis could only strengthen his desire to press home the initiative he had seized in January and scotch the flat tax before Douglas could revive it, along with GMFI, by talk of benefits almost all round. Consultation and the long route would have to wait or be applied to minor details. It was now or never.

The others in the Ad Hoc Committee and the rest of the Cabinet likewise had every reason for haste. Overwhelmingly they wanted the public rift between their two major figures closed up tight by shared decisions taken with all possible speed. Regardless of whether they favoured a Lange or a Douglas version of unity, they wanted the external face of agreement for sheer self-preservation. Collectively they constituted a forcing house for compromise; but the most adamant debaters, the ministers most at home in economics, lent strength to the Douglas side.

Cabinet's Compromise and the Disguised Defeat of the Prime Minister.

As a Cabinet they could not gainsay their Prime Minister on the issue of the flat tax, bathed in publicity as it was. But they could drive the top and standard rates of progressive taxation so far down to 33 per cent and 24 per cent that the effect would be only to modify and moderate the flat tax concept. With a remaining element of deficit built in by the size of the tax cuts, pressure would continue to be exerted for more stringency and 'reforms' in social welfare and pressure for continued privatisation to reduce overseas and, at times, internal public debt. Eventually, indeed, there would have to be a rise to 12.5 per cent in regressive GST but that was put off. Roger Douglas could live easily enough with all that if he so chose. He would have been less satisfied with the fate of the GMFI scheme which was shrunk, stripped of its more expensive supplemental aspects, and left simply as a 9 per cent rebate up to a maximum of $855 per year for the lowest earners. Thereafter the rebate decreased in steps once earnings climbed above $9,500 but it still provided an element of progressivity at the lower levels although with eligibility yet to be determined. On the other hand, the rate of taxation for resident companies was to come down to 28 per cent and for non-resident companies to 33 per cent, so business was treated generously just as Douglas had planned.

These core decisions and many lesser ones were announced by the Finance Minister on 10 February 1988[70] most firmly in the name of the Cabinet and as implementations of the 17 December Statement. Their announced purposes were to 'confirm the tax environment for businesses for 1988-1989', to assist 'business and individuals' to plan ahead, to have a fiscal impact which would be 'positive in 1988-1989', and to allow 'the Government sufficient time' to consider other tax and income maintenance issues arising from 17 December, a task the Ad Hoc Committee and Cabinet would perform. Of consultations with Caucus, the Party or more generally there was no sign. Nor had Cabinet waited for the working papers of the Royal Commission or their *Report*. Lest executives in welfare departments have missed the thrust of the measures, however, there was a message for those who could translate the arid, abstract and veiled language of the time: 'In the medium term the continued attainment of improvements in the structural fiscal position will require further attention to be given to the quality and level of government spending and revenue.'

It was plain which tendency within Cabinet and which of the two contestants and their support groups had carried the day in the Ad Hoc Committee, then Cabinet as a whole. Business at home and investors abroad could not only breathe easily again, they could celebrate. New Zealand's well-to-do and especially the very wealthy few had suffered a fortnight's uncertainty lest their 'cloud-capp'd towers' should dissolve and fade.[71] Yet here they were restored, admittedly with the named tower—'flat tax'—gone, but they remained many and substantial and utterly satisfactory. Now what was necessary was to see to it that this very low level of progressive taxation became normal, even sacrosanct as somehow an achievement of reform and essential for future economic recovery. The fact that the top levels of direct taxation fixed were lower than in Australia, or Margaret Thatcher's Britain, or even than the local, state and federal taxation of Reagan's America, all went unadvertised. It was said instead that they made New Zealand 'competitive'. The recovery which competitiveness was to bring has yet to come four and more years on. Yet those direct tax levels have stayed intact, not just for the rest of Labour's troubled term, but through two sets of rougher, more painful cuts in national superannuation, welfare, health, education and housing by the Labour Cabinet's National successors.

Radical change in the balance between progressive and regressive taxation and sudden shifts in the levels and targeting of the two kinds of taxation have fundamentally altered the mix of institutions, values, laws and expectations which constitute a political culture. The whole structure of New Zealand's system of welfare is being reduced and pushed out of familiar shape by the pressure of an insufficient, and what is, in New Zealand's past experience and political culture, a deliberately unbalanced system of taxation. The same pressure reinforces the thrust to shrink the state which is expressed in privatisation and this has been done in a manner entirely without precedent in New Zealand's political history.

We have seen how Labour's Cabinet had accomplished this revolution without manifestos, without informed electoral choice, without the concurrence of party organisations and despite a check from its Prime Minister. National's Cabinet has repeated and intensified much of the process, this time with rather more Caucus rebellion and two resignations from that body but with only one ejection of a Cabinet Minister as yet.[72] Another outcome has been the heavy electoral rejection of one government, and an unprecedentedly rapid rejection in the initial opinion polls assessing the next government. The disillusion and dismay which these successive blows at democratic confidence have produced has been reflected in the demand for new systems in Parliament and new methods of election. It is patent that pressure on one or several parts of a political culture is felt throughout the entire system.

Notes

1. R. M. Chapman, 'Political Studies and Elections', Address to the 1987 Conference of the New Zealand Political Studies Association, pp. 9-18; and further unpublished research based on *The General Election 1984*, *The General Election 1987*, and *The General Election 1987, Amended Enrolment and Voting Statistics*... [the E9 series], (Government Printer, Wellington, 1984, 1987 and 1989). For background see R. M. Chapman, 'Political Culture: The Purposes of Party and the Current Challenge', in Hyam Gold, (ed.), *New Zealand Politics in Perspective*, 2nd edition (Auckland 1989), pp. 14-32. [Reprinted here as Chapter 19. Ed.]
2. *New Zealand Herald (NZH)*, 6 November 1990, p. 3.
3. Roger Douglas and Louise Callan, *Toward Prosperity* (Auckland, 1987), p. 30.
4. Hon R. O. Douglas, *1987 Budget, Part l: Speech and Annex* (Wellington, 18 June 1987), p. 12.
5. The Treasury, *Government Management, Brief to the Incoming Government 1987*, Vol. 1 (Wellington, 1987), pp. 109-13.
6. Roderick Deane, 'Reforming the Public Sector' in S. Walker, (ed.), *Rogernomics: Reshaping New Zealand's Economy* (Wellington, 1989), pp. 120, 124-5.
7. New Zealand Government, *Government Economic Statement, 17 December 1987* (Wellington, 1987), pp. 4-13.
8. Hon R. O. Douglas, *1986 Budget, Part 1: Speech and Annex* (Wellington, 31 August 1986), p. 15.
9. Rt Hon David Lange, Transcript, 'Press Conference, 28 January 1988', 32 pp., esp. pp. 3, 4.
10. Hon R. O. Douglas, 'Press Conference, 31 January 1988',12 double pp., esp. pp. 8, 11.
11. Hon R. O. Douglas, 'Press Statement, 4 February 1988', 6 pp., plus 7 pp. annexed, p. 6 and *passim*.
12. Hon R. O. Douglas, Announcement of details re 'Business and Company Tax Reform/Indirect Taxation/Personal Tax', 10 February 1988, 4 pp., *passim*.
13. Bruce Jesson, *Fragments of Labour: The Story Behind the Labour Government* (Auckland, 1989), pp. 105-9.

14 Murray McLaughlin, 'The Year of Living Dangerously, The PM talks about a tumultuous year at the top', *NZ Listener*, 24 December 1988, pp. 20-1.
15 Office of the PM, 'Second Lange Ministry—24 August 1987, The Cabinet'; Schedule of additional responsibilities; Parliamentary Under-Secretaries, 4 pp.
16 *Sunday Star*, 8 November 1987, p. A2.
17 *NZH*, 9 November 1987, p. 8.
18 *Auckland Sun*, 7 November 1987, p. 5.
19 *NZH*, 9 November 1987, p. 8.
20 *Auckland Sun*, 7 November 1987, p. 5.
21 *Auckland Sun*, 9 November 1987, p. 9.
22 *Auckland Sun*, 9 November 1987, p. 1.
23 R. M. Chapman, *The Political Scene, 1919-1931* (Auckland, 1969), pp. 62-5. Also see Richard Mulgan, 'The Changing Electoral Mandate' in Martin Holland and Jonathan Boston, (eds.), *The Fourth Labour Government*, 2nd edition (Auckland, 1990), pp. 11-21.
24 *NZH*, 6 November 1987, p. 1.
25 *Auckland Star*, 16 November 1987, p. A8.
26 Pat Walsh, 'The State Sector Act 1988', in J. Boston, J. Martin, J. Pallot and P. Walsh, (eds.), *Reshaping the State, New Zealand's Bureaucratic Revolution* (Auckland, 1991), pp. 61-3 and *passim*.
27 *NZH*, 25 February 1988, p. 5.
28 The New Zealand Herald exclusively published 'For the record' and 'Unedited' a five-part series of letters between the Prime Minister and his Minister of Finance under the headings 'Dear David'... and 'The Douglas Dossier'. They were: Lange (L.) to Douglas (D.) 'About' 1 December 1987 and D. to L. 3 December 1987: pubd. *NZH* 31 December 1988, Sect. 2, p. l & pp. 1-2. L. to D. 6 January 1988, L. to D. 11 January 1988; & D. to L. [A] 15 January 1988, D. to L. [B] 15 January 1988: pubd. *NZH* 3 January 1989, Sect. 2, p. l; p. 1 and pp. l-2, p. 2. L. to D. 18 January 1988, D. to L. 19 January 1988: pubd. *NZH* 4 January 1989, Sect. 2, p. 1 and p. 2. D. to Deputy PM, Rt Hon Geoffrey Palmer, 21 January 1988: pubd. *NZH* 5 January 1989, Sect. 2, p. l and *NZH* 7 January 1989, Sect. 2, p. 2. L. to D. 21 January 1988: pubd. *NZH* 5 January 1989, Sect. 2, p. 1. D. to L. [A] 1 February 1988, D. to L. [B] 1 February 1988: pubd. *NZH* 7 January 1989, Sect. 2, p. 1 and pp. 1-2. Subsequent references to specific letters omit publication details.
29 D. to L. 3 December 1987.
30 L. to D. 'About' 1 December 1987.
31 L. to D. 'About' 1 December 1987.
32 D. to L. 19 January 1988.
33 Cabinet Office, C0(87)9 'Cabinet Committees: Structure and Membership', 24 August 1987, Timetable, p. 1; terms of reference and membership, Cabinet Policy Committee, p. 7. Issued to press by Deputy PM, 25 August 1987.
34 D. to L. [A] 1February 1988.
35 D. to L. [B] 15 January 1988.
36 Office of the PM, 'Second Lange Ministry—24 August 1987', 4 pp. On Hon Stan Rodger: see Rt Hon D. Lange, 'Prime Minister Announces Cabinet Changes', 7 September 1988, Expenditure Review to be conducted by Douglas, Caygill, Rodger, p. 2; and see 'Cabinet List: 8 November 1988' for Rodger's promotion to rank fifth and succeed Prebble.
37 D. to L. [B] 15 January 1988.
38 L. to D. 21 January 1988.

39 D. to Palmer. 21 January 1988.
40 D. to L. [B] 15 January 1988.
41 L. to D. 18 January 1988.
42 Lange, 'Press Conference, 28 January 1988', pp. 2-3.
43 D. to L. [B] 15 January 1988.
44 *Government Economic Statement,* 17 *December 1987,* 67 pp., esp. p. 5.
45 Lange, letter of 21 December 1987.
46 Lange, 'Press Conference, 28 January 1988', p. 6.
47 L. to D. 11 January 1988.
48 Lange, 'Happy New Year', letter to all members of Caucus, 14 January 1988, 4 pp.
49 D. to L. [A] 15 January 1988.
50 D. to L. [B] 15 January 1988.
51 Rt Hon Sir Ivor Richardson, 'Press Statement, 18 January 1988', pp. 1-2.
52 Lange, 'Royal Commission on Social Policy', press release, 18 January 1988, 1p.
53 L. to D. 18 January 1988.
54 D. to L. 19 January 1988.
55 Lange, 'Dear Member,' 19 January 1988, 1 p.
56 D. to Palmer. 21 January 1988.
57 L. to D. 21 January 1988.
58 D. to L. [A] 1 February 1988.
59 Douglas, 'Press Statement 4 February 1988', p. 4.
60 Lange, 'Press Conference, 28 January 1988', Cabinet and Caucus days, p. 1; quotations, pp. 3-4; related questions, pp. 5-13, 20-6, 32.
61 Lange, interviewed in *NZ Listener,* 24 December 1988, p. 21.
62 D. to L. [B] 1 February 1988.
63 Douglas, 'Press Conference, 31 January 1988', pp. 8-12.
64 'Rt. Hon David Lange, Prime Minister; Hon Roger Douglas, Minister of Finance, 1 February 1988, Press Statement', 2pp.
65 Douglas, 'Minister welcomes credit rating confirmation', 3 February 1988, 1p.
66 Douglas, 'Press Statement, 4 February 1988', 6pp. of text plus 7pp. annexed.
67 Lange, Douglas, '1 February 1988, Press Statement', p. 2.
68 Douglas, 'Press Statement, 4 February 1988', p. 4.
69 D. to L. [B] 1February 1988. Note the contrast with Standard and Poor's 3 February verdict. They would have observed international comment on Lange's 28 January deferments.
70 Douglas, Announcement, 10 February 1988, 4pp., *passim.*
71 *The Tempest,* IV.i.
72 [Gilbert Myles, MP for Roskill, resigned in 1991; and Hamish MacIntyre, MP for Manawata, resigned the same year. They formed the Liberal Party which became part of the Alliance. Winston Peters, Minister of Maori Affairs and MP for Tauranga, was dismissed from Cabinet in 1991 and later was expelled from the National caucus. In 1993 he resigned and successfully fought a by-election as an Independent, later founding the New Zealand Party. Ed.]

Bibliography of the Published Works of Robert Chapman
(excluding reviews and poems)

Books
New Zealand Politics in Action. The 1960 General Election (London, Oxford University Press, 1962). With W. K. Jackson and A. V. Mitchell.

New Zealand in the Twenties: Social Change and Material Progress (Auckland, Heineman Educational Books Ltd., 1969). With E. P. Malone.

The Political Scene 1919-1931 (Auckland, Heineman Educational Books Ltd., 1969).

Marginals '72: An Analysis of New Zealand's Marginal Electorates (Auckland, Heinemann Educational Books, 1972).

Edited Works
An Anthology of Zealand Verse (London, Oxford University Press, 1956; Great Neck, New York, Granger Book Co., 1979). With Jonathan Bennett.

Ends and Means in New Zealand Politics, University of Auckland, Bulletin No. 60, History Series No. 7 (Auckland, 1961).

Studies of a Small Democracy. Essays in Honour of Willis Airey (Auckland, Blackwood and Janet Paul Ltd. for The University of Auckland, 1963). With Keith Sinclair.

Reports to Government
The Broadcasting Future of New Zealand (Wellington, Government Printer, 1973). With Kenneth Adam, John Robson and Dorothea Turner.

Broadcasting and Related Telecommunications in New Zealand: Report of the Royal Commission of Inquiry (Wellington, V.R. Ward, Government Printer, 1986). With Judge Michael Brown, Elizabeth Nelson and Laurence Cameron, CBE.

Articles and Book Chapters
(excluding short newspaper articles)
'Marx and the Corn King', *Landfall*, Vol. 3, No. 3 (September 1949), pp. 257-69. With Keith Sinclair.

'The Writers' Conference', *Landfall*, Vol. 5, No. 3 (September 1951). With W. H. Oliver, John Reece Cole and Robert Chapman, pp. 220-6. (Chapman's contribution is on pp. 224-7).

'Fiction and the Social Pattern: Some Implications of Recent New Zealand Writing', *Landfall*, Vol. 7, No. 1 (March 1953), pp. 26-58. Reprinted in Wystan Curnow (ed.), Essays on New Zealand Literature (Auckland, Heinemann Educational Books, 1973), pp. 71-98.

'No Land is an Island: Twentieth Century Politics', in Keith Sinclair (ed.), *Distance Looks Our Way: The Effects of Remoteness on New Zealand* (Hamilton, Paul's Book Arcade for the University of Auckland, 1961), pp. 42-62.

'The Decline of the Liberals', in Robert Chapman (ed.), *Ends and Means in New Zealand Politics* (Auckland, University of Auckland, Bulletin No. 60, History Series No. 7 1961), pp. 18-24.

'New Zealand Since the War: 8 Politics and Society', *Landfall*, Vol. 16, No.3 (September 1962), pp. 252-77.

'Willis Thomas Goodwin Airey', in *Studies of a Small Democracy. Essays in Honour of Willis Airey* (Auckland, Blackwood and Janet Paul Ltd. for The University of Auckland, 1963, pp. 1-9. With Keith Sinclair.

'The Response to Labour and the Question of Parallelism of Opinion, 1928-1960', in Robert Chapman and Keith Sinclair (eds.), *Studies of a Small Democracy. Essays in Honour of Willis Airey* (Auckland, Blackwood and Janet Paul Ltd. for The University of Auckland, 1963), pp. 221-54.

'Psephology', *University of Auckland Gazette*, 5:2 (July 1963), pp. 3-5.

'L'Entente Incordiale', *Comment*, Vol. 4, No. 3 (April 1963), pp. 38-45.

'The "No Change" Election', *Comment*, Vol. 5, No. 2 (January 1964), pp. 8-10.

'How is our Political System Working?' *New Zealand Listener*, 26 September, 1969, p. 11.

'The Mechanics of Representation', *New Zealand Listener*, 24 October, 1969, pp. 9 and 27.

'The 1969 Election', *Comment*, Vol. 10, No. 4 (April 1970), pp. 14-8.

'Election '72: Why the Change Came', *New Zealand Listener* (18 December, 1972), pp. 18-9.

'The Politics of Change', *National Business Review* (4 August 1976 -13 October 1976).

'The Case of the Pulled Punch: The 1978 Election', *Comment*, New Series, No. 6 (February 1979), pp. 17-20.

'On Democracy as Having and Exercising a Clear Choice of Government', in J. Stephen Hoadley (ed.), *Improving New Zealand's Democracy* (Auckland, New Zealand Foundation for Peace Studies, 1979), pp. 85-95.

'From Labour to National', in W. H. Oliver (ed. with B. R. Williams), *The Oxford History of New Zealand* (Oxford, The Clarendon Press; Wellington, Oxford University Press, 1981), pp. 333-68.

'New Zealand Defers Decision: Robert Chapman Reviews the 1981 General Election and Ponders its Consequences', *Comment*, New Series, No. 16 (August 1982), pp. 11-18.

'The Politics of Division?' in Graham Bush (ed.), *New Zealand—A Nation Divided?* (Auckland, The University of Auckland, 1983), pp. 95-110.

'Voting in the Maori Political Sub-System, 1935-1984', in Annex, Appendix B, *Report of the Royal Commission on the Electoral System: Towards a Better Democracy* (Wellington, 1986, B-83-108, plus 20 graphs).

'Political Culture: The Purposes of Party and the Current Challenge', in Hyam Gold (ed.), *New Zealand Politics in Perspective*, 2nd edn. (Auckland, Longman Paul, 1989), pp. 14-32.

'A Political Culture Under Pressure: The Struggle to Preserve a Progressive Tax Base for Welfare and the Positive State', *Political Science*, Vol. 44, No. 1 (July 1992), pp. 1-27.